MISSIONAL APOLOGETICS

Cultural Diagnosis and Gospel Plausibility
in C. S. Lewis and Lesslie Newbigin

DAVID FEDDES

Christian Leaders Press
www.christianleaderspress.com

Missional Apologetics: Cultural Diagnosis and Gospel Plausibility in C. S. Lewis and Lesslie Newbigin
Copyright © 2012 David Feddes
Published by Christian Leaders Press
Monee, Illinois
www.christianleaderspress.com

Printed in the United States of America

Cover design: Christina Harris

ISBN: 0615621562
ISBN-13: 9780615621562

You are the light of the world.

Acknowledgements

Professors Harold Netland, Craig Ott, and Robert Priest were the first readers of this material and offered helpful suggestions. Professor Paul Hiebert, of blessed memory, aided in some preliminary research and opened his home to me many times. My mother, Nell Feddes, applied her meticulous eye to the manuscript. My wife, Wendy Feddes, and our children patiently endured my neglect during the many hours I spent researching and writing. Henry Reyenga encouraged and aided publication. I thank each of you.

Contents

CHAPTER 1

Missionaries to the West

Much of the Western world is far from Christian faith and practice. This book explores the efforts of C. S. Lewis and Lesslie Newbigin to understand and address the West as a post-Christian mission field. Both men were keen observers who looked with missional eyes and developed a cultural diagnosis of the West. Both men devised strategies for showing the plausibility of the gospel in the context of Western culture.

The West as Mission Field

Lesslie Newbigin, after decades of mission work in India, returned to England in 1974. He was dismayed at the degree to which British society had abandoned Christian convictions. Newbigin spent the last 24 years of his long life pondering and writing about "what would be involved in a genuinely missionary encounter between the gospel and the culture that is shared by the peoples of Europe and North America" (1986b, 1). He repeatedly raised the question he once overheard an Indonesian Christian ask: "Can the West be converted?" (1986a, 1; 1987, 1; 1994a, 108).

Newbigin urged Christians to study the nature of non-Christian Western culture as missionaries study other non-Christian cultures. He regarded mission to the West as the highest priority for mission in his time, citing two main reasons. First, post-Enlightenment Western culture, posing as a neutral process of modernization, had unmatched

1

power to infiltrate and replace traditional cultures worldwide. Second, this culture was more corrosive and resistant to the gospel than any other culture except Islam (1986b, 20; 1989b, 213). Newbigin warned that without a missionary encounter with the culture of modernity, eventually the forces which had neutered and marginalized Europe's churches were "bound to have the same effects in the third world as they have had in Europe" (1994a, 185).

Decades earlier, professor and author C. S. Lewis also described Britain in missionary terms. "Our present task," Lewis insisted in a 1945 speech, "is chiefly to convert and instruct infidels. Great Britain is as much part of the mission field as China." As missionaries to overseas peoples "would be taught their language and traditions," so British church leaders would "need similar teaching about the language and mental habits of your own uneducated and unbelieving fellow countrymen" (1970, 94). "Churches should frankly recognize that the majority of the British people are not Christians" (1952, 101). Lewis even spoke of acting as "missionary to the priests of one's own Church" (1967, 223).[1]

Like Newbigin after him, Lewis noticed "the un-christening of Europe" (1962, 13) and perceived modernizing forces antithetical to Christianity spreading beyond the West. A character in a 1946 Lewis novel said that in Britain, "the Christians are but a tenth part of the people." Countries elsewhere in Europe "are even as Britain, or else sunk deeper still in the disease." The problem was not confined to the West. "The poison was brewed in these West lands but it has spat itself everywhere by now" (1946, 292-293). Also like Newbigin, Lewis contended that Christianity met stronger resistance in the post-Christian West than in pre-Christian cultures (1962, 13-14; 1970, 172).

Lewis and Newbigin, based mainly on their experiences and perceptions of British society, each developed a reading of Western culture. Newbigin defined "modern Western culture" as "the culture that is shared by the peoples of Europe and North America, their colonial

---

[1]My parenthetical references and my reference list at the end of the book do not always identify the original form or date when material first appeared. Lewis wrote many articles, speeches, and personal letters, which were later collected in books. Similarly, some of Newbigin's books are collections of articles and speeches given on various occasions over the years. In such cases, parenthetical references in this book cite a date and page number from the published anthology (which readers can more easily access), not from the original piece. However, sometimes I also specify in the body of my text the original title, occasion, or date of an item.

and cultural offshoots, and the growing company of educated leaders in the cities of the world" (1986, 1-4). Lewis, without stating a precise definition, operated with a similar working definition of the West. A native of Northern Ireland and a long-time resident of England, Lewis offered many observations about his specific context but also spoke broadly of "the West" and of the modern age as bringing "the greatest change in the history of Western Man" (1962, 17, 22). Both Lewis and Newbigin viewed Britain as part of a wider "Western" panorama, and they saw key religious changes as related in some manner to modernization and to intellectual shifts associated with it.

Missional Apologetics

In this book I explore key elements of Lewis's and Newbigin's missional apologetics. While identifying a range of significant developments in Western societies as each man perceived and experienced them in his respective time and place, I focus especially on the place rationality occupied in each author's depiction of growing unbelief and in each author's recommendations for Christian witness to the West.

Lewis is renowned as an apologist, while Newbigin is known among pastors and scholars of missions as one of the foremost missionary leaders and thinkers of the 1900s. Yet Newbigin the missionary may be seen as an apologist (Hunsberger 1998, 11-12; Smith 1999; Wainwright 2000, 335-389; Weston 2004, 232), and Lewis the apologist may be viewed as a missionary (Jolley 1997; Mitchell 1998; Musacchio 1997; Ryken 1997). Both Lewis and Newbigin were missional apologists to the post-Christendom West. They were both *missional*, in that they viewed Western culture as a non-Christian entity that needed to be analyzed and understood through missionary eyes, just as missionaries seek to understand any other non-Christian culture to which they are bringing the gospel of Jesus Christ. Both Lewis and Newbigin engaged in *apologetics*, in that they tried in various ways to show the plausibility and rationality of Christian belief.

Lewis and Newbigin both wrote with a sense of the context they sought to address. They did not produce one-size-fits-all approaches that would be equally suitable for every culture. Lewis engaged in successful context-specific apologetics (Netland 1988, 296). Lewis's work targeted British society during the mid-1900s. Newbigin too sought to address a particular context: the late twentieth century West (plus, perhaps, some aspects of other cultures to the degree that they had been westernized). Therefore, in looking at apologetic dimensions in Lewis and Newbigin, we must pay close attention to the particularities of their context, noting how they perceived their culture and what they considered to be appropriate responses. Much of this book accordingly focuses on context-specific apologetics, though some theoretical, transcultural elements in Lewis and Newbigin are also discussed.

Both men were British citizens, yet both saw themselves as missionaries to Britain, crossing cultural boundaries to reach non-Christian people in a post-Christian culture. Each presented himself as speaking from the perspective of an outsider steeped in a different culture: Lewis as a medievalist and self-proclaimed specimen of "old Western man" (1962, 23-24), and Newbigin as a missionary to India whose long-time absence from Britain gave him an outsider's perspective on the Britain to which he returned decades later (1986b, 1; 1994a, 67). Thus these two prominent Christians perceived themselves in missionary terms, addressing a culture in which they felt somewhat out of place: feeling close enough for an insider's understanding, yet feeling distant enough to offer an outsider's diagnosis.[2]

Neither author styled himself an expert in theology or social analysis. Lewis called himself "a very ordinary layman" (1952, 6), writing "as one amateur to another (1958, 2). Newbigin said, "I can make no claim either to originality or to scholarship" (1989a, x). Given the broad learning of both men, such self-deprecation may have been partly a rhetorical ploy to attract "ordinary" people while disarming scholarly critics. However, the modesty was not entirely feigned or groundless. Both Newbigin and Lewis had reason to be modest about their credentials in some areas they addressed. Even so, both men possessed rare alertness, breadth of reading, and range of experience. Both left an imprint on the way contemporary Christians seek to provide a gospel witness in Western societies. Both men are well worth studying.

---

[2]The Oxford establishment's antipathy to Lewis involved "a collision between the Christian mind and the secular mind," but it may also have involved cultural difference, "a collision between the Irish mind and the English mind. . . . Lewis's rich dialectical combativeness and his taste for inflating the particular to the status of the universal go against the grain of the respectable English preference for niggling at particulars in isolation, for not leaping to conclusions, for avoiding what may lead to head-on intellectual conflict, for discouraging the whipping out of polemical swords, the unfurling of unambiguous creedal banners. The English 'establishment' prefer blunting sharp edges in controversy and greasing the works of social and intellectual interchange with the oil of non-commitment" (Blamires 1998, 19-21).

Lewis's Life and Impact

C. S. Lewis (1898-1963) taught at Oxford from 1925 until 1954. Then he accepted a chair at Cambridge as Professor of Medieval and Renaissance Literature, serving in that post until shortly before his death. Lewis produced scholarly works that were highly regarded by fellow academicians and that still remain in print as major contributions to literary studies. These included *The allegory of love: A study in medieval tradition* (1936), *English literature in the sixteenth century, excluding drama* (1954), and *The discarded image: An introduction to medieval and Renaissance literature* (1964).

Lewis gained fame as a Christian apologist and fiction writer. After rejecting Christianity in his teens, he became a Christian early in his career at Oxford and sought to advance the faith. In the 1940s, he explained and argued for Christianity in a number of radio broadcasts, later published as *Mere Christianity* (1952). Lewis presented Christian claims at many military bases during World War II. From 1942 until 1954, he served as president of the Socratic Club at Oxford, a weekly forum to debate the intellectual case for and against Christianity. Besides *Mere Christianity*, Lewis's directly apologetic works included *The problem of pain* (1955a [1940]) and *Miracles: A preliminary study* (1960b [1947]). Also, *The abolition of man* (1996 [1944]), though not explicitly advocating Christianity, argued for objective natural law as opposed to subjective relativism.

Lewis wrote fiction in several genres, always with an apologetic dimension. He produced a science fiction trilogy suffused with Christian themes: *Out of the silent planet* (1938), *Perelandra* (2003 [1944]), and *That hideous strength* (1946a). He portrayed demonic temptation in *The Screwtape letters* (1960c [1942]) and depicted self-chosen damnation in *The great divorce* (1946b). In the early 1950s, Lewis wrote a series of seven fantasy books, the Chronicles of Narnia, some of the top sellers in publishing history. These books center around a Christ figure, the lion Aslan. Lewis's final work of fiction, *Till we have faces* (1956), retold the ancient myth of Psyche in Christian terms of sin and repentance.

Lewis, an Anglican, did not profess to be an evangelical, yet he remains the most influential writer among American evangelicals. *Christianity Today* polled subscribers on which book besides the Bible had most affected their spiritual lives. Lewis's *Mere Christianity* received more than double the votes of any other. In the category of all-time favorite novel, the Chronicles of Narnia, *Perelandra*, and *Till we have faces* appeared in the top twelve. No other writer has had comparable influence (Maudlin 1993). In 2000, *Christianity Today* readers voted *Mere Christianity* the best book of the twentieth century. Even if one thinks the book does not merit such adulation, one must reckon with Lewis's enormous impact. Many evangelical leaders acknowledge Lewis's influence on them (for instance, Colson 1976, 112-129; Packer 1998; Pinnock 1995, 107; Plantinga 2000; Vanhoozer 2005a; 2005c).

Besides evangelicals, Christians from various traditions value Lewis as a resource for witness to the contemporary West. Orthodox Bishop Kallistos Ware lauds Lewis as an "anonymous orthodox" (1998, 68-69). Roman Catholics such as Peter Kreeft (1994; 1998) and Thomas Howard (1987) draw on Lewis. Pope John Paul II read several of Lewis's books and quoted Lewis in his sermons (Sayer 1988, 239). American Cardinal Avery Dulles placed a lengthy quote from Lewis opposite the title page of his magisterial *A history of apologetics* (2005a). Indeed, Dulles wrote that Lewis was "probably the most successful Christian apologist of the twentieth century" (2005b, 15). As Lewis influenced Christians from many traditions, he also helped motivate some to become missionaries.[3]

Despite Lewis's vast influence and his own sense of being a missionary, missiology (the scholarly study of missions) has largely ignored Lewis. Careful study of Lewis can provide help in grappling with practical and theoretical concerns relevant for missiology. His practical experiences in missions included not only his publications but also radio broadcasts, addresses to military personnel, correspondence with thousands of inquirers, and frequent dialogue with university students and professors. His writings addressed many areas vital for missiology, such as theology of religions, the relationship between pre-Christian myths and Christian truth, the respective roles of rational clarity and ritual mystery, the interaction between religion and culture, the eternal destiny of adherents of other religions, the dynamics of translating the gospel into various languages and idioms, the evils of colonialism, the pitfalls of missionary paternalism, and the relation between divine revela-

---

[3]Lyle Dorsett says he was told by Presbyterian pastor Rodman Fridland that "in 1958 the Committee on Ecumenical Missions and Relations (COMAR) surveyed 415 missionaries in the United Presbyterian Church. Among other questions, they asked, 'Who was the most influential person in your becoming a missionary?' Fifty percent of those on the mission field wrote 'C.S. Lewis' on the questionnaire" (Dorsett, 2004, 21). I tried without success to find a copy of the survey, so I cannot confirm the accuracy of the reminiscence.

tion and social manifestations of Christianity. Notwithstanding the abundant mission-related elements in Lewis's thought and practice, it seems rare for missiologists to publish on Lewis.

Conversely, few Lewis specialists have used the tools and perspectives of missiology to produce major studies of Lewis's understanding of his mission field. Missiologically significant dimensions of Lewis, as sampled above, are plentiful—indeed, far more than I intend to address. In this book, I touch upon this wide variety of matters only insofar as they bear on the specific focus of my study of Lewis: his cultural diagnosis of his mission field and his view of the role and limits of rationality in an appropriate response. I hope that this book contributes a fresh mission perspective to Lewis studies, even as I bring a key dimension of Lewis to mission studies.[4]

Newbigin's Life and Impact

Lesslie Newbigin (1909-1998) came from an affectionate Christian home in Scotland. Though he rejected Christianity in his teens, he returned to the faith, joined a Presbyterian congregation, and during his university days was active in the Student Christian Movement (SCM). Newbigin married Helen Henderson, a daughter of missionaries to India, and the Newbigins served as missionaries in India from 1936 to 1959 and from 1965 to 1974.

[4]Of 93 doctoral dissertations on Lewis, it appears none has been written for a department of missiology. Published books on Lewis include biographies (Jacobs 2005; Green and Hooper 1974; Sayer 1988; A. N. Wilson 1990) and encyclopedic collections of essays that summarize writings by and about Lewis, highlight elements of his thought, and identify key associates (Duriez 2000; Hooper 1996; Schultz and West 1998). Two anthologies offer recollections from people who knew Lewis (Como 1992; Gibb 1965). Other books focus on Lewis's fiction and contributions to literature (Adey 1998; Carnell 1974; Downing 1992; Howard 1987; Myers 1994; Schakel 1984; Walsh 1979). Some authors offer overviews and analyses of Lewis's thought (Kilby 1964; Holmer 1976; Kort 2001; Vaus 2004). Additional books trace Lewis's Spirit-suffused worldview (Payne 1995), his interaction with mysticism (Downing 2005a), and his social ethics (Meilaender 1978).

Closer to my specific area of inquiry, Aeschliman (1998) and Kreeft (1994) discuss materialistic scientism and the deterioration of Western civilization as portrayed in Lewis's *The abolition of man*. Some authors trace Lewis's arguments for Christianity (Purtill 1981; Lindsley 2005; Reppert 2003) or develop a philosophical polemic against Lewis's arguments (Beversluis 1985). Burson and Walls (1998) compare Lewis's apologetic with Francis Schaeffer's. Two anthologies of essays explore various dimensions of Lewis as a Christian witness with an evangelistic vision (Menuge 1997; Mills 1998).

Newbigin was a leader in the ecumenical movement. In India he pressed for unification of churches that had been started by Presbyterian, Congregational, Methodist, and Anglican missionaries. When the merged bodies became the Church of South India in 1947, Newbigin was ordained as a bishop. In 1948 Newbigin served as a consultant at the formative meeting for the World Council of Churches (WCC). He was deeply involved in the International Missionary Council, became its chair, and in 1958 helped bring it into the WCC. From 1961 to 1965, Newbigin lived in Geneva and directed the WCC's Division of World Mission and Evangelism. He also edited the *International Review of Missions*.

After returning to India and ministering there for another decade as Bishop of Madras, Newbigin retired at age 65 and settled back in England. From 1974 to 1979 he was professor of ecumenics and missiology at Selly Oak Colleges, Birmingham. Retiring from that post at age 70, he became pastor (without pay) of a tiny United Reformed congregation in the Winson Green area of Birmingham, which he served from 1980 until 1988.

A prolific lecturer and writer, Newbigin wrote many articles and books during his years away from Britain. *The household of God* (1953) advocated missional, ecumenical ecclesiology. *Honest religion for secular man* (1966) upheld faith in a personal God and confidence in Scripture while applauding some elements of secularization. *The finality of Christ* (1969) insisted on the uniqueness of Jesus and the need to continue calling all peoples to conversion. While teaching at Selly Oak during his first years back in England, Newbigin published *The open secret: An introduction to the theology of mission* (1995a [1978]).

From the early 1980s onward, Newbigin's books focused on mission to the West: *The other side of 1984: Questions for the churches* (1983); *Foolishness to the Greeks: The gospel and Western culture* (1986b); *The gospel in a pluralist society* (1989a); *Truth to tell: The gospel as public truth* (1991); *Proper confidence: Faith, doubt, and certainty in Christian discipleship* (1995b); and *Truth and authority in modernity* (1996b).

Newbigin's long missionary career, his prominence in the International Missionary Council and the World Council of Churches, and his many lectures, articles, and books make him, beyond dispute, a major figure among missiologists. The strand of Newbigin's work that stands out as one of his most distinctive and influential contributions to missiology has been his emphasis on mission to the West and his analysis of Western culture, rationality, and epistemology (how we know what we know).

Newbigin has influenced leaders and inspired movements. For instance, megachurch pastors Tim Keller (2001) and Mark Driscoll (Driscoll and Breshears 2008, 218) and authors John Armstrong (2010) and Nancy Pearcey (2008) draw heavily on Newbigin. Various movements have sprung from Newbigin's address to the West. The Gospel and Our Culture movement has networks in Britain, the United States, Canada, New Zealand, and South Africa, seeking to cultivate missionary engagement appropriate for each of these societies. Books in The Gospel and Our Culture Series seek to address the gospel to North American culture. Also noteworthy are the Missiology of Western Culture Project and the book series Christian Mission and Modern Culture. The original impetus for these various projects and publications came from Newbigin's launch of The Gospel and Our Culture Programme in the United Kingdom during the early 1980s. It may be noteworthy that this network later merged with the C. S. Lewis Society (Foust and Hunsberger, 2002, 324-325). The fact that British admirers of Lewis and Newbigin banded together makes it all the more appropriate for this book to juxtapose the views of Lewis and Newbigin on rationality in mission to Britain and the West.

Newbigin prioritized mission to the West and called epistemology central; yet, despite his influence among many missiologists, there is a lack of major missiological works probing into Newbigin's views on rationality and epistemology in connection with mission to the West. Various articles in periodicals or small portions of books deal in some way with Newbigin's gospel for the West in connection with his views on epistemology and apologetics. Some of these are helpful, but their brevity precludes the kind of in-depth analysis possible in a longer treatment. This book adds to Newbigin studies by focusing at length on Newbigin's view of rationality in mission to Western culture, and by comparing Newbigin's views to Lewis's.[5]

---

[5]Major books about Newbigin include biographies (Wainwright 2000; Jackson 2001) and a study of his implicit theology of cultural engagement (Hunsberger 1998). These books deal only briefly with Newbigin's views on epistemology and apologetics in mission to the West. A book by Foust deals with "the missiological approach to modern Western culture" in the work of Newbigin and Dean E. Walker (2002a). However, that work focuses mainly on Christology, restoration, and unity, not on epistemology and apologetics as such. Epistemologically relevant fruits of Foust's study appear in a brief essay on Newbigin's epistemology as "a dual discourse" (Foust

Mapping Out this Book

By examining and comparing original writings of C. S. Lewis and Lesslie Newbigin, this book portrays two prominent approaches to missional apologetics. These approaches are explored with particular attention to the nature and role of plausibility and rationality in each author's cultural diagnosis and missionary prescription for the post-Christendom West.

Christianity's decline in much of the West is one of the foremost challenges for contemporary mission to address. Lewis and Newbigin represent two leading figures in mission to the West. By locating them in a changing cultural context and exploring their perceptions of that context, by clarifying their views on the nature, role, and limits of reason, and by placing their approaches side by side for comparison and evaluation, this book may contribute to missionary understanding of the West. It may heighten awareness of cultural contexts and enhance intentionality in exercising the apologetic dimension of gospel witness.

The book has eleven chapters. In this introductory chapter, I have shown the urgency that both Lewis and Newbigin felt for approaching the West as a mission field. I have identified both men as practitioners of missional apologetics, and I have briefly sketched each man's life and impact.

In chapter 2 I examine how Lewis and Newbigin viewed the Christendom of Europe's past and their perceptions of how the situation was changing before and during the time in which each was writing. I also place alongside their analyses relevant scholarship from sociologists of religion, social historians, and missiologists who have written about Christendom and subsequent cultural and religious shifts. The main aim of chapter 2 is to show how Lewis and Newbigin each located his particular context within the larger sweep of European history and saw his own times in relation to the earlier Christendom era.

In chapters 3 and 4, I sketch developments in the twentieth century British context that Lewis and Newbigin encountered firsthand in their settings or commented on in their analyses of the West in their times.

2002b). *A scandalous prophet: The way of mission after Newbigin* (Foust, et al. 2002) is comprised of over 20 short pieces from various authors. Of twelve doctoral dissertations focused on Newbigin, only Smith's (1999) involves a lengthy attempt to explore and evaluate Newbigin's apologetics. However, Smith's approach is exclusively philosophical and theological, not missiological; he says little about cultural context. Also, Smith misreads Newbigin to be an evidentialist apologist.

Chapter 3 identifies key trends: quantitative declines in British church involvement and Christian belief, a major societal shift toward post-Christian sexuality, and changes produced by Britain's loss of colonial control, increased immigration, and higher levels of diversity. Chapter 4 highlights what was happening in influential institutions: school, home, media, government, and church. Both chapters include observations from various scholars, but most of the material is comprised of what Lewis and Newbigin themselves saw in their contexts, with particular attention given to where each author linked elements of his context to matters of belief and rationality. These chapters are meant to convey a multifaceted sense of what each author grappled with in the cultural setting in which he was trying to commend the Christian faith, identifying ways in which the two missionaries' settings and perceptions differed from one another as well as ways they overlapped. This provides a broad cultural grounding for the more specific focus of the following chapters on intellectual obstacles and opportunities in mission to the West.

Chapters 5, 6, and 7 zero in on Lewis. In chapter 5, I trace Lewis's diagnosis of thought patterns prevalent in his context that obstructed Christian plausibility. I show how he profiled the mindsets of three groups: working-class people who were intelligent but not highly educated, modern people more generally, and educated elites. In chapter 6, I explore his epistemological views, his observations about various ways our minds grasp something of reality. In chapter 7, I examine Lewis's apologetics. I identify his tactics for defending and commending Christianity, and I show his recurring emphasis on plausibility and personhood.

Chapters 8 and 9 turn the spotlight onto Newbigin. In chapter 8, I survey Newbigin's diagnosis of Western thought patterns in the late 1900s that posed major challenges to the gospel. I describe his major concerns about scientism and religious pluralism, and his contention that both problems sprang from the epistemology of Descartes and the Enlightenment. In chapter 9, I present Newbigin's prescription for epistemology and apologetics, noting particularly his insistence that all knowing is relational and must take God's revelation as its starting point. Newbigin's epistemology and apologetics are treated in a single chapter, whereas in dealing with Lewis, one chapter is devoted to his epistemology and another to his apologetics. My reason for devoting fewer pages to Newbigin than to Lewis and for not having a separate chapter on Newbigin's apologetics is quite simple: Newbigin did not

11

produce nearly the variety or amount of apologetic material that Lewis did.

After chapters devoting considerable space to detailed study of views expressed by Lewis and Newbigin, chapters 10 and 11 seek to distill things into compact, relevant form. Chapter 10 describes and evaluates key similarities and differences between Lewis and Newbigin in their diagnoses of intellectual hindrances to Christianity, their epistemological views, and their recommendations for apologetics. In the eleventh and final chapter, I briefly reflect on some considerations relevant for contemporary missional apologetics in Western societies.

Although Newbigin and Lewis are deceased, their influence lives on. If book sales are any indication, Lewis continues to connect with millions of people in the West and beyond. Newbigin's writings find fewer readers than Lewis's, but those who read Newbigin tend to hold key church positions: professors, pastors, evangelists, and missionaries. Many of these find his diagnosis of Western culture persuasive and his suggestions for mission valuable. Lewis and Newbigin remain significant figures in mission to the contemporary West, so it seems fitting and timely to study two such prominent missional apologists, not just separately but juxtaposed in a way that may enrich understanding of both. Their common concerns and similarities of context intersect enough to make comparison possible, yet they differ sufficiently from one another in their diagnosis and prescription to make a study of contrasts significant and stimulating.

CHAPTER 2

Christendom and Its Passing

Lewis and Newbigin each believed that throughout his own lifetime, Britain and other Western societies were in an ongoing process of moving further and further from a Christendom that had previously existed. Both authors expressed opinions about Christendom, its passing, and changes that were occurring even as they wrote. This chapter traces how each author located his particular context within the larger sweep of European history and saw his own times in relation to an earlier Christendom era.

Such areas of inquiry have drawn considerable scholarly attention. Missiologists discussing the West contrast the era of Christendom with post-Christendom. In a similar vein, sociologists and social historians who study and debate changes in Western religion often take past Christendom as a baseline against which to compare more recent times.[1]

In this chapter I examine how Lewis and Newbigin viewed the Christendom of Europe's past and their perceptions of how the situa-

---

[1] The Missiology of Western Culture Project (1992-1997) was a joint effort of missiologists and specialists from various disciplines. Among the publications arising out of this project is a collection of essays by various authors discussing *The decline of Christendom in Western Europe* (McLeod and Ustorf 2003). McLeod's introductory chapter provides a crisp description of Christendom, plus a concise survey of a wide spectrum of academic opinion about the nature and causes of Christendom's decline. McLeod's summary of scholarly literature ably combines range, brevity, and balance.

tion was changing before and during the times in which they were writing. I locate their perspectives against a backdrop of wider scholarly discussion about Christendom and about cultural and religious shifts away from it. I show that Lewis's and Newbigin's views on Christendom and its passing related closely to their diagnosis of the mission field they were addressing and to the nature and role of plausibility in witnessing to a post-Christendom context.

Definition of Terms

I use the term "Christendom" as shorthand for a situation in which the church was closely intertwined with government and other institutions. Christian rhetoric shaped and legitimized public discourse, and membership in society virtually made a person "Christian." Starting with Constantine, Christianity came "into alliance with the powers that be," as Hugh McLeod explains. By the end of the fourth century, most among the Roman elite adopted Christianity and prohibited other religions. Integrating the masses into the church "was much more long drawn out." In private some people continued to practice other religions long after they were outlawed. "But a pattern of relations between church and state and church and society had been established" and would be repeated as Christianity spread to other places.[2]

> For the next 1500 years most Christians learnt and practiced their faith in the context of 'Christendom'. That is, they lived in *a society where there were close ties between the leaders of the church and those in positions of secular power, where the laws purported to be based on Christian principles, and where, apart from certain clearly defined outsider communities, every member of the society was assumed to be Christian.* (McLeod 2003, 1; italics mine).

My usage of "Christendom" is similar to McLeod's definition.

---

[2]Christendom always had its opponents, even among Christians. Ever since the fourth century, observes McLeod, there have been some Christians who "opposed the identity between church and society or over-close links between church and state, or between the church and social elites. . . . [They] saw these associations as damaging to the church: 'Christendom' meant that the church was subjected to state interference, that it was forced to admit into membership those who were not true Christians, and that it was under pressure to condone contemporary customs and values which were unchristian. Since the radical Reformation of the sixteenth century there have always been Christians in western Europe who have insisted, as a matter of principle, that the church should remain independent of the state and that Christians must not use coercion to enforce their beliefs" (McLeod 2003, 1).

Speaking of "the post-Christendom West" does not entail that Christian beliefs and practices have disappeared in the West, or that Christianity's public influence has vanished, leaving no vestiges of the older Christendom. Rather, "post-Christendom" means that the church is no longer widely seen as a primary authority to direct and legitimate other social institutions, church teaching is no longer taken to be the main standard for belief and behavior, and members of society are no longer assumed to be Christian by default.

Scholarly Views of Christendom's Decline

Scholars debate reasons for Christendom's decline and disagree about when the most decisive shift occurred. But few disagree that the relation between Christianity and European society by the late 1900s was very different from what had been the case for many centuries of Christendom. "The decline of Christendom has been a very long drawn out process," says McLeod, "and the historian can distinguish between several distinct stages." First, the state began to tolerate more than one form of Christianity. Second, anti-Christian ideas were openly published. "Third was the separation of church and state. The fourth and most complex phase has been the gradual loosening of the ties between church and society" (McLeod 2003, 5). This loosening of ties has been both institutional and discursive. Formerly Christianity provided "a common language, shared by the devout, the lukewarm and even the secretly skeptical . . . and which provided generally accepted concepts and symbols." However, Christendom's decline "has meant that Christianity has been gradually losing its status as a lingua franca, and has tended to become a local language used by those who are professing Christians, but not understood by others" (2003, 11).

An influential line of thought has explained the decline of Christendom in terms of "the secularization thesis," which contends that modernization weakens religion. Comte, Durkheim, and Weber were early teachers of this view. In the 1960s, prominent secularization theorists asserted that wherever modernization and pluralization spread in the world, religious decline was likely to follow (Berger 1967, 107-109; B. Wilson 1966, 12-14). Some contemporary scholars, such as Steve Bruce, still contend for a strong version of the secularization thesis that "modernization creates problems for religion" (2002a, 2).

A growing number of specialists, however, have questioned the broad claim that modernization weakens religion. Peter Berger, noting

American religiosity, Islamic resurgence, evangelical expansion in various nations, and growth in other religious communities (2001b, 445), has altered his earlier view and says that most sociologists of religion "agree that this theory has been empirically falsified" (2005, 112). Berger sees a largely religious world with two major exceptions: Europe, and a global educated elite holding key positions in many nations (1999, 9-11; 2001a, 194; 2003; 2005, 112-114).

Various scholars have proposed alternatives to the strong version of "the secularization thesis." Supply-side thinkers (mostly American) flatly reject the notion that modernization weakens religion. They take potential religious demand to be constant and explain variations in the strength of institutional religion in terms of whether religious suppliers are competitive and offer sufficient quality. In their estimation, Christendom's suppression of religious competition weakened Christianity in Europe. Supply-siders contend that Europe was never very Christian in the past, and that it is as religious now as it has ever been (Cox 2003; Stark and Iannaccone 1994, 241; Stark and Finke 2000). An avowedly postmodern perspective asserts that Christianity did not gradually fade in the course of modernization but that a sudden 1960s shift in sexual morals and gender roles dealt a death blow to British Christianity (Brown 2001). A less tidy but perhaps more nuanced account depicts the relationship between religion and modernization as dialectical and undulating, rather than as unidirectional (Martin 1991, 467; 2005a, 8-12; 2005b, 146). Still another line of thinking highlights a shift away from institutional and associational forms of religion toward subjectivized religiosity (Davie 1994; 1999; 2001; Heelas and Woodhead 2005).

Scholarly accounts vary, yet few deny the reality of at least one type of secularization: differentiation of various social spheres and public institutions from ecclesiastical control. Differentiation may be viewed as reducing religious authority, without entailing less religious zeal or belief at the individual level (Chaves 1994). It may also be viewed not just as an impersonal, irreversible process but as the reversible outcome of a contest between contending persons and groups (Smith 2003, McLeod 2000, 28-29, 84-85; Neuhaus 2005; Ramachandra 2005, 488; Sommerville 2003, 305).

Some think differentiation reduces the societal importance and authoritative public voice of religion (Dobbelaere 1999, 232; Lambert 1999, 331; 2004, 43; Voye 1999, 287). However, José Casanova discusses a counter-trend of "deprivatization," in which individual religiosity becomes more politicized and public spheres undergo "renormativization" by religiously derived principles (1994, 5-6). If churches no longer seek compulsory power through the state, this does not necessarily mean religion has been marginalized (Casanova 1994, 220). Indeed, past attempts to preserve religious coercion may have backfired. When European churches resisted differentiation of various spheres from ecclesiastical ties and strove to prolong Christendom, the unintended result was to reinforce an impression that Christianity fostered oppression, thus alienating many Europeans from churches (Casanova 1994, 29; Chadwick 1975, 107-139; Hervieu-Leger 2001, 118).

In this book, I am focusing on the views of C. S. Lewis and Lesslie Newbigin; I am not trying to provide a thorough analysis of wider academic discussion about Europe's transition from Christendom to post-Christendom. But I have offered this brief sketch of scholarly literature because both Lewis and Newbigin commented on Christendom and on religious changes associated with modernization. Moreover, Newbigin drew directly upon scholarly discussions of secularization, and his views shifted from one end of the sociological spectrum to the other, as we shall see. With a range of academic viewpoints as a backdrop, I now trace what Lewis and Newbigin said about Christendom and its passing.

Lewis's Perspective

Lewis did not use the particular terms "Christendom" and "post-Christendom" as deployed by some contemporary scholars; however, he used similar terminology with a considerable overlap of meaning. European history could be divided roughly into three eras: "the pre-Christian, the Christian, and what may reasonably be called the post-Christian." Lewis spoke of "the christening of Europe" as an epochal change by which a culture previously shaped by classical paganism gave way to a culture pervaded by professedly Christian ideas and institutions. He also spoke of Europe's "un-christening," a "cultural change" that was "even more radical" and "more profound" than the earlier "christening." Lewis thought this "un-christening" had been underway from about the 1830s onward. He stated, "Of course the un-christening of Europe in our time is not quite complete; neither was her christening in the Dark Ages" (1962, 12-14). There were "lots of skeptics" during the Christian period and "lots of Christians now," noted Lewis. "But the presumption has changed." Formerly, "some kind and degree of religious belief and practice were the norm: now, though I would gladly believe that both kind and degree have improved, they are the exception" (1962, 19-20). At times Lewis could lament "the apostasy of the greater part of Europe from the Christian faith" (2007, 365; see also 1946a, 293). Yet he was reluctant to glorify the earlier Christendom; his knowledge of its faults prevented simplistic nostalgia.[3]

From Constantine to the 1500s

Lewis had misgivings about the way Christendom became established in Europe. He wrote, "I sometimes have a feeling that the mass-conversions of the Dark Ages, often carried out by force, were all a false dawn, and the whole work has to be done over again" (2004b, 948). Lewis also questioned whether widespread belief in some Christian truths during the medieval era necessarily entailed real faith. The "assumed background" was a "particular world-picture" which included *"coarser factual* elements of Christianity" along with "Feudalism, Ptolemaic Astronomy, Neo-Platonic Demonology etc."[4] Intellectual acceptance of "the Redemption & Heaven & Hell as fact" did not necessarily have "religious significance" in a setting where "the climate of opinion" made intellectual acceptance almost unavoidable. It could be merely "knowing Christ according to the flesh" (2004b, 953-954).[5]

---

[3] Lewis was not a professional sociologist or missiologist, but in matters related to the many centuries of European Christendom, his expertise was considerable. As a reader of a vast array of texts written in Greek, Latin, French, Italian, German, Old Icelandic, Old Welsh, Old English, and Middle English (Heck 2005, 18), Lewis acquired a rare breadth and depth of acquaintance with various eras and societies in European history. As a literary historian, Lewis studied various dimensions of history and was thus aware both of positive and negative elements during Europe's Christendom phase.

[4] In recent discussion among sociologists of religion, Rodney Stark similarly questions how genuinely Christian the masses ever became during the ages when their rulers and power structures were "converted." Before Constantine, contends Stark, Christianity "was spread by rank-and-file members through their social networks," but after Constantine the focus shifted to "professional missionaries who were, for the most part, content to baptize kings." Stark asserts that "the first era of real Christian missions ended some time in the fourth century," as "the missionizing spirit of the rank-and-file" was "allowed to decay," and it did not rekindle until monolithic Christendom gave way to religious competition. Only then did Christian groups again become "'bottom-up', mass movements" (2001, 107, 116).

[5] Recent sociological debates over the nature and causes of religious change in Europe involve differing views on individual religiosity under Christendom. Bruce views the Middle Ages, if not as "a Golden Age of faith," at least as a high point of

In *The discarded image* (1964) and elsewhere, Lewis wrote appreciatively of the world picture he saw as prevalent in the Middle Ages among educated people and perhaps among many of the uneducated as well. But he did not depict medieval European cosmology as thoroughly Christian, nor did he nostalgically call for a return to it. Lewis spoke of "Pagan elements embedded in" medieval cosmology which were "subtly out of harmony" with Christianity. In his estimation, medieval intellectuals' appreciation of their model of the universe was rarely fused with "intense religious feeling of a specifically Christian character" (1964, 18-19).[6] Lewis also recognized that modern science had exposed major errors in the medieval understanding of the universe, thus making it impossible to go back to it. Therefore, despite his delight in many elements of "the Medieval Model," Lewis explicitly stated that he did not recommend a return to it (1964, 122).

Another dimension of the Middle Ages which Lewis did not want to resurrect was its philosophy. While some of his contemporaries thought a revival of Thomism would help to renew Christian thought, Lewis frowned on attempts to restore scholastic philosophy. Lewis

---

religious influence (1995, 418-419; 2002, 45-59). Stark, however, sees the Middle Ages as a time of largely apathetic, ignorant clergy who failed to connect with the peasants comprising most of the population. Few people attended church faithfully, and their beliefs—though "religious" in many respects—were not particularly Christian (Stark 1999, 255-260; Stark and Iannaccone 1994, 241-244). C. John Sommerville says that scholarly disputes about popular levels of orthodox belief or church involvement in the Middle Ages miss the point. Religion back then, according to Sommerville, was not so much a matter of faith as of culture—of deeply embedded assumptions and customs. "The disappearance of medieval religious culture was so complete that we can't even imagine that lost world. We assume that religion is a thing to think about when it used to be a way of thinking. That is the secularization that deserves to be considered the biggest change in the last several millennia" (2002, 367). Of these three assessments of medieval religion, Sommerville's appears closest to Lewis's view.

[6]Jesuit scholar Peter Milward, a former student of Lewis, contends that Lewis's reconstruction of the medieval model does not do justice to its Christian character. Lewis focuses too narrowly on "classical pagan authors or those Christian authors who most reflect pagan influence," while failing to give due weight to the profoundly Christian outlook of "eminent representatives of mediaeval thought." Where vestiges of classical paganism remained in some medieval writers, these were usually peripheral to their interests, argues Milward. What Lewis depicted as the medieval model "isn't a mediaeval model at all but a mere relic from late classical literature." In Milward's judgment, Lewis as a Protestant was "on the modern side of 'the Great Divide,'" reflecting the bias of Oxford's "Greats" curriculum toward classical paganism and Protestantism, and thus unable to recognize the authenticity of Catholic Christianity in the Middle Ages (Milward 1995, 80-85).

held some things in common with Aquinas and valued some aspects of scholastic thought, but he regarded scholasticism as an excessively rigid intellectual system and expressed his distaste for all such systems. Moreover, Lewis viewed every movement in philosophy as temporary and therefore thought it would be a foolish tactic to tie Christian credibility too tightly to any system which was bound to fade: "we have no abiding city even in philosophy: all passes, except the Word" (2004b, 176, 188-189).

In Lewis's 1954 inaugural lecture as Professor of Mediaeval and Renaissance Literature at Cambridge, he called himself (with tongue partly in cheek) a "spokesman of Old Western Culture," a historical "specimen" comparable to a Neanderthal or a dinosaur (1962, 23-24). But it would be a misreading to suppose that Lewis lived in the past or sought to turn back the clock to some point in the medieval era.[7] Even though he thought the past contained much that could be studied for instruction and delight, Lewis did not seek to restore any past system of philosophy or theology, nor did he pine for an older, supposedly pure Christian cosmology or an imagined age of universally devout faith.

From Catholic to Protestant

As Lewis did not idealize an era when a united Catholic church tried to forge a Christian society, so he did not glorify the Reformation era or the Church of England. He described Calvin as "an unhesitating doctrinaire, ruthless and efficient." From "the original Protestant experience" of grace, Calvin raised "all the dark questions" and used extrapolation to arrive at pitiless answers (1954, 42-43). Lewis portrayed Henry VIII as demon fodder (1960c, 154) and spoke of "that whole tragic farce which we call the history of the Reformation" (1954, 37). In his estimation, the theological questions disputed during that time had "no significance except . . . on a high level of the spiritual life." Mature, godly scholars with ample time for private discussion might have been able to reach a balanced understanding without rending the church. But instead the theological questions became entangled with "a whole complex of matters theologically irrelevant" and "attracted the fatal attention both of government and the mob. . . . Each party increasingly

---

[7]For instance, a Lewis contemporary, E. L. Allen (1945, 318), derided Lewis for operating as though "a return to the Middle Ages in its most superstitious phases is the best that can be done to commend Christianity to our time."

misunderstood the other and triumphed in refuting positions which their opponents did not hold" (1954, 37). Nearly everyone still took for granted a theocratic polity—which Lewis regarded as "the worst corruption" of government (1986, 40)—and almost all assumed the responsibility of enforcing their version of true religion through persecution of any who disagreed (1954, 39).

Most of England's population switched from Roman Catholic to Protestant in a relatively short time. Lewis did not think this could be fully explained in terms of "the hypothesis that most sixteenth-century Englishmen had no religion at all" and merely did government's bidding. Religion was "ubiquitous" but "not very theological." Lewis noted that people not specifically discussing religion operated with "the assumption, unemphasized because it is unquestioned, that every event, every natural fact, and every institution, is rooted in the supernatural. . . The writers do not argue about it; they know" (1954, 38).[8] Lewis suggested that most English people at the time had a similar mindset. "If so, its centre did not lie where the controversial divines teach us to look. It is significant that changes in ritual seem to have provoked more opposition than changes in doctrine" (1954, 38-39).

Under the polity of the time, says Lewis, it was widely assumed that one's "beliefs, like his actions, were to be ruled by his Betters." The common person still had a conscience and a religion—a conscience burdened by various failings and "a religion deeply concerned with the state of the crops and the possibility of making a good end when his time came. But the great controversies were too hard for him." Far removed from pope and king, such a person had more immediate contact with the local squire and parson. If rituals did not change drastically, suggested Lewis, the national switch from Roman Catholic to Protestant did not mean a sudden, radical change in most people's folk religion (1954, 39-40).[9]

---

[8]Lewis was not just offering a hasty generalization about the writers of the 1500s. According to Alan Jacobs (2005, 184), Lewis had read *every* sixteenth century book in the vast collection of Oxford's Duke Humfreys Library during his two decades of researching and writing *English literature in the sixteenth century, excluding drama* (1954), the volume he contributed to *The Oxford history of English literature*.

[9]Milward disputes the notion that Reformation-era changes "largely went over the heads of most Englishmen." Rather, Henry VIII "dealt the deathblow to mediaeval England." Milward says Lewis "fails to see what a deep revolution was brought about within a few years not only in religion, but also in the laws and customs of Englishmen and in the way they came to look at the world around them" (1995, 43).

Lewis did not view any earlier era of Europe's history as a pure specimen of the good old days. Far from praising, and pining for, an imagined past golden age of Christianity, Lewis lamented, "Long have we erred. In reading the history of Europe, its destructive succession of wars, of avarice, of fratricidal persecutions of Christians by Christians, of luxury, of gluttony, of pride, who could detect any but the rarest traces of the Holy Spirit" (2007, 278). That is hardly high praise for Christendom's Christianity.

Christendom's Decline

Even though Lewis did not regard any era of European Christendom as a golden age, he believed that between the 1830s and his own time, a fundament cultural shift had been underway, constituting "the greatest change in the history of Western Man." This change involved at least four elements: alterations in the exercise of political power, shattering novelty in the arts, religion becoming exceptional rather than normal, and the psychological effect of "the birth of the machines" (1962, 18-22).

From about the 1830s onward, suggested Lewis, a post-Christian ethos came increasingly to characterize Europe. An earlier shift in thought among intellectuals occurred "somewhere near the end of the seventeenth century, with the general acceptance of Copernicanism, the dominance of Descartes, and (in England) the foundation of the Royal Society." But for quite some time this change among elites had only a limited effect on "our culture in general."[10] Up into the 1800s, "the tone of the common mind remained ethical, rhetorical, juristic, rather than scientific. . . . Science was not the business of Man because Man had not yet become the business of science." But then a major change accelerated, as scientific thought increasingly came to affect "everyone's daily life." New technologies proliferated and changed the way people lived. Moreover, humanity was increasingly subjected to scientific analysis and control as Darwin began "monkeying with the ancestry of Man, Freud with his soul, and the economists with all that is his" (1962, 16-17).

---

[10]Owen Chadwick similarly distinguishes between an intellectual shift among some European elites during the Enlightenment and a more widespread secularization in the 1800s. As Chadwick puts it, "the problem of secularization is not the same as the problem of enlightenment. Enlightenment was of the few. Secularization is of the many" (1975, 9).

In Lewis's view, this massive, multidimensional shift did not necessarily mean a decrease in the vitality of real faith or the number of genuine followers of Christ, but it did mean that Christianity was operating within a new setting and encountering new challenges. More will be said in later chapters about these specific challenges and Lewis's strategy for addressing them. Here I will note Lewis's reticence to regard visible changes in "religion" as accurate measures of genuine faith, and his reluctance to generalize about the state of religion in "the West."

Lewis, aware of declines in ritual observance and church attendance in Britain from the early 1900s to mid-century, did not think this necessarily showed a decline in real faith during that period. He recalled his own experience as a young atheist in 1914, being confirmed in church and taking communion "in total disbelief," largely to comply with social expectations and to avoid conflict with his father (1955b, 161). Lewis did not view higher levels of outward conformity in that earlier part of the 1900s as evidence of widespread faith.[11] In a 1953 letter, Lewis described Christians as a minority but expressed uncertainty whether real Christians had become fewer in recent decades. The main change from thirty years earlier was that "nominal Christianity has largely died out, so that only those who really believe now profess. The old conventional church-going of semi-believers or almost total unbelievers is a thing of the past." The fading of nominal Christianity meant fewer children reared to be Christian, he observed, but more adult conversions (2007, 326).

In a November 1946 article, "The decline of religion' (1970, 218-223), Lewis wrote about the religious situation at Oxford, noting that evidence could be found for contrary claims. Some evidence pointed to a terminal decline of religion among the younger generation, while other evidence indicated a revival of interest.

A frequently cited indicator of decline was that campus chapels which had been full back in 1900 were nearly empty in 1946. However, noted Lewis, attendance had plummeted at the very moment chapel was no longer compulsory. People with no desire to worship dropped out; a few devoted Christians remained. The end of compulsion did

---

[11]McLeod's recent scholarship on religious change in Europe makes a similar point: "Statistics of church attendance or participation in communion provide the best evidence of the extent and distribution of attachment to the various churches. They cannot, however, be used as evidence for religious belief or a lack of belief' (2000, 173).

not produce a different spiritual condition but only exposed what had long been true.[12] According to Lewis, this typified the supposed "decline of religion" throughout England.

Throughout the first half of the twentieth century, observed Lewis, visible Christian practice had dropped significantly in every social class and in every region. This was often regarded as a sign that the nation had gone from a Christian to a secular mindset during that period. But Lewis asserted that popular books written in the 1800s manifested an outlook as secular as that of the mid-1900s. With few exceptions, neither writers nor readers of that earlier period focused on eternity or looked for a supernatural salvation.

> One way of putting the truth would be that the religion which has declined was not Christianity. It was a vague Theism with a strong and virile ethical code, which, far from standing over against the 'World', was absorbed into the whole fabric of English institutions and sentiment and therefore demanded churchgoing as (at best) a part of loyalty and good manners and (at worst) a proof of respectability. (1970, 219-220)

As compulsion and social pressure lessened, churchgoing levels came to more accurately reflect the number of real believers seeking Christ. Lewis hinted that nineteenth-century forms of political and social pressure had been propping up a façade of religiosity that lacked the substance and strength to hold its own against opposition, or to stand on its own after the social and political props were removed. If nineteenth-century "anti-clerical and anti-theistic forces" had faced "a solid phalanx of radical Christians," the faith's influence on public institutions and its attraction for individuals might have held firm. "But mere 'religion' . . . has little power of resistance. It is not good at saying No" (1970, 220).[13]

---

[12]Some have wrongly claimed that Lewis idealized the late 1800s or early 1900s. For instance, John Wain asserts that Lewis's "chief allegiances" were to the Edwardian age he grew up in, resulting in "withdrawal from the age he lived in. . . . He was fighting a perpetual rear-guard action in defense of an army that had long since marched away" (1992, 71-73). But Lewis, though opposing a radical cultural break from all ties to the heritage of the past, did not seek to replicate decades that he bluntly depicted as deeply flawed by imperialistic politics, cutthroat economics, social pomposity, and widespread religious hypocrisy.

[13]Chadwick (1975) and McLeod (2000) offer important discussions of what they term "secularization" in Europe during the latter half of the 1800s. Chadwick describes social factors in the rise of anticlericalism (1975, 107-139). He also discusses various elements of "the intellectual problem" that confronted religion in that era

The decline of such religion could be a blessing in some respects, observed Lewis. He recalled earlier times when "'Religion' (as distinct from Christianity) was too vague to be discussed . . . and so mixed up with sentiment and good form as to be one of the embarrassing subjects." But as "religion" declined, such social and sentimental embarrassment diminished, and issues became clearer. Christianity could at least be identified as a distinct intellectual option.[14] Open discussion could even lead to conversion. In Lewis's view, the fading of English "religion" might have negative social effects, such as increased public impurity, police brutality, and incivility among political opponents. But it would not necessarily make "conversions to Christianity rarer or more difficult." Rather, it would make "the choice more inescapable" (1970, 220).

Along with the decline of "religion," Lewis saw young intellectuals in 1946 showing more interest in Christianity than had been the case in 1920. Though pleased about this, he expressed two cautions. First, he noted that heightened interest and even intellectual assent did not necessarily mean the conversion of England or of any individual. Conversion required a change of will resulting from divine intervention. While Lewis emphasized this, he differed from "those who would therefore conclude that the spread of an intellectual (and imaginative) climate favorable to Christianity is useless." When a person comes to the crisis point of either accepting or rejecting Christ, the inner battle is best fought under conditions in which "his reason and imagination are not on the wrong side." Those who cultivate a favorable climate—"the propagandist, the apologist"—are doing useful preparatory work, and these "mere Christian intellectuals" should keep pursuing their modest task. However, intellectual renewal would lead to greater, lasting results

---

(1975, 143-266). While Chadwick seeks to describe social and intellectual aspects of *The secularization of the European mind in the 19th century*, McLeod's stated aim is to trace "the secularization of European *society*" [emphasis his] during that period, showing what happened among the masses and in "the relationship between religion and public institutions" (McLeod 2000, 12).

[14]Lewis may have been partly right about such a change, but open discussion of Christian claims and the possibility of conversion were still regarded with distaste by Oxford's establishment and by many other English people. Lewis experienced this personally. He told former student Harry Blamires, "You don't know how much I'm hated." Blamires observes, "Unspoken rules of academic decorum required one to be decently secretive about religious convictions" (1998, 16-21).

only if the Lord sent "the *Preacher* in the full sense, the Evangelist, the man on fire, the man who infects" (1970, 221-222).

Second, Lewis warned that part of the mid-1940s interest in Christianity might be little more than intellectual fashion, which could change overnight. Real conversions would last, he said, but fashionable interest in Christianity would fade. Real and lasting Christian revival might be occurring, but if so, it would "work slowly and obscurely and in small groups." The climate of warm interest would pass; opposition would grow. "That is why we must cherish no picture of the present intellectual movement simply growing and spreading and finally reclaiming millions by sweet reasonableness." The opposition would "quite likely be *called* Christianity" (1970, 222-223).

In a 1958 article "Revival or decay" (1970, 250-253), Lewis addressed claims that the West was experiencing a growing interest in religion during the 1950s. In his estimation, more willingness to discuss religion did not prove more devotion but more indecision. Such indecision could be more comfortable than real Christian commitment or consistent atheism. The conversion of some among the literary elite was unlikely to affect the wider population, argued Lewis, because "the Intelligentsia (scientists apart) are losing all touch with, and all influence over, nearly the whole human race."

Some optimists about religious ascendancy supposed that excessive faith in science no longer gripped people's minds as it once had done, noted Lewis, but in his experience, many people outside the intellectual elite still tended to expect science and education to put right whatever was amiss with humanity. Moreover, his personal encounters with atheists, Theosophists, believers in UFOs, British Israelites, Spiritualists, Pantheists, and saintly Christians persuaded him that it would be more helpful to speak of "religions" than of "religion." If any one trend stood out in his variety of contacts, it was superficiality and failure to ask ultimate questions. Many generalizations about religion in "the West," Lewis suggested, owed more to rehashes of books and articles than to firsthand contact with people.

> Is there a homogeneous West? I doubt it. Everything that can go on is going on all round us. Religions buzz about us like bees. . . . Meanwhile, as always, the Christian way too is followed. But nowadays, when it is not followed, it need not be feigned. That fact covers a good deal of what is called the decay of religion. Apart from that, is the present so very different from other ages or "the West" from anywhere else? (1970, 253)

A Shift in Default Assumptions

Lewis was wary of attempts to mark the level of genuine Christian vitality in any society or era. Even so, he perceived major differences between Christendom and the post-Christendom context he was living in. Various institutions of society no longer based their authority and norms on Christian claims—or, indeed, on any transcendent, objective source. Basic Christian factual claims were no longer widely assumed to be true, in contrast to a long era when such claims could almost be taken for granted by most European writers, without further argument or investigation (2004b, 953-954). In the newer social and intellectual setting, as Lewis viewed it, the factual claims of Christianity and the influence of the divine had little place in common thought and discourse. The default pattern of belief, conveyed and reinforced institutionally and interpersonally, had shifted. In Lewis's words, "Supernaturalism, even if false, would have been believed by the great mass of unthinking people four hundred years ago, just as Naturalism, even if false, will be believed by the great mass of unthinking people today" (1960b, 10).[15] In Christendom, the reality of the supernatural, the objective authority of moral law, and the truth of Christian creeds were held as common assumptions, with little dispute or need for persuasion. In post-Christendom modernity, other assumptions held sway.

In this new setting with its new default assumptions, belief in basic Christian teachings would usually involve individual reflection and decision about contested claims.[16] Therefore, thought Lewis, Christian

---

[15]For Lewis, "Naturalism" was not necessarily atheistic; it could also be pantheistic. The assumption was that Nature is not the handiwork of a purposive, personal God who created all things and might choose to act upon his world from the outside, either through special providences or miracles (1960b, 130-133, 252, 268-272).

[16]Lewis's view is paralleled in some respects by the later sociological theory of religion proposed by Peter Berger in *The Sacred Canopy* (1967). Where Lewis spoke of what is "believed by the great mass of unthinking people" in a society, Berger applied the technical terminology of "plausibility structure" to the social base for regarding some things as self-evident and socializing the next generation in similar assumptions. Like Lewis, Berger held that Christendom's monopolistic plausibility structure no longer prevailed and that Christian belief was becoming increasingly dependent on individual, conscious choice. In a subsequent book, Berger labeled this necessity of choice *The heretical imperative* (1979a). Berger, writing after Lewis died, obviously did not influence him, but Berger did influence Newbigin. Newbigin explicitly interacted with *The heretical imperative* in *Foolishness to the Greeks* (1986b, 10-18), and he implicitly drew upon Berger's work in emphasizing the social construction of knowledge and in frequently using the term "plausibility structure."

witness would often need to make preparatory space, or a preliminary case, for claims that, in an earlier era, might have been accepted as obvious. Default assumptions contrary to Christianity would need to be disproved or at least made to seem less obvious, and Christian claims would need to be portrayed as plausible and important. Otherwise, the gospel message would be unlikely to gain a hearing among a population who had largely come to assume that Christianity was implausible and outdated.

Newbigin's Perspective

Newbigin, like Lewis, saw Western societies moving further from Christendom in various ways, including a shift in default assumptions. Newbigin's specific assessment of cultural developments, his weighting of their impact, and his recommendations for Christian witness were not always identical with Lewis's, as we shall see. But, like Lewis, he saw Christendom fading and had mixed feelings about the change.

Newbigin's evaluation of Christendom and his ideas about secularization shifted significantly over the years. During the 1950s and 1960s, Newbigin could criticize Christendom, rejoice in the advance of secularization, applaud missionaries' secularizing impact, and relish the occasion for a renewed missionary stance on the part of the church. But he could also—especially after the 1960s—lament post-Christendom social and religious disintegration, portray secularization (and the missionary contribution to it) more negatively, and say more positive things about Christendom. At no time, however, did he state that a return to Christendom was possible or desirable.

Criticizing Christendom, Celebrating Secularization

Writing in the 1950s and early 1960s, Newbigin spoke of "the breakdown of Christendom." He understood Christendom as "the synthesis between the Gospel and the culture . . . by which Christianity had become almost the folk religion of Western Europe." Over a thousand-year period, "the peoples of Western Europe . . . had the Gospel wrought into the very stuff of their personal and social life, so that the whole population could be conceived of as the *corpus Christianum*. That conception is the background of all the Reformation theologies." This *corpus Christianum*, contended Newbigin, suffused all aspects of European life but was isolated from the non-European world and was oblivious to its missionary calling (1953, 11). "Christendom almost lost consciousness of the world which was still waiting to be evangelized" (1961, 110).

Even when Christendom's synthesis of Christianity and European culture was in the process of disintegrating, its legacy continued to shape churches, mostly in an unhelpful manner. According to Newbigin, an ecclesiology inherited from Christendom lacked a properly missionary identity as revealed in Scripture and was not suited to the context of non-European lands nor to the post-Christendom European context.[17] Newbigin remarked on the rise of anti-Christian movements in Europe and declared that the majority of Western Europeans either deliberately rejected or passively ignored the Christian faith. Even as the twentieth century marked "the global spread" of a "new technical civilization" originally birthed within Christendom, it also marked "the end of Christendom. The period in which Christianity was the folk religion of the peoples of Western Europe is at an end." At just the moment when Western culture was affecting "almost the whole of mankind," that culture was itself disintegrating and bringing disintegration to ancient non-Christian cultures. In making these assertions, Newbigin added a passing remark that a fair assessment should reckon with "the remarkable revival in the life of the churches in the United States in the past decade" (1961, 15). However, at that point he did not expand on how the American context differed from Europe, nor did he comment on how American churches might differ from Christendom-shaped ecclesiology.

In the 1960s, secularization—somewhat variously defined—was a prominent concept among social scientists and among some church leaders, especially in the ecumenical movement. Newbigin accepted the sociological claim that secularization was "a universal fact." He declared, "The most significant fact about the time in which we are living is that it is a time in which a single movement of secularization is bringing the peoples of all continents into its sweep" (1966, 11).[18] He also

---

[17]To date the fullest examination of Newbigin's missionary ecclesiology is by Michael Goheen (2000). See p. 192-198 for a discussion of Newbigin's views on Christendom as an obstacle to the church's missionary awareness and on new difficulties raised when Christendom gave way to a public doctrine shaped by the Enlightenment.

[18]A widespread belief in global secularization reached the height of its influence among sociologists in the 1960s. Berger, for instance, spoke of "a global phenomenon of modern societies" in which religious institutions and symbols had a declining impact on social structures, cultural symbols, and individual consciousness. This

went along with much of the ecclesiastical tendency to endorse secularization. Newbigin depicted in a positive light "the withdrawal of more and more areas of human experience from direct reference to religion" (1963, 56). In a chapter on "Missions and the secularization of human life" (1963, 56-67), he said that secularization "could be a liberating process" which the church should not regret: "The challenge of man's coming of age has to be accepted." [19] Christendom-shaped mission efforts had launched educational, medical, and social institutions, but these aspects of life were being secularized. Christian missions, enthused Newbigin, "had been the great instrument of secularization in the midst of the ancient religious societies of Asia and Africa." This, he suggested, should help European Christians to find secularization less menacing (1963, 58-59). Nostalgia for Christendom might be understandable. "But we have to accept gladly the way God leads us," leaving Christendom behind as a "passing phase" and recognizing that "the 'desacralizing' of great areas of human life is all part of the journey by which God leads the world to the ultimate issue of faith or unbelief in Jesus Christ" (1963, 67).

In *Honest religion for secular man* (1966), Newbigin continued to depict "Western Christendom" as the historical situation in which Christianity had become "folk religion" and "the Church had become the religious department of European society rather than the task force selected and appointed for a world mission" (1966, 103). He proclaimed a new situation in which the church must ask what it means "to be God's people in a secularized world" (1966, 107). While Newbigin opposed radical theologians' denial of a personal God and reduction of the gospel to a demythologized secularism, he saw much to appreciate in secularization. He distinguished between "'secularism' as a closed system of belief and 'secularization' which is a historical process." Secularization in-

---

"global secularization process" was occurring, he claimed, because industrial society is an inherently secularizing force (Berger 1967, 107-109). In a similar vein, Bryan Wilson saw both Britain and the United States as secularized, and he held that in other societies around the world with different religious traditions, similar secularizing forces were advancing along with modernization (Wilson 1966, 12-14). One of the few sociologists to openly differ from the secularization thesis prevalent in the 1960s was David Martin (1965).

[19]At a 1957 mission conference, Newbigin lectured on "the work of God in the world outside the Church." According to Newbigin (1985a, 152-153), a conference participant, A. T. van Leeuwen, made the thesis of that lecture the starting point for his book *Christianity and world history* (1964). This book, in turn, exerted undue influence on Newbigin's own thinking in the 1960s, as he later admitted (1985a, 254).

volves "the withdrawal of areas of life and activity from the control of organized religious bodies, and the withdrawal of areas of thought from the control of what are believed to be revealed religious truths." At the same time, it included "the increasing assertion of the competence of human science and technics to handle human problems of every kind." Newbigin argued that this could "be seen as man's entering into the freedom given to him in Christ, freedom from the control of all other powers, freedom for the mastery of the created world which was promised to man according to the Bible" (1966, 8-9).

In lectures delivered in 1966 and published in 1969 as *The finality of Christ*, Newbigin observed that "many of the changes for which missions had laboured in the past are now being carried through with far greater success by secular agencies" (1969, 45). A chapter on "The gospel as a secular announcement" asserted "the integral connection between the impact of the biblical conception of God upon Asia and the process of secularization," insisting that "the real clue to the meaning of the process of secularization is to be found in the Gospel. Rightly understood, the process of secularization is an extending of the area of freedom wherein man has the opportunity to understand and respond to what God has done for the world in Jesus Christ" (1969, 63).

Throughout this period, Newbigin could rejoice that secularization freed people from sacral societies and made faith more a matter of personal decision, even as he expressed cautions. But Newbigin's "secular flirtation" did not last. Secularization's good side, suggests Geoffrey Wainwright, was more evident to Newbigin when India was on his mind, when Christian mission was threatened by Hindu nationalism. But after returning to Britain, the downside of secularization came to dominate Newbigin's thinking as he saw "the disastrous results of Christendom's collapse in British society" (Wainwright 2000, 354).

Rethinking Secularization

Even before he returned to England, Newbigin was already souring on secularization, due in part to his "shattering experience" of the Uppsala assembly of the World Council of Churches in 1968. The radicalized gathering at Uppsala seemed to be a case in which theological embrace of secularization led to repudiation of evangelism, denigration of the church's importance, and reduction of the gospel to sociopolitical radicalism. Faced with this jarring development, Newbigin's longtime devotion to church and evangelism proved stronger than his temporary and qualified approval of secularization. "It was probably the Uppsala assembly that sealed Newbigin's disillusionment with secularizing theology" (Wainwright 2000, 354).[20]

In *The open secret*, first published in 1978, Newbigin declared that "with the radical secularization of Western culture, the churches are in a missionary situation in what once was old Christendom" (1995a, 2). In this statement *secularism* (as a closed system of thought excluding the divine) was no longer clearly distinguished by Newbigin from *secularization* (as a historical process by which the sacral society of Christendom and other "ontocratic societies" had been desacralized).

Newbigin came to doubt the viability or desirability of an interconnected world linked by global secularization. In 1985 he wondered,

> Is there really emerging a secular "world community" which will be held together by the science, technology, commerce and political ideas of post-Enlightenment Europe? Twenty years ago I thought so, but now I am not sure. . . . I do not now believe that the "modern" secular culture of the post-Enlightenment West has an assured future. It seems to me to show all the signs of disintegration. (1985a, 254)

By the later 1980s, Newbigin had come to share in a shift of opinion among some sociologists about the outcome of modernization. These sociologists rejected "the secularization thesis" that had been so widely influential. The thesis had asserted that modernization would bring disenchantment of individual consciousness.[21] But this had failed to occur, in the opinion of some observers. In line with this change of scholarly opinion, Newbigin described the West as not "a secular socie-

---

[20]At Uppsala, Newbigin found that many enthusiasts for secularization angrily called for radical social and political upheaval while mocking eternal salvation. Meanwhile, Donald McGavran's "deafening barrage about the unevangelized millions of the world" struck Newbigin as "counter-productive." Even those WCC delegates who wanted to emphasize "the unfinished evangelistic task" were leery of being "aligned with the high-pressure propaganda of the 'Church Growth' school." Many delegates seemed to view the church as a "dubious institution" that was remote from the world's real needs and was hardly worth enlarging (Newbigin 1985a, 231-232).

[21]According to Weber, disenchantment comes in tandem with rationalization. People assume that "there are no mysterious incalculable forces that come into play, but rather that one can, in principle, master all things by calculation. This means that the world is disenchanted. One need no longer have recourse to magical means in order to master or implore the spirits, as did the savage, for whom such mysterious powers existed. Technical means and calculations perform the service" (Weber 1948, 139; cited by Bruce 2002a, 29).

ty" but a "pagan society" with all sorts of religious and quasi-religious beliefs and practices (1986b, 20). While atheistic principles shaped the reigning public philosophy (1986b, 65), private consciousness remained incurably religious, though seldom true to biblical faith.

In 1988 Newbigin delivered the lectures that would be published as *The gospel in a pluralist society* (1989a). He devoted one lecture to attacking "the myth of the secular society" (1989a, 211-221). Newbigin said that Max Weber and those in his wake had claimed that modernization caused disenchantment and that "the farther any society moves along the road of rationalization, industrialization, and urbanization, the more certain it is that religion will have a receding role in that society." However, continued Newbigin, sociologists had shown that in the society where these processes had gone farthest—the United States—religious belief was more than holding its own (1989a, 211-212).

Newbigin had been struck by *The sacred in a secular age* (Hammond, 1985), an essay collection which he characterized as "an almost unanimous confession that the belief which was accepted uncritically up to ten or twenty years ago, namely that the process of modernization would necessarily lead to the decline of religion, was totally mistaken" (1989a, 213). Newbigin cited Rodney Stark's thesis that the breakup of one religious group's hegemony over society would not bring a post-religious era but would instead "lead to a resupply of vigorous other-worldly religious organizations" (Stark 1985, 146; quoted in Newbigin 1989a, 213). In line with Stark, Newbigin asserted, "There are needs of the human spirit which simply must be met." Thus religions emphasizing the supernatural appeared to be flourishing, while those that "tried to accommodate as much as possible of the rationalism of the Enlightenment would decline" (1989a, 213).[22]

A second essay from *The sacred in a secular age* that impressed Newbigin was Robert Wuthnow's discussion of the correlation between religious belief and careers in the natural and social sciences. Exposure to higher education had an inverse relationship with holding basic religious beliefs, observed Wuthnow, but "it is the irreligious who are selected into academic careers in the first place, not that the process of being socialized into the academic life causes them to become less and less religious" (Wuthnow 1985, 191; quoted in Newbigin 1989a, 214).

---

[22]As Stark and Finke (2000, 276) would later phrase it, "whatever the intellectual merits of . . . modernized religion, it is clearly a failure on sociological grounds—in its inability to motivate and sustain religious organizations or activity."

Another significant finding was that those engaged in the natural sciences were far more likely to believe and practice religion than those in the social sciences and humanities. Wuthnow suggested that the irreligion of those in the human sciences—"the least scientific disciplines"— might indicate that "scientists in these fields may adopt an irreligious stance chiefly as one of the boundary-posturing mechanisms they use to distance themselves from the general public and thereby maintain the precarious reality of the work they do" (Wuthnow 1985, 199; quoted in Newbigin 1989a, 215).[23]

Such considerations prompted Newbigin to reject as untrue "the idea that secularization is an irreversible process which must lead to the inevitable marginalization of religion." He also charged that "the secularization theory has been accepted uncritically by Christians to justify a social institution." A secular society proffered escape from "the tyranny of dogma," offered "an accepted framework of shared rationality," and held out "the hope of peace among the warring religions and ideologies" (1989a, 215). But the result was "not a secular society but a pagan society . . . the age which called itself secular has produced an unprecedented crop of new religions. The secular society is a myth" (1989a, 220).

Thus, along with Newbigin's sharp turn away from theological enthusiasm for secularization came a drastic change in his sociological assessment of secularization. In echoing Stark's definition and wholesale rejection of "the secularization thesis," Newbigin swung from one end of the spectrum of sociological opinion to the other. Stark has continued to make his case vigorously (Stark 1999; Stark and Finke 2000).[24] However, he does not represent a consensus. Some sociologists, such as Bruce, remain close to the older extreme, holding a strong version of

[23]A similar discussion of the relationship between religion and science appears in Stark and Finke (2000, 52-55). They present evidence akin to Wuthnow's and see merit in his suggestion of "boundary-posturing mechanisms" among social scientists.

[24]Stark declares, "To classify a nation as highly secularized when the large majority of its inhabitants believe in God is absurd" (1999, 254). But it may be less absurd than Stark—or the later Newbigin—might think. If a majority of survey respondents say they believe in a god of some sort, this does not disprove massive religious decline. When belief is held with less clarity and certainty, when it has less influence on public discourse and personal conduct, when religion is taken less seriously, then its importance has declined. If secularization is taken to mean religious decline, though not complete demise, I think the evidence indicates secularization in Britain, even though "the secularization paradigm" may be mistaken at some points about the causes of such decline or its irreversibility.

the secularization thesis that "modernization creates problems for religion" (Bruce 2002a, 2) and insisting that religion has little meaning or attraction for most Europeans (Bruce 1996, 234). Other scholars, though questioning or modifying grand theories about secularization, nonetheless recognize real and widespread changes, in which religion has come to have a reduced or non-existent role in social spaces that were once filled with religious discourse and governed by religious norms (Brown 2001; Chaves 1994; Davie 1994; 2000; 2002a; Martin 2005a; Smith 2003).

Of special interest here is Berger, given Newbigin's engagement with Berger, and Berger's stature as the foremost sociologist to recant his earlier advocacy of a strong version of "the secularization thesis." Even Berger does not go so far as Stark. Although Berger holds that the world is largely religious, he still identifies two major secularized exceptions: Europe, and a "Europeanized" educated elite worldwide (1999, 9-11; 2001a, 194; 2003; 2005, 112-114). Newbigin went further than Berger in rejecting the sociology of secularization, portraying even Europe not as secular but as growing more religious:

> The present century has in fact witnessed a marked growth in religiosity in Europe. It is true that this has not been expressed in Christian terms. But in the forms of many new religious movements, in the enthusiasm for Eastern types of religious belief and practice, in the revival of various ancient forms of pagan religion, and in the enormous popularity of astrology among European peoples, there is a luxuriant growth of religion in what is called the secular society. (Newbigin 1994a, 148)

Mapping Newbigin's understanding of secularization can be difficult. Not only did his views swing from one extreme in the 1960s to another by the 1980s, but his newer view seems to contain tensions and inconsistencies.[25] Newbigin could claim that European religiosity increased (in altered, non-Christian form) during the 1900s, yet at the same time he could also lament that religion had been reduced to a matter of personal preference and loosely held opinion. Even if one

[25]Like Newbigin, sociologist Grace Davie makes statements about European religion that are hard to harmonize. Sometimes she suggests that Europe is becoming differently religious, not less religious (1999, 65). At other times, Davie implies that religion in Europe—particularly in Britain—is not merely different but less than it was at a previous time, and less than in most other places today. She says that "taking faith or religion seriously is becoming, increasingly, the exception rather than the norm in British society" (1994, 70).

considers only Newbigin's writings after his return to England, terms such as "secular," "secularization," and "secular society" seem to shift in meaning from one page to another, without giving the reader notice and perhaps without Newbigin himself taking sufficient notice. He could deny that European society was secular, even while insisting that atheism ruled Europe's public life.

Perhaps the later Newbigin's view on secularization could be summarized thus: Europe's public standards for rational plausibility and rules for policy appealed to shared secular principles, consistent with atheism, but its people were far from secular in their private beliefs and behaviors. Trying to account for this paradox was a key part of Newbigin's diagnosis of the West, and he placed high priority on developing a Christian rationality that did not dichotomize public and private, as we shall see in later chapters.

Appreciation of Medieval Christendom

As Newbigin's views of secularization changed, his attitude toward Christendom also shifted. Newbigin remained somewhat ambivalent toward medieval Christendom, but in his later years he stressed its positive side more than he had done earlier. He placed less emphasis on Christendom's lack of missionary identity, stressing instead the pervasiveness of Christianity in all dimensions of medieval thought and life. When Newbigin sketched a profile of modern European culture in chapter 2 of *Foolishness to the Greeks,* he contrasted maladies of post-Enlightenment culture—point by point—with what he manifestly regarded as healthier characteristics during the Middle Ages.[26]

- "Medieval thought saw divine purpose manifest everywhere in the world of nature." All study occurred in a creedal framework confessing God's revealed purposes. In contrast, modernity's explanatory framework excluded purpose.

---

[26]Newbigin emphasized "the discontinuity between the Christendom and post-Enlightenment church," says Goheen. But some missiologists who build upon Newbigin point out "the continuity that also exists between these two periods." In Goheen's estimation, "The very reason the church takes a privatized role in western culture is because of its Christendom legacy. In Christendom the church found a place for itself within the constellation of powers within the culture; in the Enlightenment the place is much reduced but the mindset of establishment remains. This contributes to Newbigin's ambivalent interpretation of Christendom" (Goheen 2002, 197-198).

- The "old picture of how things are" was "derived from the Bible" and was dramatized "in the medieval mystery plays." In contrast, modernity's world picture ignored the possibility of miracles or providential intervention.

- "Medieval society was held together by a complex network of reciprocal rights and duties." In contrast, modernity's abstract, individualistic notion of "human rights" ignored relationships and responsibilities.

- "Medieval people believed . . . that final happiness lay on the other side of death. They did not expect it in its fullness on this earth." In contrast, modern culture fixated on this brief life in its "pursuit of happiness," making it "that much more hectic, more fraught with anxiety than it was to the people of the Middle Ages."

- In the Middle Ages, rights and duties, being rooted in mutual relationships, were finite. In contrast, modernity's "quest for happiness is infinite," with the nation-state being viewed as the guarantor of people's myriad demands and expectations.

- Medieval Christians, "taught by the Bible" and centered on "the will and purpose of God," saw history moving toward Jesus' second coming, the final judgment, and the holy city of eternal perfection. In contrast, post-Enlightenment culture "transferred the holy city from another world to this," counting on human achievement rather than divine gift.

- In premodern Europe, "as in contemporary premodern societies," farming and craftsmanship were mainly carried on "for the use of the family or the local community." In contrast, the modern economy ignored relational ethics and was ruled by money and market mechanisms (1986b, 26-30).

In contrast to the late twentieth century West, Newbigin looked back to "a time when public truth as it was understood and accepted in Europe was shaped by Christianity ... Europe was a Christian society in the sense that its public truth was shaped by the biblical story with its center in the incarnation of the Word in Jesus." The church provided "the integrating power for a new social order" after classical civilization collapsed. This yielded "enormous consequences for good. . . . It created the Christian civilization of Europe. But it also led the Church into the fatal temptation to use the secular power to enforce conformity to Christian teaching" (1989a, 222). While rejecting that age's coercion,

Newbigin came to affirm Christendom's best intentions and accomplishments, including its rationality which rooted public truth in the Christian story.

In this chapter, we have seen how Lewis and Newbigin, each in his own way, depicted how the West had been changing from the Christendom of the past to the context in which they were writing. In the next two chapters, we turn to more detailed consideration of some key elements of the twentieth century British context that were related to Christian vitality and plausibility (or lack thereof), and we examine Lewis's and Newbigin's experiences and perceptions of these things in their respective settings.

CHAPTER 3

Britain in the 1900s:
Three Key Trends

Lewis and Newbigin were both born near the start of the twentieth century: Lewis in 1898, Newbigin in 1909. Although born only a decade apart, Newbigin outlived Lewis by many years. Lewis died in 1963 and did not see the final third of the century. Newbigin, on the other hand, lived until 1998 and thus had opportunity to interact with more recent intellectual, social, political, and religious developments. Each man formed a reading of Western culture in his time, based partly on experiences and perceptions of British society.

Much can be learned through careful examination of each author's context in Britain. We can better grasp what each saw as the challenges and needs of the West in his own era. We can see the wider societal context in which issues of rationality and plausibility were enmeshed, thus steering clear of a reductionism that explains nearly everything in terms of the history of ideas, and instead gaining some proportion and perspective on where intellectual matters fit in the larger picture of lived realities and social arrangements. We can also identify some aspects of the British cultural context that influenced, or were influenced by, more specifically intellectual elements—at least as perceived by Lewis and/or Newbigin. At the same time, we can gain a sense of the degree to which similarities or differences between the two men's times and settings may have affected their respective views on what constituted major challenges to the Christian faith and the sort of responses each favored.

In this chapter and the next, I trace some developments in Britain (and sometimes beyond) that occurred at various stages of the 1900s. This chapter identifies some key trends: quantitative declines in British church involvement and Christian belief; societal shifting toward post-Christian sexuality; and changes produced by Britain's loss of colonial control, increased immigration, and higher levels of diversity. Chapter 4 highlights the roles played by influential institutions: school, home, mass communication, government, and church. I have selected these particular trends and institutions for discussion not only because many scholars have stressed their importance but also because Lewis and Newbigin, each in his respective time and location, commented on them.

Throughout these two chapters, I arrange my findings in a recurring format. Each of the areas under consideration is presented in a similar pattern: first comes a short introductory sketch rooted in scholarly hindsight, followed by a section about Lewis's perceptions and a section about Newbigin's perceptions. The material is arranged in this manner so that the reader can more easily compare and contrast Lewis's and Newbigin's perceptions in each dimension, aided by a backdrop of somewhat more objective accounts as provided by specialists in British history and sociology of religion.

Along the way, I have identified ways in which Lewis's mid-1900s setting in Britain differed from the setting Newbigin encountered in the century's final decades. I have also noted similarities between the two periods. I have identified tendencies that were already present by mid-century and intensified in the 1960s and beyond. I have included observations from Lewis and Newbigin about things in their context that they saw as relevant for the condition of Christian faith and witness—even if, in some cases, these things were not directly linked to specific issues of rationality and plausibility. (After all, part of gaining a proper perspective on the role of rationality is to be aware of its limits and of how people and societies are shaped by more than just ideas.) At the same time, I have taken special care to highlight where Lewis and Newbigin explicitly linked elements of their context to matters of belief and rationality. The wide-ranging cultural observations presented in these two chapters provide a broad, multifaceted foundation for the more specific observations in later chapters about plausibility, epistemology, and reasonable witness.

Quantitative Decrease of Christianity

Lewis and Newbigin both perceived that the church in Britain was on a downward trajectory quantitatively. Their perceptions are supported by the findings of sociologists and historians. Scholars depicting religious change in Britain between 1900 and 2000 differ over details or causal factors, but they largely agree that church attendance declined throughout the century, as did levels of church affiliation, Christian beliefs, and rites of passage. By the end of the century, only a small and shrinking segment of Britain's population retained close ties to orthodox, institutional Christianity.

Back in the mid-1800s, roughly half of British adults attended church on an average Sunday (Bruce 2002a, 63-64). Church attendance and membership remained quite stable until the late 1880s. From then until World War I, attendance dropped, even as membership held fairly steady (McLeod 2000, 179-181, 199-201). Thus by Lewis's and Newbigin's early years, British church attendance was already in decline. Lewis and Newbigin, however, both came from families who still attended church (Lewis 1955b, 7; 2004b, 702); Newbigin 1985a, 3). Church attendance kept declining throughout the first half of the twentieth century, but only gradually, dropping from 19 percent in 1903 to 15 percent in 1951. Then came "a short 'blip' of growth in the 1950s" (Heelas and Woodhead 2005, 139). From the 1960s onward, a growing number of Britons from all age cohorts abandoned even occasional church attendance; declines were sharpest among those who reached adulthood after 1960 (Tilley 2003). Attendance declined more steeply with each new generation. Congregations grayed and shrank. By 2000, only 7.9 percent of the population attended church on an average Sunday, and a disproportionate number of them were elderly (Brierly 2000, 28, 95; Bruce 2002a, 63-64; Heelas and Woodhead 2005, 41, 139).

Up through the 1950s, many who seldom or never attended church still remained members and sent their children to Sunday school. Despite declining attendance from the late 1880s onward, church membership actually peaked in 1905, and declined only modestly for decades afterward. In the 1950s membership was stable, perhaps even increasing, but from the 1960s onward there was "a near-nightmarish quantitative slide" (Hastings 1991, 580). Paul Heelas and Linda Woodhead estimate British church membership at 33 percent in 1900, 29 percent in 1930, 24 percent in 1960, and 12 percent in 2000 (2005, 139). Sunday school participation, like membership, declined gradually from 1900 until 1960, then plummeted (Brown 2001, 188). For the century, British Sunday school attendance dropped from 55 percent in 1900 to 4 percent in 2000 (Bruce 2002a, 68).

As church attendance and affiliation declined, belief in Christian basics also declined. Surveys in the 1940s and 1950s indicated that 43 percent of the British population affirmed belief in a personal God. By the 1970s that percentage dropped to 32 percent, and then held quite steady, with 31 percent in the 1990s still professing belief in a personal God. A substantial part of Britain's population believed in God as impersonal spirit or life force, edging up from 38 percent at mid-century to 40 percent by the 1990s.[1] Those not professing belief in any God rose from 10 percent in the 1960s to 15 percent in the 1970s and 27 percent in the 1990s. There were also significant declines of belief in Jesus' deity, Satan's reality, life after death, and biblical authority (Gill, Hadaway, and Marler 1998, 508-514).[2]

Other quantitative indicators of Christian decline included lower levels of participation in church-based rites of passage. As late as 1950, about 63 percent of English babies were baptized in the Church of England. This dropped to 53 percent in 1962 and 27 percent in 1993 (Bruce 2002a, 70). By 2000 the number was under 20 percent, whereas back in 1900 the estimated level was 61 percent (Brown 2006, 4). The number of marriages dropped 35 percent in the period from 1970 to

---

[1]The most recent surveys appear to indicate that Britons continue to move away from theistic belief in a personal God. The 2000 "Soul of Britain" survey found that just 26 percent believed in "a personal God," while 44 percent either agreed with belief in "some sort of spirit or life force" or "there is something there" (Heelas and Woodhead 2005, 73). In the same survey, just 8 percent accepted the label "convinced atheist," but 10 percent said "agnostic" and 28 percent identified as not spiritual or religious (Bruce 2002a, 193).

[2]British sociologists of religion differ over whether declining belief has been more often a cause, or a consequence, of declining church attendance. Davie thinks a drift from Christian beliefs is usually a consequence of lower attendance, which in turn may stem from a general decline in voluntary public association (1994; 2002b). Others reverse the direction of causation and contend that declining belief (whether rejection or indifference) more commonly causes people not to attend church (Bruce 2002a; 2002b; Voas and Crockett 2005). Robin Gill offers evidence of "life-style, rather than cognitive, reasons for not going to church." In a 1955 BBC survey, only 3 percent who had stopped attending church said it was because they had stopped believing in Christianity. According to Gill, "A previous generation was reared on the popular Protestant adage that 'you don't have to go to church to be a good Christian,'" thus encouraging "a pattern of indifference to church-going within an overall canopy of cognitive commitment to Christian belief" (Gill 2002, 335-337).

2000. Of those who did marry, fewer solemnized their marriage in a church ceremony. In England and Wales, religious weddings declined from over 70 percent of marriages in 1960 to less than 40 percent in 2000. Church baptisms, weddings, and funerals remain a preference in the mindset of much British folk religiosity (Bailey 1989, 154; Lambert 2003, 71), but participation has plummeted.

Lewis's Perceptions

Lewis made little direct reference to statistics on church involvement, and the sharpest quantitative declines occurred in the 1960s and beyond, after Lewis had died. This may seem to indicate a major change that Lewis was not alive to witness. If, as stated above, church attendance in 1951 stood at 15 percent on an average Sunday, that number was halved by 2000. Considered from another angle, however, the 92 percent level of non-attendance in 2000 is not so different from the 85 percent level of non-attendance in 1951, when Lewis was going strong. Lewis was aware that the vast majority of Britons did not worship regularly. Moreover, Lewis spent four decades in university settings with lower proportions of worshipers than the wider population. Lewis saw campus chapel attendance shrivel as soon as it was no longer compulsory. It may be fair to say that in Lewis's particular setting, he was exposed to very low levels of church participation that anticipated the extremely low levels which would come to characterize Britain more generally in later decades.

Most surveys of belief occurred after Lewis's death, and even those available in his time were seldom cited by him. However, Lewis did offer his impressions of prevailing beliefs. Based on his contacts with people, he thought impersonal pantheism was popular in Britain (1960b, 136-137, 269). Already in the 1940s, Lewis said in his BBC radio talks, "A good many people nowadays say, "I believe in a God, but not in a personal God" (1952, 140). Lewis was aware that different meanings might be attached to such words.[3] In contacts with less edu-

---

[3]Variations in how people understand words such as "personal" and "impersonal" can make it hard to design survey questions with enough validity and reliability to produce a statistically precise profile of religious belief. Thus, in discussing evidence that fewer Britons believe in "a personal God," Heelas and Woodhead caution, "Much survey data seems too open to interpretation for determinate conclusions to be drawn." Still, some weight must be given to quantitative findings that many in Britain label themselves as "spiritual" rather than "religious" and are unlikely to affirm "a personal God" (Heelas and Woodhead 2005, 73-74).

cated British people, Lewis found that "personal" could mean "corporeal" (2004b, 675) and "impersonal" could mean "incorporeal" (1973, 7). Thus, in some cases, not professing belief in a "personal" God could mean something quite different than it might seem to an educated observer trying to measure people's beliefs. Still, Lewis thought noncommittal belief in an indefinite, impersonal force was widespread.

Atheism struck Lewis as a force to reckon with.[4] Even though it was the stated conviction of only a small fraction of Britons during his lifetime, atheistic assumptions shaped many aspects of thought. Atheist intellectuals wielded influence disproportionate to their numbers, aided by popularizers of the social and natural sciences. Even if atheistic arguments did not lead most British people to profess themselves to be "convinced atheists," such arguments could make Christian belief seem less plausible. Consequent weakening or suspension of Christian belief could produce indefinite, indifferent attitudes toward religious claims, leading to a vague pantheism barely distinguishable from practical atheism. Lewis's two main apologetic targets, therefore, were atheism and pantheism (2007, 125-126).

Newbigin's Perceptions

Newbigin, living in Britain from 1974 until his death in 1998, saw firsthand the accelerated aging and emptying of churches at a denominational level and at a local level. A Presbyterian before leaving for India and always an ecumenist, Newbigin felt that upon returning to Britain, he should join the group from which he had come. "This was the more attractive since the Presbyterian and Congregational . . . had become one in the United Reformed Church" (1985a, 243). Newbigin was elected URC Moderator for 1978-1979 and visited many congregations. He found qualitative bright spots, but quantitatively he saw that the URC "was small and had lost many members" (1985a, 245).[5]

---

[4]Lewis himself had been an atheist; W. T. Kirkpatrick, the tutor who shaped Lewis's thinking as a teen, was an atheist; Janie Moore, the older woman he lived with for decades, was an atheist until her death; and atheists and agnostics abounded in Lewis's university context. Yet his interactions with military personnel and BBC listeners led him in 1945 to state—correctly—that clear, committed atheism was not widely held (1970, 101).

[5]For a time British Christians hoped the ecumenical movement would lead to church unity, renewal, and growth. But churches associated with the movement fared even worse than others. The United Reformed Church, Newbigin's denomination, lost nearly 30 percent of its members and about 40 percent of its clergy from 1975 to

From 1980 until 1988 Newbigin—then in his seventies—served as part-time pastor for a congregation of aging white people that had been slated for closing, located in the Winson Green area of Birmingham. Although congregants were loyal, other British-born whites were very hard to reach, greeting evangelism with cold contempt. Neighborhood immigrants welcomed religious discussion but did not convert (1985a, 248-249; 1994a, 49). Newbigin said he could not claim numerical success. He characterized his congregation as "small and vulnerable," which he took to be typical of similarly situated churches (1994a, 47). The congregation had just 18 members when he began and 27 members eight years later when leadership passed from Newbigin to an Indian pastor (Goheen 2000, 104).

With regard to belief, Newbigin (like Lewis) took note of both atheism and pantheism in Britain. Indeed, he viewed the two as similar: "There is no great difference between saying 'God is everything' and saying 'There is no God'" (1994a, 145). In denying ultimate personality and purpose, pantheistic Eastern thought fit with naturalistic modern scientism (1986b, 39). During Newbigin's last decades, he denied that the ideology of a secular public square was accompanied by atheism in personal belief. Survey evidence would support his claim that committed atheism remained relatively rare. However, when Newbigin said British people had become more religious—though not more Christian—in the 1900s (1994a, 148), he may have depended too much on sociologists who denied secularization. He may also have underestimated the utter indifference of many who still claimed belief in some sort of God but opted in growing numbers for the least definite, least demanding belief statements offered on questionnaires.[6] Rather than

1989 (Badham 1994, 491; Gilbert 1994, 514). No matter how worthy or evangelistic the original ecumenical vision may have been, denominational mergers in practice tended to be unions of already declining bodies that declined even faster after merging (Gilbert 1980, 127).

[6]Bruce contends that the usual outcome of secularization is not decisive denial of God but casual indifference (2002a, 192-194, 240). Britons who affirm a spirit or life force mostly do so not from positive attraction to Eastern thought but "from a vague commitment to remain spiritual after the content of Christianity has been given up." Fewer people care enough about religion to give it much thought. Faced with options on a survey, "they pick the least specific response . . . that leaves them with the greatest freedom" (Bruce 2002a, 137-138). Heelas and Woodhead take newer spiritualities more seriously than Bruce does. Yet they caution against "the misleading impression that sacred activities are growing overall" (2005, 47-48). "Our findings support those—most notably Bruce—who see secularization continuing in Britain" (2005,

echoing the claims of some sociological theorists bent on debunking secularization, Newbigin's sense of white Britons' cold dismissal of his evangelistic efforts in Birmingham might have been a more representative indication of religious indifference among Britons in the late 1900s.

Post-Christian Sexuality

Changes in British sexual morals became increasingly evident throughout the 1900s, with the most quantifiable and public changes occurring in the latter decades. As "marriage both declined and secularized" from the 1960s onward, the percentage of births out of wedlock increased eightfold, from 5 percent in 1960 to 40 percent by 2000 (Brown 2006, 31-36). Government censorship of sexually explicit material "fell apart," especially after Penguin Books was acquitted of indecency charges in 1960 for publishing D. H. Lawrence's *Lady Chatterley's Lover*. In 1967 the government liberalized divorce laws and decriminalized blasphemy, homosexuality, and abortion. This "frenzy of legislation," says Brown, "effectively de-Christianised and liberalised British law and society" (2006, 267).

Lewis's Perceptions

Even before these visible, public changes that historians and sociologists can measure, major shifts may have already been underway.[7] Lewis surely thought so. In *The Pilgrim's Regress*, published in 1933, Lewis lampooned the pornographic literature of "the Dirty Twenties" and the Freudian attempt to debunk sexual repression and to make sexual desire the hidden explanation for so many things (1989, 52-53, 59).

---

55). Kirk suggests that "Europeans are largely confused." They mostly settle for pragmatic materialism; but if trouble comes, many "hedge their bets" with religious resources. If such religion evolves into a more elastic spirituality of inner consciousness, it can be "quite compatible with philosophical naturalism" (2005, 133).

[7]Brown depicts the 1960s as an abrupt rupture in British religiosity, "a sudden plunge into a truly secular condition" (2001, 1). He uses avowedly postmodern methods of discourse analysis to contend that Britain remained pervasively Christian beyond the midpoint of the twentieth century. Brown argues that "the keys to understanding secularisation in Britain are the simultaneous de-pietisation of femininity and the de-feminisation of piety from the 1960s" (2001, 192). However, the public changes of the 1960s highlighted by Brown arose from attitude shifts that began much earlier, most of which Lewis recognized. Already by the late 1800s, argues McLeod, middle class religion was declining, perhaps due partly to Darwinism and biblical criticism, but due mainly to "the reaction against 'puritanism' . . . what came to be called 'Victorianism'" (2000, 201).

During his youth and early adulthood prior to conversion, says Lewis, he felt no guilt about his sexual desires and activities (1955b, 69).[8] He thought this had become characteristic of many others in his time.

In a 1945 speech, Lewis told Welsh Anglican clergy that it would be "useless" to deploy the example of fornication to awaken a sense of sin in the unconverted. "They are mostly fornicators, but then they do not feel fornication to be wrong. . . . I do not myself think we can expect people to recognize it as sin until they have accepted Christianity as a whole" (1970, 96). In a 1955 letter, Lewis observed that the harmful aspects of fornication which formerly made it obviously uncharitable could no longer be argued against it, "now that contraceptives have removed the most disastrous consequences for girls, and medicine has largely defeated the worst horrors of syphilis." No objection to fornication would remain "unless one brings in the whole supernatural and sacramental view of man" (2007, 600).

Speaking on the BBC in the early 1940s, Lewis noted that public opinion was more tolerant of extramarital sex and homosexuality than at any point "since Pagan times" (1952, 90). He declared, "If people do not believe in permanent marriage, it is perhaps better that they should live together unmarried than that they should make vows they do not mean to keep" (1952, 97). Lewis did not think the government's divorce laws should compel a predominantly non-Christian population to abide by a Christian view of marriage; rather, "the Churches should frankly recognize that the majority of the British people are not Christians and, therefore, cannot be expected to live Christian lives." Lewis favored two versions of marriage, one for all citizens, the other for church members (1952, 101-102).[9]

---

[8]Lewis's youthful letters mention his sadomasochistic fantasies (e.g., 2004a, 268, 271, 276, 283, 313, 320). In early adulthood, prior to conversion, Lewis began living with an older woman, Janie Moore, the mother of a friend killed in World War I. She was separated from her husband but not officially divorced. Biographers find considerable evidence to suggest that Lewis's relationship with her was sexual for the first few years, though Lewis never said so, and no conclusive proof has been set forth. After his conversion, Lewis continued to live with Mrs. Moore and to provide for her until she died in 1951.

[9]Ironically, Lewis himself would later marry in two stages, civil and ecclesiastical, with both stages flouting the relevant institutional authority. His civil marriage took place solely to circumvent British law, which required that Joy Davidman Gresham, an American citizen, would have to leave Britain—unless she had a British husband. So Lewis entered civil marriage in 1956 as a legal fiction without consummating the union. Then, after falling in love, Lewis wanted to marry Joy in an ecclesiastical rite,

Open homosexuality, its decriminalization, and ecclesiastical debates about gay unions became prominent on the public agenda after Lewis's death, but Lewis was already thinking about such matters in his context. He perceived pederasty to be common among the youths at his boarding school in 1913 (1955b, 88).[10] He knew various homosexual men, including his dearest friend, Arthur Greeves (Jacobs 2005, 56). He thought the church should continue to view homosexuality as a sin.[11] However, it was not the state's business and should not be punished as a crime. Lewis saw a two-front battle: fighting for persecuted homosexuals "against snoopers and busybodies," but also fighting "for ordinary people *against* the widespread freemasonry of the highbrow Homos who dominate so much of the world of criticism and won't be very nice to you unless you are in their set" (2007, 1154). He thought homosexuals had disproportionate clout in intellectual circles.

Lewis suggested that many forms of depicting or engaging in sexual activity should be exempt from government interference, at least in a context where so many people no longer believed in Christian morality. In the aftermath of the trial over *Lady Chatterley's Lover*, Lewis wrote a 1962 article "Sex in literature" (1986, 105-108). He suggested that a nation's laws must sooner or later conform to the prevalent morality of its population; otherwise, jury trials would become farcical or impossi-

---

contrary to Anglican Church law prohibiting remarriage by a divorced person (such as Joy) whose former spouse was still living. When Lewis asked his bishop's approval, the answer was no. On March 21, 1957, Lewis requested a young priest, Peter Bide, to perform a church rite on the spur of the moment in the hospital where Joy was a cancer patient. Bide did so, was subsequently rebuked by his bishop, and promised never to do such a thing again. Thus, in this instance, Lewis was part of the growing tendency to rank individual choice above the clear intent of civil and ecclesiastical directives. Incidentally, Lewis's radio remark that the state should not enforce a church view of marriage contributed to a rift in his friendship with J. R. R. Tolkien, and Lewis's marriage to Joy further widened the rift with Tolkien (Jacobs 2005, 274-279).

[10]Lewis may have overestimated the actual extent of pederasty at Malvern (Sayer 1988, 39). But even if Lewis misread the situation, my point still stands: same-sex coupling came to Lewis's attention long before homosexuals went public in later years.

[11]Lewis wrote in a 1954 letter, "I take it for certain that the *physical* satisfaction of homosexual desires is sin." Indeed, a Christian with homosexual tendencies should not enter "mock- or quasi-marriage with a member of one's own sex even if this does not lead to any carnal act." He also noted among homosexual males of his acquaintance a tendency, "the moment they find you don't treat them with horror and contempt, to rush to the opposite pole and start implying that they are somehow superior" (2007, 471-472).

ble. But while Lewis favored changes in government laws, he opposed redefinition of church standards for sex. Bishop J.A.T. Robinson was among the "expert witnesses" who testified at the *Chatterley* trial. Robinson said of the book's adultery, "I think Lawrence tried to portray this relation as in a real sense something sacred, as in a real sense an act of holy communion." Lewis, already at odds with Robinson's theology, sarcastically mused about the bishop's qualifications as "an expert in the general nature of good and evil." Modernist clergy, charged Lewis, went beyond saying that the law of the state should not be concerned with such evils; these churchmen did not regard such things as evils at all. Christian morality differed from that of "the modern intelligentsia—who supply 'expert witnesses.'" (1986, 105-108).

In Lewis's last article, published in *The Saturday Evening Post* of December, 1963, he remarked on "what the whole western world seems to me to have been doing for the last 40-odd years." Sexual impulses had come to hold "a position of preposterous privilege." Moral restraints were discarded in the name of a "right to happiness"—often taken to mean "simply and solely 'sexual happiness.'" Lewis spoke of two eventual consequences. A "ruthless war of promiscuity" would produce a society "adverse to women" (1970, 317-322). Also, the future could bring an ideology of unbridled autonomy:

> Though the 'right to happiness' is chiefly claimed for the sexual impulse, it seems to me impossible that the matter should stay there. The fatal principle, once allowed in that department, must sooner or later seep through our whole lives. We thus advance toward a state of society in which not only each man but every impulse in each man claims *carte blanche*. (1970, 322)

In brief, Lewis saw various links between post-Christian sexuality and the intellectual realm. Arguments against Christian sexual standards were being advanced by academic elites, abetted by modernist clergy, and diffused in popular culture. Approval of non-marital sex meant apologists would have to show sin's reality to people without arguing from violation of sexual standards (standards which in earlier times had been widely affirmed even when disobeyed). Sexual license, in turn, could open the way for a wider intellectual shift, with moral relativism and personal autonomy dominating all areas, not just the sexual.

Newbigin's Perceptions

Newbigin, unlike Lewis, lived to see Britain's steep decline of church weddings and of marriage generally, the enormous increase in illegitimate births, the decriminalization of most sexual behaviors, and the growing ecclesiastical rifts that were triggered by disputes over sexual ethics, especially homosexuality. Curiously, however, these developments did not figure prominently in his cultural analysis of the West. In the 1960s Newbigin criticized "a kind of religion which limits Christian obedience to a very narrow range of personal and domestic relationships" (1966, 135). Such criticism may have been true enough in the abstract, but it showed little strategic sense that a sexual revolution was underway, posing a high-priority challenge in the realm of "domestic relationships."

Newbigin dismissed as misguided "the attempt to deduce a binding law on the subject of divorce from the recorded teaching of Jesus." We must reckon not with "any supposed eternal laws or principles," but with "the living Lord." Christian conduct "is not simply deduced from timeless truths" revealed in the Bible; "there will be different patterns of conduct for Christians in different times and places" (1966, 141-143). This may be true in a limited sense when discussing some aspects of contextualizing the gospel, but it appears in a book which, by Newbigin's own account (1985a, 199), was meant to address issues raised by Bishop Robinson. If Newbigin saw any link between Robinson's sexual relativism and his denial of a personal, transcendent God, Newbigin did not say so. Since our focus in this book is on the nature and role of rationality, we should note in this context Newbigin's antipathy to "eternal laws or principles" and his distaste for deductive inference from biblical propositions or timeless truths. This note would continue to sound in his subsequent writings.

In later years, Newbigin partnered with pro-life Presbyterians in the United States and spoke of abortion as "killing a child" (Wainwright 2000, 435-436). He plainly denounced "the irresponsibility of contemporary sexual ethics, the slaughter of unborn infants for mere convenience, and the easy dissolution of the most sacred bonds of marital fidelity, parental authority and filial obedience which are the very stuff of true human community" (1985b, 11). This statement, though strong and clear, was a brief aside, a single sentence in a 15-page lecture about a different topic. Given Newbigin's convictions and activism against elements of the sexual revolution, he said surprisingly little about such matters in his works specifically devoted to sketching a cultural diagnosis of the West.

Newbigin often spoke in general terms of the West's relativism and nihilism, and he probably considered sexual libertinism an instance of this—but that was seldom stated in his sketch of the culture. He spoke of increasing diversity leading to a growing sense that different cultures have different standards of right and wrong, making it hard for a diverse society to uphold any common standard (1989a, 55). But many immigrants from other cultures were in fact closer in their sexual ethic to the Christian tradition than millions of native Britons who chose to jettison the sexual standards taught by their forebears.

Newbigin often decried a separation of values from facts, and he attributed this mostly to flawed theories of knowledge, as we shall see in chapter 8. He did not discuss the possibility that people wishing to give free reign to their sexual urges might have strong motivation to make values a matter of personal preference, to regard as baseless opinion the theological facts standing behind older sexual mores, and to prefer a vague god within, not a transcendent God who commands obedience.[12] Whereas Lewis had earlier viewed the trend toward sexual license as a wedge that could open the way to a philosophy of autonomy in other dimensions of life, Newbigin treated philosophical factors as primary, and sexual license as a secondary symptom of philosophy. He did not explore whether shifts in sexual attitudes might be a cause, not just an effect, of intellectual and religious changes.

De-colonization, Immigration, and Diversity

During the 1900s, various parts of Britain's empire became politically independent nations. Not only did British control over its colonies fade, but a growing number of people from those areas immigrated to Britain and had a growing impact there. Britons increasingly came to see the imperial past as shameful (and some saw missions as imperialistic). Many came to view multicultural respect, rather than imperial dominance, as the proper approach in international relations. In Britain's internal affairs, too, a multicultural ideology gained strength, due in part to the growing presence of immigrants from other cultures.

---

[12]Rejection of traditional standards for family, gender, and sexual expression "has been a major cause of disaffiliation from the congregational Christianity that supported these roles" and a turn toward subjectivized religiosity and ethics (Heelas and Woodhead 2005, 117-118; see also Davie 1994, 33-35).

This had intellectual and religious implications. In the second half of the twentieth century, asserts Brown, Christianity's former hegemony gave way to a sense that a range of religious traditions were underpinning a multicultural, multiracial society (2006, 2).[13]

Ethnic and religious diversity increased in Britain after 1947 with the arrival of refugees from the Indian subcontinent, followed by immigrants from various parts of the former empire (Badham 1994, 494; Nielsen 1989, 226). Newbigin's Britain in the late 1900s was more diverse than Lewis's at mid-century. Even so, in the 2001 government census, only 8 percent of Britons did not classify themselves as White, and only 5.5 percent professed adherence to a non-Christian religion (National Statistics 2006, 20-21). The new *ideology* of diversity may have attained influence greater than Britain's actual *demography* of diversity.

Britons who abandoned Christianity seldom aligned themselves with another religion. British Jews became so few in number and so assimilated to the surrounding culture (Campbell 1994) that they comprised barely .5 percent of the British population by the year 2000 (National Statistics 2006, 66). A miniscule .3 percent of Britons called themselves Buddhists, nearly all of immigrant stock (Green 1989). Hindus in Britain strove to maintain caste unity and distinctiveness within the British context (Knott 1989). Only 1 percent of Britain's total population called themselves Hindu (National Statistics 2006, 61).

Islam likewise attracted few Britons of non-Muslim background. Still, of Britain's non-Christian religious groups, Muslims were the largest at about 3 percent of the population (National Statistics 2006, 21). Muslim birthrates, intensity of commitment, and ability to control socialization of children within a subculture strengthened Muslims' position relative to other British religious groups (Gilbert 1994, 521). In 1951 Muslims in Britain numbered only 21,000; that number swelled to 1.6 million in the 2001 census, with many not assimilated nor satisfied with British society (Peach 2006). Wary of secular schools, many preferred schools of their own (Hussain 2004), raising concerns that Muslim schools were not preparing children for a pluralist society (Badham 1994, 498; Nielsen 1989, 234-235).

---

[13]Paul Badham says Britain had reached such a degree of religious and ideological pluralism by the 1990s that any religious consensus—or even a frame of reference for seeking consensus—was unattainable (1994, 488-496). In Davie's judgment, however, the direct impact on most Britons of exposure to new varieties of culture and religion "should not be exaggerated." Britain's ethnic minorities were concentrated in urban pockets, while most areas remained "uncompromisingly mono-cultural" (1994, 25).

With only 5.5 percent of Britons affirming a non-Christian religion in 2000, it might seem that minority religions remained of negligible importance. But their presence gave occasion for schools to present religion in a pluralistic manner less favorable to Christianity. Moreover, youthful demography and higher birthrates portended future growth.

Diversity engaged Lewis's attention somewhat, and Newbigin's still more, but both focused mainly on how diversity affected Britain's white majority with Christian roots.

Lewis's Perceptions

Most of Britain's increase in non-whites of other religions came after Lewis's death. By 1963 significant immigration had occurred, but much more was still to come, and the multiplicative effect of higher birthrates among immigrants lay mostly in the future. Still, as a professor, Lewis encountered a student body that included a higher percentage of persons from other countries than was the case in Britain's general population. Students from overseas increased after World War II. In a 1950 letter, Lewis observed that Oxford was flooded by students from all over the world (2007, 45). In fact, Lewis used money from his book royalties to help pay tuition (anonymously) for African students (2007, 853).[14]

Sometimes Lewis sounded very much like a white man with few personal ties to people of color. In *The pilgrim's regress*, written in 1933, naked brown girls and black girls were allegorical figures for sexual temptation and pornography (1989, 29-30, 53). On the BBC in the early 1940s, Lewis compared his own oft-brushed but poor teeth to the fine teeth of a (hypothetical) "healthy young Negro who never used toothpaste at all" (1952, 177). His children's books of the early 1950s depicted Northern nations as more free and humane than cruel territories in the South. "Dark, bearded men from Calormen" were the evil forces attacking "the fair-haired men of Narnia" (1994b, 26). Blond-

[14]Although Lewis never traveled beyond Europe, he was interested in non-European peoples and in the growth of Christianity among them. He had extensive correspondence with his brother, a military officer stationed for a time in China; with Peter Milward, a missionary in Japan; and with Dom Bede Griffiths, a missionary in India. Lewis declared, "Christianity is for all men, not simply for modern Western Europeans" (2004b, 393). He affirmed that Chinese and Indian Christianity were vitally important for the wholeness of Christian identity and thought (2004b, 842; 2007, 408). He once mused that for the church, "all the valuable future may lie with the Christened Chinaman" (2004b, 747).

haired heroes battling dark-skinned evildoers may have been be a staple of European fairy tales, but non-whites could hardly be expected to appreciate such depictions. Lewis also used the terms "uncivilized" and "savage" (e.g., 1960d, 54; 1970, 54) to describe non-literate peoples, although such peoples often had rich oral cultures. Even admirers of Lewis must concede that such language showed the author's limited personal contact with other ethnicities and lack of sensitivity to how such words might strike them. Lewis (unlike Newbigin) had no experience of living in a predominantly non-white community, and it sometimes showed.[15]

Nevertheless, Lewis was no bigot devoted to white superiority. Living during the dissolution of much of the British Empire, Lewis was painfully conscious of imperialist colonialism and racism. He knew that these evils weakened Christianity's plausibility in other countries and in Britain itself, and he repudiated such sins. *Out of the silent planet* (1938) portrayed the pomposity and cruelty of interplanetary colonizers looking for new places to invade and new races to exploit. Lewis denounced crimes against people "differing from us in features and pigmentation" (1960d, 90).[16]

All too often, religious talk had served as a cloak for greed: "we Westerners preached Christ with our lips, with our actions we brought the slavery of Mammon" (2007, 278). Churches and missionaries sometimes were complicit in sinning against peoples from other ethnic and religious backgrounds. "'Gun and gospel' have been horribly combined in the past. The missionary's holy desire to save souls has not always been kept quite distinct from the arrogant desire, the busybody's itch, to (as he calls it) 'civilize' the (as he calls them) 'natives'" (1960d, 90).

[15]Lewis sensed that without cross-cultural experience or fluency in any non-European languages, he was limited in key respects. Writing in 1956 to a fellow scholar, Chinese Buddhist Hsin-Chang Chang, Lewis lamented knowing "no languages that are not closely related to one another." Chang, conversant with Eastern and Western languages, was better positioned to be "aware of the nature of Language simply as such" (2007, 764).

[16]Lewis declared, "All over the earth the White Man's offence 'smells to heaven': massacres, broken treaties, theft, kidnappings, enslavement, deportation, floggings, lynchings, beatings-up, rape, insult, mockery, and odious hypocrisy make up that smell (1967, 158-159). The British Empire's hypocritical paternalism had "nauseated the world." Lewis mocked "the white man's burden" and mourned the evils it had produced. White claims to superiority would be "a roaring farce" if there had been "no broken treaties with Redskins, no extermination of the Tasmanians, no gas-chambers and no Belsen, no Amritsar, Black and Tans or Apartheid" (1960a, 46-47).

Past sins had undermined Christianity's plausibility. "Large areas of 'the World' will not hear us till we have publicly disowned much of our past. Why should they? We have shouted the name of Christ and enacted the service of Moloch" (1960a, 49). It is clear, then, that Lewis opposed racism, nationalism, paternalism, and cultural imperialism, and that as an apologist he tried to improve Christianity's credibility in Britain and elsewhere by distancing the genuine gospel from such evils.

It is equally clear that Lewis spoke as a white person to other white people. Besides clumsy references to brown temptresses and dark Calormene invaders, Lewis's very confessions of white guilt showed that he was speaking as a white to other whites. Even when he wrote *about* non-white oppressed peoples, he still spoke *to* white oppressors labeled "us." British whites were the ethnic group Lewis knew best and addressed most directly.

Although major non-Christian religions had a relatively small number of adherents in the Britain of Lewis's era, Lewis took an interest in other religions and knew some adherents personally. He was acquainted with a number of Hindus (2007, 776), sought to understand Hinduism, and regarded Hinduism and Christianity to be "the only two serious options for an adult mind" (1967, 96). He read the *Analects* of Confucius (2004b, 881; 2007, 72). He studied Buddhist writings (1952, 177). He tried to understand something of Zen, though he admitted finding it "utterly opaque" (2007, 1378). He read the Koran, as well as material by an Arab Christian showing the significance of the crucifixion for Muslims (2007, 1322). Lewis considered the views of his Jewish contemporaries (2004b, 941; 2007, 1042). His wife, Joy, was born Jewish. David Gresham, Lewis's stepson, eventually opted for education in a Jewish school (paid for by Lewis) and aligned himself with Judaism.

Lewis also knew people who became involved with alternative religious groups and ideas of more recent origin.[17] He knew spiritualists and occultists (1955b, 59, 174-175, 203). His dearest friend, Arthur Greeves, joined the Baha'i faith for a time (Hooper 1996, 665). A former student converted to a westernized version of Sufism and tried to persuade Lewis (2004b, 204, 1053). His close friends Owen Barfield

---

[17]Some wonder whether alternative spiritualities in recent years signal a "spiritual revolution" (Heelas and Woodhead, 2005). But Voas and Crockett contend that alternative spiritualities "were at least as common in the past," citing a variety of groups and movements that attracted people in the early part of the century (2005, 25). Lewis observed that unconventional religiosities were plentiful in his time (1970, 253).

and A. C. Harwood were leading figures in Anthroposophy (1955b, 206-208; 2004a, 670-671).[18] Lewis was no expert on world religions or alternative spiritualities, but he had a lively interest in them, a range of reading about them, and a variety of personal contacts with adherents.

In his public speaking and published writing, Lewis sometimes *discussed* other religions but seldom directly *addressed* adherents of those religions. He tended to categorize other religions and dispose of them summarily through a process of elimination. Muslims and Buddhists would not accept—nor even want to discuss—Lewis's brusque claim that "Islam is only a Christian heresy, and Buddhism a Hindu heresy" (1967, 96). Confucians would be repelled by a claim that their beliefs and ethics comprised a mere "philosophy for aristocrats." Devout Jews would hardly be persuaded by Lewis's quick dismissal, "All that was best in Judaism . . . survives in Christianity." Practitioners of African folk religions would not be won over to Christianity by Lewis's one-sentence diagnosis that their religion lacked a "philosophical, ethical, and universalizing element." Worshippers in India would not meekly grant Lewis's claim that Christianity is superior to Hinduism because Christians unite ritual mystery with universal, rational ethics, while such things are separated from each other in different Hindu castes (1970, 102-103).

Such stark characterizations would have been ineffective if Lewis had been addressing committed believers in those religions, but he was targeting Britons with tenuous Christian ties or no specific faith. Even before increased immigration brought more adherents of various world religions to Britain, there was a growing awareness among Britons of a multiplicity of religions in the world. Such a dizzying array of possibilities could be seen by some people as a reason to regard all religions as equally implausible, and to see Christianity as just one myth among others.[19] Lewis himself felt that way before his conversion (2004a, 230-231). Others might think all religions to be equally plausible and equally

[18]For more on the Anthroposophy of Lewis's friends and his interactions with them, see Adey (1978), Barfield (1965), Harwood (1992), and Lindskoog (1998).

[19]Netland shows that for five centuries, the West became more involved with other cultures and gave more thought to other religions. Even before immigration increased, Confucianism, Hinduism, and Buddhism received wide exposure in the West, especially through books. By the late 1800s and early 1900s, declining confidence in Christian truth was accompanied by increased willingness to look into other religious traditions and to draw (often selectively) upon their ways of understanding (Netland 2001, 93-123).

authoritative as sources of partial insight into ultimate reality. As an apologist to British whites departing from their Christian heritage, Lewis tried to show that the field of religious choices was not really so crowded or confusing and that Christianity stood out from the rest.[20]

His way of classification and elimination, without nuance or depth, might help his target audience to see religions not as a multitudinous muddle but as a small number of basic options. People with little direct exposure to any religion besides Christianity might go on to conclude that if they were to consider an alternative to scientific materialism or vague pantheism, they could skip lesser contending religions and focus on Christianity as the top candidate. Lewis's insistence on presenting "mere Christianity"—a unity, not a perplexing array of denominations and doctrinal differences—was also intended to simplify and clarify, to cut through the complexity and variety of beliefs, in order to present a clear choice.

Lewis regarded post-Christian naturalism—whether pantheistic or materialistic—to be the main opponent and alternative to Christianity in Britain. If British people were to be won to Christianity, most would need to be won away from post-Christian vague religiosity or material-ism, not persuaded to switch allegiance from another major religion. If British churchgoers were tempted to abandon Christianity, the main temptation would not come from one of the other world religions but from naturalism in its materialistic or vaguely pantheistic guise. Lewis poured his energies into battling naturalism, not because he saw it as a more worthy opponent than non-Christian religions, but because it was the competing worldview he knew best from experience and consid-ered most likely to enmesh his white British contemporaries.

In short, Lewis had some exposure to religious diversity in his con-text, but he engaged white Britons' post-Christian naturalism (scientific materialism or westernized pantheism) more deeply than he engaged the claims of major non-Christian religions. He had some exposure to ethnic diversity, but he understood whites better than he understood non-whites. He cherished the increasingly international, multicultural

---

[20]Already in 1922, a growing tendency among Britons to view Christianity as just one among many religions prompted G. K. Chesterton to write *The everlasting man* (1993). This work was Lewis's favorite popular apologetic (Lewis 1955b, 223; 2004b, 823; 2007, 72). According to Chesterton, "its thesis is that those who say that Christ stands side by side with similar myths, and his religion side by side with similar reli-gions, are only repeating a very stale formula contradicted by a very striking fact" (Chesterton 1993, 7).

character of the church, resulting from mission endeavors around the world; but he saw European imperialism and missionary missteps as blows to Christian credibility that must be addressed by apologists.

Newbigin's Perceptions

Newbigin's interest in other peoples began early. In the 1930s, while still in Britain, Newbigin participated in the Glasgow International Club and "formed many Indian and African friendships" (1985a, 24). Up to that time, his experience of diversity resembled Lewis's: he met individuals from other cultures in a British university context. But Newbigin's subsequent experiences of diversity would go far beyond Lewis's.

For decades Newbigin lived in India among a non-white, non-Christian majority. He engaged in street preaching and conversations with people who were strongly attached to their own religion (1985a, 55). He studied in a Hindu monastery and "learned to see the profound rationality of the world-view of the Vedanta" (1985a, 57). He was in India during the last years of British rule and the first decades of independence, among people for whom the end of colonialism loomed large (1961, 9-10). As an ecumenical leader, Newbigin met Christians from many nations and was involved in dialogue with representatives of other religions. Living in Geneva from 1961 till 1965 while serving with the World Council of Churches, he found himself among "hosts of foreign diplomats, civil servants and employees of multi-national companies" (1985a, 211). After Geneva, Newbigin spent another decade in the cultural kaleidoscope of India. Newbigin's time in India and his ecumenical exposure to Christians from many nations heightened his consciousness of anti-colonialist sentiment and of the evils that had been committed by imperial powers.[21]

Upon returning to England, Newbigin taught from 1974 to 1979 at Selly Oak Colleges, which had "a rich mix of races, nations and denominations" (1985a, 242). He lived in Birmingham, a magnet for immigrants and home to some of Britain's highest concentrations of devotees of non-Christian religions (National Statistics 2006, xvii). Newbig-

---

[21]Polemics against colonialism may have been distorted and exaggerated at times, observed Newbigin, but it was undeniable that "the western white man has been guilty in recent centuries of genocide, wholesale exploitation of subject peoples, the opium wars, the slave trade, the colour bar, apartheid and the use of weapons of mass destruction on civilian populations" (1969, 112).

in ministered from 1980 through 1988 in Birmingham's Winson Green neighborhood, populated with "mostly Hindus, Muslims, and Sikhs" (1994a, 46, 49). Ethnic and religious diversity was a more immediate and pressing reality for Newbigin at that time and place in Britain than it had ever been for Lewis.

Even in the 1990s, non-whites and adherents of non-Christian religions comprised only a small minority of Britain's total population. But while most areas remained "uncompromisingly mono-cultural" (Davie 1994, 25), Newbigin's immediate context was largely non-white and rooted in non-Christian religions. This setting, along with his past experiences in missions, made Newbigin especially alert to diversity-related issues in the West. Indeed, his sense of the degree and impact of diversity in Britain may have been inflated somewhat by a setting that was not typical for most of Britain.

Newbigin said that after World War II, European society had moved "a long way toward the same kind of religious pluralism" as he had seen in India. In earlier times, there had been "no significant non-Christian presence" in Britain except for the small community of Jews. Back then, evangelism was a matter of "calling people back to their spiritual roots." But the situation had changed. Big cities had sizeable "communities of Hindus, Sikhs, Buddhists, and Muslims." White Britons found that many of their new neighbors were "much more godly, more devout, and more pious than the average native Christian." Some thinkers concluded that Christian evangelism should not be directed toward such people but that it should, in effect, be intended "for whites only," a notion which seemed odd to Asian Christians living in British cities (1989a, 3-4). Newbigin felt that England's general public stereotyped the foreign missionary as "a destroyer of precious cultures, a stooge of the imperialists." British Christians had become timid and concerned not to impose their faith on others. Even missionary societies talked about interchange, not evangelism (1994a, 177-179).

"Cultural pluralism"—acceptance of demographic diversity—was all too often accompanied by "religious pluralism," which Newbigin defined as "the belief that the differences between the religions are not a matter of truth and falsehood, but of different perceptions of the one truth" (1989a, 14). Timidity to evangelize, said Newbigin, was partly due to church people being intimidated by "the modern scientific world-view" into thinking that traditional Christian teaching was no longer believable. But an additional reason for such timidity was the notion that respect for religious minorities "precluded any kind of evangelism." Newbigin attended a Birmingham meeting of a group called "All Faiths for One Race." He recalled, "It was typical that all those present were Christians and that a clergyman among them described missions as 'theological racism'. I was provoked into advising him to beware of theological fornication!" (1985a, 243-244).[22]

As Newbigin attended meetings of church leaders who disparaged missions, he also participated in meetings of school officials who seemed anxious "lest any child should become a committed Christian as the result of religious education" (1985a, 244). In 1975 the Birmingham City Council, noting that many students in public schools came from homes professing a non-Christian religion, approved a new syllabus for religious education. The professed aim was to foster critical awareness of religious and moral aspects of human experience, not to advance the truth claims of any particular religion. Newbigin's friend John Hick played a role on the Standing Advisory Committee on Religious Education. Hick's theological convictions had shifted over time from Christian orthodoxy to thoroughgoing pluralism.[23] His pluralistic theology left its imprint on school policy.

Newbigin saw that the schools' purportedly inclusive policy in fact enshrined definite dogma: Hick's brand of pluralism. Hick's place on the committee was later filled by Newbigin (Goheen 2000, 108; Thomas 1996), 13-14). Newbigin's committee participation did not influence school policy to move away from pluralism in religion classes or from secularism in the rest of the curriculum, but it did influence Newbigin. It gave him opportunity to hear directly from Muslim parents who did not want their children assimilated into such thinking, and Newbigin was prompted to wonder why Christians would be content to assimilate (1990, 1). The committee experience heightened Newbigin's sense that mission to the West could not ignore the role of schools in shap-

[22]If Newbigin's experiences in Britain indicated that many church leaders had lost their nerve for evangelism and missions, that impression was only strengthened by his perception of concurrent trends in the World Council of Churches, which he loved so much. Newbigin saw the WCC and its leadership sliding toward a misguided ecumenicity which embraced all religions, thus denying the uniqueness of Christ and the necessity of Christian missions (1985a, 231; 1994b, 1994c).

[23]For a brief account in Hick's own words of his theological pilgrimage and a concise case for his pluralistic stance, see Hick (1995, 29-59). A former student of Hick, Harold Netland, provides an evangelical account of Hick's journey and a detailed rebuttal of Hick's pluralistic position (2001, 158-177, 212-246). Many more works by and about Hick are identified in Netland's notes and bibliography.

ing minds (more about that in the next chapter). It also made him all the more eager to challenge the religious pluralism of Hick and others (see 1989a, 155-183; 1995a, 160-189).

Newbigin saw British Muslims as offering "much more vigorous testimony" in public affairs than Christians were doing. He declared that both faiths, as minority positions "in a society dominated by the naturalistic ideology," shared "a common duty to challenge this ideology." Christians could be grateful for the bold Muslim critique of public policies that excluded God. Christians ought to be "as confident and clear" as Muslims in challenging reigning assumptions and should "seek afresh a vision for the future of a society shaped by the Christian gospel" (Newbigin, Sanneh, and Taylor 1998, 22-24). This would require attention to epistemology, plausibility structures, and the nature of public truth.

As the Muslim presence in the West could be a blessing, it also posed a threat to the future viability of societies no longer grounded in Christianity. Newbigin warned of "powerful new religious fanaticisms" that were gaining strength because of the "internal weaknesses" of the "liberal, secular democratic state" (1989a, 223). British citizen Salman Rushdie had to go into hiding after his book *The Satanic Verses* provoked Muslim decrees demanding his death. Noting that "Western liberal writers" were outraged, Newbigin doubted whether their complaints were backed by anything that could "withstand the determined onslaught of those who hold firm beliefs about the truth." He saw this as an indication that Christians should "welcome some measure of plurality but reject pluralism." British society needed an intellectual foundation more solid than naturalism or pluralism (1989a, 244).

With all of Newbigin's cross-cultural experience and observations related to the diversity of cultures and religions in Britain, his writings on mission to the West did not directly address non-Christian, non-Anglo immigrants with the gospel, nor did he offer much guidance to churchgoers on how to witness to neighbors of the various religions.[24] Instead, Newbigin focused more on how whites from a Christian background were responding to growing diversity by shrinking from evangelizing others, by not insisting that their own children receive Chris-

---

[24]As Jenny Taylor observes, Newbigin showed heightened interest in Islam in his later writings, but the emphasis was on Islam's public role in Britain. He offered few specifics about witnessing to Muslims or converting them to Christianity (Taylor 2002, 216).

tian schooling, and by assuming that public policy should be formed without reference to God's reign in Christ. While Newbigin's direct exposure to religious diversity exceeded Lewis's, Newbigin's missiology for the West did not speak directly to ethnic and religious minorities in Britain; rather, he focused on the impact their presence had on white Britons from a Christian background. Such people, he believed, had long tended to doubt Christianity and to reduce it to a matter of personal opinion rather than truth for all; the growing presence of other religions in Britain brought out this tendency more strongly. Thus he saw a need to engage the ideology of religious pluralism and examine its intellectual roots.

CHAPTER 4

Britain in the 1900s:
Five Influential Institutions

The previous chapter discussed three trends: quantitative decline of church involvement and Christian belief, movement toward post-Christian sexuality, and increasing diversity. It is worth noting that diversity, in itself, would not necessarily entail decline for Christian belief and behavior. The faith can thrive amid cultural and religious variety. Christianity existed for centuries before Christendom took shape, and many parts of today's world never had Christendom but have millions of Christians (McLeod 2003, 1-5). Even so, it is important to recognize that European Christianity not only lost direct coercive power but also—especially in the 1900s—lost discursive influence to maintain Christian memory in institutions such as school, home, media, government, and even the church itself (Davie 2000, 38-114). This chapter considers developments among these influential institutions, noting especially Lewis's and Newbigin's perceptions within their respective settings.

School

By 1900 universities "had become established as the main arbiters of intellectual orthodoxy" (McLeod 2000, 288-289), and the universities' "orthodoxy" was agnostic, not biblical. The secularism dominating most disciplines in higher education had a growing effect on all levels of British education as the century unfolded.

63

The 1920s and the 1960s marked two phases of particularly bold departure from Christianity. The 1920s involved a "craving for vitality and sensation" and a "collapse of deference" (Mews 1994, 466). In the 1920s agnosticism openly reigned as "intellectual orthodoxy" among university elites, "an apparently irresistible consensus" created by Darwin, Marx, Nietzsche, Freud, Durkheim, and Frazer (Hastings 1991, 222-223). Still, most Britons in the 1920s did not attend universities. University education became more common by the 1960s, so the anti-authority, anti-orthodox attitude common to both eras reverberated more widely in the 1960s than in the 1920s (Hastings 1991, 585).[1]

For much of the 1900s, British primary and secondary schools were still expected to acquaint pupils with Christianity. The 1944 Education Act required schools to provide religious education and to begin with an act of worship (McLeod 2003, 10; Brown 2006, 166). Until the 1960s, schools "intended to produce children with a better knowledge of Christianity," says Davie. Since 1960 the schools, whether state-run or church-run, grew vaguer in the objectives for their classes on religion, tending toward comparative religions.[2] By the 1990s, Church of England schools had "no measurable effect on attitudes towards Christianity" compared to schools with no religious affiliation (Davie 1994, 133-134). Abandoning a Christian catechesis model and instead offering tidbits about various religions resulted in ignorance of Bible stories and church history among the young (Davie 2000, 180). By the late 1900s, most schools allowed little opportunity for biblical faith to be clearly and compellingly presented in religion classes. Meanwhile, most subjects were taught without reference to Christian claims. Universities were more secular still (Bebbington 1992b).

---

[1]Secular "orthodoxy" was not confined to Britain or Europe but also affected American higher education. In *The secularization of the academy* (Marsden and Longfield 1992), various scholars trace how Christianity, a leading force in higher education well into the 1800s, became peripheral or entirely absent. The book's main focus is on the United States, but essays on British and Canadian universities are also included. *The secular revolution* (Smith 2003), another anthology, depicts the distancing from Christianity that occurred in several academic disciplines and social institutions in the United States. Special attention is given to specific groups and persons vying for influence.

[2]An exception is the recent appearance in Britain of a "growing number of 'Christian' schools—sometimes attached to house churches and sometimes of American origin—which nurture children in a convinced and articulate doctrinal environment. They are sought after by a particular group of parents in order that home and school may become mutually reinforcing" (Davie 1994, 136).

Lewis and Newbigin experienced firsthand the challenge that schools could pose to Christian plausibility. Already in the early 1900s, even before the open and official changes in education that would later occur, Lewis and Newbigin both abandoned the faith of their parents while in British boarding schools. In both cases, the social setting as well as the intellectual climate played a role in making Christianity seem implausible to them.

Both students abhorred the separation from home and the experience of school life. Lewis often expressed his loathing for all three boarding schools he attended. He compared school clothes to prison uniforms (1955b, 23). He hated these schools even more than the frontline trenches of World War I (1955b, 96, 113; 2007, 1325). Newbigin, for his part, felt "utter desolation" entering a Quaker boarding school. "There is no way of describing it, for it is just darkness with no light at all" (1985a, 4).

Along with experiencing a sense of trauma and separation from familial roots at school, Lewis and Newbigin were influenced by the teaching. Both were carried along not so much by direct claims as by implicit assumptions. Lewis remembered how a matron's vague, speculative spiritualism and occultism "blunted all the sharp edges of my belief . . . altering 'I believe' to 'one does feel.'" In studying Greek and Roman classics, Lewis found that teachers and textbooks took for granted that religions "were sheer illusion . . . a kind of endemic nonsense into which humanity tended to blunder." Christianity was "a fortunate exception . . . labeled True," but no grounds were given to support this claim. "No one ever attempted to show in what sense Christianity fulfilled Paganism or Paganism prefigured Christianity" (1955b, 62-63). Eventually "escaping school," Lewis resided with an ex-Presbyterian, atheist tutor, for whom he maintained lifelong respect. The tutor, Kirkpatrick, never directly attacked religion in Lewis's presence, but Lewis's unbelief was strengthened by Kirkpatrick's rationalism and library—especially Frazer's *The Golden Bough*, which accounted for religions in terms of anthropology (Lewis 1955b, 132-148; 2004b, 702).

Going through school a decade after Lewis, Newbigin "abandoned the Christian assumptions of my home and childhood" as he became immersed in contrary assumptions. "From my chemistry teacher I learned that 'life is a disease of matter', and ... I imbibed a broadly deterministic view of history." Everything could be explained without reference to the divine. Therefore, "'God' was no longer a tenable hypothesis" (1985a, 5-6).

Both Lewis and Newbigin would later return to belief in God and commit their lives to Jesus Christ—and both were aided in their conversion by reading books that offered compelling cases for religious belief and by conversations with highly intelligent friends in a university setting (Lewis 1955b, 212-237; 2004a, 976-977; Newbigin 1985a, 6, 10, 13). But the books that helped most were not assigned by teachers, and the conversations that helped most did not occur in classrooms. For the rest of their lives, Lewis and Newbigin expressed concern that British education and intelligentsia posed a serious challenge to faith.

Lewis's Perceptions

British education became patently less Christian at every level of schooling in the decades after Lewis's death, but the university—Lewis's specific context—was already in his lifetime almost as pervasively and openly non-Christian as other levels of schooling would later become. Lewis spent his adult life as an educator.[3] He saw all around him how educational institutions, through direct teaching and implicit assumptions, could induct students into patterns of thought that were antithetical to Christian belief. Chapter 5 traces some of the intellectual currents—often flowing through schools and universities—that Lewis saw in his context as challenges to Christianity's plausibility. What will be discussed here are some other aspects of schooling noted by Lewis which did not involve actual teaching and did not directly attack Christian intellectual positions but were at odds with Christian spiritual formation and thus indirectly influenced the intellectual realm as well.

Of his own experience, Lewis wrote, "Spiritually speaking, the deadly thing was that school life was a life almost wholly dominated by the social struggle." He wondered if Britain's "bitter, truculent, skeptical debunking, and cynical *intelligentsia*" might have developed such attitudes earlier in life amid the social competition of schools that "very few of them liked" (1955b, 107-108). Seeing the battle for grades and social standing during the time of a young person's life that "nature meant to be free and frolicsome," Lewis asked, "Is this the way to breed a nation in psychological, moral, and spiritual health" (2007, 17)?

[3]Joel Heck (2005) provides a book-length discussion of Lewis's experience as an educator and his views on education. Recollections from some of Lewis's former students and professorial colleagues are included in Como's anthology (1992, 33-106).

In his 1955 essay "Lilies that fester," Lewis denounced the manner in which "cultured education" was becoming a passport into "a new, real, ruling class: what has been called the Managerial Class." Teachers served as gatekeepers for "the unofficial, self-appointed aristocracy of the *Cultured*" by prescribing certain aesthetic preferences and analytic methods. Only students who conformed to such canons of taste and rationality would get the good marks needed to gain entry into "the Managerial Class" (1960d, 41-45).

Much modern education was a form of mass production and bureaucratic control (1955b, 97)—and Lewis liked "bats much better than bureaucrats" (1960c, x).[4] Lewis's fictional villain Feverstone declared, "A real education makes the patient do what it wants infallibly: whatever he or his parents try to do about it" (1946a, 42). Schools herded the young in groups dominated by peer pressure and moved them all step by step through a curriculum sequence like units on an assembly line, mass-producing mediocre souls with minimal individuality or spiritual aspiration. This process could manufacture multitudes of unthinking prey for demons, imbued with "imperturbable conceit and incurable ignorance" (1960c, 164-168). Lewis had in mind not just British but American education (1960c, 152).[5]

The more education was funded by government taxation and controlled by government regulation, the further such tendencies would go. Screwtape boasted, "Penal taxes, designed for that purpose, are liquidating the Middle Class, the class who were prepared to save and spend and make sacrifices in order to have their children privately educated" (1960c, 168). The more education became a function of centralized state power, the less space would be allowed for Christianity in schools. In 1946 Lewis predicted that English government in coming decades would not "tolerate any radically Christian elements in its State system of education." Christianity was antithetical to "omnicompetent government." The ongoing trend "towards increasing state control" meant that authentic Christianity would "be treated as an enemy" in fact if not yet in words (1970, 118).[6]

---

[4]As Wesley Kort observes, "The two most evil structures Lewis describes are both bureaucracies: N.I.C.E. in *That Hideous Strength* and the 'lowerarchy' of hell in *The Screwtape Letters*" (Kort 2001, 45).

[5]Lewis remarked in a 1961 letter that "the arguments against both day-schools and boarding schools are equal and unanswerable" (2007, 1289).

[6]British government's high degree of centralization and regulation of education has made it harder for British parents than for American parents to influence local

Although Lewis warned about the impact of bureaucracy and government on schools, he sometimes downplayed such things and emphasized that what really mattered was whether or not the teachers themselves were Christians. Even if a school curriculum was structured to disregard religion, Christianity would still be conveyed to students if enough teachers were Christians. Conversely, even a curriculum structured to include religion would only inculcate cynicism and unbelief if teachers were not Christians. "We have, in the long run, little either to hope or to fear from the government. . . . Let the abstract scheme of education be what it will: its actual operation will be what the men make it." Little good would come from campaigns to bring structural change to "large schools on which a secular character is already stamped." The main problem with British education was that Britain had too few real Christians. The most practical way to change education would be to convert recent graduates and adults: "If you make the adults of today Christians, the children of tomorrow will receive a Christian education" (1970, 117-119).

In this section we have seen several ways that Lewis perceived Christian plausibility to be negatively impacted by schooling, even apart from the content of teaching. Social competition and cruelty in schools made people—especially the most educated—grow up to be bitter and skeptical, quick to debunk and slow to believe. Schools were gatekeepers imposing the intellectual and aesthetic criteria of a self-perpetuating "cultured" class, thus putting pressure on students' minds and blocking non-conformists from pathways to positions of wide influence. "Democratic education," championing equal opportunity for all, used bureaucratic methods of standardization and control that tended to stifle individuality, stunt intellectual excellence, and suppress spiritual exploration. The shortage of committed Christians in British society generally, and among teachers particularly, meant too few op-

---

government schools (Berger 2001b, 448). It has also been harder to establish parent-controlled Christian schools or to home school. In Britain even church-run schools "are constrained by a national curriculum," and private schools must comply with examination boards (Bruce 2002a, 223-224). Thus, as state policy moved farther from Christian grounding, so did state-regulated education at all levels. In a society where government aims to be religiously neutral, the more government gets involved in the affairs of other social institutions, the harder it is for those institutions to bear a Christian imprint and to perpetuate Christian discourse. In post-Christendom Europe, the vast extent of state power may be a more serious challenge to Christianity than the limits of the church's institutional power.

portunities for students' minds to be shaped by encounters with exemplars of faith.

Newbigin's Perceptions

In the century's final decades, when Newbigin was living back in Britain, schools at all levels were much less likely than in earlier times to host Christian worship or to make Christianity the main focus of classes on religion. Throughout the century, educational trends away from Christianity intensified, and were reinforced by growing ethnic and cultural diversity in the latter decades. By the time Newbigin was writing about mission to the West, most schools had openly abandoned any pretense that religion classes aimed to cultivate Christian belief or that other subject areas reflected a Christian worldview. Newbigin's perception of thought patterns prevalent in the West (and propagated in its schools) will receive closer attention in chapter 8; this section, though touching upon such things, focuses mainly on institutional policies and practices of schools as Newbigin saw them.

Even in the 1960s, when Newbigin was viewing secularization positively as liberation of various spheres of life from domination by religious institutions, he saw no way for a school to be religiously and morally neutral. In subject after subject, the content of teaching would change if Christianity was no longer the foundation of European learning. For centuries the Bible had provided the framework for teaching world history in European schools, said Newbigin, but not anymore (1966, 20). The secular state would face its biggest challenge in education. It was impossible, insisted Newbigin, for a school not to convey "accepted convictions about behavior and about values" (1966, 130-131).

The later Newbigin, having rejected the notion of a secular public square free from any reigning ideology, insisted more strongly than ever that it was impossible for schools to be neutral. Students' minds would be "shaped by a very definite creed," and it would not be Christian (1994a, 166). Schools were agents of the reigning plausibility structure. British public schools were dominated by "a powerful education lobby" which disallowed teaching Christianity as truth (1988a, 191). American public schools were teaching secular humanism (1988a, 188). Public educational institutions in the West were not allowed to teach as fact that a loving, wise God created and redeemed humanity, but they were required to teach as fact the evolutionary dogma that humans resulted from "a ruthless struggle for survival in which the secret of progress is the destruction of rivals" (1988b, 152). It was a fact that DNA governed human nature; it was mere opinion that the purpose of human existence is to glorify God and enjoy him forever (1986a, 4; 1987, 4; 1989a, 15).

Religion classes were still required by law in Britain's schools. Although "this had always been understood as meaning Christian education," that was no longer the case. Students were to study religions as "aspects of differing cultures, not to accept any of them as accounts of how things are," wrote Newbigin. "It seemed obvious to me that the alleged 'objectivity' effectively concealed the real commitment of the practitioner of this kind of teaching, a commitment to the accepted values of the consumer society of which he was a part" (1985a, 244). With the growing number of students from Hindu, Sikh, and Muslim families, teachers were supposed to "teach 'religion' as an aspect of culture rather than as a vision of truth." Meanwhile, other subjects in the curriculum were supposedly conveying not mere "culture" but "the way things really are," thus ruling out of order any questioning of those "factual" claims from a religiously grounded intellectual position (1983, 62).

Some religious parents, especially Muslims, objected that their children were being taught "to look down and not to look up." Newbigin thought Christians should offer a similar objection (1990, 1). He saw a need for children to be trained to understand and tolerate the different faith commitments of their fellow citizens even if they believed them to be false. Such teaching could not be based on a secular epistemology which enthroned autonomous human reason and excluded divine revelation. It also could not happen in "a fully Islamic society," where "the teaching in public schools of religious beliefs contrary to those of Islam must be suppressed." Only the gospel could ground such a society, for according to the gospel, "God has provided a space and time during which there is freedom to disbelieve and to disobey the rule of God, and in which the reality of the rule of God is known as a matter of faith but not of sight" (1996, 5). However, Western societies and schools were not invoking this Christian intellectual basis for accepting religious diversity.

Pluralism was the creed for religion classes (1985a, 244-245; 1988a, 191). In other classes, the atheistic assumptions of the modern scientific worldview reigned (1986b, 38; 1989a, 15, 24, 42; 1994a, 166). In all subjects but religion, truth was taken to be objective and clearly known;

anything contradicting it was wrong. In religion classes, on the other hand, belief was subjective and any opinion was as good as another (1986a, 5).[7] Perceiving the schools in this way, Newbigin saw an urgent need to show that the "knowledge" produced by science was not so objective or certain, and that the "beliefs" rooted in Christian faith were not so subjective or uncertain. He thought that legal battles over the content of the school curriculum were expressions of a deeper "malaise of our culture," which could only be attacked "at the place where we ask about what it means to know, about epistemology" (1988a, 193). This identification of epistemology as the most basic problem was a refrain that sounded again and again in Newbigin's missional diagnosis of the West.

Home

Intergenerational transmission of Christian thought and life involves not just school but also home. In the twentieth century, the custom of prayer before meals and bedtime vanished from most British homes (Brown 2006, 4-5). Bible reading at home "faded away" (Hastings 1991, 666).[8] In 1999 only 18 percent of Britons thought it important that children share their parents' faith (Lambert 2003, 71). The fact that fewer university students found Christian basics plausible may have been a result not just of what happened at school but of what did *not* happen at home. "Family background helped sustain undergraduate religiosity long into the twentieth century," but a "collapse in the reli-

---

[7]Newbigin's perception of religion classes in British schools may have been affected by what he earlier witnessed in the *Sarvodaya* system of elementary education in India. Each day began and ended with an act of common worship, using "prayers and meditations drawn from the sacred books and traditions of all the religions. The names of Ram, Jesus, Allah, Buddha, etc. are used indifferently." Such worship was meant to express "the true essence of religion in which men of all kinds can find their unity." It was based on belief that beneath the various expressions of religions lay a single reality that grounded the real truth in all of them. Newbigin cautioned against being deceived by the "appearance of benevolence and openheartedness" in treating all religions as the same, for this in fact involved its own dogmatic claim about religious truth (1961, 32-35). This observation would later be echoed in Newbigin's critique of Hick and of religious pluralism in British schools: the rhetoric of tolerant inclusiveness masked the enshrining of a definite religious dogma.

[8]Martin finds that "in modern Christianity there is a significant absence of supportive family ritual." He wonders whether most Protestantism tends to be too inward and individualistic for consistent intergenerational transmission (Martin 2005a, 56).

gion of the home" accelerated in the 1960s, so that university students born after that time were much less likely than their parents to have had even a shred of religious training (Bebbington 1992b, 267).

British Christianity since mid-century had a generational half-life: each new generation had only half the levels of attendance, affiliation, and affirmation of Christian doctrines as true and important, compared to the previous generation. Homes with unchurched parents produced 97 percent unchurched offspring. Homes with one churchgoing parent raised 23 percent churchgoers. Homes with two churchgoing parents (monthly minimum) produced a 46 percent level of churchgoers in the next generation. (Voas and Crockett 2005, 17-22). Theologically liberal parents were unlikely to pass any faith to their children (Bruce 2001b, 99-100). Conservative Protestants' children remained more likely to hold Christian beliefs and go to church (Bruce 1996, 85).

Lewis's Perceptions

Lewis wrote a foreword to B. G. Sandhurst's *How heathen is Britain?* (1946). Sandhurst contended that Britain's younger generation had no inherent incapacity for accepting Christian claims. The young were not at fault; rather, "it was lack of home training and school instruction which did the damage." Especially problematic were middle-aged parents and schoolmasters "who rose to manhood during the deplorable twenties" and whom the next generation was now counting on for answers (Sandhurst 1946, 156-157).[9] In Lewis's foreword (reprinted in Lewis 1970, 114-119), he agreed with Sandhurst that the new generation was not being taught effectively by parents and teachers.

> If the younger generation have never been told what the Christians say and never heard any arguments in defence of it, then their agnosticism or indifference is fully explained. There is no need to look any further: no need to talk about the general intellectual climate of the age, the influence of mechanistic civilization on the character of urban life. And having discovered that the cause of their ignorance is lack of instruction, we have

[9]Sandhurst discussed findings from 2,000 questionnaires filled out by cadets, young men age 18-22, with whom he had spent a few sessions presenting Christian claims. About half agreed that their forebears had been right to believe in Christ as divine, though in many such cases, belief was vague. Of those not initially believing, many changed their minds when presented with basic Christian claims and a cogent case for them. Most said they had never previously been shown any reasons to believe Christianity (Sandhurst 1946, 1-45).

also discovered the remedy. There is nothing in the nature of the younger generation which incapacitates them for receiving Christianity. If any one is prepared to tell them, they are apparently ready to hear. (1970, 115)

Emphasizing that each generation is taught by the previous one, Lewis observed that the beliefs of youth in the 1940s were "largely the beliefs of the Twenties," and that the beliefs of future youth in the 1960s would echo those of the 1940s (1970, 116).

Lewis saw the home as a potential counterbalance to the baneful systems of "educationalists." Planners since Plato had dreamed of a centralized society with "every child a bastard raised by a bureau." Lewis was glad that home nurture and a child's individual spirit often resisted and overcame such controllers (1996, 71; see also 2004b, 934). Yet Lewis did not view home as a cure-all, and he criticized those who portrayed it that way.

Writing in the *Church of England Newspaper* in 1945, Lewis blasted "a sentimental tradition" promoted by some preachers who talked "as if 'home' were a panacea, a magical charm." This phony view was inherited from the 1800s, said Lewis, when "some people thought that monogamous family life would automatically make them holy and happy." This notion, so out of touch with the often sinful and painful realities of family life, made Christian preaching less plausible, observed Lewis. Hearing such falsehoods made audiences, especially the young, stop listening. Family life "converted and redeemed" could "become the channel of particular blessings and graces," but Lewis thought it urgent "to stop telling lies about home life and to substitute realistic teaching" (1970, 282-286).[10]

As the post-war 1950s in Britain brought a boom of marriages, births, and rhetoric about family, Lewis kept warning that idolization of the home opposed Christian commitment and contradicted lived realities. He saw nominally Christian families becoming upset if one of them became devoted to God.[11] Meanwhile, some popular art was por-

---

[10]Brown contends that by the early twentieth century, most British religiosity was "liberated from conversionism" but retained a nineteenth century emphasis on the home (2001, 87). Brown claims Christianity died in Britain during the 1960s when women left behind old roles and family ideals. But perhaps the deadly illness set in earlier when Christ and conversion came to matter less than a sentimentalized, culture-bound view of the family.

[11]Angry opposition to a family member's devotion to the divine is a major theme in *Till we have faces* (Lewis 1956) and in *The four loves* (Lewis 1960a).

traying happy homes as the supreme good. "How many of these 'happy homes' really exist?" asked Lewis, denouncing "the odiousness of nearly all those treacly tunes and saccharine poems in which popular art expresses Affection" (1960a, 61-62). Lewis's life ended before the feminist movement and the youth-based counterculture reached critical mass in the 1960s. But he pinpointed the false exaltation of the home against which many would soon revolt in disgust. Lewis would not have joined the revolt, but he felt the disgust.

In opposing idolization of home life, Lewis at times may have tended toward the opposite extreme: individualistically discounting the impact of parents. Lewis's main emphasis was on converting individuals one at a time, not on family solidarity and home discipleship passing faith from parents to children.[12] Lewis recognized that fewer children were getting basic Christian instruction as nominal Christianity continued to fade, but he viewed more adult conversions as a counterbalancing trend (2007, 326, 507).

In short, Lewis saw Christian plausibility affected by the home in various ways. He thought many parents were not conveying Christian teaching or giving arguments for its truth. He perceived that some preaching portrayed the family implausibly, thus losing credibility with the younger generation, who knew their homes did not match pulpit rhetoric. Lewis saw a need for realistic teaching and family transformation, yet in his tendency to focus on individual conversion, he may have underestimated the long-term harm to Christian belief and plausibility in Britain when homes failed to transmit Christianity.

Newbigin's Perceptions

Newbigin recalled from his childhood days that his father "never failed to take time for prayer in the morning" (1985a, 3). When he himself was a young man groping his way back from unbelief toward faith, one of his first steps was to take up daily prayer and Bible reading (1985a, 10). In 1992 he testified to a German audience that his precious

---

[12]Lewis lost his mother when he was nine, was not close to his father, spent his formative years in boarding schools or with a tutor, had no children of his own, and, by his own admission, did not enjoy being with young children. During most of his adult years, Lewis's "home" bristled with the dysfunctions of his alcoholic brother Warren and the aging atheist Mrs. Moore (Jacobs 2005; Sayer 1988; Wilson 1990). Such background may have contributed to Lewis's distaste for sugary words about happy homes. It may also have kept him from adequately seeing the impact homes often had in furthering faith or unbelief.

time each morning in Scripture cleared his vision to see things differently from "the stories that the world is telling about itself" (1994a, 204-205). In Newbigin's personal experience, daily devotions at home made a vital contribution to seeing Christianity as more plausible than alternate rationalities and accounts of the world. Yet in his cultural critique, Newbigin was surprisingly silent about the decrease of devotional acts in British homes and the concurrent slide in Christian belief from one generation to the next. His missional diagnosis of the West said more about church and societal structures than about the home.

Newbigin did speak of trends beyond the home that relegated the home to less significance and corroded intergenerational ties. He depicted "a sort of atomizing process" that came with urbanization. The individual became less attached to family or neighborhood and instead became "a sort of replaceable unit in the social machine." Newbigin contended that the modern city loosened people from old ties "wherever western civilisation has spread in the past one hundred years" (1953, 3). Development—technical, industrial, economic—"encourages the younger generation to think differently from its parents" (1966, 14).

During his final decades, living back in Britain and offering a profile of Western culture, Newbigin noted that one characteristic of capitalist societies is the "disintegration of family life" (1986b, 113; 1989a, 223). His publications during this period included some remarks about factors that decreased parental influence on children. A major factor was "the new conception of education as a responsibility of the state." One consequence of ever-expanding government was an ever-shrinking role for the family. "The transmission of traditional wisdom in families from the old to the young is replaced by systems of education organized by the state and designed to shape young minds toward the future that is being planned" (1986b, 28-29). Modern societies "set up public educational systems by which children are taken away from their parents" and immersed in a mechanistic rationality which disregards God's purposes (1986b, 38).

The decrease of parental influence in rearing godly children was due in part to government and its schools, said Newbigin, but parents were not free of blame. "Parents ask [schools] for religious instruction for their children, but it does not take the children long to discover that the parents do not believe what they want the children to learn" (1983, 61-62). If Christianity was not held as fact at home, religious "values" taught in school would have little credence with the young. (The fact-value split was perpetrated by Newbigin's usual suspect, Enlightenment epistemology.) Children needed parents who believed Christianity as fact and did what was necessary for their children to receive Christian education. Newbigin lauded thousands of American parents who, rather than immerse their children in public schools' "false account of the world and of human life," instead set up parent-controlled Christian schools (1988a, 193). Such schools were extensions of the home, not of the state.

Newbigin often emphasized relatedness over autonomy. The Bible, unlike Indian or modern Western thought, did not "see the human person as an autonomous individual" but in relationships "between man and woman, then between parents and children, then between families and clans and nations." Belief and salvation did not occur in isolation but through relational ties (1989a, 82). Newbigin made this theological point but did not offer a corresponding diagnostic assessment of specific home practices. He did not discuss how parental ritual, instruction, example, and treatment of children could make Christianity seem reasonable and attractive, or unreasonable and repulsive, to the young.

Newbigin insisted that the church must "claim the high ground of public truth" and not be limited to "only the private and domestic aspects of life" (1989a, 222). But Newbigin's analysis of Western culture may have erred in the opposite direction: it was largely concerned with the public sphere to the neglect of the domestic. Public trends can affect home ties—but home devotion (or lack thereof) can also have public ramifications. Modern rationalities can undermine the influence of the home—but the home's influence can also counter modern rationalities and inculcate a different sense of what is believable.

In his missiology for the West, Newbigin repeatedly stressed the congregation as the "only real hermeneutic of the gospel" (e.g., 1989a, 227, 232; 1994a, 42, 153, 176); he said nothing of the Christian home as a hermeneutic of the gospel. This is ironic, for in the first chapter of his memoirs, the proportions were reversed. Newbigin fondly recalled his parents' piety and love but did not mention any boyhood memory of church. Even after he left home and lost Christian belief while in boarding school, his home heritage remained a magnet pulling him toward Christian truth. He could not stop wondering "whether belief in God was possible," and it was while visiting his parents' home that he read two books that "made a reasonable case for belief," helping him see "that Christian faith was not irrational" (1985a, 6). In short, the home loomed larger in Newbigin's experience than in his theorizing.

Media

Mass communication had a major impact in the twentieth century through technologies such as print, radio, film, television, and internet. Media had considerable power over what would come to people's attention and what they would find believable.

In the 1920s, the British government assigned control of radio to the British Broadcasting Corporation. BBC policy excluded "contentious religious themes from the airwaves. Evangelizing evangelicals were defined as contentious." When television started in the 1930s and then became widespread in the 1950s, evangelicals were still denied access, despite their protests (Bebbington 1993, 207). Roman Catholics also objected to unfair BBC treatment (Brown 2006, 136). Broadcast outlets allowed little room for contested doctrines or direct "proselytizing" by a particular church.

In the 1940s, Lewis's BBC broadcasts helped make him a major figure in Britain. His access to the BBC may have depended in part on the fact that he fit within the parameters of acceptability that the BBC upheld at the time.[13] Lewis disavowed any intent to recruit for a particular church body and stressed his intent to present only what Christians agreed upon (1952, 6). He did not advocate the pricklier positions of evangelicals, deemed by the BBC to be unfit for public consumption.[14]

---

[13]Justin Phillips (2002) offers an account of the BBC's engagement with Lewis. Phillips stresses the Christian ethos of the BBC's founding and the Christian intent of key BBC figures who put Lewis on the air. The BBC's Broadcast House, built in 1931, was inscribed with a dedication to God and a "prayer that good seed sown may bring forth a good harvest" (2002, 16). Eric Fenn, Lewis's producer, was a Presbyterian minister and an activist in the Student Christian Movement. James Welch, the Director of Religious Broadcasting who originally invited Lewis to speak on the BBC, was eager for credible Christian messages. Welch had been a missionary in Nigeria and earned a Cambridge Ph.D. in anthropology (Phillips 2002, 22-23). He wrote to Lewis about the "need of a positive restatement of Christian doctrine in lay language" (Phillips 2002, 80). These BBC officials clearly wanted to advance Christianity. At the same time, their ecumenical zeal, together with regulatory policy, resulted in a decided preference for generically Christian programs, impeding a church body from airing its own distinctive message or recruiting members.

[14]Lewis, though lionized by many evangelicals, differed from positions distinctive of many evangelicals in his time. He did not insist on faith in Christ as necessary for salvation; rather, Lewis suggested that people from other religions might be saved by Jesus without actually believing in Jesus (1952, 65; 1970, 102; 2007, 163, 245-246). He did not teach justification by faith alone. He treated substitutionary atonement as merely one atonement theory which might be helpful to some but not to others (1952, 57; 2007, 1476). He did not proclaim an inerrant Bible (1958, 109-110; 2007,

As time passed, British media increasingly excluded not only the "contentious" claims of evangelicals and Roman Catholics but also the kind of centrist "mere Christianity" such as Lewis had presented. From mid-century onward, radio and television tended to grant decreasing space for direct Christian messages and to feature more and more material that implicitly undermined Christianity or even explicitly contradicted and ridiculed the faith. Although the government-sponsored BBC originally claimed to present "Christian values" common to "all religious bodies," it remained an instance of "state control of new media," and over time allowed less and less opportunity to present distinctively Christian themes (Brown 2006, 181-182). Religious programs became increasingly "bland and devoid of either theological content or proselytizing zeal" (Gilbert 1994, 512-513).

In the 1960s open mockery of Christianity became increasingly frequent on TV, says Brown. Such fare had previously existed in some local music halls, but the impact was vastly magnified when government-sponsored television, reaching nearly every British home, lampooned Christianity and laced programs with profanities and sexual content. Even the "God-slot" moved away from vaguely innocuous, devotional religion into featuring prominent clergy who challenged key tenets of Christian faith. "Television was showing the British people how to reject religion" (Brown 2006, 227-229). Such media trends reflected and reinforced a widening divide between Christianity and popular culture, "one of the most important aspects of twentieth-century secularization in England" (McLeod 2000, 286).[15]

Lewis and Newbigin, each in his own time and context, offered observations on mass communication and its effects. Both spoke not just about specifically Christian or anti-Christian messages but about how media indirectly shaped minds and attitudes.

961, 1044-1046, 1436-1437). He did not challenge geological theories of earth's history or biological theories of human origins (1958, 115; 2004b, 962; 2007, 141, 157).

[15]Perhaps in mass communication, as in education, Christian influence was hampered not so much by the weakening of a state church as by the strengthening and centralization of state control in various spheres (Berger 2005, 117). Instead of "a plethora of local initiatives," as in the United States, Britain had a centralized "monopoly of the airwaves" (Bebbington 1994, 379). According to Bruce, broadcasting is vital for maintaining a religious worldview and subculture. One reason religious groups are stronger in the U. S. than in Britain is that the two nations have "different regulatory regimes." For most of the 1900s, British media did not "allow particular religious organizations or communities to produce programmes that represented their views" (Bruce 2002a, 223-227).

Lewis's Perceptions

Lewis thought Christians using media to make faith plausible and attractive for their audience should not shy away from being contemporary and colloquial. He praised the religious radio dramas of his friend Dorothy Sayers (Lewis 2004b, 572-573, 577). Her fresh, everyday renderings made Bible stories come alive for contemporary listeners. When some people objected to Sayers's alleged irreverence, Lewis derided "'cultured' asses . . . who are always waffling about reverence" (2004b, 586). Archaic or highbrow language would not necessarily be more reverent, but it would damage Christianity's plausibility among moderns by conveying a sense that the faith was only a cultural artifact from the past.

Discussing his own BBC programs, Lewis could complain that the strict time constraints required him to make difficult doctrines fit "the Procrustes' bed of neither more nor less than fifteen minutes" (2004b, 502). Yet he recognized, with gruff humor, that the plain talk required by the radio medium kept him from using academic abstractions about things of which he knew little. "I could do it for a Bamptom Lecture, but this d—d colloquial style is so intrinsically honest that I can't conceal *in it* my ignorance" (2004b, 598). [16]

Besides commenting on Christian-themed programming, Lewis offered wide-ranging remarks on various media and their impact on the mind. Rapid communication could bring tragic reports each day from all over the world, he noted, far exceeding the amount of trouble that people would directly encounter in their local setting. Lewis thought this "imposed a burden on sympathy for which sympathy was never made," making the world "simply *too much for* people," including himself. [17] Trying to take in the whole modern world numbed the heart and befuddled the mind—especially as World War II dawned (2004b, 350).

In a wartime context, people were eager for media reports but could also be skeptical and cynical. According to Lewis, nearly all military personnel he met on trains in Britain regarded newspaper stories

---

[16]Phillips asserts that working with BBC radio professionals and their sensitivities to audiences "helped Lewis with his clarity of expression and his economy of words" (2002, 127). In radio, "words have to make sense right away" (Phillips 2002, 235).

[17]Mission agencies and charitable organizations sometimes speak of "compassion fatigue" among supporting constituencies. People exposed to a steady dose of tragedies in the mass media—and in the mass fundraising appeals of agencies—find it increasingly hard to feel sympathy for the latest woes that befall people they have never met, and many of the accounts they hear may even come to seem implausible.

about Nazi atrocities as mere propaganda to "pep up" troops and fuel the war effort, nothing more. Disbelief toward government and media had become so rampant that even true accounts of real horrors were brushed aside by people who had become jaded by verbal efforts to mobilize public support.[18] Such distrust of authority and dismissal of words could make people resistant not only to media reports but to other forms of persuasion as well (1986, 48-49; see also 1958, 29). A general cynicism could undermine the plausibility of many kinds of claims—including the claims of the gospel.

Lewis blasted newspapers as bundles of distortions or outright lies (2007, 114; 1967, 117) that fostered "an incurable taste for vulgarity and sensationalism" (1955b, 159). Intellectuals who read "the leading articles" were more likely to be "the dupes of their favourite newspapers" than less educated people who only read the sports. At least sports reports were usually true (1986, 49). Meanwhile, clergy who tried to be relevant by sermonizing on social and political issues usually revealed little except what newspaper they happened to be parroting, thus undermining the spiritual authority of their office and diminishing the credibility of their claims on theological matters (1970, 94).

The popular press could spread false assumptions and ideologies. Popular science writers and novelists could be agents of a scientism that Lewis was eager to combat (2004b, 236-237, 918).[19] Popular periodicals could propagate the myth of evolutionary progress even after many intellectuals had abandoned it (1967, 127-128).

According to Lewis, mass communication—even when its content was not specifically evil—could become an obstacle to Christian belief by its sheer pervasiveness and power to distract. Screwtape spoke of Satan's "kingdom of Noise" and his plan to fill the universe with noise (1960c, 103, 146). News, entertainment, and advertising crowded out silence, solitude, and "any train of thought that leads off the beaten

---

[18]Doris Myers states that militaristic propaganda in Britain during World War I had excessively vilified Germany and glorified British heroism, while glossing over the grim realities of mutual slaughter in the trenches. Wartime idealism—often supported by churches—gave way to postwar disillusionment in the 1920s and beyond. "Lewis's often-noted refusal to read newspapers suggests that he shared the postwar disillusionment with language that replaced public idealism and excitement" (Myers 1994, 3).

[19]Thomas Peters (1998) describes the broad impact of H. G. Wells's fiction and Lewis's efforts to counter such scientism with popular science fiction of his own.

track," thus making it "extremely easy" for moderns to avoid God (1967, 227).

When considering film, Lewis recognized much technical skill but disliked what he perceived as too much stimulation and too little aesthetic and moral excellence.[20] As film became a fixture in millions of homes during the 1950s via the medium of television, complaints arose that the young were wasting too much time on television. Lewis responded by saying that their newspaper-reading parents had a worse diet (2007, 1178). He may have been right that the older generation was too quick to ignore its own flaws and to complain about the next generation. Still, in hindsight, it appears that television surpassed any power newspapers ever had to occupy people's time and alter their perceptions.

To distill into one sentence Lewis's observations on mass communication in relation to Christian plausibility: he thought Christians could witness plausibly in modern media and idioms, but he saw Christian plausibility challenged when media overwhelmed sympathy, fostered cynicism, misled audiences, or distracted them from thoughts of God.

Newbigin's Perceptions

In contrast to Lewis, who died when television was still relatively young, Newbigin experienced the full reality of an era in which television had become the dominant form of mass communication, occupying much of people's discretionary time and attention.[21] As a local pastor visiting neighborhood homes in the 1980s, said Newbigin, he was "forced to recognize that the most difficult missionary frontier in the contemporary world is . . . the frontier that divides the world of biblical faith from the world whose values and beliefs are ceaselessly fed into

[20]Lewis wondered what Walt Disney's talent might have produced if he "had been educated—or even brought up in a decent society" (2004b, 242). In 1951 Lewis said that he found film "an astonishingly ugly art. I don't mean 'ugly' in any high flying moral or spiritual sense, but just disagreeable to the eye—crowded, unrestful, inharmonious" (2007, 105). After seeing The forbidden planet in 1956, he was struck by "the contrast between the magnificent technical power and the deplorable level of ethics and imagination" (2007, 783).

[21]Living in 1960s Geneva, Newbigin wisecracked that a developed society is one which "prefers sitting round a television screen listening to songs about detergents," rather than the communal dances and singing of "undeveloped" societies (1966, 14). In 1986 he said that even in Birmingham's poorest neighborhoods, "Every home has a television, and this provides, for most of the time, the visible center of life in the home" (1994a, 40).

every home on the television screen" (1985a, 249). In a nutshell, he perceived TV to be purveying paganism, monopolizing attention, and redefining reality.

A secular society, declared Newbigin, would have no supreme ideology and would offer no overarching vision of the good life. "If that is so, ours is certainly not a secular society." He alluded to statistics that "something like 90% of the population spends at least three-quarters of its free time glued to the television screen." Addictive images of the good life "are being ceaselessly pumped into every living room in the country." The programs and advertisements presented "an image of the good life more powerful than anything Islam or mediaeval Christendom ever managed to fasten on an entire population. Ours is not a secular society, but a society which worships false gods" (1986a, 6).

In arguing that no society can be truly secular, Newbigin not only cited sociologists who were rejecting previous versions of secularization theory, but he also offered television as evidence against secularization. Agreeing with Calvin that the human mind is "an image-factory," Newbigin insisted that no society is secular and neutral, that every society holds up models for emulation, and that in the West these models are "very easy to identify. They are presented hour after hour on the television screens in almost every home in the land." These images displayed society's conception of the good life and were "fueled by the most powerful commercial interests in society" (1989a, 219). Mass communication was a powerful proselytizer on behalf of the modern Western worldview, at odds with Christian presuppositions and doctrines.

> Every person living in a 'modern' society is subject to an almost continuous bombardment of ideas, images, slogans, and stories which presuppose a plausibility structure radically different from that which is controlled by the Christian understanding of human nature and destiny. The power of contemporary media to shape thought and imagination is very great. Even the most alert critical powers are easily overwhelmed. (1989a, 228-229)

In 1990 Newbigin spoke of "a vast entertainment industry designed to save us from the anxieties that would arise if we had a lot of time to think about serious matters."[22] He observed that technology, after re-

---

[22]Long before Newbigin warned about televisions (or Lewis about newspapers) as dangerous distractions from ultimate concerns, the seventeenth century apologist Pascal (1966) commented on humanity's aversion to stillness and the compulsion to

ducing menial labor and freeing time for leisure, had to solve the problem of filling up leisure time. Modern people had to be "continuously entertained" and "perpetually amused." He compared television to soma in Huxley's *Brave new world*, labeling TV "the delightful drug which keeps us happy and saves us from asking questions about ultimate meaning"[23] Newbigin warned that television was altering our sense of reality. "We move towards the point where there is no real world out there to be explored and known, only the world of the self, its imaginings and fantasies. The world of television becomes more real than the world of our everyday life." In such a culture, an event was "not real till you see it on television" (1990a, 3). A screen determined plausibility or lack thereof.

Newbigin spoke of "a world full of assumptions about what is true."[24] This world of assumptions was formed "through all the means of education and communication existing in a society." In the West, control of schools and media meant power over thought. "The question of power is inescapable." Therefore, Christian citizens must "seek access to the levers of power," not leave education and mass media to governmental and business interests, which supported a world of assumptions antithetical to Christian faith (1989a, 224).

For Newbigin, in summary, mass communication posed a challenge to Christian truth and rationality by presupposing and propagating an idolatrous plausibility structure, by constantly amusing and distracting minds from God, and by altering what would be regarded as important and real. Because power issues were unavoidable, Christians had to find fitting ways to exert influence in mind-molding realms such as schools and media. Christian witness that neglected such structural matters would be inadequate.

---

pursue various diversions that crowded out thoughts of God and the human condition. Diversions mentioned by Pascal included gambling, theater, dancing, tennis, hunting, billiards, and cock fighting. Moreover, serious activities—algebra, business pursuits, political administration, and military expeditions—could also serve as distractions (see especially *Pensees* #132-139).

[23]Newbigin here acknowledged drawing upon Neil Postman's *Amusing ourselves to death* (1985). Postman's jeremiad is especially scathing toward television with a purportedly serious aim. He argues that television, by the very nature of the medium, turns almost anything it touches—education, politics, religion—into entertainment.

[24]Berger (1967, 3-52) writes about religion in relation to social processes of "world-construction" and "world-maintenance." A social world is experienced by those within it as objectively real. Newbigin's language here about living within a social world of unquestioned, seemingly objective assumptions owes much to Berger.

Government

The impact of government has been alluded to already at various points in this study. The fading of Christendom, discussed in chapter 2, involved major changes in the relationship between church and state. As direct church influence on the state and other societal spheres decreased, the nation-state increased its involvement and influence over those spheres. In chapters 3 and 4, government's role in twentieth century Britain has been a recurring theme, involving such things as legislative changes related to the sexual revolution, colonial rule and post-colonial immigration policy, and control of education and mass communication. Here I explore in a more sustained way political factors (besides those previously mentioned) that were important for Lewis and Newbigin in their respective contexts, highlighting where they saw implications involving reason and plausibility.

Lewis wrote in times when Britain was either at war or recovering from war. Through the military draft, the government compelled millions to join the services. By requiring production of tanks, planes, and munitions, the government dominated vast sectors of industry. Through rationing of food, fuel, and other commodities during and after the war, the government controlled distribution and consumption. Modernization may have previously set in motion processes of societalization and rationalization, leading to expansion of government command and control.[25] But conditions of war and economic crisis accelerated these tendencies. Thus Lewis wrote in a context of vastly expanding government power.

By the 1980s and early 1990s, when Newbigin was writing about mission to the West, conditions had changed. Britain was not under attack or suffering from shortages. Many Britons thought government had become too big, too intrusive, and too expensive. High inflation and unemployment were increasingly blamed on government interference, not on government inaction. British Prime Minister Margaret Thatcher, like American President Ronald Reagan, slashed social spending and reduced regulations. Thatcher sought to shrink government's role in the economy, the media, and other spheres. Some church leaders fought these changes as unjust to the poor and contrary

---

[25]In *societalization*, local communities lose influence to industrial enterprises, impersonal government bureaucracies, and urban anonymity. In *rationalization*, various dimensions of life are viewed in terms of "technological consciousness," valuing procedure, control, and efficiency (Bruce 1996, 43-52; 2002a, 13, 117).

to the common good (Badham 1994, 499; Brown 2006, 288-289). It was in the context of these governmental changes—indeed, in heated opposition to them—that Newbigin began his major output of lectures, articles, and books critiquing Western culture in missional terms (Newbigin 1993c, 250-256).

Lewis's Perceptions

For Lewis, specific government policies were less a concern than overall trends. Four troubling tendencies were: (1) excessive expansion of government power, (2) church entanglement in politics, (3) obsession with vast crises rather than God and the soul, and (4) a modern political atmosphere which made monism seem more plausible than Christian theism. In each case, Lewis identified elements related to intellect and rationality.

Lewis saw unbridled government power rising from an intellectual shift which discarded moral reason and past precedent. In "the modern theory of sovereignty," the state saw itself as the source of law and thus could make any law it pleased. Many societies in earlier times had thought government "should hardly legislate at all" but should only "administer a pre-existing law" which was "given in the divine reason or in the existing custom." The new theory transferred the seat of political power "from the reason which humbly and patiently discerns what is right to the will which decrees what shall be right." As government felt free to "create its own 'ideology,'" individuals in society could not use objective moral reason against the state's self-justifying ideology (1954, 47-50).

Nazis, Fascists, and Communists were not the only threats Lewis saw. In a 1943 essay, "The poison of subjectivism," he contended that many democratic political planners and scientists were just as eager to manipulate and condition people according to values created by experts (1967, 11). In 1944 Lewis published *The Abolition of Man* (1996). He warned that government coercion in tandem with scientific planning—not anchored in the objective moral standards of practical reason—could produce a ruling group whose powers to condition and control people would effectively destroy what makes people human. Lewis made the same point in his 1946 "fairy-tale for grownups," *That Hideous Strength* (1946a).

In a 1958 article "Willing slaves of the welfare state," Lewis observed that two world wars and economic concerns had moved government to "take over many spheres of activity once left to choice or chance." This endangered "a freeborn mind." People would hardly dare think independently "when the State is everyone's schoolmaster and employer." Intellectuals had already "surrendered first to the slave-philosophy of Hegel, then to Marx, finally to the linguistic analysts." Politicians might become "the scientists' puppets." A technocratic welfare state might have dire consequences for individual cognition and feeling.

> To live his life in his own way, to call his house his castle, to enjoy the fruits of his own labour, to educate his children as his conscience directs, to save for their prosperity after his death— these are wishes deeply ingrained in white and civilised man. Their realization is almost as necessary to our virtues as to our happiness. From their total frustration disastrous results both moral and psychological might follow. (1970, 311-316)

A second concern of Lewis regarding government was the danger of church entanglement in politics. Lewis wanted the church to keep its distance from the state and not jeopardize the integrity and credibility of gospel truth by linking it with any national or political agenda. After the onset of war with Germany, Lewis thought it right for Britain to fight, but he did not want the church to equate Britain's cause with God's (2004b, 272, 391). He wrote, "I see no hope for the Church of England if it allows itself to become just an echo to the press" (2004b, 278).[26] Lewis insisted that no political ideology become part of the Christian creed. He predicted that "both a Leftist and a Rightist pseudo-theology" would develop—"the abomination will stand where it ought not" (2004b, 327). In 1953 Lewis wrote, "I think almost all the crimes which Christians have perpetrated against each other arise from this, that religion is confused with politics. For, above all other spheres of human life, the Devil claims politics for his own, as almost the citadel of his power" (2007, 358). Exalting political fervor to theological status conflicted with both reason and revelation.

---

[26]Lewis's speeches and radio broadcasts during World War II were perceived by some to be his contribution to the war effort. But Lewis insisted, "I had no concern with public morale at all. I was writing [radio scripts] purely as an apologist" (2007, 628). He was eager to avoid any appearance that his apologetic work served the agenda of any party or nation. When the Churchill government in 1951 intended to recognize Lewis in its Honours List, Lewis politely declined, saying that he did not want to strengthen the perception among some that "my religious writings are all covert anti-Leftist propaganda" (2007, 147).

A third government-related tendency that Lewis saw in his context was people's excessive focus on politics, international affairs, and global crises. Lewis regarded the eternal destiny of souls as more important than the temporal fate of civilizations (1967, 144; 1960c, 170). He felt that people of his time thought too much about national and world affairs, which they could seldom grasp or influence, and too little about the local setting where they were called to act (2004b, 843-844).[27] Lewis lived in times of dreadful conflict and crisis, but he did not want instability or danger to be the main object of attention or lead to an obsession with questions of survival. Rather, he hoped that the fragile state of nations and the world would prompt people to look beyond this world. In his 1942 essay "First and second things," Lewis wrote that for the past thirty years, the highest goal of civilization had been to preserve civilization. This not only drew attention away from what was truly ultimate but also jeopardized civilization itself. For civilization to survive, it might need to be placed second to something else, and "that immediately raises the question, second to what? What is the first thing?" (1970, 278-281).

As the cataclysmic upheavals of the world wars gave way to the growing menace of the Cold War, Lewis wrote a 1948 essay, "Living in an atomic age." He noted worries among political observers that future conflicts among nations could involve atomic bombs, and warnings from scientific experts that global cooling might soon produce "another of those periodic ice ages." Lewis contended that such dangers, rather than provoking panic about personal survival or the survival of civilization, should serve as reminders that every person will die, every society will perish, and the world itself will end at some point. These inescapable facts, made harder to ignore in times of crisis, meant that the ultimate question was not whether bombs or global cooling might destroy civilization but "whether 'Nature'—the thing studied by the sciences—is the only thing in existence" (1986, 75). For Lewis, apologetics was not just gathering evidence to support the right answers, but helping people to focus on the right questions. Worries about nuclear

---

[27]Lewis granted that Christians should try "to ensure a good government and to influence public opinion," but much had to be left to those whose task it was to govern, without always second-guessing them. Most people knew too little of "history and strategy" to know better than their officials. Acquiring the needed expertise would exceed most citizens' capacities or cause them to neglect their non-political callings (2004b, 251).

catastrophe or climate change had a lower priority for Lewis than the relationship of an eternal soul to God.[28]

A fourth government-related concern of Lewis was the manner in which the political context could make the very existence of a personal, supreme God seem less plausible than monism. Lewis believed that intellectual worldviews and theories not only shaped political trends but were shaped by them.[29] He contended that among "the great mass of unthinking people today," embrace of egalitarianism and rejection of monarchy made it harder for moderns to believe in a universe in which the supernatural God reigned as King over the earthly realm.[30] "Supernaturalism is the characteristic philosophy of a monarchical age and Naturalism of a democratic" (1960b, 10). Naturalistic monism, whether materialist or pantheist, appealed to the modern heart's "hankering for a universe which is all of a piece, and in which everything is the same sort of thing as everything else—a continuity, a seamless web, a democratic universe" (1960b, 40).[31] Modern nation-states and ideologies of

---

[28]Mitchell (1998, 3-5) provides additional evidence from Lewis's writings and from those who knew him, showing Lewis's surpassing concern for saving souls.

[29]For instance, Lewis said Darwinism gave scientific support to a pre-existing political myth of progress. "If no evidence for evolution had been forthcoming, it would have been necessary to invent it. The real sources of the myth are partly political. It projects onto the cosmic screen feelings engendered by the Revolutionary period" (1960d, 103).

[30]Britain still had (and has) a monarch, but by Lewis's time the real rulers were elected officials and appointed technocrats. The monarch's stature was mainly symbolic and nostalgic, with little governing authority. It may be worth considering whether this view of the monarchy was mirrored in many Britons' view of the Christian God: a symbolic and nostalgic vestige of the past, neither to be entirely abolished nor humbly obeyed. Suggate speaks of "the Englishman's abiding disinclination to abandon his attenuated Christianity" along with "his polite refusal to embrace a more vibrant form" (1994, 471). Davie points to a British notion of "an *ordinary* God" who has no real effect on daily affairs (1994, 199).

[31]A striking instance of projecting pro-democratic, anti-monarchical feelings onto the universe is Phillip Pullman. A popular author of fantasy for the young, Pullman detests Lewis and writes stories intended to counter "the nauseating drivel in Narnia" (quoted in Jacobs 2005, 307). According to Pullman, the monarchical myth of the kingdom of Heaven, shorn of its unbelievable and non-existent divine King, must give way to "the republic of Heaven" in which we all are equally autonomous and free to pursue our own Heaven here and now. We must find joy and meaning exclusively in this life and this world by pursuing our physical and intellectual passions, confident that "we are not subservient creatures dependent on the whim of some celestial monarch, but free citizens of the republic of Heaven" (Pullman 2001, 658)." The "republican myth" accepts "the overwhelmingly powerful evidence" for "blind

both Left and Right purported to treat all people as equal—indeed identical—and made all equally into units of a system to be managed by controllers. This blend of democracy and totalitarianism tended to destroy personality and individuality, thus meshing most comfortably with a religious outlook of monism, also dubbed "everythingism" by Lewis. "Everythingism is congenial to our minds because it is the natural philosophy of a totalitarian, mass-producing, conscripted age. That is why we must be perpetually on our guard against it" (1960b, 270).

Thus, in at least four key areas, Lewis saw links between his political context and matters of rationality and Christian plausibility. (1) Modern politics was replacing moral reason with sheer assertion of power and appeal to technical expertise. (2) Partisan zealotry could infiltrate Christian teaching and produce syncretistic idolatry contrary to both reason and revelation. (3) Worries about the survival of "civilization" could crowd out top-priority questions about God and the supernatural realm. (4) Political blending of egalitarianism and totalitarianism fostered a cognitive style more favorable to monism than Christian theism.

Newbigin's Perceptions

Two of Newbigin's concerns about government in the context of the later 1900s were idolatrous market ideology and state-sponsored scientism. He saw both threats rising largely from Enlightenment epistemology's displacement of Christian rationality.

Newbigin perceived an idolatrous market ideology at work when Reagan and Thatcher reduced domestic programs and increased military spending and nuclear weapons in the early 1980s. The new political context fueled old fires in Newbigin. He had long thought about government in its relation to economics and military power.[32] By Newbig-

---

and automatic" evolution instead of a Creator King. This does not mean humans have no purpose; rather, belief in evolution allows us to take our own consciousness as the sole source of purpose. "We might have arrived at this point by a series of accidents, but from now on we have to take charge of our fate" (Pullman 2001, 665).

[32]Newbigin recalled that his beloved father "was always struggling with the question of how to apply his Christian faith to the day-to-day issues of business and politics." Though owning a fleet of ships, Newbigin's father was a "radical" who kept moving further in a socialist direction as he grew older; he also abhorred militarism (1985a, 2-3). Newbigin, as a student, visited factories, tenements, and mining communities, growing in concern for people in poverty (1985a, 11-12). At Cambridge he read intensively in economics (1985a, 18). In the throes of the Great Depression, "it

in's own account, the political situation was a major motivation for launching "The Gospel and Our Culture" movement and writing about epistemology and mission to the West. Under Thatcher's government, "things which were simply taken for granted in the years following the war were being swept aside." A sense of obligation to other citizens, regard for public service, desire for public consensus, long-term government planning, respect for the BBC as "one of our greatest institutions"—all were being "swept contemptuously aside in favour of commitment to private gain. Market forces were to have final sovereignty over our lives" (1993c, 250). Perceiving "a replay of what happened in the 1930s" under Hitler, Newbigin thought the church was "dealing not with a political programme but with an idolatry. We were coming into a confessional situation" (1993c, 250).

With the approach of 1984—the date made famous in advance by Orwell's ominous book—Newbigin worked with a British Council of Churches study group and produced his first publication on mission to the West, *The other side of 1984* (1983). He denounced the nuclear arms race and said the prospect of nuclear war forced upon modern consciousness the fearful question, "Is there a future for civilization as we know it?" (1983, 4) He depicted Britain's "reaction against state supported welfare schemes" as a form of cynicism "which in effect pampers the rich at the expense of the poor" (1983, 58). These and other ills stemmed from Enlightenment assumptions that needed to be uprooted by questioning "contemporary assumptions about what is involved in knowing" (1983, 60).

---

seemed that the capitalist system was collapsing." Newbigin was initially impressed by young German National Socialists who seemed "a breakaway from European capitalism;" only later did he recognize Nazi aggression (1985a, 23-24). Throughout the 1930s, Newbigin saw "an inescapable contradiction between Christianity and capitalism." He half believed Soviet Russia "had created a more just economic order." The young Newbigin held socialist and pacifist positions, from which he later drew back somewhat (1985a, 36, 46). But he would always remain quick to see capitalism and militarism as idols to be opposed by the gospel.

Newbigin's vehemence against attempts by Reagan and Thatcher to reduce the welfare state was heightened by his immediate context during the 1980s. Winson Green was one of the poorest areas in Britain, with "very high unemployment" (1994a, 40). People there seemed likely to be among the hardest hit by budget cuts and deregulation of industry. Having spent much time "in the decaying areas of a city like Birmingham, one is moved not just to cool analysis but to hot anger," declared Newbigin (1985b, 173).

In his 1984 Gore Lecture, "The welfare state" (1985b), Newbigin said he felt "emboldened to speak of a Christian perspective on the welfare state by the fact that Christian thinking contributed much to its conception and development in this country." He blasted "the domesticated version of Christianity" which did not apply Christ's lordship to "the public affairs of nations." He argued that "our society is trying to operate on two mutually contradictory principles—an economy based on the idea that wants create rights and a welfare system based on the idea that *needs* create rights." Enlightenment assumptions had led to stressing rights without relational reciprocity and to splitting public from private. Such presuppositions needed to be replaced by "Christian dogma" as the ground for public life (1985b, 173). Trying to be evenhanded, Newbigin criticized both left and right. Yet the upshot was that he judged Thatcher's rollback of government spending and regulation to be a manifestation of idolatrous market ideology. Recalling the Barmen Declaration's confession of Christ fifty years earlier in the face of Nazi ideology, Newbigin asked,

> Is the Church in Britain today prepared to use the same language to those who claim that politics and economics are governed by laws with which theology has nothing to do, who denounce Christian bishops when they speak a word of testimony to the truth as it is in Jesus in the context of contemporary economic and political events? Or have we been so seduced by the ideology of the Enlightenment . . . that we are no longer able to use such language? (1985b, 182)[33]

---

[33]Newbigin's "prophetic" fury against those who wanted to reduce the welfare state in the 1980s is strikingly different from Lewis's concern about growing enslavement to the welfare state during and after World War II. Lewis's concern came mainly from distrust of state coercion and dislike of clergy politicking, not from personal greed or ideological faith in laissez faire capitalism. Lewis pointed out that the ancient Greeks, Old Testament Jews, and medieval Christians had all "told us not to lend money at interest: and lending money at interest—what we call investment—is the basis of our whole system." Lewis would not conclusively declare interest wrong but thought it noteworthy that three great civilizations had condemned "the very thing on which we have based our whole life." If we could visit a "fully Christian society," said Lewis, we would "feel that its economic life was very socialistic." However, this virtuous and voluntary socialism in which all worked hard and shared generously, powered by love for God and neighbor, was not to be equated with coercive socialism, powered by government regulation and redistribution. Moreover, Lewis considered it "silly" for "the clergy to put out a political programme." The application of Christian principles to matters of state, economics, and education must come from

In *Foolishness to the Greeks*, Newbigin—seldom given to understatement—warned that Thatcher's and Reagan's policies would "destroy our societies" (1986b, 122). With Iran's revolution under Ayatollah Khomeini fresh in his mind, Newbigin empathized with the Islamic aim of counteracting "the European Enlightenment" but rejected the Muslim "sacralizing of politics." At any rate, contended Newbigin, Iranian Islam was not as bad as America's Reagan-supporting Moral Majority, whose alleged confusion of political policy with the cause of Christ was "more dangerous than the open rejection of the claims of Christ in Islam." The Moral Majority was "only a further development of the ideologizing of politics that stems from the Enlightenment" (1986b, 116).

In the late 1980s, the Soviet Union and other communist regimes in Europe collapsed, while the American and British economies prospered. Whether or not this had anything to do with Reagan and Thatcher, it became harder to credibly claim that socialism and market capitalism were equal and opposite errors. In 1991 Newbigin still opposed "the contemporary ideology of the free market"—but as "something good being corrupted." Recent events had driven home the lesson "that free markets are the best way of continuously balancing supply and demand" (1991, 76). Earlier Newbigin had depicted Adam Smith as maker of the capitalist idol (1985b, 179), but now Newbigin said, "Smith himself recognized that free markets would only work for the common good if certain moral principles permeated society." Smith's successors—not Smith—had detached economics from ethics. Economics, separated from moral obligation and the supremacy of Christ, meant surrender to "the pagan goddess of fortune" and "demonic powers (1991, 76-77).

Lewis had dreaded becoming "willing slaves of the welfare state." Newbigin was incensed by Thatcher's reductions in the welfare state. Lewis had complained that British leftists were "wolves in sheep's clothing. Of those who work injustice in politics many say they are building the Kingdom of God" (2004b, 868). Newbigin admired those in that earlier era who had seen "the creation of the welfare state as the proper social expression of the Christian faith" (1985b, 175). Lewis had

---

Christian statesmen, economists, and schoolmasters, not from bishops, "just as Christian literature comes from Christian novelists and dramatists—not from the bench of bishops getting together and trying to write plays and novels in their spare time" (1952, 78-81).

feared that growing government and increasing collectivism during and after the world wars would smother freedom and individuality, and indirectly foster monism. Newbigin feared that the shift away from collectivism toward a greater emphasis on individual freedom and initiative which occurred under Thatcher would enshrine idolatrous market ideology and indirectly reinforce an unbiblical epistemological dichotomy between public truth and private opinion.

A second major governmental concern of Newbigin had much more in common with Lewis: the specter of state-sponsored scientism. Although Newbigin fought against reductions of government-run programs in Britain, he also expressed wariness of excessive faith in government and devotion to the nation-state.

> The nation-state has taken the place of God. Responsibilities for education, healing and public welfare which had formerly rested with the Church devolved more and more upon the nation state. In the present century this movement has been vastly accelerated by the advent of the 'welfare state'. National governments are widely assumed to be responsible for and capable of providing those things which former generations thought only God could provide—freedom from fear, hunger, disease and want—in a word: 'happiness'. (1983, 14-15)

Making "the pursuit of happiness" a fundamental right had produced a "revolution of expectations" in which most people saw government as guarantor of the right to happiness (1983, 55). As usual for Newbigin, Enlightenment thought was the root problem. "The Enlightenment gave birth to the hope of an earthly utopia to be achieved by the liberation of reason and conscience from the shackles of dogma, and by the application of the scientific method to the exploitation of nature and the ordering of society" (1983, 59).

Endless pursuit of happiness meant unlimited demands upon the nation-state, which took God's place as the source of all good things. Faith in science and government to produce an earthly utopia at some point in the future had opened the way for totalitarian states "to extinguish the rights of the living for the sake of the supposed happiness of those yet unborn." A less extreme outcome was to value the young over the old and to jettison traditional wisdom in favor of "systems of education organized by the state and designed to shape young minds toward the future that is being planned" (1986b, 27-29).

Newbigin, like Lewis, perceived technocratic bureaucracy to be growing. Bureaucracy expressed and reinforced a rationality of abstract, cause-and-effect calculation without regard for personhood or purpose. In the economy and the legal system, justice had to be blind to personal relationships and regard people as anonymous, interchangeable units. "In its ultimate development, bureaucracy is the rule of nobody and is therefore experienced as tyranny" (1986b, 33). One challenge for British society was to express "the mutual responsibility which all must share for all in a more personal and face-to-face manner," something Newbigin saw the government's welfare bureaucracy as unable to do (1983, 58).

Newbigin insisted that the church, in mission to the West, must relate the Christian faith to public issues, not just focus on saving individual souls (1986b, 132). The church must not allow an epistemological split between public truth and private opinion to block its missionary witness to God's reign in every sphere of life, including government. "We cannot do without a theologically grounded Christian doctrine of the state," insisted Newbigin, even as he confessed to being unsure exactly what this would involve. "We are in a new and unprecedented situation, a new missionary frontier" (1994a, 73).

Church

Of all institutional challenges for Christianity in Britain, the church itself may have posed one of the hardest. The institution charged with preserving and propagating the faith often undermined it instead. A major change was "a different view of the Bible" (Worrall 1988, 83). Higher criticism of Scripture, formerly limited mainly to intellectual circles, entered public discussion after the 1890s. Many clergy openly embraced Darwinism (Brown 2006, 73-76). Seminaries and departments of religious studies may have harmed the Christian cause even more than state-controlled schools did.[34] Failure to uphold Christian basics became common in longstanding denominations (Badham 1989, 23).

Bishop J.A.T. Robinson's *Honest to God* (1963) "was a vital event in the making of post-Christian Britain." Robinson and other radical theologians offered a gospel so "vacuous" that many Britons who formerly had been vaguely undecided about Christianity made up their minds and abandoned even a nominal link to church. Also, in the name of being "prophetic," radical theologians pushed leftist ideologies of

---

[34]"Religious studies could itself be a symptom of secularization" (Bebbington 1992b, 269). "The professional study of religion was a more efficient cause of secularization than the natural sciences" (Sommerville 2003, 371).

liberation which repelled many (Gilbert 1980, 123). In Britain and elsewhere, church groups which jettisoned traditional beliefs in favor of theological modernism declined numerically.

Meanwhile, in many parts of the world, religions which emphasized traditional certainties and supernatural realities attracted a considerable following in the latter part of the 1900s, with Christian evangelicalism among the foremost. A measure of this occurred in Britain. The evangelical movement gained strength inside and outside longstanding church groups (Davie 1994, 70, 199-200).[35] By 2000 an estimated 37 percent of congregations in England could be characterized as evangelical. However, while some spoke of an evangelical upsurge, evangelical churchgoers in Britain declined by 3 percent in the 1990s (Brierley 2000, 67). Evangelicals continued to become a larger proportion of British churchgoers but not of the total population. During the late 1900s in Britain, black immigrants and their children were far more likely than whites to be religious and attend church, so they occupied an increasingly important place in British Christianity (Brown 2006, 291). Afro-Caribbean churches in Britain—most of them Pentecostal—were marked by evangelistic dynamism and growth (Badham 1994, 491-494; MacRobert 1989).

As documented in chapter 3, British church attendance was in decline from the late 1880s onward. However, so long as school, home, and media continued to present Christian basics in some form, orthodox belief remained fairly high—though often it was probably not vibrant faith. But when Christianity fell silent in other influential institutions, and when key church leaders publicized their own non-Christian ideas, popular belief and behavior departed more swiftly from Christian moorings. Lewis and Newbigin both had much to say about the church and Christian plausibility in their respective times.

---

[35]According to David Bebbington, evangelicals in Britain and the United States had similar core characteristics and followed parallel trajectories in the twentieth century. Four hallmarks emphasized in common were conversion, active outreach, Scripture, and atonement through the cross. Both movements hit a low point around 1940, feeling marginalized by the ecclesiastical mainstream. However, Bebbington suggests, even then the movement had two hidden strengths: sympathy toward evangelical aims among a great many people attending mainline churches, and vitality of evangelistic efforts targeting youth. In contrast to American evangelicals, British evangelicals tended to frown on church splits more than Americans did, and British evangelicals influenced society at large less than their American counterparts did, due largely to less numerical and financial strength and a more restrictive political system (Bebbington 1994).

Lewis's Perceptions

From his conversion until he died, Lewis opposed church leaders who denied historic orthodoxy. [36] Lewis saw no worse enemy to Christianity than religion which gutted Christian belief and emptied Christian churches but still claimed to be Christian.

> The truth is we shall never get on till we have stamped out "religion" . . . as it is called—the vague slush of humanitarian idealism, Emersonian Pantheism, democratic politics and material progressiveness with a few Christian names and formulae added to taste like pepper and salt—it is almost the great enemy. If one can't talk to a Christian then give me a real believing member of some other religion or an honest clear-headed skeptic . . .
> One can at least get sense out of them. (2004b, 657)

Clergy who contradicted orthodoxy made the faith implausible to people inside and outside the church, so a Christian apologist had to distinguish Christianity from pseudo-Christianity.

Lewis's fiction repeatedly skewered theological modernism.[37] His non-fiction and letters did likewise. This may seem surprising in light of Lewis's oft-stated resolve not to take sides publicly in disagreements between different varieties of Christians (1952, 6, 157; 1970, 60; 2004b, 257, 801; 2007, 1133). But Lewis regarded modernists not as Christians but as "semi-Christians" (2007, 325, 1012). Many people—"some of them clergymen"—were gradually ceasing to be Christians but kept the Christian label (1952, 46, 176). Those who wanted Christianity without miracles were abandoning Christianity for "mere 'religion.'" Consulting New Testament scholars was like going "as sheep among wolves. Nat-

---

[36]While Lewis castigated liberal church leaders, he rejected the notion that "the present wide-spread apostasy must be the fault of the clergy, not of the laity." He denounced "the modern assumption that, for all events, 'WE', the people, are never responsible: it is always our rulers, or ancestors, or parents, or education, or anybody but precious 'US', WE are apparently perfect & blameless. Don't you believe it" (2007, 333). People were responsible for their own folly if they followed false leaders.

[37]In 1933 Lewis's first Christian book, *The pilgrim's regress*, lampooned Mr. Broad's disregard for "mere orthodoxy" (1989, 118). In 1941 *The Screwtape letters* depicted a vicar who delighted demons by watering down the faith to make it more acceptable to his congregation, with the result that they were shocked to find he believed less than they did, and many left the church (1960c, 73). In *That hideous strength*, the fanatical preacher Straik denied the afterlife and equated the kingdom of God with utopian revolution (1946a, 78-80). In *The great divorce*, a modernist bishop denied Jesus' resurrection and was rewarded with academic praise, loftier positions, and higher pay. After death, he preferred endless theological debate in hell to the beatific vision (1946b).

uralistic assumptions, beggings of the question . . . will meet you on every side—even from the pens of clergymen" (1960b, 218, 267). Higher critics bore primary responsibility for undermining historic orthodoxy, said Lewis. The Church of England had little future unless someone served as a missionary to its demythologizing, unbelieving priests (1967, 205, 223).[38]

Lewis faced his fiercest opposition from "'liberal-minded religious people" (2004b, 707), "all the Bultmann, Niebuhr, Norman Pittenger class" (2007, 1359). Those who prided themselves on being "undogmatic" struck Lewis as "the most arrogant and intolerant" (2007, 112). For instance, apologetics professor Norman Pittenger criticized Lewis for traditionalism and "irrational fideism." [39] He complained that Lewis took the Scriptures in "their literal verbal sense" rather than "in the light of the best possible critical analysis." Pittenger slammed Lewis's *Miracles* as "one of the worst books ever written on this subject" and called Lewis "a dangerous apologist and an inept theologian" (1958a, 1104-1107).

In his published "Rejoinder to Dr. Pittenger," Lewis avoided a showdown over theological differences. Instead, Lewis slyly suggested that Pittenger was a careless reader and an ineffective apologist. Lewis stated that his own aim was to reach people who were not helped by revivalist emotionalism or by "the unintelligible language of highly cultured clergymen." He said that if he used a style like Pittenger's, such people would not understand him and would suspect him of deception

---

[38]Lewis detested modernistic religion even among non-Christian faiths: "how much more one has in common with a *real* Jew or Muslim than with a wretched liberalizing, Occidentalized specimen of the same category" (2007, 249). Modernistic Christians and modernistic Muslims could casually share drink and conversation, not because both were so charitable despite creedal differences, but because "both abandoned their creeds and cultures and are now two ordinary standardised, urban, cinema-fed, materialistic, denationalised wops." This new basis of agreement might at least seem to bring "political and humanitarian gains," but Lewis wondered whether in the long run such religious vacuity might leave people vulnerable to whatever demonic ideology might come along (2004b, 328-329).

[39]Pittenger authored more than fifty books, often stressing that modern knowledge is not compatible with traditional Christian beliefs. After Lewis died, Pittenger supported the sexual revolution of the 1960s. In 1967 Pittenger published a book calling for Christians to approve homosexuality and later declared his own homosexuality (Hooper, in Lewis 2007, 985, note 192). At the time of his clash with Lewis in the late 1950s, Pittenger's theological deviations from historic Christianity were more public than his sexual deviations.

(1970, 177-183).[40] In private letters, Lewis was harsher: Pittenger's main problem was not just unclear language but apostasy. [41]

As Lewis neared the end of his life and was forced by failing health to retire from his professorship, Bishop Robinson became the latest cleric to attack orthodox belief. "English religion of the 1960s will always remain more associated with *Honest to God* than any other book" (Hastings 1991, 536-537). In March, 1963, *The Observer* published an excerpt, titled "Our image of God must go," arguing against anthropomorphic conceptions of a personal God. In response, Lewis wrote a brief piece in *The Observer* (24 March 1963) asking, "Must our image of God go?" He treated Robinson dismissively, saying that Christians had long ago "abandoned belief in a God who sits on a throne in a localized heaven." Lewis called Robinson "very obscure" and suggested that if the bishop sounded heretical, it might come more from "a failure to communicate" than from actual heresy (1970, 184-185). As with Pittenger, so with Robinson: Lewis's article depicted his opponent as an unclear writer rather than as a dangerous apostate. However, Lewis's private letters showed his antipathy toward the bishop and his "nonsense" (2007, 1422, 1425, 1468).

Letters to Malcolm: Chiefly on prayer was the last book Lewis wrote before his death. He included a sarcastic dig at the simplemindedness of Robinson's Woolwich flock if they needed to be told not to seek a god in the sky (1973, 74). Countering Robinson's insistence that Christianity needed to stop regarding God as a personal entity and drop all anthropomorphic language about him, Lewis insisted that all language is metaphorical, and that most attempts to escape anthropomorphism about God merely exchanged lively, personal metaphors for dead, impersonal metaphors (1973, 21-22).

[40]Lewis's rejoinder delighted a reader who had benefited from Lewis and saw Pittenger as "a surprisingly poor example of learned liberalism." This reader wrote to *The Christian Century* and declared an urgent need for apologists like Lewis: "We need theologians, preachers and journalists who have experienced the heart of the gospel and who can 'get it across' to the man in the street who thinks of most churchmen as either an obscure medieval remnant or unintelligible contemporary eggheads" (van Heerden 1958, 1485).

[41]*The Christian Century*, which had published Pittenger's attack, struck Lewis as "a pretty nasty periodical" (2007, 985). Lewis could respect "an honest unbeliever" more than "such a Mr. Facing Both Ways" (2007, 999-1000). Lewis found it disgusting that "while contradicting nearly every article of the Creed, he continues to *receive money* as a professor of Christian Apologetics . . . how can a man endure to be what he is?" (2007, 1007).

Lewis had Robinson and similar theologians in mind in the final chapter of *Letters to Malcolm* when he spoke of "liberal Christians" who could not accept most articles of the faith but were "extremely anxious that some vestigial religion which they (not we) can describe as 'Christianity' should continue to exist and make numerous converts." These liberals added no intellectual heft to naturalism but could only offer "an ineffectual echo" to the open unbelief of more able and influential naturalists (whether secularist or pantheist). Clergy attacks on Christian doctrine made headlines, asserted Lewis, not because they offered fresh thought but only because news media (eager for sales) hyped the spectacle of church leaders attacking the very teachings they had sworn to uphold. If anti-supernatural Christianity was supposed to be more plausible to modern skeptics, it was worth asking whether any skeptics were ever converted by it (1973, 118-119).[42]

Another area Lewis perceived misguided rationality to be infecting the church was in the nascent movement calling for women to be ordained as Anglican priests. Lewis said that ordaining women as priests would be "the very triumph of what they call 'practical' and 'enlightened' principles" (2004b, 860). In a 1948 article, Lewis wrote that the proposed change might make the church "much more rational" but less like a church. Lewis focused on the representative role of a priest.[43] He predicted that ordaining women as priests would eventually lead to "a different religion" involving prayers to "Our Mother which art in Heaven." Mathematical-style rationality and the modern state might regard men and women as interchangeable neuters; however, in the church, "we are not homogeneous units, but different and complementary organs of a mystical body." Sexual difference and marriage were meant "to symbolize to us the hidden things of God. . . . We have no authority to take the living and semitive figures which God has painted

---

[42]Lewis raised a similar question in his "Rejoinder to Dr. Pittenger," asking: "What methods, and with what success, does he employ when he is trying to convert the great mass of storekeepers, lawyers, morticians, policemen and artisans who surround him in his own city?" (1970, 183). Pittenger huffed in response that a crass appeal to numbers was no way to measure apologetic excellence (1958b). Indeed, Lewis's success in swaying so many people was what upset Pittenger in the first place: Lewis's eloquence "deceives those who are not instructed and misleads many who are" (Pittenger 1958a).

[43]Lewis did not object to women doing pastoral tasks such as counseling, administration, or preaching. But Lewis saw a priest primarily in sacramental terms as "a double representative, who represents us to God and God to us" (1970, 236).

on the canvas of our nature and shift them about as if they were mere geometrical figures" (1970, 234-239).

While Lewis opposed what he saw as rationalistic distortion of Christianity, he also shied away from unthinking, rote authoritarianism. In a December 1931 letter, shortly after becoming a Christian, Lewis spoke of a contemporary Puritanism whose spirit and system "was ignorant. It could give no '*reason* for the faith that was in it'." Such rigid, unreasoning religion was "the form which the *memory* of Christianity takes just before it finally dies away altogether, in a commercial community: just as extreme emotional ritualism is the form it takes on just before it dies in a fashionable community" (2004b, 23).

Lewis was uncomfortable with Karl Barth's impact in Britain. In a 1940 letter, Lewis spoke of theology marked by "the horrible ferocity and grimness of modern thought." Young Christians at Oxford had been reading "a dreadful man called Karl Barth, who seems the right opposite number to Karl Marx. 'Under judgment' is their great expression. . . . They don't think human reason or human conscience of any value at all." Even if this stern theology was "substantially right," said Lewis, "the total effect is withering" (2004b, 350-352).[44] In his 1943 preface to *The pilgrim's regress,* Lewis identified Barth with a tendency which "exaggerates the distinctness between Grace and Nature into a sheer opposition and by vilifying the higher levels of Nature (the real *praeparatio evangelica* inherent in certain immediately sub-Christian experiences), makes the way hard for those who are at the point of coming in" (1989, 12). Rather than the Barthian emphasis on revelation as contradiction, Lewis often stressed continuity: incarnation, vicariousness, and resurrection were prefigured in processes of nature and in other religions (1960b). Reason could serve pre-evangelism.

As Lewis saw it, a major problem with theologians and preachers of his time was that they were not effective communicators. They were not stating the gospel in the ordinary vocabulary of their hearers. Before discussing "the problem of communication on a grand, philosophical level," it was necessary first to pursue the basic task of grasping people's actual usage of words, to make sure of speaking their language.[45] Many preachers tended to use "incantory words" that were

---

[44]Lewis's impressions were based on Barthians he met, not on Barth's writings. He stated in 1958, "Barth I have never read, or not that I remember" (2007, 980).

[45]Theologians who ignore cultural aspects of translation and communication may jump to excessively negative theological assessments if their audience does not re-

understood only within their circle. Lewis therefore recommended avoiding "vogue-words" such as "under judgment, existential, crisis, and confrontation... They are like a family language, or a school slang." Such language could befuddle outsiders and delude insiders into thinking they understood something of which they really had no clear conception at all (1970, 254-257).

In brief, Lewis perceived that the church was largely botching the task of making Christianity plausible. Those who tried to make Christianity plausible by revising its content to fit naturalistic rationalism were producing a different religion and destroying the church's identity and credibility. Meanwhile, those who stressed revelation as a contradiction to human reason and conscience were making it harder for people to find the gospel persuasive or attractive. In many cases, neither modernists nor orthodox were speaking the language of non-theologians. Some used the verbiage of academic specialists; others parroted formulations from centuries past, rather than translating the gospel into the vernacular.

Newbigin's Perceptions

Like Lewis, Newbigin encountered theological modernism and sought to uphold historic orthodoxy. Unlike Lewis, Newbigin considered Barth helpful for mission. Newbigin saw British churches as syncretistic, not only in their handling of specifically intellectual matters, but in their failure to combine ecumenicity with evangelism.

Newbigin wrote *Honest religion for secular man* (1966) to counter *Honest to God*. Newbigin dismissed Robinson's notion that one could deny a personal God and still claim that love is ultimate reality and the ground of our being. "What is love if there is no lover?" (1966, 88) Using an approach that would be echoed in his later writings about mission to the West, Newbigin declared, "We cannot persuade ourselves any more of the existence of God. That era of human history has ended. But neither can we persuade ourselves of the truth of the very abstract statements in which Bishop Robinson tries to preserve some echoes of the

---

spond as hoped. Failure to communicate may be attributed (by orthodox and neo-orthodox) to humanity's idolatrous antipathy toward God, or (by liberals) to a need for replacing traditional Christian belief with more palatable ideas. Lewis wanted theologians of all stripes first to examine their own failure to speak in the vernacular, rather than too quickly resorting to sweeping theological explanations of why the Christian message was not getting through.

Christian faith."[46] Newbigin insisted on the need to move "from the language of argument to that of testimony." Using general human experience to argue for God's existence and goodness would leave one "in the world of unbelief" (1966, 89).

> We cannot argue ourselves into knowledge of another person. That person must meet us, and we must learn by speech, action, event, to know that person in the concreteness and particularity of his person. The Christian testimony is that God has so acted, so spoken, so given himself for us in Jesus, that we know that he loves us, and that that knowledge is constantly confirmed and enriched through the events of daily life. To say this is to say something that belongs to a different order of statement from the statement that ultimate reality is personal, even though the latter might be a legitimate deduction from the former. (1966, 89)

In this book, Newbigin also responded to other theologians who tried to offer their own theological formulations—allegedly more relevant and believable for moderns—to replace the biblical God. For instance, Bultmann's *Kerygma and myth* (1962) came under fire from Newbigin for exalting individualism and existentialism in place of Jesus' real resurrection and biblical faith "in a God who acts in history." Timeless faith detached from history, such as Bultmann wanted, was "characteristic of ancient paganism" (1966, 49). An especially noteworthy feature of *Honest religion for secular man* is that it was the first of Newbigin's writings to draw upon Michael Polanyi's *Personal knowledge* (Newbigin 1966, 79-88). Polanyi's epistemology would appear again and again in Newbigin's missiology for the West during the 1980s and 1990s.

After Newbigin moved back to Britain, he came to view Karl Barth as a valuable mentor for mission to the West.[47] Newbigin's 1982 com-

---

[46]Newbigin was working in Geneva for the World Council of Churches at the time. In his memoirs, Newbigin remarked that Robinson spoke for those who wanted to remain Christians without God. Newbigin "loved and respected John Robinson" and, at Robinson's request, had shared in his consecration as bishop. But Newbigin sensed the "theological earthquake" caused by Robinson's book and viewed it as "an attack on the very centre of the Christian faith. It left no room for a truly personal God." Newbigin knew of ministers who forsook their calling after reading Robinson's book (1985a, 198-199).

[47]Back in the 1930s, as a young man trying to understand the essentials of the gospel as expressed in Romans, Newbigin had consulted various commentaries and found Barth's "incomprehensible" (1985a, 30-31). At various points in Newbigin's career, he had met Barth and had even chaired theological groups that included Barth

mentary on John—published shortly before the start of his outpouring of works on mission to the West—was laced with Barthian ideas and catchphrases. For instance, "Religion is unbelief" (1982b, 13, 102). "Revelation must involve contradiction" (1982b, 81, 93, 107, 170, 206). Newbigin's writings on mission to the West would be suffused with a Barthian antipathy to the notion that rational arguments or other religious traditions could be preparations to meet Christ.[48]

Newbigin had long viewed syncretism as a danger to Western churches (1963, 29), and upon returning to England after decades in another culture, his diagnosis became more trenchant. "It would be hard to deny that contemporary British (and most of western) Christianity is an advanced case of syncretism" (1983, 23). Chapter 8 explores in more detail what Newbigin meant by such a statement and how it related to rationality and epistemology, but here I will highlight two aspects of Newbigin's British context in which he perceived the church to be adjusting itself to "modern western civilization" instead of issuing an authentically missionary challenge. Insisting that "every Christian must be both evangelical and ecumenical" (1982a, 146), Newbigin lamented that (1) the ecumenical movement was ignored by some in Britain and that (2) evangelistic outreach was abandoned by others.

Newbigin noticed that some Britons in the 1980s opposed the World Council of Churches. He attributed this to the WCC's "sustained insistence on justice for the poor, the oppressed and the forgotten," which posed a threat to "the comfortable identification of Christians with the established order." Newbigin saw opposition to the

---

himself (1985a, 115-116, 131-132, 139-140). During those many years, Newbigin had read quotes and summaries from Barth, and these had not impressed him. But in 1974, after returning to Britain, he read Barth's entire *Church dogmatics*. He found Barth "enthralling" and viewed his own new-found appreciation for Barth as "a needed preparation" for the mission to the West that occupied the last decades of Newbigin's life (1985a, 241-242).

[48]Ironically, Newbigin's appreciation for Barth grew strong at a time when many others' enthusiasm for Barth had faded. Newbigin had been living outside Britain during the period when Barth's influence was at its height among British preachers. By the time Newbigin returned to England and experienced a newfound enthusiasm for Barth, perhaps British churches had already tried Barth and found him wanting. Badham contends that Barthian neo-orthodoxy weakened the Christian cause in Britain because Barthian "distrust of human reason" made it "relatively rare to find any systematic or reasoned preaching about God" in Anglican churches. Without an apologetic "defending propositional claims," faith lacked content to differentiate it from non-faith (Badham 1989, 26).

WCC among "many church people in the rich world" as "piercingly clear evidence of the unrepented sin of our society" and of "jealously guarded denominational sovereignty" (1985a, 253).[49] Newbigin perceived a tendency among evangelical churches to privatize religion and focus on personal salvation while ignoring God's reign in such matters as church unity and poverty relief—yet another result of the Enlightenment's baneful dichotomy between public and private.

Newbigin also saw problems among people who tended to be less evangelical. He noted among many white congregations a lack of confidence in gospel history as really true and vitally important for all peoples, resulting in a lack of faith and evangelistic zeal. He contrasted this to Britain's non-white churches with recent immigrant roots. "We have not had the boldness that, for example, our black-led churches in Birmingham show, to recognize the story that the Bible tells as the real story, the true story, the story that explains who we really are, where we come from and where we are going" (1994a, 152).

By the 1990s, Newbigin had increasing interest and ties with Pentecostals and other evangelicals. In 1994 he charged WCC head Konrad Raiser with "ecumenical amnesia" for abandoning the missionary roots of the ecumenical movement and seeking to include non-Christian religions under the umbrella of ecumenicity. Newbigin pointed out that evangelical churches and movements were "growing and showing increasing breadth of vision in their approach to the whole range of contemporary human problems," while bodies holding positions similar to Raiser's were in decline, numerically as well as theologically. "It would be heart-breaking if the WCC should in truth become, what some already claim to see in it, only the organ of those parts of the church that are in decline" (1994b, 4-5).

Newbigin, as shown further in chapter 8, asserted that epistemological assumptions from the Enlightenment pervaded the "syncretistic" Western church in both liberal and conservative branches. He expressed Barthian disdain for apologetic arguments that tried to build

---

[49]Newbigin wrote these words at about the same time he was calling for a Barmen-style declaration in response to Thatcher's policies, so economic and political matters were much on his mind. It seems fair to say that unrepentant sinners were not the only people outraged by the World Council of Churches; people who valued biblical orthodoxy objected not only to the WCC's leftist political utterances but also to its doctrinal deviance and denial of missions. Indeed, Newbigin himself, on other occasions, could severely criticize the WCC and the ecumenical movement for these very failings.

upon reason or conscience rather than simply testifying to revelation. Newbigin saw an urgent need to develop sound views of epistemology and rationality, of truth and biblical authority, and of a missionary church community displaying gospel reality publicly, plainly, and plausibly—thus attracting individuals and addressing public structures.

The writings of Lewis and Newbigin were too vast and varied for all their perceptions of twentieth century Britain to be encapsulated and arranged under a mere eight headings, as I have done in these two chapters. In selecting and summarizing, I have omitted much. In organizing these materials for purposes of clarity and comparison, I have inevitably imposed a tidiness that does not fully capture the complexity and ambiguity of the two authors and their settings. Even so, these chapters have given some indication of the British context as each perceived it in his particular time and place, and some basis for understanding and comparing their readings of Western culture in relation to matters of epistemology and plausibility. The chapters that follow build upon these findings as we trace Lewis's views and Newbigin's views on the nature and role of rationality in each author's cultural diagnosis and missionary prescription for the post-Christendom West.

CHAPTER 5

Lewis's Diagnosis of Problematic Thought Patterns

This chapter considers Lewis's diagnosis of thought patterns in his context that obstructed Christian plausibility. Elements of his diagnosis can be gleaned from wide-ranging remarks in various writings, such as the perceptions examined in chapters 2, 3, and 4. But Lewis also wrote some pieces with the express purpose of profiling the mindset of his mission field and its major intellectual challenges. After briefly reviewing findings from earlier chapters, we focus on writings in which Lewis specifically diagnosed (1) the "mental habits" of what he termed "the English 'Intelligentsia of the Proletariat,'" (2) the "mental climate" of modernity more generally, and (3) intellectual patterns among educated elites.

As shown in chapter 2, Lewis thought Europe's "un-christening" had been underway from about the 1830s onward. A massive cultural shift became widespread during the Industrial Revolution and its aftermath. Religion declined, though in Lewis's opinion, the religion that declined was not clear, vibrant faith but nominal Christianity, a vague theism with an ethical code barely distinguishable from British culture and respectability. Lewis saw religious belief and practice becoming the exception, not the norm. Christian claims were no longer simply presumed true. To be Christian would henceforth involve more conscious deliberation and a decision to go against more widespread assumptions.

Lewis's perceptions of key trends, presented in chapter 3, included the sense that Christian belief and practice were becoming less common as naturalism prompted more people to become atheistic, agnostic, vaguely pantheistic, or susceptible to a profusion of cults or the occult. Growing rejection of Christian sexual standards resulted in less sense of sin and aided a wider intellectual shift in the direction of moral relativism and personal autonomy. Britain's growing awareness of other cultures and religions became an occasion for many from Christian background to question whether Christianity was any truer than other faiths. Lewis saw such questioning, mixed with guilt over imperialism, as a problem for apologists to address. All the while, Lewis directed his own apologetic efforts mainly toward white Britons with tenuous Christian ties or no specific faith.

Chapter 4 traced Lewis's views of important institutions and their ramifications for Christian plausibility. Lewis saw schools hampering Christian belief as a non-Christian approach was explicitly taught or implicitly assumed; as school competition and cruelty made British intellectuals prone to bitterness, skepticism, and debunking; as educational bureaucracy cultivated conformity and suppressed spiritual aspiration; and as too few teachers were genuinely Christian. Lewis saw few homes teaching Christianity or giving reasons to believe, even as sugary sermons portrayed home life implausibly. He believed mass media had possibilities for plausible witness using contemporary idioms, but found it more common for Christian plausibility to be undermined when media overloaded the human capacity for sympathy, furthered cynicism, deceived audiences, or diverted them from ultimate issues. Lewis thought that modern government was exalting unrestrained political and technical power above moral reason; that political ideology could infect theology and crowd out reason and revelation; that obsession with a nation's or civilization's survival could be a distraction from the supernatural and eternal; and that political pursuit of equality and mass control tended to inculcate a monistic rather than theistic mindset. The church, rather than making the gospel plausible, was too often watering down the gospel, or else was not speaking people's language plainly and not addressing their questions persuasively.

Thus far the observations we have considered from Lewis about cultural and intellectual factors have been lifted from a broad and varied spectrum of his writings. Now we zero in on what Lewis said when he set out specifically to profile intellectual patterns in his context and deliberately diagnosed key challenges to Christianity's believability.

Mental Habits of Intelligent Proletarians

In a 1945 speech "Christian Apologetics" (1970, 89-103), Lewis described common thought patterns and attitudes that Christian witnesses had to reckon with. In 1948, he gave a similar account in his article "Difficulties in presenting the Christian faith to modern unbelievers," later reprinted as "God in the dock" (1970, 240-244). In both pieces, Lewis noted that his experience was limited. His analysis, he stressed, was based partly on conversations with university students but mainly on contacts with Royal Air Force personnel—most of them English, not Welsh, Scottish, or Irish. Few were highly learned academicians, so Lewis could call them "uneducated" (1970, 94, 98). However, most had technical skills and a smattering of basic science. Lewis summed up their intellectual and social location by calling them "the English 'Intelligentsia of the Proletariat.'" Witness to the less intelligent, said Lewis, would require "quite a different approach" than his (1970, 240). Also, people ministering in other regions of Britain or addressing other segments of society might find that some of his observations would not be true of their audience. Making clear these caveats, Lewis offered a profile of non-academic but intelligent people he encountered.

One thing that struck Lewis was the variety of non-Christian religious beliefs among such persons. In his experience among academicians, materialism had seemed the only major opponent. But among the less educated, he found all sorts of religious views. Even professions of Christianity were often vague and tainted with pantheistic notions (1970, 240-241). Many did not take Christianity's truth claims to be of "infinite importance." Rather, they thought that "a certain amount of religion is desirable but one mustn't carry it too far." They also tended to assume that various religions could be equally true and could bring salvation apart from Jesus. Although Lewis saw partial truth in other religions and allowed that some people might go to heaven through Jesus without explicit knowledge of him in this life, he saw an urgent need to "attack wherever we meet it the nonsensical idea that mutually exclusive propositions about God can both be true" (1970, 101-102).

Another characteristic of the English proletariat, asserted Lewis, was extreme skepticism about history. Events and ideas from "The Old Days" seemed unimportant and unreal. Indeed, speculation about prehistoric times—seen as "science"—had more credibility than documented history. Lewis had formerly thought that the main obstacle to belief in the gospels would be refusal to accept miracles. But it was more common to disbelieve events in the gospels just because they happened long ago (1970, 94-95, 241-242).[1]

An additional challenge involved language. Church leaders could not assume that they understood, or were understood by, their neighbors. Words commonly used by clergy with a particular meaning in mind could have quite a different meaning in the minds of most unchurched people without higher education. Christian communicators needed to learn the language of uneducated unbelievers in England, just as missionaries to people in an African culture had to learn their language. Christian speech needed to be conducted in the vernacular, speaking directly in the uneducated audience's vocabulary. Words that required detailed explanation would induce boredom or even arouse distrust (1970, 94-99, 242-243).

Another huge barrier was that people lacked a sense of sin. Early in the Christian era, preachers addressed Jews, Gentile ethical monotheists, and Pagans, all of whom could be assumed to have some sense of guilt and would thus be able to hear the gospel of forgiveness as good news. Modern people, however, tended to blame problems on anyone but themselves. The proletariat were even more self-righteous than the elite, said Lewis, though he allowed that the educated might just be better at hiding their pride. People with little sense of sin would see little need for the gospel remedy. Indeed, rather than fearing God's judgment, they took it upon themselves to judge God (1970, 95, 243-244).

Elsewhere in Lewis's writings, mention was often made of these same four "mental habits" among the less educated: plural spiritualities in addition to materialism (1955b, 174-175; 1970, 253; 1980, 28; 2003, 80); disregard of history (1955b, 208; 1962, 21; 1970, 200-207; 2003, 28; 2007, 1371); a different language from that of most clerics (1970, 254-257; 1973, 6-7; 2004b, 674-675; 2007, 1006-1007, 1359); and shameless obliviousness to sin (1986, 57; 2004b, 470; 2007, 365-366).

---

[1]Lewis lamented "'chronological snobbery,' the uncritical acceptance of the intellectual climate common to our age and the assumption that whatever has gone out of date is on that account discredited" (1955b, 207). Lewis suggested that chronological snobbery had become especially prevalent since "the birth of the machines" during the Industrial Revolution. A different "climate of opinion" had been "imposed . . . on the human mind" by "a new archetypal image. It is the image of old machines being replaced by new and better ones." Into all dimensions of thought and life seeped the assumption that the new rendered the old obsolete (1962, 21-22; see also 1989, 159-160).

Modernity's Mental Climate

In a somewhat different cultural profile, Lewis widened his focus and discussed more broadly "Modern man and his categories of thought" (1986, 61-66). Lewis wrote this paper (unpublished until 40 years later) in October, 1946, at Bishop Stephen Neill's request, for the Study Department of the embryonic World Council of Churches. Lewis spoke of ways in which "the public mind" of his time differed from the intellectual "predispositions" of people addressed by Christ and the apostles, and he sought to identify causes for the shift. The earliest missionaries could expect most people to already believe in the supernatural, to be aware of sin and afraid of judgment, and to hold that "the world had once been better than it was now." In contrast, asserted Lewis, "The world which we must try to convert shares none of those predispositions. In the last hundred years the public mind has been radically altered" (1986, 61). Lewis suggested six underlying causes.

First, a "revolution in the education of the most highly educated classes" had occurred. Formerly, European education had been grounded in "the Ancients" and had introduced students to "the better elements of Paganism." This made people more open to piety, tradition, and the discovery of valuable truth in ancient writings. It also gave exposure to values unlike those of "modern industrial civilization." Abandoning the teaching of ancient classics tended "to isolate the mind in its own age; to give it, in relation to time, that disease which, in relation to space, we call Provincialism." This fostered the modern habit of regarding old writings, including biblical writings, as not worth believing (1986, 62).

Second, women's liberation meant "fewer exclusively male assemblies." This brought "many good results" but "one bad result." Young men in the company of women would be preoccupied with impressing the opposite sex and would neglect "prolonged and rigorous discussion on ultimate issues." Any serious discussion that did occur would focus on psychological and social matters linked with "the intense practicality and concreteness of the female," not on the "disinterested concern with truth for truth's own sake, with the cosmic and the metaphysical," which Lewis thought more typically masculine. Thus, as women joined men in universities and other formerly male-only settings, there was "a lowering of metaphysical energy" that "cuts us off from the eternal" (1986, 62-63).

Third, "Developmentalism," originating in "Darwinianism," extended evolution far beyond "a theorem in Biology" and made it "the key principle of reality."[2]

To the modern man it seems simply natural that an ordered cosmos should emerge from chaos, that life should come out of the inanimate, reason out of instinct, civilization out of savagery, virtue out of animalism. . . . The modern mind accepts as a formula for the universe in general the principle 'Almost nothing may be expected to turn into almost everything' without noticing that the parts of the universe under our direct observation tell a quite different story. . . . [T]his view is not incompatible with all religion: indeed it goes very well with certain types of Pantheism. But it is wholly inimical to Christianity, for it denies both creation and the Fall. Where, for Christianity, the Best creates the good and the good is corrupted by sin, for Developmentalism the very standard of good is itself in a state of flux. (1986, 63-64)

Fourth, "the Proletariat in all countries . . . has consistently been flattered for a great many years."[3] As self-satisfaction increased, shame at sin decreased.[4] People thought about "God's duties to them, not

---

[2]In "The funeral of a great myth," Lewis described the cosmic Myth of evolution as "one of the most moving and satisfying world dramas which have ever been imagined." Among its many attractions, the Myth pleases those who want to debunk virtue as mere instinct, and at the same time appeals to those who prefer to think "vice is only undeveloped virtue." The Myth "soothes the old wounds of our childhood" by telling us that we, coming later in time, are better than our fathers. "The Myth pleases those who want to sell things to us." Modern manufacturers want people to have "a new everything every year. The new model must always be superseding the old. Madam would like the *latest* fashion." Moreover, the Myth has political resonance. "It arose in the Revolutionary period" and "would never have been accepted" except for "the political ideals of that period." The Myth helps to obscure the obvious fact that "any given change in society is at least as likely to destroy the liberties and amenities we already have as to add new ones." Therefore, the modern political Left and political Right, in constantly pressing for changes of their own devising, both have "a vested interest in maintaining the Myth" (1967, 118-128).

[3]In 1961, after 36 years of university teaching, Lewis noted that "many modern undergraduates" in literature knew very little of the Bible or the classics, yet they bristled if someone told them so. They seemed to "have been so long shielded and softened by flattery that they can no longer bear unexpurgated criticism" (2007, 1234).

[4]The widespread failure to feel sin and shame was attributed to two other reasons in *The Problem of Pain*: (1) Ethics had been reduced to kindness, and other virtues had been disregarded. Most people did not "feel anything except kindness to be really

their duties to Him." God's duties had very little to do with eternal salvation. God's job was to bring security, prevent war, and raise the standard of living. "'Religion' is judged exclusively by its contribution to these ends" (1986, 64-65).

Fifth, people were "becoming as narrowly 'practical' as the irrational animals." When telling "popular audiences" that he believed Christianity to be "objectively *true*," Lewis found that they were "simply not interested in the question of truth or falsehood. They only want to know if it will be comforting, or 'inspiring', or socially useful." Closely related to this was a distaste for doctrine and an "unconsciously syncretistic" notion that "'all religions really mean the same thing'" (1986, 65).

Sixth, such "unhuman Practicality," together with vague impressions of what Freud or Einstein said, had produced "Skepticism about Reason . . . a general, and quite *unalarmed*, belief that reasoning proves nothing and that all thought is conditioned by irrational processes." In conversations with people, Lewis found that some accepted "without dismay the conclusion that all our thoughts are invalid" (1986, 65-66).

These were "the main characteristics of the mental climate in which a modern evangelist has to work." Lewis thought it might be necessary "to re-convert men to real Paganism as a preliminary to converting them to Christianity."[5] Meanwhile, relativistic skepticism could be not

---

good or anything but cruelty to be really bad," and it was easy to wrongly think themselves kind if they were merely comfortable, had no reason to be upset, and thus could feel vaguely benevolent at no cost to themselves. (2) Due to "the effect of Psycho-analysis on the public mind," people got the impression "that the sense of Shame is a dangerous and mischievous thing... But unless Christianity is wholly false, the perception of ourselves which we have in moments of shame must be the only true one; and even Pagan society has usually recognized 'shamelessness' as the nadir of the soul. In trying to extirpate Shame we have broken down one of the ramparts of the human spirit" (1955a, 44-45). Loss of shame at one's own sin was accompanied by loss of "the invaluable faculty of being shocked" at others' evils (1986, 57). Contrary to much psychology, Lewis insisted in a 1960 letter, "To feel guilty, when one is guilty, and to realise, not without pain, one's moral and intellectual inadequacy, is not a disease, but commonsense" (2007, 1134-1135).

[5]Lewis elsewhere contended that post-Christian people were in a worse position than pre-Christian Pagans. He stated that "many men of our time have lost not only the supernatural light but also the natural light which pagans possessed." Christians needed to work not only at preaching the gospel but also at preparing people for the gospel. "It is necessary to recall many to the [rational and moral] laws of nature *before* we talk about God. . . . Moral relativity is the enemy we have to overcome before we tackle Atheism. I would almost dare to say 'First let us make the younger generation good pagans and afterwards let us make them Christians" (2007, 365-366).

only an obstacle but also an opportunity for Christians: "the fact that we are coming to be almost the only people who appeal to the buried (but not dead) human appetite for objective truth, may be a source of strength as well as of difficulty" (1986, 66).

Intellectual Patterns Among Educated Elites

Lewis recognized that the West's mental climate was not entirely produced by the influence of intellectuals. Even so, Lewis thought that ongoing shifts in thinking among educated elites had contributed significantly to the wider mental climate. Skeptical debunking, scientism, and mindless mysticism were three trends among intellectuals that fostered broader thought patterns inimical to Christianity.

Emptying the Universe, Abolishing Man

As Lewis looked around at his fellow intellectuals and looked back over Western intellectual history, he saw a growing tendency for analytic thinking to displace mythic, animistic, and anthropomorphic conceptions and to divide aspects of thought that had once been unified. He spoke of "the deathlike, but indispensable, process of logical analysis" in which "nature and spirit, matter and mind, fact and myth, the literal and the metaphorical, have to be more and more sharply separated, till at last a purely mathematical universe and a purely subjective mind confront one another across an unbridgeable chasm." Lewis contended that "if thought itself is to survive," this gap must be closed (1960b, 262-263).

When medieval intellectuals looked up, they saw not just space, but "the heavens," "resonant with music" (1964, 99, 112). Heavenly bodies were moved by celestial Intelligences, not just by inanimate laws (1964, 115). Earthly things could be influenced by intelligent powers and were suffused with meaning and purpose. Medieval artists viewed the universe as splendid and fascinating, in contrast to modern artists who saw their task as making a dull, lifeless, mathematical universe splendid by their own genius (1964, 204, 211).

Near the end of the 1600s came perhaps the sharpest change in "the history of thought" among educated elites, said Lewis. The universe came to be viewed in mechanical and strictly mathematical terms. Questions of meaning were excluded from scientific study (1962, 16). The practical success of the new science arose from a strict methodological focus on phenomena that could be precisely measured and controlled. Over time the new way of seeing things among intellectuals spread to the wider population and replaced the older view of the universe as "tingling with anthropomorphic life . . . a festival not a machine." The initial outcome, wrote Lewis, was a form of dualism, not materialism. "The mind, on whose ideal constructions the whole method depended, stood over against its object in ever sharper dissimilarity" (1954, 3-4). When Western thinkers removed from the objective world all properties except the mechanical and mathematical, they transferred those other properties to human subjectivity. Lewis spoke of "that great movement of internalisation, and that consequent aggrandisement of man and dessication of the outer universe, in which the psychological history of the West has so largely consisted" (1964, 42).

The process did not stop with humanity's exaltation, however. The human subject itself turned out not to be safe from mechanistic reductionism. After transferring so much from object to subject, "the subject himself is discounted as merely subjective; we only think that we think. Having eaten up everything else, he eats himself up too" (1964, 215). In his 1952 essay "The empty universe," Lewis depicted Western intellectuals nearing the disastrous conclusion of "a single one-way progression" in the history of thought. Formerly the universe seemed "packed with will, intelligence, life and positive qualities." Next, such qualities were treated not as objectively inherent in the universe but as subjective "sensations, thoughts, images or emotions." After inflating the subject at the expense of the object, the final, most devastating step was to debunk the subject (1986, 81-82).

> While we were reducing the world to almost nothing we deceived ourselves with the fancy that all its lost qualities were being kept safe (if in a somewhat humbled condition) as 'things in our own mind'. Apparently we had no mind of the sort required. The Subject is as empty as the Object. Almost nobody has been making linguistic mistakes about almost nothing. By and large, this is the only thing that has ever happened. (1986, 83)[6]

Mechanistic determinism in the physical and biological sciences, behaviorism in psychology, and logical positivism and linguistic reductionism

---

[6]In a 1954 letter, Lewis wrote, "Don't imagine that the Logical Positivist menace is over. . . . At the Socratic [Club] the enemy often wipes the floor with us" (2007, 462). However, Lewis fared better than he thought. Even Norman Pittenger, who attacked much of Lewis's apologetic work, later remarked that Lewis "saw through the absurdity" of logical positivism and linguistic philosophy (Pittenger 1981, 17).

among philosophers and literary critics were seen by Lewis to be symptoms of the broad, ongoing intellectual movement toward an empty universe and a hollow humanity.

The utter skepticism inherent in reductionistic thinking was impossible for most people to maintain for more than a few moments, said Lewis. Thinking was impossible without presupposing that thoughts referred to reality (1986, 82-83). Thus many debunkers—inconsistent with their reductionistic assumptions—continued to deploy thinking and argument and to assume that their knowledge was objective.

While trying to stop short of debunking their own thinking, debunkers were quicker to dismiss moral sentiment. Their epistemology had no room for emotion as a vital human capacity for detecting and interacting with objective reality, and their ontology denied the existence of any external standard by which an emotional response could be right or wrong.[7] "On this view, the world of facts, without one trace of value, and the world of feelings without one trace of truth or falsehood, justice or injustice, confront one another, and no *rapprochement* is possible" (1996, 32). Debunkers of conscience and emotion wanted to retain head (thought) and belly (appetite) but not heart (trained moral sentiment) (1996, 36).

Applying natural science's methodology to the study and control of humans, warned Lewis, would destroy the humanity of both the controlled and the controllers, resulting in "the abolition of Man" (1996, 74). The elite's "extreme rationalism," by debunking all motives—including, inevitably, their own—would make them "creatures of wholly irrational behavior," with no standard beyond their impulses. "Nature, untrammeled by values, rules the Conditioners and, through them, all humanity. Man's conquest of Nature turns out, in the moment of its consummation, to be Nature's conquest of Man" (1996, 76).

---

[7]In *The abolition of man*, Lewis lamented how intellectuals' disastrous errors were being foisted upon students unawares. Lewis specifically targeted "*The Green Book*," his label for *The control of language* (King and Ketley, 1939). Lewis saw this school textbook as smuggling into young minds the reductionistic assumptions of atheist Oxford literary critic I. A. Richards (Lewis 2004b, 811). According to Doris Myers, Richards denied "the existence of mental faculties such as will, emotion, and cognition" and maintained that there was "simply the activity of the nervous system." The instincts and desires of the nervous system needed to achieve equilibrium, and good art had value in bringing this about "without assenting to traditional or ethical religious values" (Myers 1994, 31). Myers helpfully places Lewis in the context of his debates with literary scholars who tried to replace religion with literature, even as they made literature a mere byproduct of physical urges.

Scientism

Lewis did not oppose technology as such, but he saw pursuit of technological power without ethics as "a cancer in the universe" (2004b, 594).[8] Lewis opposed scientism, but he did not oppose the sciences, kept in "their proper place" and properly regarded as "hypotheses (all provisional) about the *measurable* aspects of *physical* reality." Scientific views had to be considered along with "the quite different pictures we get from Theology, Philosophy, and Art." These pictures could complement each other. If discrepancies arose among them and no solution appeared, some matters might need to be left in suspense, rather than assuming science to be right and other pictures wrong (2004b, 1010-1011). Science pursued "those specialised inquiries for which truncated thought is the correct method." Such "truncated thought" could have avoided naturalism only by continual correction from other sources. "But no other source was at hand, for during the same period men of science were coming to be metaphysically and theologically uneducated" (1960b, 65-66).

In Lewis's portrait of Western intellectual history, modern science arose in a time when astrology and magic had become widespread among intellectuals. Astrology implied that humanity's destiny was totally determined by non-human forces; ultimately, humans could do nothing to alter their destiny. Magic, by contrast, involved humanity in the pursuit of unlimited power and control; nothing could stand in the way of human power. Both approaches, despite differences, had one thing in common: abandonment of "an earlier doctrine of man. That

---

[8]Biologist J. B. S. Haldane represented the sort of scientism Lewis opposed. According to Haldane, "If science is to improve man as it has improved his environment, the experimental method must be applied to him." Religious objectors would hinder "experimental inquiry into the human mind." However, if man mustered the will for "taking his own evolution in hand," Haldane saw "no theoretical limit to man's material progress but the subjection to conscious control of every atom and every quantum of radiation in the universe. There is, perhaps, no limit at all to his intellectual and spiritual progress." Science had to be pursued "as the thing of all things most supremely worth doing," or else "man and all his works will go down into oblivion and darkness" (Haldane 1928, 302-305). Haldane complained that according to Lewis, "The application of science to human affairs can only lead to hell" (Haldane 1946, 34). In a response to Haldane (which Lewis never sent or published), Lewis said he was attacking "scientism," not science (1982, 71). Lewis denied that he thought "scientific planning will certainly lead to Hell." Rather, knowing modern people's respect for science, he was saying that "any effective invitation to Hell will certainly appear in the guise of 'scientific planning'—as Hitler's regime in fact did" (1982, 74).

doctrine had guaranteed him, on his own rung of the hierarchical ladder, his own limited freedom and efficacy: now, both the limit and the guarantee become uncertain—perhaps Man can do everything, perhaps he can do nothing" (1954, 13-14). Scientism involved the worst elements of these two incompatibles: the fatalistic determinism that marked astrology, and the conscienceless domination to which magic aspired.

Magic and modern science were not opposites but close relatives, insisted Lewis. "The evil reality of lawless applied science" could be viewed as "Magic's son and heir" (1960b, 245)—or as its twin. The magic twin failed; its scientific twin succeeded. But though results differed, the motive was the same: "to extend Man's power to the performance of all things possible." For thinkers in earlier times, "the cardinal problem had been how to conform the soul to reality, and the solution had been knowledge, self-discipline, and virtue." However, for magic and applied science, the problem was "how to subdue reality to the wishes of men," and the solution was "a technique," to be pursued even if it involved doing things previously considered disgusting and immoral (1996, 83-84; see also 2004b, 475).

It was a serious error—common among "little scientists, and little unscientific followers of science"—to think that the full reality of an object could be known when it was "stripped of its qualitative properties and reduced to mere quantity." Great minds recognized that such "an artificial abstraction" omitted important dimensions of reality (1996, 79). A healthy science would be "continually conscious that the 'natural object' produced by analysis and abstraction is not reality but only a view" and would constantly be "correcting the abstraction." Such science "would not do even to minerals and vegetables what modern science threatens to do to man himself. When it explained, it would not explain away." If the trend among elites continued, they would explain away explanation itself (1996, 85-86).[9]

Lewis believed that materialistic scientism could endanger science itself. If too many scientists despaired of objective truth, they would become indifferent to it and pursue "mere power" (1946a, 203). In earlier times, people expected to find law in nature because they believed in a divine Lawgiver. This laid the foundation for science. But as this

[9]Michael Aeschliman (1983) and Peter Kreeft (1994) expand upon Lewis's critique of scientism. Mary Midgley cites Lewis and develops similar themes in *Science as salvation* (1992).

belief faded, Lewis suggested that belief in uniformity and intelligibility might not survive long without it. Some scientists were already giving up claims to truth and were instead asserting merely that their science gave practical results. "We may be living nearer than we suppose to the end of the Scientific Age" (1960b, 169).

Increasingly reductionistic assumptions among intellectuals, bolstered by the practical success and prestige of science, had a growing impact on the wider population. In 1942 Lewis spoke of how materialism had become the popular creed of Western Europe (1970, 25). Lewis tempered this assessment somewhat after many encounters with Royal Air Force personnel and thousands of letters from his readers and radio listeners. In 1948 he wrote that "materialism is only one among many non-Christian creeds" among the English (1970, 240-241). Even so, Lewis still saw reductionistic materialism as a major opponent, dominant among intellectuals and affecting many of the less educated masses (1960b, 10).

Monism and Mysticism

Any approach that made the universe meaningless, and humanity mindless and guiltless, made it harder for Christianity to gain a hearing. This applied not only to reductionistic scientism but also to "muddy heathen mysticisms which deny intellect altogether" (1980, 28). Scientism and "heathen mysticisms" had in common not only rejection of Christian revelation but also departure from healthy cognition and conscience. Scientism and pantheism were not so far apart; both ultimately undermined rational distinctions and moral differences, thus embracing power as its own justification and losing the self to Satan (2003, 77-82; 2004b, 594).

Lewis saw an ever-present danger in Monism, also labeled "Everythingism."[10] Such thought viewed everything as self-existent, regarded particular things as less important than the totality, and even regarded particularity as illusory: everything was ultimately one. "Thus the Everythingist, if he starts from God, becomes a Pantheist; there must be nothing that is not God. If he starts from Nature he becomes a Natu-

---

[10]Some intellectuals, while striving to be Christian apologists, could be complicit in exchanging Christianity for monism. Jesuit thinker Teilhard de Chardin's synthesis of Christianity with evolutionary thought struck Lewis as "evolution run mad" (2007, 1137) and "biolatrous" (2007, 1186). Teilhard's thought manifested "a dangerous (but also commonplace) tendency to Monism or even Pantheism" (2007, 1190).

ralist; there must be nothing that is not Nature. He thinks that everything is in the long run 'merely' a precursor or a development or a relic or an instance or a disguise, of everything else" (1960b, 269). Monism, whether pantheistic or naturalistic, denied individuality and personality, thus rejecting a personal God and abolishing the human person.

Lewis wrote of a widespread "philosophical preconception," rooted in Kant, that reality must have just one level, as in monism; or else, "as 'religion' conceives it," two levels—at most—that were totally separate. There could be no connection between the two levels and no other kinds of beings between. This excluded belief in angelic beings, miracles, and bodily resurrection. It ruled out direct divine action in the physical world and in historical events, even as it denied the possibility of human thought categories applying in any way to the "spiritual Something." Thus it was assumed that "the first step beyond the world of our present experience must lead either nowhere at all or else into the blinding abyss of undifferentiated spirituality, the unconditioned, the absolute" (1960b, 252).

Lewis granted the utter transcendence of "the ultimate Fact, the fountain of all other facthood, the burning and undimensioned depth of the Divine Life" (1960b, 253). But he insisted that the transcendent God had created spirit beings lower than Himself yet higher than beings in our natural world; that God acted in the physical world through miracles and providence; that God created human capacities for relating to the divine; that God revealed something of himself in human language; that God united himself to human nature in the Person of Jesus Christ; and that faith, prayer, sacraments, and obedience could be forms of experiencing and participating in the divine life.

Lewis's diagnosis was not just an academic exercise for him. As a missionary eager for others to believe in Christ, Lewis saw a need for Christian intellectuals to buck the currents of thought among many intellectuals and to foster "the spread of an intellectual (and imaginative) climate favorable to Christianity" (1970, 221). Such an endeavor could help to prepare other intellectuals to come to know God in Christ. It could help less educated non-believers to escape anti-Christian "mental habits" that had flowed to them, at least in part, from intellectual elites. It could also provide some protection and encouragement for less learned Christians. Believers with deep learning had to "be able to meet the enemies on their own ground." Failure to do so "would be to throw down our weapons, and to betray our uneducated brethren who have, under God, no defence but us against the intellectual attacks of the heathen" (1980, 28).

Having considered Lewis's diagnosis of thought patterns prevalent in his context, we turn in the next chapter to Lewis's own epistemological views. Then, in chapter 7, we explore apologetic strategies and tactics that Lewis favored.

CHAPTER 6

Lewis's Epistemological Views

One's approach to missional apologetics is bound to be influenced by his epistemological convictions, whether those are explicitly stated or tacitly assumed. His diagnosis of problematic thought patterns in his context, as well as his prescription for what apologetic tactics to use, depend to a large extent on his views of rationality and of ways in which our minds grasp something of reality. This chapter sketches Lewis's epistemological views. Lewis wrote no treatise systematically outlining his epistemology, but he often remarked on various aspects of human knowing. I have grouped such observations into five main areas: (1) logical and moral reason; (2) metaphor, imagination, and myth; (3) virtue-dependent knowing; (4) authority, tradition, and Scripture; and (5) constructs and reality.

Logical and Moral Reason

Lewis used the word *reason* in a number of ways. Sometimes he used *reason* as a broad term for "human thought," the ability of human consciousness to perceive, remember, notice connections, and make inferences (1967, 82-83). In certain contexts, Lewis used *reason* as a narrower label for "the faculty of grasping self-evident truths or logically deducing those which are not self-evident" (2007, 129). Besides using the term *reason* to denote deductive logic or "theoretical reason," Lewis also affirmed "practical reason," the capacity for knowing not just *is* but *ought*, for discerning moral value as an imperative for practicing right action (1967, 101, 107; 1996, 46). Lewis used the word *reason* with a range of meanings, but it always denoted a faculty of discernment.

This rational faculty for discernment, insisted Lewis, must be accepted as a given. It could not be established by argument or refuted by reducing various dimensions of reason to mere epiphenomena of biochemical processes (1955b, 208; 1967, 99). "If the value of our reasoning is in doubt, you cannot try to establish it by reasoning. . . . Reason is our starting point. There can be no question either of attacking or defending it" (1960b, 33). In presupposing the validity of logical reason and moral reason, Lewis held to an objective, eternal reality which was prior to, and the source of, human inference and conscience.

Logic and Logos

When Lewis spoke of reason in the narrower sense, he often termed it *logic*. By *logic* Lewis usually meant basic principles, such as non-contradiction, and fundamental rules of inference, such as modus ponens. He insisted that no field of science, nor any other branch of knowledge, could advance without logic or discredit logic. Experimental verification and empirical generalization in science depended on "the validity of logic," and "all knowledge whatever depends on the validity of inference."[1] If inference, in principle, "reveals only how our cortex has to work and not how realities external to us must really be, then we can know nothing whatever." Granted, "we often make false inferences and while we make them they feel as certain as the sound ones." But "accidental errors" could be corrected "by further reasoning," whereas "if inference itself . . . were a merely subjective phenomenon," no knowledge would be possible. "Logic," asserted Lewis, "is a real insight into the way in which real things have to exist. In other words, the laws of thought are also the laws of things" (1967, 84-86). No knowledge of reality could violate the laws of logic. Self-contradictory claims would be "intrinsically impossible," "impossible under all conditions and in all worlds and for all agents" (1955a, 15-16).[2]

---

[1]Along the same line, Mary Midgley declares, "Science cannot stand alone. We cannot believe its propositions without first believing in a great many other startling things, such as the existence of the external world, the reliability of our senses, memory and informants, and the validity of logic. If we do believe these things, we already have a world far wider than that of science" (Midgley 1992, 108).

[2]Even God could not bring about intrinsic impossibilities, said Lewis. This was no denial of God's omnipotence; logical contradictions were merely "meaningless

In positing the validity of human logical reasoning, Lewis affirmed the objective reality of a Reason that was the source of intelligence in humans and of intelligibility in the universe. "Unless all that we take to be knowledge is an illusion, we must hold that in thinking we are not reading rationality into an irrational universe but responding to a rationality with which the universe has always been saturated" (1967, 88).[3] In Lewis's younger days, he had held to materialism; but he became convinced that this "left no room for any satisfactory theory of knowledge." He reached a point where he was utterly unable to regard thought as a mere byproduct of material processes and conditioning. "Unless I were to admit an unbelievable alternative, I must admit that mind was no late-come epiphenomenon; that the whole universe was, in the last resort, mental; that our logic was participation in a cosmic *Logos*" (1955b, 208-209). For the rest of his life, Lewis insisted on external, objective Reason as the basis and standard for logical reasoning.

Morality and the Tao

Lewis understood reason, conceived more broadly, to include not just the logical faculty but also the human capacity to make value judgments. Before modern times, asserted Lewis, all first-rate thinkers viewed value judgments as rational and linked to objective reality (1967, 100). Emotional reactions of approval or disapproval could be in accord with reason or contrary to reason. Around the world, various peoples in various eras held "the doctrine of objective value, the belief that certain attitudes are really true, and others really false, to the kind of thing the universe is and the kind of things we are." As they held a similar *concept* of objective value, the core *content* of their moral judg-

---

combinations of words. . . . Nonsense remains nonsense even when we talk it about God." Lewis's insistence on the law of non-contraction even in relation to God was tempered by the realization that "human reasoners often make mistakes." We might think a claim to be self-contradictory and intrinsically impossible, when in fact that claim did not involve a real contradiction; conversely, we might suppose something to be possible that was really a logical absurdity. Even so, this danger of misapplied logic did not mean sound logic would have no bearing on statements about God; rather, it required "great caution in defining those intrinsic impossibilities which even Omnipotence cannot perform" (1955a, 16).

[3]Midgley cites these words of Lewis and asserts, "Acknowledging matter as somehow akin to and penetrated by mind is not adding a new, extravagant assumption to our existing thought-system. It is becoming aware of something we are doing already." She derides "the humbug of pretending that we could carry on intellectual life in an intrinsically unintelligible world" (Midgley 1992, 13).

ments was also similar. Lewis termed this shared concept and core content "the *Tao*" (1996, 27-33).[4]

Some moderns claimed that different cultures had such different standards that there was no morality common to humanity as a whole. Lewis called this a "resounding lie" and asserted the "massive unanimity of the practical reason in man."[5] Studies of various cultures showed "the same triumphantly monotonous denunciations of oppression, murder, treachery and falsehood, the same injunctions of kindness to the aged, the young, and the weak, of almsgiving and impartiality and honesty." There were some differences between cultures, and "even blindnesses in particular cultures—just as there are savages who cannot count up to twenty." But the overall picture indicated "exactly what we should expect if good is indeed something objective and reason the organ whereby it is apprehended—that is, a substantial agreement with considerable local differences of emphasis and, perhaps, no one code

---

[4]In speaking of "the *Tao*," Lewis borrowed a key term from Chinese thought, but his thinking was shaped more by Europe's natural law tradition than by "the *Tao*" as conceived in China. Lewis endorsed Confucius' call to prize "harmony with Nature," and he wrote that in the Chinese understanding, the Way to be followed by humans ought to be in accord with the eternal Way from which all things received being. (*Tao* is often translated into English as "the Way.") At the same time, Lewis wrote that the Chinese conceived of the *Tao* as "the abyss that was before the Creator Himself" (1996, 30). Lewis, as a Christian, did not grant that anything preceded the Creator, but in *Abolition* he still chose the terminology of "the *Tao*" rather than "natural law." He thought that for the Westerners he was addressing, "natural law" carried too much baggage of misunderstanding and controversy. He believed that "the *Tao*" would be a more neutral term for Western readers, free of past associations and thus better able to serve as a label for an objectively grounded, cross-cultural, common morality. However, Lewis's decision to use "the *Tao*" instead of "natural law" produced two unfortunate consequences: "Although his book *The Abolition of Man* is perhaps the greatest work on natural law in the twentieth century, most scholars of natural law have never heard of it, and quite a few people who do read it mistakenly suppose that he endorsed the Eastern philosophy of Taoism" (Budziszewski 2003, 13).

[5]Lewis thought some anthropologists, especially in earlier times, had fostered skepticism about a common morality by downplaying similarities, by focusing on the most variable elements, and by "treating the savage as the normal or archetypal man." But Lewis contended that people whose mental and moral capacities were untrained or stunted were to be seen as exceptions. He did not "attach much significance to the diversity and eccentricity (themselves often exaggerated) of savage codes. And if we turn to civilized man, I claim that we shall find far fewer differences of ethical injunction than is now popularly believed" (1967, 73-74). Moreover, recent "anthropologists and missionaries are less inclined than their fathers to endorse your unfavorable picture even of the modern savage" (1955a, 61).

that includes everything" (1967, 106-107; see also 1952, 19; 1955a, 50; 1996, 93-109).

Lewis asserted that the concept of objective morality, along with the content of specific imperatives recognized in most cultures, had to be accepted as axiomatic. "Unless the ethical is assumed from the outset, no argument will bring you to it" (1967, 75). Widely shared moral judgments had to be accepted "as rational—nay, as rationality itself— as things so obviously reasonable that they neither demand nor admit proof" (1996, 52-53).

> I believe that the primary moral principles on which all others depend are rationally perceived. We 'just see' that there is no reason why my neighbour's happiness should be sacrificed to my own, as we 'just see' that things which are equal to the same thing are equal to one another. If we cannot prove either axiom, that is not because they are irrational but because they are self-evident and all proofs depend on them. Their intrinsic reasonableness shines by its own light. (1960b, 54)[6]

When Lewis spoke of "the *Tao* ... Natural Law or Traditional Morality or the First Principles of Practical Reason or the First Platitudes" (1996, 55), he meant not that moral maxims are known by all without being taught but that "they express fundamental truths about human nature" (Meilaender 1978, 197). As Lewis put it, "In the *Tao* itself, as long as we remain within it, we find the concrete reality in which to participate is to be truly human: the real common will and common reason of humanity, alive, and growing like a tree, and branching out, as the situation varies, into ever new beauties and dignities of application" (1996, 82). Thus, to live within the *Tao* was to express one's nature as a human.

In calling the axioms of logic and morality self-evident, Lewis did not claim that their truth was obvious to everyone at a glance or that moral knowledge would come automatically. Lewis stressed moral education: teaching the young right principles and training them in rightly ordered moral sentiments. With proper initiation into the *Tao*, people

---

[6]Whether or not downplaying "savage codes" indicates "a kind of provincialism in Lewis," says Meilaender, "another question is more important. Can this judgment be reconciled with his epistemological position? If the truths of the *Tao* are simply seen, how is it that some do not see them? Individual exceptions can be explained. ... But exceptions of whole societies would be more difficult to account for. Of course, it remains an empirical question whether and how many such societies there are" (Meilaender 1978, 194).

would be in a position to recognize the inherent rightness and axiomatic nature of moral platitudes. "That is what he means by referring to them as self-evident. Knowledge of these maxims, for those who acquire it, is direct" (Meilaender 1978, 200).

Just as Lewis believed that logical reasoning was grounded in a "cosmic or super-cosmic Reason," he believed that "the Reason in which the universe is saturated is also moral" (1967, 91). Human conscience was "an offshoot of some absolute moral wisdom." There must be "a supernatural source for our idea of good and evil," just as there must be "a supernatural source for rational thought" (1960b, 60).

The absolute objectivity of the *Tao*, or natural law, did not necessarily entail that an abstract, impersonal entity was held to be as ultimate as God or even above God, contended Lewis. "God neither *obeys* nor *creates* the moral law. The good is uncreated; it never could have been otherwise; it has in it no shadow of contingency." This much was recognized by some pagan thinkers. But Christians, "favoured beyond the wisest pagans," knew the absolute good to be not just a law but the eternal, mutual love of Father, Son, and Spirit, "the positive infinity of the living yet superpersonal God" (1967, 109-111). Absolute good was neither above God nor created by God but was "the necessary expression, in terms of temporal existence, of what God by His own righteous nature necessarily is. One could. indeed say of it *genitum, non factum* [begotten, not made]: for is not the *Tao* the Word Himself, considered from a particular point of view?" (2007, 1227)[7]

Correcting Without Rejecting

For Lewis, to posit absolute, unchanging (yet living and personal) Reason as the ground for logical reason and moral reason in humans did not make human logic and morals perfect. In logical reasoning, "we frequently make false inferences: from ignorance of some of the factors involved, from inattention, from inefficiencies in the system of symbols (linguistic or otherwise) which we are using, from the secret influence of our unconscious wishes or fears." Therefore, it was necessary "to combine a steadfast faith in inference as such with a wholesome skepticism about each particular instance of inference in the mind of a hu-

---

[7]This quote comes from a 1961 letter of Lewis to Clyde Kilby. Lewis was addressing objections from Harvie Conn (1960) to Lewis's concept of the *Tao*. It is worth noting here that Chinese Bible translations of John 1 speak of the pre-incarnate Word (λόγος) as "the *Tao*" (Netland, private communication).

man thinker." To be "sceptical about Reason itself" assumed that "reality contradicts Reason." In contrast, admitting human fallibility assumed the need—and possibility—for specific "human imperfections of Reason" to be corrected by "total Reason." True reasoning would correct flawed reasoning, not by utter contradiction, but by showing mistakes and incorporating "whatever was already rational in your original thought. You are not moved into a totally new world; you are given *more* and *purer* of what you already had in a small quantity and badly mixed with foreign elements. To say that Reason is objective is to say that all our false reasonings could in principle be corrected by more Reason" (1967, 91-92).[8]

Moral values, similarly, were rooted in "the ultimate Reason," but humans were prone to mistakes about morality. Therefore, Lewis considered it "reasonable to combine a firm belief in the objective validity of goodness with a considerable skepticism about all our particular moral judgments." Awareness of a constant need for correction had a double implication: "that our moral judgments are partly wrong and that they are not merely subjective facts about ourselves—for if that were so the process of enlightenment would consist not in correcting them but abandoning them altogether" (1967, 93).

Such correction and growth could occur not only in the moral insight of individuals but of cultures and of humanity as a whole. Lewis admitted that in lumping together "the traditional moralities" of various cultures, one would find not only important areas of agreement but "many contradictions and some absurdities." Correction and further development were needed—not wholesale debunking or reinvention of morality (1996, 56).

Lewis rejected Freudian claims "that all thoughts are psychologically tainted at the source" by unconscious complexes. He also dismissed Marxist assertions that all "thoughts are 'ideologically' tainted at the source" by economic and social interests. All sane people had always believed "that some thoughts are tainted and others not." Only moderns would "assume without discussion *that* [someone] is wrong and then distract his attention from this (the only real issue) by busily explaining how he became so silly." (Lewis labeled this tendency "Bul-

---

[8]In a 1941 letter, Lewis granted "our fallibility as reasoners" but insisted, "A refusal to claim infallibility does not reduce us . . . to sheer nescience. The fact that we *may*, after all, have made a mistake does not justify us in expecting of God things which our best thinking pronounces to be impossible" (2004b, 461).

verism," after its imaginary inventor). By contrast, Lewis insisted that "you can only find out the rights and wrongs by reasoning—never by being rude about your opponent's psychology" (1970, 271-274).

Lewis dismissed the notion that truth is only what people are conditioned to believe or that "'good' means whatever men are conditioned to approve" (1967, 111). He granted that thinking, as an activity of the brain, was affected and often limited by physical factors. He also affirmed that "the moral outlook of a community can be shown to be closely connected with its history, geographical environment, economic structure, and so forth." But he thought such facts fit well with his understanding of humanity's incomplete but real participation in absolute rationality and morality. "A man's Rational thinking is *just so much* of his share in eternal Reason as the state of his brain allows to become operative... A nation's moral outlook is just so much of its share in eternal Moral Wisdom as its history, economics etc. lets through" (1960b, 61-62).

In Lewis's view, awareness of physical, psychological, and social influences on thought and conscience should stimulate diligent inquiry and humble willingness to be corrected, not serve as an excuse to deny objective truth and morality. Some scientists said logic was "merely subjective" and sought "not to know what is there but simply to get practical results." Still, most research aimed to grasp reality and could not let logic dissolve into subjectivism. Therefore, denial of "theoretical reason" was not all that common. However, denial of "practical reason" was far more widespread: morality was debunked as "the feeling we have been socially conditioned to have" (1967, 99-100). Rejecting the objectivity of truth and morality often came in the guise of not being dogmatic, of keeping an open mind. Lewis countered, "An open mind, in questions that are not ultimate, is useful. But an open mind about the ultimate foundations either of Theoretical or of Practical Reason is idiocy. If a man's mind is open on these things, let his mouth at least be shut" (1996, 59).

Imagination, Metaphor, and Myth

Epistemology for Lewis involved far more than the axioms and inferences of logical and moral reasoning. The faculty of imagination, interacting with metaphor and myth, was vital for knowing, due to the incarnational character of knowable reality.

Metaphor and Sacramental Metaphysics

Most language and knowledge involved metaphor and therefore required imagination, asserted Lewis. "When we pass beyond pointing to individual sensible objects, when we begin to think of causes, relations, of mental states or acts, we become incurably metaphorical." Those who claimed to speak of such things literally, without metaphors, were in reality "driven by unrecognized metaphors." Nothing, or almost nothing, could be thought or spoken apart from imagination, "because all our truth, or all but a few fragments, is won by metaphor." Lewis wrote, "For me, reason is the natural organ of truth; but imagination is the organ of meaning." Reason could assess the truth or falsehood of a statement only if the statement had meaning—and imagination was the capacity to grasp meaning via metaphor. Meaning "is the antecedent condition of both truth and falsehood, whose antithesis is not error but nonsense." Thus, according to Lewis, "Imagination, producing new metaphors or revivifying old, is not the cause of truth, but its condition" (1939, 155-157).[9]

Metaphor was unavoidable, insisted Lewis.[10] He defined metaphor as "talking about something which is not perceptible by the five senses" through the use of "words which, in one of their meanings, refer to things or actions that are [perceptible to the senses]." It would be a mistake to regard metaphor as a mere decoration for poetry and oratory, unneeded for plain speech. "Books on psychology or economics or politics are as continuously metaphorical as books of poetry or devotion" (1960b, 114-115).[11] Philosophers' words were likewise "myth and

[9]Lewis's drew heavily on Owen Barfield (1973; see also Adey 1978).

[10]In making this assertion, Lewis was not saying that metaphorical language had no real referent, nor was he saying that a statement's meaning was coterminous with the sense-based metaphor used to convey the meaning. For instance, when someone says he grasps an argument, he does not claim that the mind has hands, or that arguments can be manually seized. "To avoid the word *grasp* he may change the form of expression and say 'I see your point,' but he does not mean that a pointed object has appeared in his visual field. He may have a third shot and say 'I follow you,' but he does not mean that he is walking behind you along a road." Each metaphor conveys nearly the same meaning and can be clearly understood without mistaking it for literal physicality. Still, each attempt to escape metaphorical wording leads only to a different metaphor (1960b, 114).

[11]For instance, psychologists avoided "unscientific" terms such as *soul* or *spirit*, with metaphorical roots in ancient words for breath. But speaking of "complexes, repressions, censors, engrams, and the like," exchanged "the *breath* . . . for *tyings-up, shovings-back, Roman magistrates*, and *scratchings*" (1939, 151; see also 1960b, 115).

metaphor," but most were unaware of this, so their thought was mastered by "the hidden myth" (1989, 171). If a scientist, eager to get beyond symbol, "deserted metaphor for mathematics, he did not really pass from symbol to symbolized, but only from one set of symbols to another" (1939, 150).[12]

Lewis understood his view of metaphor to have "metaphysical implications." All metaphor would be unrelated to truth, and thus all thinking would be nonsense, "if there is not, in fact, a kind of psycho-physical parallelism (or more) in the universe" (1939, 158). For metaphor to have meaning, there must be some relationship between human imagination and qualities inherent in the universe. This relationship, this "psycho-physical parallelism," could exist because imagination and the universe were both patterned "to reflect heavenly truth" (1955b, 167). As an ultimate Reason imbued the universe with intelligibility and humanity with intelligence, as an absolute *Tao* held the universe to moral standards and endowed humanity with conscience, so a "heavenly truth" suffused the universe with mythic radiance and gave humanity the imaginative capacity to detect and reflect that radiance. "If God chooses to be mythopoeic . . . shall we refuse to be *mythopathic?*" (1970, 67)

Lewis's view of reality was sacramental and incarnational, as various scholars observe (Adey 1998; Carnell 1998, 214; Payne 1995, 27, 144; Starr 2002, ii). A particular thing could be sacramental in relation to something higher by being "a sign, but also something more than a sign . . . because in it the thing signified is really in a certain mode present" (1980, 62). The Creator could fill the natural with meaning and make it more than just natural. Through what Lewis called Transposition, "the lower reality can actually be drawn into the higher and become part of it." The supreme case of this was the Incarnation, by

---

[12]In *Metaphors we live by*, George Lakoff and Mark Johnson assert, "Our ordinary conceptual system, in terms of which we both think and act, is fundamentally metaphorical in nature" (2003, 30). In this they resemble Lewis, and they offer considerable insight into the role of metaphor in human thinking. However, unlike Lewis, Lakoff and Johnson deny any absolute source or standard of truth, morality, and meaning (1999, 290-334; 2003, x; see also Johnson 1993). They think "evolutionary theory . . . shows that human capacities grow out of animal capacities" (1999, 17). Lakoff and Johnson—with question-begging boldness—allege that cognitive science eliminates the possibility of a mind without a body. When discussing human spirituality, they recommend panentheism, in which "empathic projection onto anything or anyone is contact with God" (1999, 566-568).

which humanity was drawn into deity (1980, 70-71). Lewis suggested that "the triple distinction of truth from myth and of both from fact. . . was part and parcel of that unhappy division between soul and body which resulted from the Fall."[13] Even so, "the sacraments existed as a permanent reminder that the division was neither wholesome nor final. The Incarnation had been the beginning of its disappearance" (2003, 122).

Myth and Art

In using the word *myth*, Lewis explicitly distinguished his usage from what anthropologists meant by myth. He did not mean just any story of pre-modern peoples that embodied their values. By *myth*, Lewis meant a story that "deals with the permanent and inevitable" (1982, 100), a story that involves "preternaturals," conveys a pattern of universal relevance, and inspires an awe-filled sense of something numinous, timeless, and vastly important, which surpasses the mind's ability to conceptualize it (1961, 43-44).

A mythic dimension in the arts could present concrete things in a way that gave the imagination a nourishing taste of permanent reality. A painting could give "glimpses of Heaven in the earthly landscape" (1946b, 80). The possibility of poetry came from "that great Imagination" who invented the world and human speech. Thus poetry could be "a little incarnation, giving body to what had been before invisible and inaudible." Poetry at its best could "somehow convey to us an inkling of supersensual and super-intellectual Reality," akin to the "*mysterium tremendum*" of religious experience (2004b, 445).[14]

---

[13]This triple distinction is treated by Charlie Starr as the key to understanding Lewis's entire epistemology. In my estimation, Starr overstates his case, yet his insights help to clarify some key aspects of Lewis's thought. Lewis "distinguishes fact as what *is* (objects or events) and truth as statements we make *about* facts." The main concern of knowledge "is not truth statements about reality but reality itself" (Starr 2002, 5, 7). "In the higher reality of heaven, truth *is* reality; in the lower reality of earth, truth is an abstraction corresponding to reality. 'Myth' in heaven is . . . the 'I Am,' palpably real and utterly factual. On earth, 'myth' reveals a glimpse of heavenly reality perceived in imaginative form" (Starr 2002, ii).

[14]Likewise, fairy tales could waken in a reader "a longing for he knows not what" and impart "a new dimension of depth" to everyday experience (1982, 38). Tolkien's *Lord of the Rings*, said Lewis, freshly illuminated the significance of things that had become overly familiar. "By dipping them in myth we see them more clearly" (1982, 90).

Lewis cautioned that those who, like himself, loved the numinous echoes in mythic art had to keep in mind the deadly danger of confusing "an aesthetic appreciation of the spiritual life with the life itself" (2004a, 906; see also 1960a, 192). Imaginative appreciation of art and myth did not of itself constitute "a beginning of, nor a step toward, the higher life of the spirit, merely an image." Since it contained "no element either of belief or ethics," explained Lewis, it would not suffice to make someone "wiser or better." Nevertheless, imaginative experience still had "the shape of the reality it reflected," and God could cause it to be a starting point leading toward belief and morality (1955b, 167).[15]

The arts were closer to "normal experience" than were the "specially and artificially purified moments of *ratio*" (2004a, 206). Almost all experience exceeded the capacity of logical definition to express it, "except thought made *deliberately* abstract for scientific purposes." Strictly definitional and scientific thought was not the norm but the exception for human perceiving and thinking.[16] "To be incommunicable by Scientific language is, so far as I can judge, the normal state of experience" (1967, 183). Propositional truth, though valuable, was at best able to express only a partial abstraction of such knowledge.[17] Knowing about (*savoir*) was not equivalent to knowledge by direct acquaintance (*connaître*). Lewis asserted that "all the arts depend on turning *savoir* into *connaître* as far as possible" (2004a, 6; see also 1961, 139). The arts at

---

[15]In Lewis's own experience, he became entranced by George MacDonald's *Phantastes* years before conversion. The "bright shadow" of holiness no longer seemed remote but was "too near to see, too plain to be understood, on this side of knowledge." Amid "the then invincible ignorance of my intellect," wrote Lewis, "my imagination was, in a certain sense, baptized" (1955b, 179-181). The impact of *Phantastes*, he said, "made it easier for me to understand how the better elements in mythology can be a real *preparatio evangelica* for people who do not yet know whither they are being led" (2004b, 453).

[16]Thus, in relation to God or even ordinary things, human efforts to grasp reality "are very far from being exhausted by the logical, the discursive, or the propositional" (Carnell 1998, 214). "The world for Lewis is not merely factual, not 'merely' anything . . . reason is unworthy of itself until it rises above 'merely'" (Kilby 1971, 25).

[17]Paul Helm likewise notes that propositional statements are selective abstractions from a more immediate, richer experience. This is the case whether a proposition concerns "the detached observing of some object in the world, or a personal relationship of mutual trust." A proposition can accurately (though not fully) represent a dimension of an object or a person, "provided we are aware of the fact of selectivity" (Helm 2000, 5). For Helm, as for Lewis, knowledge far surpasses what can be expressed in propositional form, yet the truthfulness and usefulness of propositions and logical inferences must be affirmed.

their best could give imagination a taste—not just an analysis—of concrete realities, and in doing so could also convey some hint of the ultimate Reality which was reflected in all persons and things.

Lewis perceived a rift between two kinds of knowledge that were both valuable but rarely, in our present state, united. To participate experientially in reality gave one sort of knowledge. To engage in clear, critical observation from outside an experience gave a different sort of knowledge. "As thinkers we are cut off from what we think about; as tasting, touching, willing, loving, hating, we do not clearly understand. The more lucidly we think, the more we are cut off: the more deeply we enter into reality, the less we can think." Lewis saw myth as a partial solution to this problem. "What flows to you from the myth is not truth but reality (truth is always *about* something, but reality is that *about which* truth is), and, therefore, every myth becomes the father of innumerable truths on the abstract level." Myth—unlike critical thought—could give a taste, not just an abstract description. At the same time, myth—unlike direct experience of a specific thing—conveyed not just something small and temporal but something universal and timeless (1970, 65-66).

Myth "must be grasped with the imagination, not with the intellect," wrote Lewis. "It is the sort of thing you cannot learn from definition: you must rather get to know it as you get to know a smell or a taste, the 'atmosphere' of a family or a country town, or the personality of an individual" (1989, 13). Starr rightly says that for Lewis, "Myth is epistemologically valid, even if the knowledge it reveals cannot be stated in abstract propositions" (Starr 2002, 8).

Pagan Myths as Preparation for the Gospel

Similarities between the Christian story and some pagan myths had been taken by some anthropologists as evidence that all such stories were equally false. This kind of thinking had contributed to Lewis's abandonment of Christian belief as a youth. Later, however, Lewis rejected "the anthropological argument against Christianity" and saw things from a very different angle. Christianity's resemblances to the greatest pagan myths (myths in Lewis's sense as well as the anthropological sense) did not indicate falsehood; rather, God had used the pagan myths as preparation for the gospel, "a divine hinting in poetic and ritual form at the same central truth which was later focused and (so to speak) historicised in the Incarnation" (1970, 132).[18] Key to Lewis's own conversion to Christianity was his new perception that "the Pagan stories are God expressing Himself through the minds of poets, using such images as He found there, while Christianity is God expressing Himself through what we call 'real things'" (2004a, 977). Pagan myths of savior-heroes, gods taking human form, bloody sacrifice, and resurrection, pointed ahead to Christ.

The best myths were "premonitions" (1980, 84), "pictures" (1989, 152-155), "good dreams" (1952, 54), "a real though unfocused gleam of divine truth falling on human imagination" (1960b, 218). Lewis thought the existence of such myths in many cultures was part of what John 1:9 meant in saying that the divine Word, through whom the world was made and who became incarnate in Jesus, gives light to every man (1980, 83). Demons tried to corrupt the pagan myths and partly succeeded, but elements of divine truth still got through (1958, 106; 1989, 152; 2004b, 771). Seeing myths as preparation, and gospel as fulfillment—somewhat like the relation between Old and New Testament (1958, 99-134; 1960b, 218; 2004b, 193)—struck Lewis as more reasonable than wholesale dismissal of them all. "Surely the history of the human mind hangs together better if you suppose that all this was the first shadowy approach of something whose reality came with Christ" (2004b, 35).

All things were created through the eternal Word and were partial expressions of the unfathomable riches of that Word. When the Word became flesh in Jesus, that which had been hinted at in myth entered the world of fact, yet retained mythic power. This myth-become-fact was to be not only grasped by reason but embraced by imagination.[19] The mythic dimension gave a fuller taste of reality than the factual

[18]Lewis did not dispute anthropologists' explanations that mythic belief in a dying and rising god originated from experience of agriculture; he only disagreed that this explained away the myth's connection to higher reality. When pagan poets saw the burial of a seed and the rising of a plant, said Lewis, their imaginations formed myths of a dying and rising Corn-King. The Corn-King's similarity to Christ was "not in the least unreal or accidental," for the myth was derived from a recurring pattern in nature, which in turn came from the creative Word, who in the fullness of time would become incarnate, die, and rise to life. A pattern of descent and reascent was "written all over the world" in various forms as "transpositions of the Divine theme into a minor key." Lewis declared, "The pattern is there in Nature because it was first there in God" (1960b, 180, 186; see also 1958, 105-107).

[19]The relationship of reason and imagination for Lewis is probed from varying angles by Barfield (1989), Hooper (1996, 564-575), Schakel (1984), and Starr (2002).

alone, and it touched aspects of the total person that rigorous reasoning did not. God Incarnate, "Perfect Myth and Perfect Fact," was "addressed to the savage, the child, and the poet in each one of us no less than to the moralist, the scholar, and the philosopher" (1970, 63-67).

Lewis took it as axiomatic that if God could be known, it had to be by his self-revelation, not by our speculation. Therefore, God had to be sought among various traditions in which it was claimed that God had revealed himself. As Lewis perceived a common core in the logics and morals of many cultures, so he saw a common core in their myths. "The traditions conflict, yet the longer and more sympathetically we study them the more we become aware of a common element in many of them: the theme of sacrifice, of mystical communion through the shed blood, of death and rebirth, of redemption, is too clear to escape notice." Lewis saw Christianity bringing these old themes together in a new way that "no longer revolts our conscience and our reason." It was reasonable to see Christianity as "the consummation of all religion, the fullest message from the wholly other." It was reasonable to join the church, "the only concrete organization which has preserved down to this present time the core of all the messages, pagan and perhaps pre-pagan, that have ever come from beyond the world" (1970, 144).

Virtue-Dependent Knowing

In Lewis's epistemology, virtue could be a precondition for grasping reality and could be indispensable for sustaining Christian belief. Vice could impede the capacity to know. Preoccupation with self was the worst vice (1960c, ix). This had epistemological implications, because intimate knowledge of things and persons outside oneself depended on venturing beyond the self. To love, to make moral choices, and to reason—each brought an expanded grasp of reality by carrying a person beyond preoccupation with self.

> In love we escape from our self into one other [*sic*]. In the moral sphere, every act of justice or charity involves putting ourselves in the other person's place . . . In coming to understand anything we are rejecting the facts as they are for us in favour of the facts as they are. The primary impulse of each is to maintain and aggrandize himself. The secondary impulse is to go out of the self, to correct its provincialism and heal its loneliness. In love, in virtue, in the pursuit of knowledge, and in the reception of the arts, we are doing this. (1961, 138)

135

Escaping the vice of self-absorption and becoming more truly the self God intended enabled one's faculties for knowledge to become more capacious and more accurate. What a person could know, according to Lewis, depended to a large extent on the person's stance and character: "For what you see and hear depends a good deal on where you are standing: it also depends on what sort of person you are" (1994d, 148). This was especially the case in relation to God. Growth in knowledge of God depended on growth in obedience. Lewis, echoing John 7:17, insisted, "He who does the will of the Father shall know of the doctrine" (2004b, 202, 823). Some aspects of Christianity could be known "from the outside" by non-Christians, but many things could not be understood until after a person became a Christian and made some progress in the Christian way (1952, 126).

Knowing God depended on God's initiative; we could know nothing of God unless he showed himself. Still, God showed more to some than to others. This was not because God played favorites, "but because it is impossible for Him to show Himself to a man whose whole mind and character are in the wrong condition." In the sciences, various instruments could be used to gain knowledge of physical things; but the instrument for gaining knowledge of God was the entire self. "And if a man's self is not kept clean and bright, his glimpse of God will be blurred. . . . That is why horrible nations have horrible religions: they have been looking at God through a dirty lens" (1952, 143-144).

Virtue was involved not only in gaining knowledge of God but in sustaining such knowledge. Lewis rejected the notion that "the human mind is completely ruled by reason," though he did not repudiate logic and evidence. Trying to force oneself to believe a statement if one thought the evidence bad "would be merely stupid." Lewis said, "I am not asking anyone to accept Christianity if his best reasoning tells him that the weight of the evidence is against it."[20] However, loss of Chris-

[20]Philosopher John Beversluis seizes upon this sentence and uses it as the basis for an entire book that misrepresents Lewis's belief and apologetics as "the search for rational religion" (Beversluis 1985). Beversluis's thesis is contradicted by a vast range of material in Lewis's writings. Indeed, even this very statement of Lewis appears in a context that belies the claims of Beversluis. Far from advocating strict rationalism in religion, the fuller passage insists that belief involves much more than mere reasoning and evidence. The statement Beversluis cites as the linchpin of Lewis's approach was a passing remark, a strategic comment by Lewis that he did not expect his radio listeners and readers to force themselves to perform the absurd act of believing what they saw no ground for believing.

tian belief more often resulted from mere drifting—as moods, desires, circumstances, or companions changed—than from reasoned consideration of evidence. Faith had to fight virtuously against fickleness, not against sound reason. Such faith required the virtue of "holding on to things your reason has once accepted, in spite of your changing moods." What reason initially accepted, reason alone could not sustain. A Christian had to set aside time each day to focus the mind on Christian truth. According to Lewis, "daily prayers and religious reading and churchgoing are necessary parts of the Christian life," for we need to be reminded repeatedly of what we believe. No belief "will automatically remain alive in the mind. It must be fed" (1952, 122-124).

Reason, in a moment of clarity, might be persuaded of Christian claims. But without the virtue of faith, reason would soon lose its grip on belief in Christ. "The moment rational thought ceases, imagination, mental habit, temperament, and the 'spirit of the age' take charge of you again." New thoughts recognizing Christian truth had to become habitual, and this could happen only by continual vigilance and constant training. Without such vigilance and training, a mind newly persuaded of gospel truths could easily slip back into old ruts, yielding to a familiar feeling that Christian realities were unreal (1960b, 271-272).

Oxford freshmen from religious homes who abandoned Christianity at university were usually swayed by a new context and new companions, not by new evidence. Going by appearances—what "*looks* improbable"—was more of a problem than arguments against faith. The main conflict was between faith and sight, not faith and reason. Reason was not to be rejected, but neither could it be depended on to stand firm. When caught up in sin, even preposterous arguments could sway reason against Christianity (1967, 56-57).

> Reason may win truths; without Faith she will retain them just so long as Satan pleases. There is nothing we cannot be made to believe or disbelieve. If we wish to be rational, not now and then, but constantly, we must pray for the gift of Faith, for the power to go on believing not in the teeth of reason but in the teeth of lust and terror and jealousy and boredom and indifference that which reason, authority, and experience, or all three, have once delivered to us for truth. (1967, 58)

Lewis's virtue-dependent epistemology went beyond the need for an individual to be upright and trustful. A virtuous community was also needed. All knowledge involved social ties. Without other people, knowledge would be impossible: "we need them if we are to know anything, even ourselves" (1960a, 12). A bad circle of companions could make falsehood seem plausible, evil seem admirable, and truth seem embarrassing and doubtful. But a Christian circle of companions could enable one go on believing and behaving in line with the gospel, regardless of what a hostile world might say (1960a, 114). Since a Christian was bound to be in unbelieving company at times, the individual virtue of faith had to resist social pressure, but it also had to draw regularly on Christian friendship.

To receive and retain knowledge, one needed to be a virtuous individual in a virtuous community. God showed himself "not simply to men who are individually good, but to men who are united together in a body, loving one another, helping one another, showing Him to one another." Therefore, "the one really adequate instrument for learning about God is the whole Christian community." If people bypassed community and the truths accumulated in the Christian tradition, if they instead offered a "simplified religion of their own," they had no chance to improve on what the community and tradition had already learned, and their theological novelties would soon be forgotten (1952, 144). Knowledge of God was to be gained within a virtuous community continuing over time; hence, authority and tradition would properly play a large role in Christian belief.

Authority, Tradition, and Scripture

For Lewis, reason was not antithetical to authority. "One of the things my reason tells me is that I ought to check the results of my own thinking by the opinions of the wise. I go to authority because reason sends me to it" (1967, 34). Most of our knowledge came from believing others who were in a better position to know than we were—in other words, through authority. Reliance on authority was not unique to religion. On the contrary, wrote Lewis, "Ninety-nine per cent of the things you believe are believed on authority." All statements about historical events were believed on authority; none could be proved "by pure logic" (1952, 63). Non-scientists believed scientific findings based on authority, not based on their own discoveries and deductions (1955b, 174). If an epistemology excluded beliefs based on authority, it would produce near-total ignorance. When Christian belief rested on authority, rather than on autonomous investigation, this did not make Christian belief epistemologically inferior to other kinds of belief. In Lewis's judgment, those who insisted that religious belief was acceptable only if it resulted from rigorous, autonomous reasoning were imposing a burden that was seldom imposed on other, non-religious types of belief.

Moreover, if modernity insisted that ordinary people should not accept the supernatural unless it could be proved through "abstruse reasoning," it was departing from what had been normal in earlier eras. Lewis stated, "All over the world, until quite modern times, the direct insights of the mystics and the reasonings of the philosophers percolated to the mass of the people by authority and tradition; they could be received by those who were no great reasoners themselves in the concrete form of myth and ritual and the whole pattern of life." But a century of naturalistic thinking and education had forced upon "plain men" the new burden of getting truth for themselves or going without it. For Lewis, the modern notion that religion was a matter for individuals to experience or reason out for themselves posed a deadly danger to common people, and, indeed, to society as a whole. The modern proletariat was no more spiritual or rational than common people in earlier times, yet these much-flattered moderns thought themselves spiritual and wise, with little need for the authority and the cumulative tradition derived from spiritual and intellectual giants. A society where few people had direct spiritual experiences or superb reasoning powers could still live if the right authority and tradition were heeded. Of course, if all people in a society would become seers who received direct insight from God and reasoned brilliantly, that society could live more fully. "But a society where the mass is simple and the seers are no longer attended to can achieve only superficiality, baseness, ugliness, and in the end extinction" (1960b, 67).

In seeking to discern the intellectual content of genuine Christianity, Lewis gravitated toward his usual preference for a core consensus. He felt most confident in "the vast mass of doctrine which I find agreed on by Scripture, the Fathers, the Middle Ages, modern Roman Catholics, modern Protestants. That is true 'catholic' doctrine." Lewis summarily rejected "mere modernism" for its break from the historic Christian consensus. He also granted little authority to any "provincial or local *variation* from the central, ancient tradition," whether the distinctive emphases of various Protestant groups, or the claims of "modern Romanism" about Mary, the papacy, purgatory, or transubstantiation. "What we are committed to believing is whatever can be proved from Scripture" (2004b, 646-647).

While recognizing biblical authority, Lewis emphasized that Christ, not Scripture, is the main object of faith. "It is Christ Himself, not the

Bible, which is the true word of God. The Bible, read in the right spirit and with the guidance of good teachers will bring us to Him" (2007, 246). Biblical authority could not be isolated from the tradition of the Christian community: "The basis of our Faith is not the Bible taken by itself but the agreed affirmation of all Christendom: to which we owe the Bible itself" (2007, 652-653). However, even though the Bible was accepted on the church's authority, Lewis stressed that this did not mean that "the Bible can never give us grounds for criticising the Church." The Bible was a higher authority than the church. When Lewis, as a teacher, recommended a book to a pupil, the pupil would consult the book on Lewis's authority, yet recognize that the book's author knew more about the subject than Lewis did—for Lewis himself had said so. Likewise, church authority pointed to the Bible as a still higher authority (2007, 1307-1308).

Biblical authority, for Lewis, did not mean that the Bible was perfect in every part. Joshua's "atrocities (and treacheries)" might have been evil, not divinely commanded, for the doctrine of God's goodness was more certain than the doctrine of biblical inerrancy (2007, 1436-1437).[21] Some statements in the Psalms might be wicked or self-righteous (1958, 12-33). The Bible's earliest writings were "hardly moral at all" and "not unlike the Pagan religions." These beginnings were "gradually purged and enlightened" in a process that led up to "the religion of the great prophets and Our Lord Himself. That whole process is the greatest revelation of God's true nature" (2007, 608).

Even at its highest and purest levels, Scripture could still contain errors of minor fact, thought Lewis, just as Jesus, being fully human, probably made such errors. After all, "our modern & western attention to dates, numbers, etc. simply did not exist in the ancient world. No one was looking for *that* sort of truth" (2007, 961). Lewis ruled out "the view that any one passage taken in isolation can be assumed to be inerrant in exactly the same sense as any other." One need not suppose that Old Testament "numbers of armies . . . are statistically correct because the story of the Resurrection is historically correct." Lewis thought inerrancy loomed larger in theological controversy than in personal Bible reading and Christian living. He was sure that "the over-all operation of Scripture is to convey God's Word to the reader . . . who

---

[21]Christensen (1979), writing amid heated evangelical debates over inerrancy, describes at length Lewis's views about Scripture. Christensen draws upon Lewis's writings that were published at the time but includes little from Lewis's letters.

reads it in the right spirit," but not that "it *also* gives true answers to all the questions (often religiously irrelevant) which he might ask" (2007, 1044-1046).

The Genesis creation story was "in the form of a folk tale," said Lewis. That was no flaw. The story was so deep and grasped the idea of creation so rigorously that no philosophical theory had radically improved upon it (1958, 109-110; 1960b, 51). Lewis suggested that Esther, Jonah, and Job "pretty well *proclaim* themselves to be sacred fiction," as did Jesus' parables. The Lord "meant us to have sacred myth & sacred fiction as well as sacred history." Lewis insisted that he never thought "a story unhistorical *because* it is miraculous." His sense of literary genre, not skepticism about miracles, made him see some parts of scripture as fictional (2007, 652-653; see also 1958, 109; 2007, 319).

God's Word was to be received from Scripture "not by using it as an encyclopedia or an encyclical but by steeping ourselves in its tone and temper and so learning its overall message." We might have expected or wanted God to give "ultimate truth in systematic form— something we could have tabulated and memorised and relied on like the multiplication table." But even Jesus' perfect teaching was "not given us in that cut-and-dried, fool-proof, systematic fashion." Jesus' sayings—"paradox, proverb, exaggeration, parable, irony; even the 'wisecrack'"—came in particular contexts and could not be reduced to a system. "It may be indispensable that Our Lord's teaching, by that elusiveness (to our systematising intellect), should demand a response from the whole man, should make it so clear that there is no question of learning a subject but of steeping ourselves in a Personality, acquiring a new outlook and temper, breathing a new atmosphere," and thus being reshaped in his image. Similarly, observed Lewis, God gave Paul many gifts but not the gift of clear, orderly exposition. Paul's letters, with their "turbulent mixture of petty detail, personal complaint, practical advice, and lyrical rapture, finally let through what matters more than ideas—a whole Christian life in operation—better say, Christ Himself operating in a man's life." Likewise, Old Testament imperfections may have been needed for us to re-live with the Jews God's gradual revelation, "to feel the very contention between the Word and the human material through which it works," and to elicit "our total response" (1958, 111-114).

Lewis's epistemology regarding Scripture stressed the personal over the systematic and sought to be properly receptive to metaphor as well as literal assertion. Jesus' death, while a physical fact, also had an impact that no single image or definition could fully capture. In a 1963 letter, Lewis wrote, "I think the ideas of sacrifice, Ransom, Championship (over Death), Substitution etc. are all images to *suggest* the reality (not otherwise comprehensible to us) of the Atonement. To fix on any *one* of them as if it contained and limited the truth like a scientific definition would in my opinion be a mistake" (2007, 1476).

Language about God was always analogical. It was not possible to get behind the analogy to "a purely literal truth. All we can really substitute for the analogical expression is some theological abstraction." Abstractions (such as divine impassibility) could be somewhat useful as warnings not to make absurd deductions from metaphorical analogies, but abstract negations about God could not convey what was positively expressed in "the sensuous, organic, and personal images of Scripture." Lewis suggested two guidelines for exegesis: "1) Never take the images literally. 2) When the *purport* of the images—what they say to our fear and hope and will and affections—seems to conflict with the theological abstractions, trust the purport of the images every time." Our abstractions are themselves analogies that model spiritual reality "in legal or chemical or mechanical terms." Attempts to demythologize Christianity were actually "'re-mythologising' it—and substituting a poorer mythology for a richer" (1973, 51-52).

The Bible's anthropomorphisms—"man-like images"—were less misleading than other kinds of images. Man, contended Lewis, is the highest of things we know by our senses. Though God is "unspeakably different" from us, he is even more different from "images of shapeless mists and irrational forces" that accompany supposedly sophisticated attempts to advance beyond "a personal God" (1960b, 118). While all biblical language about God involved analogy and metaphor, this did not diminish its revelatory character or truthfulness. God was not less than a metaphor could express but infinitely more.[22] Of utmost im-

---

[22]Lewis thought that in the history of language, "words did not start by referring merely to physical objects and then get extended by metaphor to refer to emotions, mental states and the like. On the contrary, what we now call the 'literal and metaphorical' meanings have both been disengaged by analysis from an ancient unity of meaning which was neither or both." Lewis observed, "Some people when they say that a thing is meant 'metaphorically' conclude from this that it is hardly meant at all... This mode of interpretation I regard, frankly, as nonsense. For me the Christian doctrines which are 'metaphorical'—or which have become metaphorical with the increase of abstract thought—mean something which is just as 'supernatural' or shocking after we have removed the ancient imagery as before" (1960b, 123-125).

portance for Lewis, the metaphorical nature of anthropomorphisms meant not that God was sub-personal but that he was super-personal.

In addition, the fact that language about God must be metaphorical did not entail that accounts of "the miracles of the Incarnate God" were metaphorical (1970, 71).

> Events on the historical level are the sort of things we can talk about literally. If they occurred, they were perceived by the senses of men. Legitimate 'explanation' degenerates into muddled or dishonest 'explaining away' as soon as we start applying to these events the metaphorical interpretation which we rightly apply to the statements about God . . . the assertion that Jesus turned water into wine was meant perfectly literally, for this refers to something which, if it happened, was well within the reach of our senses and language. (1960b, 126)

Likewise, Jesus' resurrection involved facts that came through into ordinary human experience "in all their literal facthood." Lewis asserted, "The local appearances, the eating, the touching, the claim to be corporeal, must be either reality or sheer illusion" (1960b, 250-251). In biblical accounts of the ascension, language about Jesus sitting down at God's right hand was metaphorical. "But the statement that the holy Shape went up and vanished does not permit the same treatment" (1960b, 254). Jesus' human nature and historical actions, as described by biblical witnesses, were literal facts. These facts incarnated a divine nature and accomplished things in the spiritual realm that could be described only metaphorically, but the facts themselves remained literal and could be described in straightforward language.[23]

---

[23]Mark Edwards Freshwater grants that Lewis was right in criticizing some aspects of New Testament research and in saying that scholars such as Bultmann were "re-mythologizing." Still, Freshwater charges that Lewis failed to prove the historicity of New Testament records or to come to grips with recent NT scholarship. Freshwater suggests that NT portrayals of Jesus' character and actions need not be accurate, and that the important thing conveyed in the New Testament is "a new vision and understanding of reality. Christianity could then be seen as Lewis saw the Old Testament, the 'chosen mythology' of God." For Freshwater, the core of Christianity is to assert a loving God and "a supernatural realm which in some sense intervenes in the world of the everyday" (Freshwater 1988, 121-128). Freshwater fails to notice that Lewis regarded only some parts of the Old Testament as chosen myth; Lewis took much to be historical (1960b, 218; 2007, 319, 652-653, 1044-1046). Moreover, Freshwater ignores Lewis's observation that NT narratives of miracles purport to describe actual events (not just a new way of looking at the universe) and that the events described are "well within the reach of our senses and language" (1960b, 126).

Constructs and Reality

Lewis was a critical realist in his epistemology. He was a realist in that he presupposed an objective basis and referent for human thought. He was critical in that he viewed all thought systems as constructs, influenced by personal and social factors, providing partial, provisional, suggestive models of reality, but never full, final, or exact replicas.

Constructs of the Cosmos

Reflecting upon ties between epistemology and cosmology, Lewis pondered what would prompt people to abandon one model of the universe and embrace another. He believed that a switch came not simply in response to "new phenomena but to a subjective demand for a new model" (2007, 1385). *The discarded image* (1964), while depicting "the Medieval Model" of the universe, also offered "reflections on the character of *all* cosmic images, including our own, which I believe people ought to consider" (2007, 1397-1398).

Great thinkers in every age, said Lewis, knew that scientific theories "are never statements of fact" but provisional hypotheses to explain observable phenomena, and that any cosmology is "only a model, possibly replaceable." Such experts, knowing each model to be "a construct of answered questions," continually "engaged either in raising new questions or in giving new answers to old ones." They did not take the prevalent cosmology as final. Lewis thought that in his own time, the less people really knew about science, the more likely they were to regard the reigning model of the universe as indisputable fact. He attributed this in large part to "a popular scientism" created by "the mass media." In earlier times, non-experts "were more aware of their ignorance than now" (1964, 14-18).

The medieval model "was not true," conceded Lewis. "But the meaning of the words 'know' and 'truth' in this context has begun to undergo a certain change." Up through the nineteenth century, "scientists and plain men"—despite some philosophers' musings—had held that "the 'truth' would be a sort of mental replica of the thing itself," that reality was something "ordinary imagination and conception could grasp." But physicists increasingly used models that were not held to be miniature replicas of reality, nor even close metaphorical analogies, but only mathematical codes or faintly suggestive riddles "like the sayings of the mystics." No longer was it possible to say we "know what the universe is like . . . no model we can build will be, in that old sense, 'like' it" (1964, 216-218).

In stressing that no cosmology could be a mental replica of the universe, Lewis also stated that a change from one model to another was as much a response to desires as to discoveries. Granted, discoveries of new facts did change particular hypotheses within a model. "But the change of the Model as a whole was not so simple an affair." The geocentric model of the universe, with much tinkering, had been able to keep up with observations. The old astronomy was not proven wrong; rather, the new seemed a simpler, better tool and appealed to "our ingrained conviction that Nature herself is thrifty." Preference also drove the shift from "from a devolutionary to an evolutionary scheme." Well before Darwin's theory, revolutionary and romantic attitudes had produced "the demand for a developing world." Only then did scientists ferret out evidence for that sort of universe. The new phenomena were not necessarily illusory, but nature "has all sorts of phenomena in stock and can suit many different tastes" (1964, 219-221). In short, "probably every age gets, within certain limits, the science it desires" (1967, 117).

Lewis thought that the human mind is affected by the prevalent cosmology of the time and culture in which the mind is located.

> But there is a two-way traffic; the Model is also influenced by the prevailing temper of mind. We must recognize that what has been called 'a taste in universes' is not only pardonable but inevitable. We can no longer dismiss the change of Models as a simple progress from error to truth. No Model is a catalogue of ultimate realities, and none is a mere fantasy. Each is a serious attempt to get in all the phenomena known at a given period, and each succeeds in getting in a great many. But also, no less surely, each reflects the prevalent psychology of an age almost as much as it reflects the state of that age's knowledge. (1964, 222)

In the future, a new model would not be constructed without evidence—but evidence would likely turn up "when the inner need for it becomes sufficiently great." Lewis, a lawyer's son, compared the construction of a cosmological model to cross-examination in court. Even if the questioner did not elicit any falsehoods from the witness, still the portion of total truth disclosed and the pattern it took would depend on "the shape of the examination." Lewis wryly remarked that "a good cross-examiner can work wonders." Of models constructed in various ages and cultures, each was to be respected but none idolized (1964, 222-223).

Perceiving every overall cosmology to be a constructed model, Lewis likewise regarded as constructs various entities posited by the sciences. In a 1956 article "Behind the Scenes," Lewis compared human consciousness to what appeared onstage in a play. He depicted the physical and human sciences as efforts to guess what was backstage, and he stressed the impossibility of actually getting backstage by scientific means to confirm whether such guesses corresponded to concrete realities. Psychologists might try to explain conscious thoughts and attitudes in terms of the unconscious, but things alleged to reside in the unconscious were, by definition, outside conscious awareness and were thus inaccessible to direct scrutiny. Physicists and biologists might account for seeing and hearing in terms of photons and sound waves affecting the nervous system; but when we look up, what our consciousness perceives is the sky, not photons; and when we hear someone speak, what our consciousness perceives is a voice, not sound waves. Whatever might be happening behind the scenes psychologically or physically, contended Lewis, we should not assume that consciousness is less real than, or can be reduced to, various backstage entities posited by science. Photons, sound waves, and the unconscious "are constructs, things assumed to account for our experience, but never to be experienced themselves." Even if probable, they remained hypothetical. Moreover, Lewis suggested, efforts to know the backstage mechanics of a stage production—even if successful—were less important than understanding the play's meaning. Such understanding depended on knowing "the teacher of the language in which this universal drama is being performed" (1970, 245-249).

Constructs of the Self and of God

Lewis insisted that consciousness has a reality of sorts, and he opposed positivistic tendencies to explain away consciousness; yet he did not deny that there is more to physical and psychological reality than seems immediately evident to consciousness. He spoke of consciousness as a façade, "the thinnest possible film on the surface of a vast deep." Although psychologists had rightly emphasized this, they had underestimated "the depth and variety of its contents." The self was a mystery deeper than its conscious surface, just as physics was a mystery deeper than seemingly solid surfaces. Penetrating to the deeps of the self or the deeps of physical objects would ultimately mean reaching "the point where something, in each case unimaginable, leaps forth from God's naked hand." God, as the ground of an individual's being and as the ground of matter, embraced and united both "in the daily miracle of finite consciousness" (1973, 79-80). Such a view, contrary to positivism, did not explain the higher in terms of the lower by making consciousness merely chemical, or by making reality merely propositional and mathematical. Rather, it made the mystery that enabled consciousness something higher: the mystery of God and his action.

Finite consciousness would be deceived unless it recognized its finiteness, its use of constructs, and the ineffable God as the ground of subject and object. The self and the physical surroundings were both façades. Physical surroundings were stage sets, and the self "a dramatic construction. . . . Normally I call this construction 'me,' and the stage set 'the real world.'" These facades would be deceptive if taken as ultimate realities, but prayer could bring awareness that "this 'real world' and 'real self' are very far from being rock-bottom realities." The aim was not to escape the "creaturely situation as a subject facing objects" but to be aware of that situation, and thus to be aware of God as the author of the whole drama, who made consciousness of self and objects possible (1973, 80).[24]

According to Lewis, "the bright blur in the mind which stands for God," as well as "the idea I call 'me,'" were constructs built by "the real I" from psychological odds and ends (1973, 78). There was a real self and a real God—on this Lewis insisted—but it was not safe to assume that the realities matched the constructs. Only God could show the real self beneath the supposed self. Only God—"the iconoclast"—could help us break through our images and ideas of him to a more authentic encounter with the living Lord. In prayer mental images of God were most helpful "when they are most fugitive and fragmentary . . . contradicting one another (in logic) as the crowded metaphors of a swift poet may do." The total effect conveyed a qualitative sense of God as

---

[24]Kevin Vanhoozer writes of *The drama of doctrine* (2005), developing at length the analogy of Christianity as a stage performance. Vanhoozer claims to offer "new metaphors for theology (dramaturgy), Scripture (the script), theological understanding (performance), the church (the company), and the pastor (director)" (2005c, xii). The stage metaphors are not exactly original with Vanhoozer. Indeed, Vanhoozer frequently draws on Lewis (Vanhoozer 2005c, 80, 180, 230, 254, 348, 363, 394). Vanhoozer's stimulating work may go overboard in using drama as *the* metaphor, rather than *one* metaphor among others.

personal and more than personal. Lewis spoke of "the wave of images . . . all momentary, all correcting, refining, 'interanimating' one another, and giving a kind of spiritual body to the unimaginable" (1973, 81-82).

Lewis valued precise, concrete, lively language over vague generalities about God. But he also understood that any attempt at greater precision in speaking of God would

> be only that of a model or symbol, certain to fail us in the long run and, even while we use it, requiring correction from other models. The humblest of us, in a state of Grace, can have some 'knowledge-by-acquaintance' (*connaître*), some 'tasting,' of Love Himself; but man even at his highest sanctity and intelligence has no direct 'knowledge about' (*savoir*) the ultimate Being— only analogies. (1960a, 174-175)

Lewis did not want his attempts at clear, concrete speech about God to be misconstrued as confidence that he had figured God out or had precisely defined God.[25]

Theology could provide a map of sorts to guide our knowledge of God and his ways. The theological map was not God, and was less real than experiences of God. Yet the map had the advantage of being based on many revelatory experiences much higher than our own. The map was necessary as a guide but must not be mistaken for the reality itself. Going to sea involved more than looking at a map; by the same token, going on a voyage without any map would be foolish and probably fatal (1952, 135-136).[26]

If world pictures produced by scientists and philosophers were at best partial, suggestive, and provisional (though in their heyday they seemed comprehensive, objective, and final), so too the world pictures constructed by theologians "turn out to be only shadows," even though they "look so solid while they last." Theological systems and doctrinal explanations, constructed in a particular time and cultural setting, might

---

[25]Lewis was wary of interpreting "one part of Scripture so that it contradicts other parts." But he also cautioned that some matters were more than our faculties could conceive or define in "a consistent formula." Scientists were wise to treat light as a wave and as a stream of particles, even though the two constructs could not be made consistent. Reality had to be self-consistent, "but till (if ever) we can *see* the consistency it is better to hold two inconsistent views than to ignore one side of the evidence." Lewis applied this to doctrines in tension, such as total dependence on grace versus the necessity of good works (2007, 355).

[26]In a somewhat similar vein, Paul Hiebert says that an epistemology of critical realism "sees knowledge as models, maps, or blueprints of reality" (1999, 76).

provide helpful hints in their setting but were bound to change as the setting changed. Systematized religious propositions, often taken to be more objective and real than participatory acts of relating to God, were less enduring and less in touch with the real that such acts. "It is religion itself—prayer and sacrament and repentance and adoration—which is here, in the long run, our sole avenue to the real." In God's presence, differences between various eras and cultures would fall away as inconsequential. Intellectual constructs and complexity could not hide us from God but would "vanish, leaving us naked in his presence" (1970, 46-47). Only then could one begin to know the true self that long lay below the surface level of consciousness: the self in its fallen squalor and redeemed splendor (1956, 291-293, 307-309).

To summarize Lewis's epistemological views, he posited logic and conscience to be capable of discerning truth, while being limited and fallible. He saw imagination as a capacity for conceiving reality through myth and metaphor. Logic, conscience, and imagination were all faculties rooted in an ultimate Reality that was personal. Much knowing depended on personal and communal virtue. Authority and tradition conveyed most of the knowledge people possessed of any subject. Christian Scripture and tradition provided reliable (though not inerrant) interaction with God's acts and personal character. Constructs of the world, the self, and the divine could aid knowing but were not exact replicas of reality.[27] This cautiously confident, emphatically personal rationality shaped Lewis's apologetics.

---

[27]Lewis's later writings may have stressed more than his earlier work the shadowy, provisional nature of most knowledge and the constructed character of our concepts about the universe, the self, and God. But this possible change of emphasis should not be construed as Lewis abandoning his earlier insistence on objective logic, morality, and beauty, nor should it be thought that only late in life did Lewis recognize that cosmologies, philosophies, and theologies are always inadequate and impermanent. The article cited in the previous paragraph, "Dogma and the Universe," was written in 1943. Still earlier, even before his conversion to Christianity, the young Lewis wrote in a 1926 letter, "No one is more convinced than I that reason is utterly inadequate to the richness and spirituality of real things; indeed this is itself a deliverance of reason" (2004a, 670-671).

CHAPTER 7

Lewis's Apologetics

Every mission field has the same basic need: for persons to live in relationship to the God revealed in Jesus Christ. But mission contexts, missionary understandings, and missionary competencies differ widely, so mission strategies differ accordingly. As a missional apologist, Lewis pursued a strategy that he considered urgent for his context, faithful to sound theology and epistemology, and suitable for his gifts. Lewis saw among white Britons a cramped mindset which assumed—usually through conditioning more than actual thinking—that God was nonexistent, irrelevant, or impersonal; and which reduced humans to irrational, amoral, impersonal bundles of sensations and urges. Drawing upon his logical and literary gifts, Lewis used various tactics to make Christianity plausible and personal. This chapter examines some important dimensions of Lewis's apologetics and shows recurring tendencies to stress plausibility and personhood.

Modest Expectations for Apologetics

Lewis considered Christianity to be plausible, not provable. He did not regard Christianity as a systematic set of propositions to be proved beyond reasonable doubt by deductive proofs or empirical data. Reality—especially reality involving human and divine personhood—was too vast, lively, and mysterious to be reduced to a static, abstract system. Moreover, arguments and evidence of the kind that could be marshaled in Christian apologetics were not capable of compelling consent from every rational person.[1] Lewis practiced cumulative case apologetics.[2] The most that could be expected was "*probable* evidence," not "mathematical certainty" (2004b, 448).[3]

Christian truth would never be "intellectually compulsive," at least not until Christ's return (1960d, 92). Christian belief in eternal life was a venture, wrote Lewis, not a demonstrable certainty. This left room for personal freedom and generosity (1973, 120-121). Christianity—like the existence of matter or the character of dear friends—was not a matter for "*demonstrative* proof" but was "far more probable than the alternatives." Was God "even interested in the kind of Theism which would be a compelled logical assent to a conclusive argument? Are *we* interested in it in personal matters?" Friendship involves trust "which is *certain* without demonstrative proof." To demand rigorous proof would indicate lack of personal confidence (2007, 75). According to Lewis, "there must always be just enough lack of demonstrative certainty to make free choice possible" (2007, 106).

Lewis did not think all Christians had to have a carefully argued basis for their beliefs. As indicated in the previous chapter, Lewis's epistemology treated authority and tradition as rational grounds for believing. Lewis also recognized that many Christians trusted the Lord based on a sense of personal encounter, apart from arguments or abstract analysis. Lewis heartily approved "thousands of simple affectional natures who begin, where we hope to end, with devotion to the person of Christ" (1967, 31). An intellectual approach could be the appointed

---

[1]This was a view Lewis held from his earliest days as a Christian. In 1931 he complained of incessant arguments in which "God might be defined as 'a Being who spends his time having his existence proved and disproved'" (2004b, 7). In 1938 he said he had never seen a proof of God or immortality that he found "absolutely compelling" (2004b, 233). Victor Reppert rightly says that although Lewis sounded at times like he was trying "to satisfy the requirements of strong rationalism . . . the reading of Lewis that fits his writing best as a whole is a reading of him as a critical rationalist" (Reppert 2003, 38).

[2]A classic delineation of the cumulative case method is philosopher Basil Mitchell's *The justification of religious belief* (1973). Mitchell was a regular participant in the Oxford Socratic Club, and in 1955 he succeeded Lewis as its president.

[3]In the divide between Christianity and naturalism, one side had to be wrong and must be misreading evidence, said Lewis. But this did not mean that the error was obvious or that those making it were irrational. Otherwise disagreement would not have persisted. Christians did "not necessarily claim to have demonstrative proof" (1960d, 15, 21).

road to God for some people, but it was not the only, or the safest, path (1980, 27). Lewis thought argument was helpful for a limited number: "Some people can be converted on rational grounds, but more can't." Rather than get flustered by this, the apologist had to accept that everything depended on God. The Lord could use apologetics in some cases but usually chose other means to draw people to himself (2007, 494).

Lewis approved preachers who used a direct, emotional "Come to Jesus" appeal, though he himself lacked the gift for it. He thought that "the ideal missionary team" might involve both an arguer and a preacher: the first to undermine intellectual prejudices against Christianity, and the second to make the evangelistic appeal (1970, 99). Lewis also thought personal testimony by non-preachers could make an impact, though again he did not feel himself gifted for that. He thought his conversion story involved too many "highbrow" philosophical issues to attract many ordinary people to Christianity (2004b, 568, 575, 605). In addition, Lewis valued non-verbal witness. People who resisted arguments "may be unable to resist *lives*" (2004b, 59). Christian conduct aided others' conversion more than preaching did (2007, 576). Real holiness would be irresistible: "If even 10% of the world's population had it, would not the whole world be converted and happy before a year's end?" (2007, 352)

It is clear that Lewis regarded apologetics as just one part, and far from the most important part, of Christian witness, even though he felt gifted and called to it. It is also clear that Lewis felt apologetics to be dangerous for his own spiritual wellbeing. The main danger came not from his opponents' arguments, but from his own best arguments. Lewis tended to find a Christian doctrine most dubious and dim right after successfully defending it (1970, 128; 2004b, 573, 730; 2007, 762). He did not take this as an indication that making a rational case for Christian truths was an illegitimate, counterproductive enterprise. Rather, he took it as a sign that apologists, though temporarily treating Christianity as a conceptual hypothesis and offering evidence and arguments for the sake of inquirers, must never base their faith on their own rational powers nor regard their own conceptual construct as the object of faith.[4] Apologists could "be saved only by falling back con-

---

[4]Lewis also thought that in God's arrangement, an apologist could help others but not himself, so that the apologist would not fall into proud autonomy but would in turn rely on other Christians to help him in his walk with God (2004b, 497, 953).

tinually from the web of our own arguments... into the Reality—from Christian apologetics into Christ himself" (1970, 103). In 1942 Lewis wrote his "Apologist's evening hymn":

From all my lame defeats and oh! much more
From all the victories I have seemed to score;
From cleverness shot forth in Thy behalf,
At which, while angels weep, the audience laugh;
From all my proofs of Thy divinity,
Thou, who would'st give no sign, deliver me.
Thoughts are but coins. Let me not trust, instead
Of Thee, the thumb-worn image of Thy head;
From every thought, even from my thoughts of Thee,
Oh thou fair Silence! fall and set me free.
Lord of the strait way and the needle's eye,
Take from me all my trumpery lest I die. (2004b, 527)

In short, strict rationalism was not the main ground of Lewis's faith nor was it the key to his apologetic strategy. The modest goal of apologetics was to make Christianity more plausible for persons of a particular type, as preparation for such persons to trust the person of Christ.

Undermining Bogus Certitudes

Christianity is bound to seem implausible to people who take for granted patterns of thought that exclude Christian realities. Lewis viewed naturalism as the reigning orthodoxy among intellectuals. Among the masses, few decisively embraced atheism, but most were under "the evil enchantment of worldliness" (1980, 7) in which God was not so much denied as ignored. Their godless worldview was less a deliberate choice or a reasoned conclusion than an assumption produced by a spirit-smothering smallness. They lived in "a tiny windowless universe" which they mistook as "the only possible universe" (1967, 31). In a cramped world where nothing was real unless it could be measured and manipulated, the unseen and eternal seemed unreal and irrelevant. Not just eternity but personality fell prey to worldly reductionism. Lewis strove to undermine bogus certitudes so that such people would rediscover the personal and become more open to the possibility of Christianity being true.

He did this partly through offering the sort of diagnostic observations and epistemological views noted in earlier chapters. Those who imbibed skepticism about religion during their schooling might become

153

more skeptical about skepticism itself if they saw how their attitudes had been shaped not by clear thinking but by schools' propaganda, nasty competitiveness, and soul-smothering bureaucracy. Those holding evolutionary monism, whether materialistic or pantheistic, might be slower to dismiss Christianity as a myth if they saw evolutionism itself as a myth that was aided by political currents and "the rise of the machines." Those who dismissed ancient insights, assuming newer is better, might feel less sure if their attitude was called "chronological snobbery," not "progressiveness." Those enthralled by scientism might have second thoughts if they learned of an old kinship between scientists, astrologers, and magicians. Those who saw science as a grand entity that could explain and control all things without reference to God might reconsider if they could see science as a cluster of provisional constructs based on a methodology of truncated thought and influenced by psychological preferences. Those who exalted autonomous reason and derided religious authority might be more open to biblical and church teachings if they realized that 99 percent of all the other things they believed had been accepted on authority.

Another way Lewis sought to undermine bogus certainties was to make them a matter of debate. His role in the Oxford Socratic Club should be seen in this light. In describing "The founding of the Oxford Socratic Club" (1970, 126-128), Lewis spoke of establishing "an arena specially devoted to the conflict between Christian and unbeliever" in which people would "follow the argument wherever it leads." Some Christians might question the propriety and wisdom of making Christianity a matter of weekly debate, vulnerable to argument. Such concern may have some legitimacy. Yet it is clear from the wider range of Lewis's writings that he did not suppose Christian truth to stand or fall from week to week, depending on the latest arguments. In making Christianity a matter of debate, he was making non-Christian thinking a matter of debate, thus undermining the settled certitude of unbelief that was too common in the university context.[5]

Perceiving naturalistic certitudes to be common among theologians and clergy, Lewis suggested that often such thinking was "not honestly come by" but was merely a matter of plunging into ideas that "seemed modern and successful" (1946b). Lewis challenged the supposedly assured results of New Testament scholarship and suggested to seminary students that higher criticism of gospel texts was just "a school of theo-

[5]See Hooper (1992) and Mitchell (1997) for accounts of Lewis's Socratic role.

logical thought" that might "blow over" at any time, as similar approaches had already faded from other disciplines. Lewis called for agnosticism of a sort: "I do not wish to reduce the sceptical element in your minds. I am only suggesting that it need not be reserved exclusively for the New Testament and the Creeds. Try doubting something else" (1967, 217, 220).

That sentence encapsulates a significant strand of Lewis's apologetic: "Try doubting something else." Become less sure of bogus certitudes that block access to the most important realities. Naturalistic monism—"everythingism," the mindset underlying both atheistic materialism and religious pantheism—had to seem less plausible in order for Christianity to seem more plausible. Lewis thought that a key part of an apologist's task in relation to unbelievers was to "undermine their intellectual prejudices" (1970, 99). Casting doubt upon widespread non-Christian assumptions would not show Christianity to be true. Indeed, Beversluis charges that in attacking the credibility of competing views, Lewis's apologetic "runs the risk of making Christianity appear to be little more than the best of a bad lot" (1985, 92). But seldom will anyone seriously consider an alternate view if they complacently take their own for granted. In a context where default assumptions ran contrary to Christian truths, anything Lewis could do to break the grip of those assumptions, or even loosen that grip somewhat, might help liberate minds and open fresh possibilities for belief.

Influencing Plausibility Structures

Lewis called for Christians to infiltrate various realms of culture, infuse them with latently Christian presuppositions, and thus influence Britain's plausibility structures. Otherwise, direct presentations and arguments for Christianity might get people's attention briefly, but then people would be "plunged back into a world where the opposite position is taken for granted. As long as that situation exists, widespread success is simply impossible." Lewis thought that materialism spread most effectively not through books directly arguing for materialistic philosophy but through materialistic assumptions pervading other books. Christians had to produce more books, not about Christianity as such, but about all sorts of things, with Christian assumptions latent (1970, 93; see also 2004b, 683; 2007, 502).

Although the salvation of just one soul mattered more than all cultural masterworks (1967, 13; 1980, 19), culture still mattered—if for no other reason than that culture shaped souls for better or worse (1980, 28). For Lewis, people were not isolated monads but cultural and social beings. Therefore, Christians had to do more than seek to persuade individuals; they had to affect the cultural milieu. "If we are to convert our heathen neighbors, we must understand their culture. We must 'beat them at their own game'" (1967, 22-23). Lewis's goal of influencing a culture's plausibility structure can be termed "indirect apologetics" (Purtill 1998, 84) or "cultural evangelism" (Burson and Walls 1998, 258).

Modern Western culture was so inhospitable to Christian claims, thought Lewis, that it might be necessary to inject the best elements of paganism into the culture before Christianity could gain a hearing. By paganism, Lewis meant "the ancient pre-Christian religions." He thought paganism was closer to reality than "the common modern pseudo-scientific attitude" (2007, 199). The best pagan philosophy upheld logic and objective morality. The best pagan myths evoked a sense of awe at the supernatural, of personality in deity, of guilt, atonement, and resurrection. Such logic, morality, and myth—so important in Lewis's own epistemology—might help undo antirational pragmatism, moral relativism, and lack of wonder or curiosity. Moreover, the study of old pagan writers could undermine chronological snobbery and foster a mentality more open to historical gospel truths. Lewis thought that the loss of classical learning in Britain had contributed to atheism among intellectuals (2004b, 93); conversely, he thought that restoration of such learning to schools and universities might alter Britain's plausibility structure in favor of Christianity.

As a way to influence the plausibility structure of academia, Lewis said that "what we very badly need is a new, frankly high-brow, periodical" that would "not be specifically Christian" but would work within the boundaries of the *Tao* (2004b, 757). He wanted this scholarly periodical "to come before the public with *no* explicitly religious pretensions at all." He wanted it to be run by Christians but also to accept articles from non-Christians writing within "the 'good Pagan' range of rationality and virtue." While stressing that he did not regard pagan standards as more important than Christian standards, Lewis said,

> I consider the tactics I have suggested more likely in the long run to do what a periodical can towards the conversion of educated people in England. In every other age the preaching of Christianity has been able to presuppose the light of nature in its hearers. . . . All these had already some kind of ethics, a be-

lief in reason, and often high standards of family, tribal, or civic duty. Where there is total scepticism the call to repentance and the promise of forgiveness *must* fall completely flat. Early Christian preachers were fighting for the Supernatural against Nature. What we are up against is the anti-Natural. The rehabilitation of the Natural (though only of course as a preliminary to its conquest by the Supernatural) seems to me the greatest service a periodical could do today. (2004b, 772-774)

In Lewis's academic lectures, he did not directly advocate Christianity; rather, he sought to nudge university scholarship toward a place where Christianity would be more plausible. For instance, the lectures comprising *The abolition of man* (1996) insisted on objective logic and morality, without saying anything about salvation in Christ.

Much of Lewis's scholarly work depicted the thoughts and attitudes of long-ago writers, whose perspectives were often decidedly closer to Christianity than to naturalism.[6] *A preface to Paradise Lost* (1942) not only told *about* Milton but helped the reader to see through Milton's eyes—that is, more Christianly. Lewis's massive *English literature in the sixteenth century* opened with a lengthy introduction tellingly titled "New learning and new ignorance" (1954, 1-65), showing that the dawning of modernity brought great losses of knowledge as well as great gains. *An experiment in criticism* showed how literature could help the reader to "see with myriad eyes" (1961, 141)—taking one beyond the cramped confines of a self shaped by scientism and presentism. *The discarded image* (1964) was more than a scholarly portrait of an outdated cosmology; it unveiled a different way of seeing the world, and suggested that naturalistic cosmology was a construct that left out many things. In reading it, marveled A. N. Wilson (at the time an agnostic and far from a devotee of Lewis), "We have actually had our picture of the universe changed for ever" (1990, 152).

Lewis's vision for influencing plausibility structures extended beyond the academy to the wider population of those less educated but still intelligent and curious. "The first step in the conversion of this country" would be the writing of implicitly Christian, affordable books

---

[6]Lewis hoped that his own discipline of English Literature would be mainly historical, a "Time Machine" to rid people of "their chronological provincialism by plunging them into the thought and feeling of ages other than their own." He was disappointed when Oxford and Cambridge turned away from such an approach for the most part (2007, 1371).

at a popular level introducing various sciences and other subjects, with the excellence to "beat the *Penguin* and the *Thinkers Library* on their own ground" (1970, 93).

In the realm of popular fiction, Lewis saw opportunities to reach individuals and culture in a way that could indirectly make Christianity more plausible and desirable. He found superb the sort of "theological shocker" produced by G. K. Chesterton and Charles Williams, and he was delighted that such "substantial edification . . . must be reaching the ordinary thriller-reader" (2004b, 198).

Employing his own imaginative and literary gifts, Lewis tried to do something similar. The genre of science fiction had been dominated by the likes of H. G. Wells and had been conveying naturalistic scientism—"Wellsianity" (1980, 79). Lewis wanted "to conquer for my own (Christian) point of view what has always hitherto been used by the opposite side" (2004b, 236-237), so he wrote *Out of the silent planet* (1938). After its publication, Lewis remarked that "any amount of theology can now be smuggled into people's minds under cover of romance without their knowing it." He thought this could be "a help to the evangelization of England," if only there were a Christian writer with more time and talent than he possessed (2004b, 262). Lewis went on to write *Perelandra* (2003 [1944]) and *That hideous strength* (1946a), "trying to redeem . . . 'science fiction'" and to offer an implicitly Christian "critique of our own age" (2007, 1178). Each story in the space trilogy contained "imaginative hypotheses illustrating what I believe to be theological truths (2007, 465).

Likewise, the Narnia books—though initially prompted by mental images unrelated to Christianity and by an author's itch to write— became a way for Lewis to "steal past a certain inhibition" that kept people from feeling the real power of the Christian story. Many, like Lewis, had been brought up in church and had often been told to feel a certain way about God and about Jesus' sufferings. "An obligation to feel can freeze feeling." Also, reverence in church was often associated with "lowered voices, as if it were something medical." In short, a certain kind of church experience could impede a heartfelt response to the gospel. "But supposing that by casting all these things into an imaginary world, stripping them of their stained glass and Sunday school associations, one could make them for the first time appear in their real potency? Could one not thus steal past those watchful dragons? I thought one could." The inhibitions that affected children's minds could "exist in a grown-up's mind too, and may perhaps be overcome by the same means" (1982, 47-48). With the gospel embedded in a fairy-tale, "the reader is taken off his guard" (2007, 1075).[7]

Most books designed to teach Christianity to children struck Lewis as "namby-pamby and 'sissie' and calculated to nauseate any child worth his salt." The Narnia books connected with some children though not others (2007, 1011). Lewis expressed "hope that the Narnian infiltration may bear a little fruit" (2007, 441). In this indirect infiltration, he did not aim at immediate conversion but, as he told George Sayer, he wanted "to make it easier for children to accept Christianity when they met it later in life" (Sayer 1988, 192). These seven fairy tales, like the science fiction trilogy, were Lewis's way of entering a popular genre, claiming cultural ground, and preparing minds to find Christianity plausible.[8]

As Lewis diagnosed declining confidence in reason and diminishing interest in truth among British people, he thought that stories might still get their attention and expand their minds in a way favorable to Christianity. With classical education fading and fewer students encountering ancient myths, Lewis sought to provide contemporary myths. Ancient myths, thought Lewis, had evoked Christ in unconscious, fragmentary fashion, but Lewis's quasi-mythic tales of Narnia and other planets were consciously written to evoke "the true myth." In addition, Lewis retold the ancient myth of Cupid and Psyche in *Till we have faces* (1956). In this, his favorite book, he evoked the power of myth, even as he portrayed the kind of resentment felt by agnostics and lukewarm Christians toward loved ones who were converted or followed a calling (2007, 590). Unlike the "frontal attacks" of his directly apologetic works, Lewis's indirect approach aimed at "catching the

---

[7]"The whole Narnian story is about Christ," explained Lewis in a 1961 letter. "*The Magician's Nephew* tells the creation and how evil entered Narnia. *The Lion etc*—the Crucifixion and Resurrection. *Prince Caspian*—restoration of the true religion after a corruption. *The Horse and His Boy*—the calling and conversion of a heathen. *The Voyage of the Dawn Treader*—the spiritual life (specially in Reepicheep). *The Silver Chair*—the continued war against the powers of darkness. *The Last Battle*—the coming of Antichrist (the Ape). The end of the world, and the Last Judgement" (2007, 1244-1245).

[8]Stephen M. Smith (1998) speaks of the Narnia books as "pre-apologetics" that move the imagination toward new assumptions, making Christianity more plausible and undermining naturalism. Smith offers examples of how the stories deflate skepticism, defuse projection theories of religion, and deny syncretistic pluralism. For more on how the Narnia books promote Christianity, see Downing (2005b), Hooper (1979), and Myers (1998).

reader unawares—through fiction and symbol" (2007, 651). Lewis's varied writings, "scholarly, fantastic, theological," could make him seem to be "a man who impersonates half a dozen authors" (2007, 891), but underlying his forays into various genres at different intellectual levels was a unity of thought and a missionary determination to do all he could to foster "the spread of an intellectual (and imaginative) climate favorable to Christianity" (1970, 221).

Direct Presentation

Not all of Lewis's apologetic work was indirect. He also sought to change minds through direct presentation of Christian claims. He prioritized "translating" the historic gospel for specific audiences to make it plain, interesting, and plausible for them. He also deployed specific lines of argument, as well as comparisons of overall worldviews, to show Christianity to be the most personal and plausible among competing hypotheses.

Audience-Specific Translation

Lewis considered it essential for apologists and preachers to know orthodox Christianity and to know their specific audience.[9] The main message was to be found in the Bible and in the authoritative core tradition of the church, not in the latest theology. The main audience was ordinary people, not clergy. Therefore, Christian communicators had to study people.[10] "The proper study of shepherds is sheep, not (save accidentally) other shepherds. And woe to you if you do not evangelize" (1967, 204). Lewis geared most of his own apologetic and theological writings toward English people who were of above-average intelligence but would not be classed as intellectuals or extremely learned. He chose

[9]Lewis urged preachers "to present that which is timeless . . . in the particular language of our own age. The bad preacher does exactly the opposite: he takes the ideas of our own age and tricks them out in the traditional language of Christianity. . . But your teaching must be timeless at its heart and wear modern dress" (1970, 93-94).

[10]Lewis detested theological modernism, but even orthodox modern theologians might "say in 10 pages of polysyllabic abstraction what Scripture or the old writers would say in a couple of sentences," or they might be so "terribly repetitive" that they would fill a book with what could have been said in a paragraph (2007, 979). Lewis opposed "watering down the message to suit" the tastes of unspiritual masses. But it was necessary to "*translate* it into terms which those who are *educationally* 'the masses' can understand." Nobody would respond to "an unintelligible call" (2007, 1358-1359).

his vocabulary level, metaphors, and brevity with such people in mind. He thought that for other types of people, other translators could do better than he could do.[11]

Lewis could marshal evidence and formulate arguments, as shown below. But he deployed argumentative methods "less often than many have imagined. More often he helps us step inside the tradition, and in doing so, he enlarges our vision" (Meilaender 1978, 240-241). Metaphor occupied a prominent place in his epistemological views, so in offering much-needed translation of Christian claims, Lewis chose metaphors and vivid analogies that would convey the message in a way that resonated with the segment of people he sought to reach. As Chad Walsh points out, "This use of analogy is no form of proof. . . . A way of looking at things has simply been proposed, and the reader finds himself, if not persuaded, at least loosened up, ready to consider a possibility that, presented in the abstract, might stir the theorizing mind but not take on a kind of everyday plausibility" (Walsh 1979, 204).

Lewis laced his sermons and non-fiction writings on Christianity with homely examples, striking similes, and lively metaphors. For many people, such language would feel more concrete and thus more plausible than abstractions. Lewis also designed some of his fiction as a vehicle for quite direct presentations of apologetic arguments and theology. The subtitle of *The pilgrim's regress* (1989) identifies it as an "apology." *The Screwtape letters* (1960c) and *The great divorce* (1946b) were both originally published serially in popular periodicals before being put into book form. Such stories were not so much literature as propaganda.[12] Lewis did not regard these works as literary on a level with *Perelandra* (2003) or *Till We Have Faces* (1956). By attaching Christian claims and arguments to a narrative framework, Lewis could elicit a sense of personal engagement and of action, of momentous *happenings* in the un-

[11]When invited to write Christian material for British factory workers, Lewis replied that he could not do so because he knew nothing of factory life. Someone in the Christian Workers Union would be more familiar with the vernacular the workers actually spoke and would have firsthand knowledge of what questions and needs to address (2004a, 674). Similarly, Lewis thought that Americans would need a translator other than himself, since their vernacular was "not quite the same as that into which I have translated. Small differences, in addressing proletarians, may be all-important" (2007, 1006).

[12]Here I use "propaganda" descriptively, not negatively: such works propagated Christianity unabashedly, without aiming at high literary finesse or philosophical rigor. They approached matters from a different angle than sermons usually did; but, like sermons, they offered explicit theology and argument propagating Christian claims.

seen world. People who shied away from sermons or essays would perhaps attend to exposition and argument if it came in intermittent doses during the course of a story. People who avoided essays might still read stories (1994a, 36). Thus Lewis sought to translate Christianity and reach people where they were, speaking language that would connect with their vocabulary and using formats that would command their attention.

Arguments from Aspects of Personhood

Lewis's arguments for theism appealed to aspects of human personhood and inner experience, not to inferences from observed patterns in the physical world. Like Pascal before him, Lewis found theistic arguments based on evidence of design in nature to be very weak, even counterproductive. A world dominated by pain, futility, and death hardly constituted obvious proof of a perfectly good and all-powerful Creator. Rather, it was the strongest case for atheism. Religion had not originated in arguments from design. Indeed, people in earlier ages—lacking modern pain relievers and technology, and with much lower life expectancy—were more familiar with pain, futility, and death than modern people. Religion had not begun as an inference from nature (1955a, 1-4; 2004b, 747; 2007, 195).

In chapter 1 of *The problem of pain*, Lewis purported not mainly to argue for Christianity but to describe its origin. He asserted that all developed religions arose in three stages, with Christianity adding a fourth stage. At the first stage, religion began with a sense of awe in the presence of the numinous. At the second stage came a sense of moral obligation and of guilt: approving a moral code yet disobeying it. Positing the numinous and the moral both involved jumps beyond any inference from physical facts. Thus the numinous and the moral either had to be mere quirks of the mind or else supernatural and revelatory. The numinous and moral were not always linked—priestly worship of gods was often separate from philosophical discussions of ethics. At the third stage of religion, the numinous being who prompted awe was understood to be the same as the being behind moral law. In many cultures, "non-moral religion, and non-religious morality," were common, yet the awesome and the moral were linked by "great individuals in all times and places," and were fully linked by one particular people: the Jews. This linkage of numinous and moral, identifying the awesome Creator with the moral Lawgiver, produced "increased health." So it

162

was either a lucky bit of craziness, or revelation. The fourth stage was a historical event, the appearance among the Jews of a man claiming oneness with the Creator/Lawgiver. According to Lewis, Jesus had to be an abominable lunatic or the incarnate Lord he claimed to be. If he was Lord, Christian claims that he died and rose again became credible, as did the claim that his death somehow changed for the better our relationship to the awesome, moral God (1955a, 4-12).

> To ask whether the universe as we see it looks more like the work of a wise and good Creator or the work of chance, indifference, or malevolence, is to omit from the outset all the relevant factors in the religious problem. Christianity is not the conclusion of a philosophical debate on the origins of the universe: it is a catastrophic historical event following on the long spiritual preparation of humanity. (1955a, 12)

Lewis said that at any of these stages of religious development, a person could rebel without logical absurdity but "not without violence to his own nature." Rejecting the numinous would cut a person off from many of humanity's great poets and prophets, from what he sensed in childhood, and from "the richness and depth of uninhibited experience." Regarding moral law as illusory would cut a person off from "the common ground of humanity." Refusing to unite the awesome with the moral, a person could pursue barbarous worship of "sexuality, or the dead, or the life-force, or the future." Denying the Incarnation, though logically an option, involved denying the goodness and sanity of the person seen by many to be the wisest and best of humans, as well as rejecting a "message from the core of reality" that was "strangely like many myths which have haunted religion," yet possessed the unexpected, rough texture of a reality we could not merely have made up (1955a, 12-13).

Lewis's approach in the introductory chapter of *The problem of pain* marked much of his directly apologetic material. Viewing the numinous, the moral, and their union as three stages in religion history that were preparatory for Christianity, Lewis evidently thought some modern individuals needed to pass through similar preparation before they could understand the gospel and receive it as good news. Viewing various human capacities and kinds of experience as signs of the divine, Lewis argued that rejection of theism, even if logically possible, tended to debunk or to violate core elements of human personhood.

Awestruck dread at the numinous was linked to desire for the infinite. Lewis used "Joy" as a technical term for "an unsatisfied desire which is itself more desirable than any other satisfaction" (1955b, 17-18). This bittersweet pang, vital in Lewis's own journey to faith, could come in conjunction with experiences of various things but was never satisfied by those things and could not be reduced to aesthetic experience. The longing drew Lewis—and could draw others—into the numinous realm, "the region of awe." It pointed to "a road right out of the self, a commerce with something which, by refusing to identify itself with any object of the senses, or anything whereof we have biological or social need, or anything imagined, or any state of our own minds, proclaims itself sheerly objective" (1955b, 221).[13]

Lewis thought that most, if not all, people had stabs of bittersweet longing. However, various intellectual movements in the 1900s had in common "enmity to 'immortal longings'" (1989, 10). Such thinking suppressed spiritual desire and implanted "the inner wiseacre, the *Jailer*," who dismissed the invitation to paradise as "wishful thinking." The proper reaction to such "sham realism" was to be even more realistic by attending more closely to one's actual experience of life with all its "quivering and wonder" (1986, 53-55). A "sensible" modern could repress that part of himself and debunk such desire as an illusion of childhood and adolescence, not to be taken seriously by grownups. However, if infinite happiness really beckoned, "it would be a pity to find out too late (a moment after death) that by our supposed 'common sense' we had stifled in ourselves the faculty of enjoying it."[14]

---

[13] In a study of Lewis's theory of spiritual longing, Carnell notes the "parallel to Anselm's ontological argument" and regards it as "Lewis's most significant contribution to Christian apologetics" (1974, 164). Unlike Anselm, Lewis suggested that "the dialectic of desire" involved not just arguing for, but living through, "a sort of ontological proof" (1989, 10). Lewis wrote, "I don't think we can initially argue from the *concept* of Perfect Being to its existence." Still, desire for the infinite was a suggestive clue. Moreover, some people had tasted something of God, and Lewis thought that the ontological argument may have arisen "as a partially unsuccessful translation of an experience without concepts or words." In trying to formulate such experience into a concept and a syllogism, "did they really, inside, argue from the experienced glory that it could not be generated subjectively?" (1967, 188) Human longings and hopes raised the question, "How could an idiotic universe have produced creatures whose mere dreams are so much stronger, better, subtler than itself?" (2007, 75) This was the thrust of a passage in *The silver chair* involving Puddleglum (1994f, 182-191). Of this passage, Lewis stated that, borrowing from Anselm and Descartes, he had "simply put the 'Ontological Proof' in a form suitable for children" (2007, 1472).

[14] Philosopher John Beversluis, true to form, suggests that people "who neither have been nor want to be 'stabbed' by this bittersweet sense of loss" are wise. Those who do experience the longing should, as they mature, learn to ignore such mislead-

Lewis reasoned, "If I find in myself a desire which no experience in this world can satisfy, the most probable explanation is that I was made for another world." Earthly blessings were never meant to satisfy desire but to awaken it to something greater (1952, 120; 1980, 8-9).[15]

As longing and wonder were subjective human capacities designed to respond to objective divine glory, so conscience was a human capacity designed to respond to objective divine goodness. This tenet of Lewis's epistemology, together with his diagnosis that few moderns felt a desperate need to be forgiven by God, moved him to produce his first radio talks focusing on "Right and wrong as a clue to the meaning of the universe."

Lewis started with the sort of appeals to fairness and common decency that crop up daily in personal relationships. Everybody uses moral language, he observed, and such talk would be empty unless it presupposed an external, objective "Rule about Right and Wrong." Our inner sense of an outer standard of right and wrong cannot be reduced to mere physical processes, biological instincts, or social conventions. We know conscience within more surely than we know such things, argued Lewis, for the thing we know best "is Man. We do not merely observe men, we *are* men." Knowing humanity from the inside, we know that we sense obligation to a moral law which we did not invent and have not obeyed. We sense that Something beyond us urges us to do right and makes us uneasy when we do wrong, and "we have to assume that it is more like a mind than it is like anything else we know—because after all the only other thing we know is matter and you can hardly imagine a bit of matter giving instructions." Therefore, it makes the most sense to regard conscience as a signal from a mind-

---

ing "inner states," rather than heeding Lewis's argument from desire. "The pursuit of Joy is a childish thing . . . it is simply adolescent disenchantment elevated to cosmic status" (Beversluis 1985, 30).

[15]Hyatt (1997) and Kreeft (1989) offer mainly positive analyses of Lewis's argument from desire. According to Kreeft, Lewis claimed to offer not an irrefutable proof but "a hypothesis that explains the data better than any other" and shows "the practical necessity of taking this desire seriously. . . . Like Pascal's 'Wager,' the argument here shows that you are a fool if you turn your back on this strong clue, this strong probability that infinite happiness exists and that you are designed to enjoy it" (Kreeft 1989, 254). Ironically, Kreeft and Beversluis—philosophers with diametrically opposite assessments of Lewis—were classmates at the same Christian Reformed high school and at Calvin College. Kreeft became Roman Catholic; Beversluis traded strict Calvinism for agnosticism.

like entity with consciousness, purposes, preferences—who, being absolutely good, "must hate most of what we do" (1952, 17-39).[16]

Lewis's moral argument (see also 1960b, 53-60) aimed to make theism more plausible and to "create, or recover, the sense of guilt" (2004a, 470).[17] The argument was personal throughout: it began in personal experience, pointed to a Being with personal traits, and aimed to awaken a personal sense of desperate need for a personal Savior.

Another dimension of human personhood Lewis linked to the divine was love. His manner of doing this was less directly apologetic than some of his other arguments, but it may still be called "the argument from agape" (Burson and Wall 1998, 181-183). This line of thinking appeared in various works (1946a, 1946b, 84-105; 1956; 1960c, 120-124; 1980, 93-105), but the clearest, fullest statement came in *The four loves* (1960a). A preliminary chapter discussed love for the subhuman, such as love of nature and love of country. Then came chapters on "the four loves" as such: family affection, friendship, eros, and charity (agape/divine gift-love). Lower forms of love could serve as training for higher forms of love and could serve as "glorious images of divine Love," but unless subordinated to God, such loves were bound to degenerate eventually into "complicated forms of hatred" which could verge on the demonic (1960a, 20). The loves could not remain themselves except with God's help, in right relation to him, and empowered by "the Divine energy" of the eternal love within the Trinity (1960a, 166, 175). Each form of natural love had to be "taken up into, and made the tuned and obedient instrument of, Love Himself." Patterned on the Incarnation, in which Christ's perfect manhood was taken into his perfect deity, "the natural loves are called to become perfect Charity and also perfect natural loves" (1960a, 184).

---

[16]N. T. Wright thinks Lewis here managed to highlight "features of human existence that are puzzling and interesting and point beyond themselves" but failed in his intent to provide an inexorable, step-by-step theistic proof: "the logic doesn't quite work" (Wright 2007, 31). Though correct about what Lewis succeeded in doing, Wright misreads Lewis's intent. Lewis did not intend to provide a rigorous, logical demonstration of God's existence. The first section of *Mere Christianity* is not titled "Morality as a proof of God" but "Right and wrong as a *clue* to the meaning of the universe" [emphasis mine].

[17]Lewis thought "most apologetic begins a stage too far on. The first step is to create, or recover, the sense of guilt" (2004a, 470). His first radio talks were "an attempt to convince people that there is a moral law, that we disobey it, and that the existence of a Lawgiver is at least very probable and also (*unless* you add the Christian doctrine of the Atonement) imparts despair rather than comfort" (2004a, 484-485).

Traits of human personhood such as deep longing, conscience, and love could, if one insisted, be regarded as mere biological byproducts "without running into flat self-contradiction and nonsense," conceded Lewis. "Whether you can do so without extreme unplausibility—without accepting a picture of things which no one really believes—is another matter." Still, since naturalists insisted on denying such vital aspects of humanity, Lewis zeroed in on the one human capacity that even a naturalist "cannot deny without (philosophically speaking) cutting his own throat," namely, human reasoning (1960b, 54). If all thoughts were nothing but physical effects caused by an evolutionary process of random change and natural selection, argued Lewis, then all our reasoning would be discredited (including the reasoning that concocted evolutionary naturalism).[18] This argument had led Lewis himself to abandon materialism (1955b, 208-209), and Lewis used variations of the argument from reason again and again throughout his life (e.g. 1960b, 17-36; 1967, 82-85, 122-123; 1970, 135-138, 274-276; 1980, 88-89; 2007, 1338-1339). [19] If "thoroughgoing Naturalism leads to self-

[18]Lewis followed an approach earlier taken by G. K. Chesterton, who wrote, "There is a thought that stops all thought," and derided epistemology rooted in Darwinian naturalism as "movements in the brain of a bewildered ape" (1990, 33). Earlier, Darwin himself had agonized over the implications of his theory for human cognition: "With me the horrid doubt always arises whether the convictions of a man's mind . . . are of any value or at all trustworthy. Would anyone trust in the convictions of a monkey's mind, if there are any convictions in such a mind?" (1887, 255) Lewis's atheist contemporary J. B. S. Haldane stated frankly, "If my mental processes are determined wholly by the motions of atoms in my brain, I have no reason to suppose that my beliefs are true" (1928, 209), a statement Lewis quoted (1960b, 22). More recently, Darwinian philosopher Richard Rorty has insisted, "The idea that one species of organism is, unlike all the others, oriented not just toward its own increased prosperity but toward Truth, is as un-Darwinian as the idea that every human being has a built-in moral compass—a conscience" (Rorty 1995, 33). Yet Beversluis slams Lewis's "argument from reason" for constructing straw men and false dilemmas (1985, 58-83). Alvin Plantinga, like Lewis, argues that evolutionary naturalism defeats itself by implying that our cognitive faculties are unreliable (1993, 194-237; 1996; 2000, 227-240). Philosopher Victor Reppert (2003) ably develops and defends Lewis's argument from reason. Reppert does not claim that "the argument from reason closes the case against naturalism" but says that it provides "some substantial reasons for preferring theism to naturalism" (2003, 128).

[19]At a 1948 meeting of the Oxford Socratic Club, Roman Catholic philosopher Elizabeth Anscombe criticized weaknesses of Lewis's argument in chapter 3 of the 1947 edition of *Miracles*, "The self-contradiction of the naturalist" (see Anscombe 1981, 224-232). This meeting coincided with Lewis becoming less involved in rigorous debate and more engaged in literary pursuits. Some have suggested that Lewis

contradiction in epistemology" (2004a, 715), it would be best to reject naturalism in favor of some form of theism that could take the mind seriously, accepting that human reason was created and illumined by God's reason.

As Lewis premised his theistic arguments on aspects of human personhood (desire, conscience, love, and reason), he defended against the main atheistic argument—that suffering was incompatible with God's existence—by invoking yet another feature of personhood: freedom. God, out of his own freedom, created angels and humans as personal beings, not automata, with freedom to choose. Some angels chose to rebel, and all humans made sinful choices.[20] Suffering resulted from living in a world afflicted by the consequences of angelic and human abuses of freedom. At the same time, God could use suffering to rouse complacent persons and to shape them in his likeness (1955a; 1960b, 196-197). Moreover, in Jesus' suffering, the Lord was personally involved in our pain (1973, 41-44; 2001, 28, 44).

When arguing not just for theism but for Christianity specifically, Lewis again appealed to personality: Jesus' personality. Jesus talked as though he was God. He did so in a context that was not pantheistic or polytheistic but strictly monotheistic: Jesus claimed oneness with the transcendent Creator. Such a shocking claim, if it were not true, would make Jesus a lunatic or a liar akin to the devil, argued Lewis. But Jesus' personality was manifestly not demented or deceptive. Therefore, since Jesus was a sane and honest man, he also had to be God with us, as he claimed (1952, 54-57; 1970, 156-160). Lewis found that many in his context were willing to discuss Jesus' deity even before hearing arguments for God's existence, and he found that this line of argument for

---

thought Anscombe's criticisms were fatal to the argument from reason and that he henceforth saw little value in apologetics as a whole. This is clearly not so, for in the 1960 edition of *Miracles*, Lewis revised chapter 3 and sharpened his argument. Moreover, even though his published writings after *Miracles* were less overtly apologetic, Lewis continued to use direct apologetic arguments in private correspondence. Indeed, in the year before his death, Lewis was still deploying a version of the argument from reason (2007, 1338-1339). For a balanced assessment of the Lewis-Anscombe exchange and its aftermath, see Christopher Mitchell's account (1997, 341-351).

[20]Alvin Plantinga articulates "the Free Will Defense" using methods of analytic philosophy in his *God, freedom, and evil* (1977). See also chapter 14 in Plantinga's *Warranted Christian belief* on "Suffering and evil" (2000, 458-499).

Jesus' deity was often effective in eliciting clear belief and decisive commitment (1970, 100-101).[21]

It is beyond the scope of this book to examine in detail each avenue of argument deployed by Lewis or to identify specific strengths and weaknesses in each. The intent of the brief overview I have given here is to show that running through Lewis's main arguments was a concentration on various dimensions of personhood as evidences for the plausibility of Christianity, though not airtight proofs of it.

Worldview Comparison

The effectiveness of Lewis's arguments did not hinge on the irrefutability of any one of them but on their cumulative force in showing the Christian worldview to be more plausible than major competing worldviews in mid-1900s Britain. Lewis's direct arguments flowed from his epistemology and his diagnosis of a depersonalizing intellectual context. He appealed to elements of universal human experience (Purtill 1981, 12-27), thus exploiting the central weakness—impersonality—of the worldviews he opposed: materialism and pantheism, both of which Lewis saw as forms of evolutionary naturalism. As Burson and Walls observe, "An impersonal worldview is hard-pressed to account for any facet of personality" (1998, 237). If Britons would stop being buffaloed by a reductionism that denied the very things they knew best and would instead take seriously human personhood, they might also come to regard personal traits as plausible pointers to the super-

---

[21]According to Beversluis, Lewis's argument makes Jesus' claims to deity clearer than they actually were, ignores theologians who interpret the claims differently, and shows Lewis to be "textually careless and theologically unreliable." Moreover, Beversluis contends that there is no logical difficulty in supposing that Jesus was mistaken about his own deity but was still a fine person and a great moral teacher. Stressing that the Jewish leaders charged Jesus not with insanity but with blasphemy, Beversluis seems to suggest that blasphemy would be compatible with good morality, and that sincere delusions of deity would be compatible with sanity (1985, 54-57). Lewis knew full well how some scholars explained away New Testament texts in which Jesus attributed deity to himself, and Lewis was aware of scholarly denials that the gospels conveyed anything of Jesus' personality. However, Lewis found the texts reliable, and he discerned in NT accounts of Jesus a "shattering immediacy of personal contact." Lewis thought such scholars were blind to the obvious, and he ridiculed Bultmann's notion that the early church did not try to present or preserve a sense of Jesus' personality. "I begin to fear that by *personality* Dr Bultmann means what I should call impersonality: what you'd get in . . . a Victorian *Life and Letters of Yeshua Bar-Yosef* in three volumes with photographs" (1967, 208-210).

personal Fount of personhood, in whose image human personhood was created (Gen 1:26-31). If people were willing to consider Christianity as a hypothesis, they might find that it embraced more of reality and made sense of more things than competing, impersonal worldviews.

Rather than merely defend Christianity against secular attack, Lewis went on the offensive and turned the tables on naturalism's leading lights. Freud tried to debunk religion as desire writ large; Lewis argued that insatiable desire indicated the likelihood of an infinite Object of desire. Darwin portrayed human cognition as a product of a random material process; Lewis took reason as a given and argued for the absurdity of Darwinian materialism. Nietzsche tried to explain away objective moral law by providing a genealogy of morals; Lewis postulated objective morality, argued for a transcendent Lawmaker, and depicted Nietzsche and his imitators as purveyors of idiotic nihilism.[22] Thus Lewis turned naturalists' weapons against them. At the very least, Lewis's arguments offered another way of seeing things besides the naturalism that dominated the public sphere.

Christianity was sometimes accused of small-minded dogmatism, but Lewis turned the tables. Naturalism was literally small-minded and based on rigid dogma. The materialist's "factual realism" was a "doglike mind" which looked at fact while excluding meaning. No evidence or argument could change such a mind so long as it remains locked in reductionism that saw everything "from below" (1980, 71). Christianity, contended Lewis, is more capacious and illuminating than naturalistic scientism: "Christian theology can fit in science, art, morality, and the sub-Christian religions. The scientific point of view cannot fit in any of these things, not even science itself. I believe in Christianity as I believe that the Sun has risen, not only because I see it, but because by it I see everything else" (1980, 92).[23]

The plausibility of the Incarnation lay in the way this doctrine made sense of many known facts. Its plausibility could not be determined by

[22]Lewis also hijacked Nietzsche's notion of the *Übermensch* (superman) and spoke of Christ as inaugurating "the Next Step" in human evolution, which was producing "the New Men" (Lewis 1952, 183-190).

[23]Again Lewis was using a tactic Chesterton had deployed. Chesterton said of the materialist, "His cosmos is smaller than our world . . . it is not thinking of the real things of the earth . . . if the cosmos of the materialist is the real cosmos, it is not much of a cosmos" (1990, 23-24). "It is we Christians who accept all actual evidence—it is you rationalists who refuse actual evidence being constrained to do so by your creed" (1990, 150).

philosophical criteria of probability such as David Hume had proposed. After all, Hume was skeptical not only about miracles but about everything else as well. If the Incarnation was real, "it was the central event in the history of the Earth." It was improbable in the sense that it happened only once—but the course of history itself happened only once; that did not make history unbelievable. "The historical difficulty of giving for the life, sayings, and influence of Jesus any explanation that is not harder than the Christian explanation, is very great." Moreover, like the discovery of a missing section from a novel or symphony that illumined and integrated all the other parts, the Incarnation illumined and integrated "the whole mass of our knowledge" (1960b, 174-176). Christianity's plausibility, suggested Lewis, did not lie in the sort of simplistic obviousness that characterized pantheism ("everything is God") or materialism ("everything is electricity"). "The doctrine of the Incarnation works into our minds quite differently. It digs beneath the surface, works through the rest of our knowledge by unexpected channels, harmonises best with our deepest apprehensions and our 'second thoughts', and in union with these undermines our superficial opinions." The Incarnation, if believed, "illuminates and orders all other phenomena" and "at one stroke covers what multitudes of separate theories will hardly cover for us if this is rejected" (1960b, 212-213).

According to Lewis, the Incarnation could not have been inferred from the character of nature, the content of sub-Christian myths, or the course of history. Yet when it happened and was made known, the Incarnation shed fresh light on nature, myth, and history. Lewis, accordingly, did not use patterns in nature (or myths derived from those patterns) as premises on which to build proofs, and he rarely used historical evidences as premises to argue, say, for Jesus' resurrection. Instead, Lewis proffered a reverse-angle apologetic: he took the Incarnation as the central claim of the Christian worldview and then showed how such a worldview illuminated and integrated nature, myth, and history. Competing worldviews made less sense of these things, besides having no room for genuine personhood.

The Logic of Personal Relations

Lewis labored to make plausible not just an idea or a thing but the super-personal God, the irreducible personhood of humans made in His image, and the vital necessity of relating to God in a personal way. Materialism, pantheism, and any other form of naturalistic monism made ultimate reality impersonal, thus making all individual personality illusory. Lewis used direct arguments and worldview comparison to contend for the personal, but even arguments premised on dimensions of personality were still *arguments*, and the premises, though referring to the personal, were still discussed as abstractions. Lewis thought this was worth doing, but he sought to do more. He beckoned human persons to a personal relationship with the tri-personal God and warned against personal demons.

Lewis suggested that "the logic of speculative thought" differed from "the logic of personal relations." Christians' assurance fed on the character of the God they were "beginning to know by acquaintance." This personal, qualitative knowledge could not be communicated to non-Christians (1960d, 29-30). Apologists thus faced a major disadvantage. Direct apologetic argument amid controversy had to avoid rich testimonial language and had to restrict itself to abstract definitions acceptable to unbelievers. "We have to try to prove *that* God is in circumstances where we are denied every means of conveying *who* God is" (1967, 180-181). Also, the difference between speculative logic and the logic of personal relations yielded different evaluations of whether a Christian's level of trust exceeded its grounds. "In relation to the philosophical premises a Christian's faith is of course excessive: in relation to what is sometimes shown him, it is perhaps just as often defective. My faith even in an earthly friend goes beyond all that could be demonstratively proved; yet in another sense I may often trust him less than he deserves" (1970, 176). Entering a relationship with God involved a leap beyond the sort of evidence that could be amassed by speculative logic. Also, continuing in that relationship involved discounting contrary evidence.

One way Lewis conveyed the leap from the logic of speculative thought to the logic of personal relations was by telling of his own conversion to belief in the living God. After various intellectual twists and turns, Lewis found that "a philosophical theorem . . . became a living presence. I was to be allowed to play at philosophy no longer . . . Total surrender, the absolute leap in the dark, were demanded."[24] Lewis

---

[24]Beversluis claims that Lewis opposed "those who advocate 'leaps of faith'" (1985, 1). Beversluis's only documentation for this claim is a reference to a secondary source that said Lewis found Kierkegaard baffling (Beversluis 1985, 70, note 1). Lewis may have been puzzled by the dour Dane, but it is abundantly clear from the excerpts I document here that Lewis did not oppose "leaps of faith."

told of "feeling . . . the steady, unrelenting approach of Him whom I so earnestly desired not to meet. . . . I gave in, and admitted that God was God, and knelt and prayed" (1955b, 227-228).

Lewis used other tactics besides autobiography to show that faith involves a personal encounter and a leap of commitment. In *That Hideous Strength*, Jane Studdock was urged "to take a leap in the dark. . . You can't know what it's like until you take the plunge . . . you can only take it on trust (1946a, 115-116). In *The Silver Chair*, Jill had to drink water in Aslan's presence, despite fear of being devoured and with no guarantee to the contrary. Then she had to walk by faith in Aslan's signs and not let anything deter her (1994f, 19-24). In *Till We Have Faces*, Orual's reasoning about the divine was worse than useless until she came to know her sinfulness and encountered the divine firsthand (1956, 294, 308).

A decisive commitment could occur only in relation to a definite deity. As we saw in Lewis's diagnosis of intelligent proletarians (chapter 5), he was concerned not only about materialism but about a hodge-podge of religious notions that were vaguely understood and loosely held, and that assumed some sort of pluralism or pantheism in which all religions were compatible. Lewis, therefore, insisted all the more upon "a concrete, choosing, commanding, prohibiting God with a determinate character," in sharp contrast to "a pool of generalized spirituality" which "excludes the 'living God' of Christianity and believes instead in a kind of God who obviously would not do miracles, or indeed anything else" (1960b, 99-100). Denying a vague "generalized spirituality," Lewis proclaimed the incarnate Christ: the ineffable God in the person of a specific, "small, solid" man (1980, 84-85).

Lewis chose to emphasize the Trinity, not just out of theological propriety but out of missional necessity. Many in Britain claimed to believe in God, but not a personal God. Lewis took this to mean that they thought God must be more than a person and that they could not accept an excessively anthropomorphic theism. However, they ended up thinking of God as less than personal, as impersonal. Lewis argued that only the Trinity believed by Christians is "super-personal," a loving unity of three divine Persons. Moreover, only Christians had an idea of how people could partake in God's life and remain themselves, without losing their individual identities, as in pantheism (1952, 140-141; 1960c, 136-137).

The initial decision to trust this super-personal God would take the believer beyond speculation into a life of obedience and devotion, involving concrete, personal contact that would give real content to ideas about God that would otherwise be hollow.

> One moment even of feeble contrition or blurred thankfulness will, at least in some degree, head us off from the abyss of abstraction. It is Reason herself which teaches us not to rely on Reason only in this matter. For Reason knows that she cannot work without materials ... The materials for correcting our abstract conception of God cannot be supplied by Reason: she will be the first to tell you to go and try experience—'Oh, taste and see!' (1960b, 143-145)

It would be folly to put ourselves "on a personal footing with God," but God himself gives us that footing when the Holy Spirit prompts us to pray to the Father. "By unveiling, by confessing our sins and 'making known' our requests, we assume the high rank of persons before Him. And He, descending, becomes a Person to us" (1973, 21).

Persistence in belief, emphasized Lewis, sometimes involved discounting "apparent contrary evidence." Although such "obstinacy in belief" might appear anti-rational, said Lewis, it was really "a logical conclusion from the original belief itself," for to suppose that God is real would be to grant that God surpasses our capacity to understand his dealings with us. Moreover, accepting Christianity involved recognizing the reality of Satan and of his deceptive power to present "evidence strong enough 'to deceive if possible the very elect.'" Having become aware of God's unfathomable ways and of Satan's powerful deceptions, Christians would be wrong to base their level of trust on their own latest assessment of evidence. In personal relationships, failure to trust a supremely trustworthy person would not be praised as excellent logic but blamed as vacillation and suspicion. To demand demonstrative certainty would eliminate the role of trust. Meanwhile, believers' faith was not groundless. They could counter apparently contrary evidence with favorable evidence. Such evidence might be found partly in external events, and more importantly in "something like a knowledge-by-acquaintance of the Person we believe in, however imperfect and intermittent it may be. We trust not because 'a God' exists, but because *this* God exists." The "logic of speculative thought" involved variations of opinion, but "the logic of personal relations" involved "variations of conduct by a person to a Person . . . the increasingly knowable Lord." Such faith, even when devastated, was "always rising from its ashes" (1960d, 13-30).

After his wife's death in 1960, Lewis found his faith in ashes—but then rising again from the ashes. Ever the missional tactician, Lewis published an account of his grieving process in order to help others. In a private letter he said of the book, "It is 'A Grief *Observed*' [emphasis his] from day to day in all its rawness and sinful reactions and follies. It ends with faith but raises all the blackest doubts *en route*" (2007, 1460). Lewis felt as though his faith collapsed like "a house of cards" (2001, 37-39, 52). But with renewed appreciation of Jesus' vicarious suffering, Lewis found he could believe again (2001, 44). He realized afresh, "I need Christ, not something that resembles him." Lewis's ideas of God, even if accurate to some degree, had to be repeatedly shattered by "the great iconoclast. Could we not almost say that this shattering is one of the marks of His presence? The Incarnation is the supreme example; it leaves all previous ideas of the Messiah in ruins" (2001, 65-66). God gave Lewis not explanation but personal assurance, the sense of "a friend just beside him in the dark" or of a Father saying, "Peace, child; you don't understand" (2001, 64,69).[25]

Intellectual assent had to blossom into a more substantial reality embraced by the heart. This was impressed on Lewis not only in a devastating loss but also in "perhaps the most blessed thing that ever happened to me" (2007, 425). In 1951 forgiveness became real to Lewis as never before. Overcome with joy, he felt that his previous belief in forgiveness had been notional and insubstantial, that he had not grasped the reality with his whole heart. He took this as an indication that "any

---

[25] Lewis's grief drove home what he had long known. Back in 1940, Lewis said that "the least tincture of the love of God" would help a sufferer more than any amount of knowledge (1955a, viii). In 1942 he prayed, "From every thought, even from my thoughts of Thee, Oh thou fair Silence! fall and set me free" (2004b, 527). In 1956 one of his fictional characters said, "I know now, Lord, why you utter no answer. You are yourself the answer" (1956, 308). Lewis could not count on the accuracy or stability of his own beliefs; ultimately, he had to rest in God. The logic of personal relations meant faith in God, not faith in one's own faith. Beversluis, as usual, misreads Lewis and contends that *A grief observed* indicated the failure of Lewis's entire apologetic career (1985, 140-167). Dulles responds, "With the vast majority of Lewis scholars, I am convinced of the opposite." Lewis had long known that "no intellectual solution could suffice to overcome the doubts that would arise in situations of grief. During the first weeks after his wife's death he experienced this insufficiency, but in the end he came to see that God was weaning him from excessive earthly attachments and inadequate concepts so that he could fix his heart more purely on the divine reality itself—on the God who surpasses all that we can think or imagine about Him" (Dulles 2005, 18).

morning a doctrine I thought I possessed may blossom into this new reality" (2007, 123). This did not mean Christian doctrines were false or that apologetic defense of them was useless; rather, it meant that the realities were more substantial and wonderful, and could be known in a more palpable way, than mere assent to propositions. Such "real belief in the truths of our religion is a great gift from God" (2007, 751). Such palpable, relational faith was vital in the logic of personal relations.

As Lewis stressed that human personhood flourishes in relation to the Person of Christ, he also warned that human personhood could be devoured by malevolent, personal demons. Lewis did this through fiction in the devilish correspondence of *The Screwtape Letters* (1960c); in various demonic persons in the Narnia books, such as the witch Jadis (1994c; 1994d), the green serpent (1994f), and Tash (1994b); and in the angels and demons of the space trilogy. Of particular note, Weston, a character first devoted to materialist scientism and then to trendy pantheism (the chief dangers Lewis saw in his British context), ended up with his personality devoured by a demon (2003, 75-83, 148).

Consistent with Lewis's fiction was his nonfiction, which often emphasized the threat that personal demons posed to human persons and to all creatures (1955a, 123). Much depravity and pain in the natural world was due to the personal sin of people and, before them, of fallen angels (1960b, 195-196). According to Lewis, all of reality is caught up in a personal battle pitting God and his holy angels against Satan and his fallen spirits. "There is no neutral ground in the universe: every square inch, every split second, is claimed by God and counterclaimed by Satan" (1967, 44). Intellectual doubts could be triggered by demonic activity (2007, 93); indeed, belief based only on reason and evidence could not last against Satan's attacks (1967, 58). The logic of personal relations required keen awareness of attacks from mighty and mysterious personal entities whose ploys had to be recognized and resisted in the wisdom and strength of the Lord, not in mere human reasoning.

The preeminence of the personal for Lewis was also demonstrated by his astonishing commitment to writing back to every person who had written to him after hearing his radio programs or reading his books (2004a; 2004b, 2007; see Dorsett, 2004). His daily correspondence took time and energy he could have invested in other pursuits, and sometimes Lewis complained of the burden. Yet this ongoing personal interaction with people kept him in touch with the concerns and vocabulary of people outside his specialized realm of academia and probably enhanced the effectiveness of his missional apologetics.

In short, Lewis used various apologetic tactics consistent with his epistemology in an effort to make Christianity plausible and personal for a context he saw as afflicted by reductionism and depersonalization. With modest hopes for apologetics, he undermined bogus certitudes, influenced plausibility structures, translated Christianity for specific audiences, offered direct arguments focusing on the personal, compared worldviews, and emphasized the logic of personal relations in knowledge by acquaintance.

Further evaluation of Lewis's diagnosis of problematic thought patterns, of his epistemological views, and of his apologetic methods will come in chapters 10 and 11, where his views are compared to Newbigin's and examined for relevance to contemporary mission. First, however, chapters 8 and 9 shift the focus to Newbigin, exploring his diagnosis of intellectual trends and his prescription for epistemology and apologetics.

CHAPTER 8

Newbigin's Diagnosis of Problematic Thought Patterns

This chapter examines Newbigin's diagnosis of thought patterns in the West that posed major challenges to the gospel. In calling on Christians in Europe and North America to engage their culture missionally, Newbigin insisted that an essential part of such engagement involved an accurate assessment of widespread assumptions about truth and rationality. He regarded scientism and religious pluralism as two dominant thought patterns that reinforced each other, typified imperialistic modernization, and stood in opposition to Christian faith. These two thought patterns, contended Newbigin, were both rooted in the Enlightenment and especially in the epistemology set forth by Descartes.

Before tracing in detail Newbigin's account of this, it may be helpful to review material from previous chapters about his perceptions of various aspects of his late-twentieth century context. As indicated in chapter 2, Christendom's passing was viewed as good riddance in some of Newbigin's earlier writings but later struck him as a considerable loss. Christendom, though flawed and too coercive, had based public truth on the Christian story. Secularized modernity, on the other hand, produced theories with no room for purpose and divine action, separated rights from relationships, pursued happiness through faith in economic mechanisms and the nation-state, and abandoned eschatological hope of a personal and collective future that would come as God's gift. Secularization, said Newbigin, had not made individual consciousness less religious. Instead, as secularization produced a public sphere shaped by atheistic principles and idolatrous greed, it produced a private spirituality open to all sorts of novel religious beliefs and behaviors. Newbigin sought to explain, and undo, the post-Christendom dichotomy between public and private.

Chapter 3 conveyed Newbigin's observations about some notable trends. He encountered firsthand Britain's sharp decline of church involvement and Christian belief. In the realm of beliefs, he noted that both atheism and pantheism held to an impersonal ultimate reality, and thus resembled each other and fit in with naturalistic modern scientism in a way that Christianity could not. Concerning the sexual revolution, he regarded sexual license as a result—not a contributing cause—of an intellectual shift. A demographic increase in cultural pluralism was seen by Newbigin as furthering an ideology of religious pluralism which downplayed differences between faiths, assumed that all faiths were complementary perceptions of the same reality, and opposed evangelism. Such an ideology among British whites stemmed from declining confidence that ultimate truth was revealed exclusively in Christ, and from a corresponding tendency to make Christianity a private opinion rather than an authoritative claim addressed to everyone. Increased exposure to other cultures and religions added momentum to this ideology, but it originated in an earlier intellectual shift. Therefore, Christians had to identify and address the origins of that shift.

Chapter 4 showed that Newbigin perceived Western institutions to be presupposing and propagating ways of thinking and acting that were not in line with the gospel. Schools were teaching religion as a slice of culture, not a vision of truth, and were teaching other subject areas as objective fact, impervious to religious challenge. Pluralism reigned in religion classes; scientism dominated all other subjects. Newbigin saw a need to address education at its epistemological roots. The home, said Newbigin, was losing influence due to modernity's atomizing effects. Also, while most parents wanted schools to teach religious values, the parents themselves did not take the gospel to be fact. (Newbigin treasured his own family roots and personal devotions, but he said little about the role family must play in Christian mission to shape minds and behavior). Modern media, especially television, inducted people into an idolatrous plausibility structure of greed, offered incessant distraction from God and from ultimate questions, and redefined reality in terms of visibility and publicity. In Newbigin's judgment, media and schools had so much power over minds that Christian witness had to deal with power issues and seek appropriate institutional influence. Newbigin saw in government dangerous tendencies to make market ideology supreme and to make the nation-state an agent of scientism. He viewed both tendencies to be largely results of Enlightenment epistemology, which had driven a wedge between public fact and private value. The church in the West, as Newbigin saw it, was syncretistic in its Enlightenment-based intellectual constructs and in its practical failure to combine public and private witness in a manner that was simultaneously ecumenical and evangelical. Throughout his remarks about the various institutions, he expressed a recurring concern about the effects of the epistemology that had dominated European intellectuals since the Enlightenment.

Underlying such observations was Newbigin's sense that an accurate diagnosis of Western culture was urgently needed. He perceived a serious gap in missiology. While multitudes of studies dealt with contextualizing the gospel in nearly every culture, the so-called "modern world" was itself a culture that was not being studied or addressed from the cross-cultural perspective of a missionary (1987, 2; 1989b, 213-214).

Newbigin considered this missiological gap to be especially serious because Western culture, with its proven corrosiveness to Christian claims, was spreading worldwide in the guise of modernization (1986b, 20; 1989b, 213). Therefore, from a global perspective, "mission to 'modernity'" would be "incomparably the most urgent missionary task" for decades to come (1989b, 214). Though rejoicing at church growth and vitality in various parts of the world, Newbigin warned that without a missionary encounter with Western culture, eventually the modernizing forces which had reduced Christianity's believability and impact in Europe would have the same impact elsewhere.[1] This likelihood increased as more Christian leaders around the world were inducted into European-style education (1994a, 185). A key task for missiology, contended Newbigin, was to call into question an imperialistic culture of modernity that was propagating scientism and religious pluralism.

---

[1]Disagreeing with Newbigin, Andrew Walls suggests that the modern and postmodern intellectual legacies of the Enlightenment are not pressing issues for non-Western Christians and are unlikely to corrode non-Western Christianity as Newbigin feared. Even though many missionaries were influenced by the Enlightenment, non-Western Christianity developed its own character and is "independent of the Enlightenment worldview," says Walls. "The principal constituents of Christian development are likely to come from the ancient cultures of Africa and Asia," and the pressing issues are war, poverty, disease, and hunger, not epistemology (Walls 2002, 145-148).

Imperialistic Modernization

Newbigin spoke of science being revered as "a kind of religion," with many people viewing "the sciences as the ultimate source of truth… as contrasted with the myths and superstitions of religion." People counted on scientific achievements, not religious promises, to save them from problems (1961, 15). Westerners had a "mechanical view of the nature of ultimate reality," and this view was reinforced by living in a society where manufacturing, commerce, and government followed mechanistic patterns (1986b, 66). Newbigin called science "the central citadel of our culture" and saw it "embodied in our political, economic, and social practice" (1986b, 79). In his judgment, "the modern scientific world-view" presupposed its own ultimate authority and relativized all religious truth claims. Newbigin, eager to turn the tables, wanted to presuppose the gospel's ultimate authority and to relativize the Western scientific worldview's claim to truth (1986b, 22, 41).

Newbigin defined the gospel as "the announcement that in the series of events that have their center in the life, ministry, death, and resurrection of Jesus Christ something has happened that alters the total human situation and must therefore call into question every human culture." He understood culture as "the sum total of ways of living developed by a group of human beings and handed on from generation to generation." He defined "modern Western culture" as "the culture that is shared by the peoples of Europe and North America, their colonial and cultural offshoots, and the growing company of educated leaders in the cities of the world." He depicted modernization not as a neutral updating of various cultures but as a "co-opting" of leaders from various cultures into the culture originating in western Europe, through the agency of universities, corporations, and media (1986b, 1-4).[2]

Sociology of knowledge, said Newbigin, showed that "our sense of what is real is, to a large extent, a function of the society in which we

---

[2]This conceptualization is challenged by Bert Hoedemaker, who charges that Newbigin's "traditional gospel/culture polarity" remains trapped in flawed assumptions (1999a, 207). Hoedemaker rejects the notion of bringing "'the gospel' from outside to 'culture'" (1999b, 228). Moreover, says Hoedemaker, "What we are inclined to call 'Western culture' is not a 'culture' in the traditionally missionary sense; rather, it is the cradle and the reflection of a complicated global process, in which so-called cultural identities are permanently created, projected, disputed, recaptured, 'cobbled together.'" Rather than frame Christianity versus modernity as a Western problem, contends Hoedemaker, we should view it in the framework of a "worldwide tension" between "a narrow functional rationality" and "'transcending' questions" (2002, 17-22).

live." The modern Western worldview was socially shaped, and it functioned as a plausibility structure just as Islam or Catholicism did. Like any plausibility structure, the Western blend of scientism and religious pluralism made it nearly impossible for individuals socialized in its certainties to see reality in a different way (1986b, 54). Those immersed in the Western plausibility structure took for granted that their views were true and beneficial—and worth spreading worldwide.

Newbigin observed that most in the West had come to view as arrogant the effort to proclaim the gospel as truth for all cultures, yet many had no such reservations about "taking Western science, technology, and political institutions into every part of the world under the name of 'world development'" (1994a, 123). Colonialism and all missions that accompanied it were denounced by guilt-laden Westerners as imperialism, but Newbigin charged that modern Western culture's program of spreading aggressive scientism, linking global markets, and demoting religion from a public role to privatized pluralism, was no less imperialistic: it was a case of one culture imposing itself on others. The Enlightenment sought to know causal relations between facts in order to gain control. As a result, "the whole thrust of our culture has been toward patterns of domination," prompting dominated groups to clamor for emancipation (1991, 22) and moving many intellectuals to adopt the postmodern suspicion of all claims to universal truth and to resist every metanarrative—except, of course, the postmodern metanarrative (1995b, 27, 83; Newbigin, Sanneh, and Taylor 1998, 151). Newbigin was fond of remarking that imperialism is the label we give to any program for human unity other than our own (1986b, 123; 1994a, 125; 1995a, 31).

Most Westerners, not recognizing the particularity and relativity of their own plausibility structure, tended to think their brand of rationality was universal and context-independent, asserted Newbigin. Many were oblivious to imperialistic undercurrents in "modernization" and "development." Western Christians and missionaries to other regions, lacking missional perspective on their own culture, had taken their modern Western culture and plausibility structure for granted. Consequently, they often failed to see how the gospel challenged their own assumptions and how the gospel could address other cultures without imposing westernization on them (1989a, 3).

The gospel, insisted Newbigin, was not inherently imperialistic. Though claiming ultimate authority, its defining revelation was not a figure of domination but Jesus Christ in the weakness of the cross, drawing all to himself (1982b, 160; 1986b, 123). Though proclaimed to all cultures, the gospel's main agents by the late 1900s were not missionaries linked to powerful interests but "the churches of the Third World which have no such power or privilege" (1989a, 158).[3] With the crucified Christ as its decisive revelation and with powerless people as its main agents, the gospel—though authoritative and universal—was decisively different from the imperialism of other projects seeking to unite all peoples. "To affirm the unique decisiveness of God's action in Jesus Christ is not arrogance; it is the enduring bulwark against the arrogance of every culture to be itself the criterion by which others are judged" (1989a, 166).[4] Consequently, Newbigin contended that the most urgent need was not to extend Western-style technocratic scientism and religious pluralism to all cultures, but to bring the gospel to all cultures including—most urgently—the West itself.

Syncretistic Church, Pagan Culture

Oblivious to this need, the Western church was failing to show the contrast between its host culture and the gospel, charged Newbigin.[5] This may have been partly a lingering legacy of Christendom—the

[3]Along the same line, Tite Tiénou states that "since people of color now represent the majority of Christians in the world, the perception of Christianity as a Western religion can be corrected. Making the case for Christianity on the basis that it is a worldwide global religion can, especially in Africa, erase the stigma of Christianity as a white man's religion. This will bring apologetic dividends," says Tiénou, for non-Western Christians can refute charges that they are agents of westernization. "The apologetic dividends of a non-European Christianity may also apply to the United States and some European countries," where in some locales more churchgoers are people of color than white (2006, 41-42).

[4]Paul Weston says Newbigin was addressing postmodern concerns about power "long before postmodernity came into focus as a cultural phenomenon." Newbigin, by stressing a cross-centered metanarrative, effectively undercut postmodern objections that every metanarrative is an attempt to dominate (Weston 2004, 244).

[5]Some hear in Newbigin a prophetic voice addressing the Western church's cultural captivity (Goheen 1999; Drew 2005; Hunsberger 1998, 4-5; Shenk 2000, 62; Van Gelder 1996; Wainwright 2000, 72-75). Walls, however, disputes Newbigin's judgment and argues that in the modern West, many Christians—especially evangelicals—appropriated the Enlightenment in ways that were a faithful "indigenization of Christianity in Western terms." Walls wryly remarks, "Syncretism is somebody else's indigenization, is it not?" Evangelicals, by distinguishing between "nominal Christianity and real Christianity," incorporated "the Enlightenment insistence on personal responsibility . . . without destroying the corporate expression of Christendom which was part of European identity" (Walls 2002, 150-152).

blend of gospel and culture which had been taken for granted as Europe's folk religion with little sense of mission. But Western culture's taken-for-grantedness grew stronger still through its success in becoming the worldwide standard for modernization, making more plausible its "claims to universal validity" (1989a, 65). Newbigin judged most Western Christianity to be extremely syncretistic (1983, 23). People in the West were "perpetually trying to fit the gospel into our culture" (1994a, 67).

Viewing the church in the West as syncretistic, Newbigin regarded the culture as pagan. Secularization did not produce a secular society free of gods. In its public ideology, the West worshiped science and the market, "gods which are not God." In private spirituality, religions proliferated (1989a, 220). European religiosity increased but was often expressed in astrology, pagan practices, and variations on Eastern religions. When rationality was equated with trust in modern science, the result was a void of meaning. Rejecting the living God left a vacuum to be filled by superstitions and idols (1994a, 148-150; 1995b, 48). Skepticism led to subjectivism, which in turn provoked strident reassertions of various faiths worldwide. Militant fundamentalisms loomed larger in public life and international politics (1995b, 35-36). Post-Christian paganism was "far more resistant to the gospel than the pre-Christian paganism with which cross-cultural missions have been familiar," contended Newbigin. "Here, surely, is the most challenging missionary frontier of our time" (1986b, 20).

When non-Christian assumptions in a culture went unnoticed by a syncretistic church, one way to unmask such assumptions would be to listen to Christians from other cultures (1986b, 22; 1987, 7; 1994a, 130).[6] Newbigin said that interacting with Christians in India showed him his own syncretism as well as theirs. Seeing a culture "with the Christian eyes of a foreigner" could provide "the Archimedean point"

---

[6]In every society, observed Newbigin, there is "a strong tendency to domesticate the gospel within the thought-forms of that society" to the point that it fails to challenge reigning assumptions and simply "becomes part of the culture." Therefore, the church in every culture could benefit from challenges presented by Christians who came from different cultures with different assumptions (1994a, 179). In Newbigin's estimation, the church in the West was especially prone to domestication of the gospel, since it had long regarded its culture as Christian and commonly regarded its role in mission as sender rather than receiver. Western Christians had largely been unable or unwilling to confront their own culture or to heed any critique from non-Western Christians.

to critique syncretism that went unnoticed by those immersed in the culture (1994a, 67-68). However, lamented Newbigin, most Western-ers—even in the ecumenical movement—had ears for those from oth-er cultures only if they had Western education, used Western language, and thus had been "co-opted into our culture." Intercultural dialogue was worth pursuing, but "we can hardly start there" in finding a stance from which to critique "Europeanism." A more useful place to begin, he suggested, was to identify modern culture's origins in the Enlight-enment and the epistemological shift—the "conversion"—that it in-volved (1986b, 21-23).

Epistemology and History

Newbigin identified epistemology as the main issue in mission to the West (1988a, 193; 1989a, 25; 1994a, 104). Enlightenment thinkers, though only a small elite, devised epistemological ideas which became "the unquestioned assumptions of millions." If a missionary elite could expose those assumptions and offer a sounder epistemology, the im-pact on church and culture could be equally far-reaching: "The 'trickle-down' model does not work with economics but it does work with ide-as" (1989b, 213-214).

Newbigin insisted that no system of rational discourse was neutral, universally self-evident, or timeless. Every belief system started with unproved presuppositions, was socially embodied, and had a history. There was no context-independent rationality that transcended all oth-ers (except divine omniscience), no neutral and certain standpoint from which to evaluate all other discourses. Western rationality was no ex-ception, asserted Newbigin. Like all other traditions, it had its own pre-suppositional framework of unchallenged assumptions, its own socially located plausibility structure, and its own history (1989a, 64-65; 1994a, 108, 143; 1994d, 80).

European culture's particular history was viewed by Newbigin as developing from the encounter between the biblical story and classical humanist thought (1995b, 3). He noted two major strands in humanist thought. The *rationalist* tradition viewed human reason as the means for grasping truth. The *spiritualist* tradition held that the human spirit, through mystical experience, could make direct contact "with the ulti-mate source of being and truth." Rationalists and spiritualists, whatever their differences, agreed that historical events could not reveal ultimate truth, that timeless truth had to be universally accessible to every human equally, and that ultimate reality was impersonal (1989a, 2).

The Bible, in contrast, recorded revelation as historical events, witnessed and transmitted by a particular community, showing ultimate reality to be personal, asserted Newbigin. Personal being could only be known to the degree that the person chose to reveal himself. So if ultimate reality was personal, human knowledge of ultimate reality depended on divine revelation and trustful listening to the story in the context of the community chosen by God to bear the revelation (1986b, 88; 1989a, 62; 1994a, 92-93; 1994d, 60). There was no basis for asserting that a philosophical construct was a better starting point for knowing than the historic person of Jesus and the historic events of his life, death, and resurrection (1982b, 47; 1995a, 166). One of Newbigin's most characteristic assertions was that the historic revelation in Christ could not fit into any plausibility structure except that of which it was the starting point and ultimate criterion (1982b, 132; 1986b, 63; 1989a, 88; 1991, 11; 1995b, 93).

New Testament writers (especially John, Newbigin's favorite) tried to convey the radical newness of Christ in the thought forms of classical culture. Generations of church fathers continued the effort, striving for the gospel to transform classical thought rather than letting classical culture neutralize the gospel (1982, 3; 1995b, 4). In Newbigin's judgment, their efforts found success as affirmations of the Incarnation and Trinity (especially in Athanasius) established a fresh starting point for knowledge, surmounted old dichotomies, and created a new plausibility structure (1991, 17; 1995b, 4). Augustine's *Credo ut intelligam* ["I believe in order to understand"] shifted the epistemological center of gravity from the classical emphasis on human discovery of impersonal reality to the Christian dependence on divine revelation of personal action and purpose. As classical culture collapsed, this new post-critical starting point provided the basis for European civilization and scientific investigation, thus preserving what was best in classical thought while transcending it (1986b, 102-105; 1995b, 6-12).

Using intellectual history as a key to understanding Western culture, Newbigin suggested that classical rationalism began making a comeback with the translation into Latin of Islamic commentaries on Aristotle. Aquinas, in his synthesis of Christianity and Aristotelian philosophy, introduced a dichotomy between two ways of knowing: faith and reason. His natural theology offered arguments from reason to make faith in God more certain. But the God allegedly proven by Aristotelian logic differed from the God of the Bible, noted Newbigin. Moreover, the philosophical proofs for God turned out to be fragile. Consequently skepticism increased. Descartes sought to defeat skepticism by using its fundamental method—radical doubt—as a new starting point from which to establish truths with absolute certainty (Newbigin 1993, 341-343; 1994d, 61-63; 1995b, 16-28). Newbigin viewed Descartes's *Cogito ergo sum* ["I think; therefore, I exist."] as an idolization of human reason, a pursuit of absolute certainty grounded "in the autonomous mind and not in the faithfulness of God," thus repeating Adam's Fall. "We are all Adam's heirs, and we in our particular culture are all heirs of Descartes" (1991, 27).

Both Augustine and Descartes sought to link Christianity and classical thought, but (according to Newbigin) Augustine made faith in God's revelation his starting point, whereas Descartes made autonomous reason his starting point. As Goheen aptly encapsulates Newbigin's analysis, "Augustine is the father of a synthesis that places the classical tradition in the context of the Biblical story. Descartes is the father of a synthesis that places the gospel in the context of the classical tradition" (Goheen 2002a, 365).

Enlightenment thinkers, taking their cue from Descartes, felt sure that "Europeans now knew the secret of knowledge and therefore the secret of mastery over the world" (1986b, 23). They applied "the geometric spirit" to every kind of knowledge. When they glorified reason, said Newbigin, "by reason they meant essentially those analytical and mathematical powers by which human beings could attain (at least in principle) to a complete understanding of, and thus a full mastery of, nature—of reality in all its forms" (1986b, 25).

The Cartesian pursuit of total certainty through a method of radical doubt was sure to fail, declared Newbigin. The goal of absolute proof was unachievable before the world's end. Moreover, the method of radical doubt could not connect with any reality and inevitably ended in skepticism and nihilism (1983, 61; 1989a, 33; 1993, 343; 1994d, 62-63). Thus the Age of Reason led, via Nietzsche, to "the age of postmodernity" (1995b, 26-27). All claims to universal truth were rejected and suspected to be sheer power grabs. The hermeneutic of suspicion was not the opposite of Enlightenment rationalism but the fruit of it, "the postmodernist development of modernism" (1995b, 83).

Newbigin viewed the West as "a culture that has sought for absolute certainty as the ideal of true knowledge but now despairs of the possibility of knowing truth at all" (1995b, 93). Among many intellectuals, postmodernism brought skepticism even about science itself, observed Newbigin. At the popular level, most people would still assume the existence of a real world, about which it was possible to be correct or mistaken. They would continue to esteem science as part of a body of public truth that all should acknowledge. However, they would regard claims about human nature, choices, and destiny as matters of mere opinion (1994a, 161; Newbigin, Sanneh, and Taylor 1998, 152). Newbigin declared, "Greek rationalism can no more provide the ultimate basis for society in the twentieth century than it did in the third and fourth" (1995a, 168).

Newbigin's historical account of rival epistemologies is not always consistent with his own key emphases or congruent with historical evidence. Given that Newbigin often emphasized sociology of knowledge, it seems ironic and somewhat inconsistent that his core analysis of Western rationality turned out to be largely an intellectual history of great minds.[7] Further, his analysis of those great minds was seriously flawed. He misconstrued the thought and impact of Descartes. His stark contrast between Augustine and Descartes was overdone, especially since Descartes's *Cogito ergo sum* came as an echo of Augustine's *Si fallor sum* ["If I err, I exist"]. Similarities of method and approach between Augustine and Descartes have long been noted by many scholars, but Newbigin took no account of these similarities.

Goheen, though appreciative of Newbigin, asserts that Newbigin's analysis was "incomplete and inadequate" in its identification of idolatrous commitment to reason as the main problem in the West. Other idols may have had a stronger grip. Moreover, says Goheen, even if ra-

---

[7]In fairness to Newbigin, it should be noted that in *Foolishness to the Greeks*, he explicitly denied that Western culture could be accounted for purely in terms of ideas:

> In attempting to sketch the broad outlines of the movement of thought that marked the birth of modern Western culture, I have spoken as if it all began in the realm of pure ideas. This, of course, would be a foolish notion. Ideas develop in a context of actual life—political and private. Without opting for either the view that ideas are primary and their political and social consequences secondary, or the view that ideas are merely a by-product of social change, one can accept the fact that there is a reciprocal relationship between them and that one does not truly account for one without attending to both. . . . plainly what we call modern Western culture is much more than a body of ideas. It is a whole way of organizing human life that both rests on and in turn supports and validates the ideas I have been referring to. (1986b, 29)

This strong statement should be given due weight; still, it remains true (as he himself conceded) that Newbigin often spoke "as if it all began in the realm of pure ideas."

tionalistic humanism was a problem to some degree, Augustine was a contributor to the problem, not a pristine paradigm of how to avoid it. Newbigin took insufficient account of "the powerful humanistic and rationalistic currents" in Augustine, and did not recognize that Augustine's synthesis of Christianity with classical thought "paved the way for Aquinas, and finally Descartes and Locke" (Goheen 2000, 417).[8]

Vinoth Ramachandra, while praising Newbigin and endorsing his main concerns, says that his sweeping statements about Enlightenment and post-Enlightenment culture were "liable to generalizations and one-sided distortions." Newbigin followed Barth in positing a radical Enlightenment rebellion of autonomous reason against divine revelation, says Ramachandra, but Newbigin bypassed scholarship arguing that modern secular culture originated in the Reformation's emancipation of public life from clerical control, he underestimated the significance of religious wars in the rise of Europe's secular culture, and he misconstrued Descartes, Locke, and others. "The attack on the Christian world view in European society had its origins far earlier than the rise of modern science and the subsequent Enlightenment," contends Ramachandra, but Newbigin largely ignored this and made rational, scientific "objectivity" the main villain (Ramachandra 1996, 156-164).

In short, Newbigin's history of Western epistemology focused too narrowly on great minds, caricatured key thinkers, and placed too much blame on autonomous reason, while neglecting other important factors that presented difficulties for Western Christianity. Nevertheless, despite deficiencies of precision and proportion, Newbigin did well to stimulate missional evaluation of the West and its assumptions about rationality. He identified some key thought patterns and presuppositions that needed to be challenged.[9]

[8]The skeptical method of Descartes had a precedent in Augustine (Groothuis 2000, 146). Foust thinks Newbigin misconstrued Augustine as a fideist. "Augustine did not assert that there is no knowledge without faith," contends Foust. "He held that a certain amount of rational evidence for Christ is necessary before one believes, but after one believes it, one can then go on to find new reasons to believe." Also, Augustine drew on neo-Platonism, raised questions about what can be believed, and spoke of a priori truths lodged in all people's memory. Thus Augustine's maxim *Credo ut intelligam* was not a charter for presuppositional fideism (Foust 2002, 157-159).

[9]Even Newbigin enthusiasts do not credit him with scholarly accuracy. Wainwright concedes lack of nuance in Newbigin, while lauding "that clarity and sharpness which often characterizes the insights and vision of pioneers and prophets" (2000, 355). In a similar vein, Shenk says Newbigin is best characterized not as a systematic scholar but as a strategic thinker focused on priority issues (2000, 59).

Excluding Teleology, Exalting Dichotomy

In attacking Cartesian epistemology, Newbigin said that contrary to its claims to establish indubitable knowledge, it rested on a "vast and unproved assumption" that we can know the truth about reality without revelation from its Creator (1994a, 159). Such an assumption required a focus on impersonal "facts" and causal connections. Questions of purpose had to be excluded, because the purpose of a thing was not immediately accessible to observation but resided in the mind of its maker and could be known only when the maker revealed his purpose or when all things reached their appointed end (1991, 22). Newbigin insisted that goodness or badness depended on whether or not something fulfilled its maker's purpose (1994a, 71). Therefore, an epistemology that began by excluding God and purpose ultimately had no ground for treating morality and religion as matters of objective fact; such things had to be relegated to the realm of subjective opinion (1994a, 161).

The "abandonment of teleology," declared Newbigin," is responsible for "vast changes in the human situation." If knowledge was comprised of "value-free facts" and purpose was not part of "the world of 'facts,'" then any notions of purpose or value could only be what people invented for themselves as matters of desire and will, with no objective standard for good and bad (1986b, 36-38; 1994a, 161). Appeals to "traditional moral values," insisted Newbigin, "rest upon a different (and older) world-view and have no basis in 'facts.'" Consequently, the masses would sink deeper and deeper into moral relativism, and manipulative elites would have no objective criteria to evaluate public goals and decisions. "In eliminating purpose from the category of 'facts,' the manipulator hands over control to whatever is the predominant force in his own nature. Man's conquest of nature turns out to be nature's conquest of man" (1986b, 78). Newbigin was here echoing C. S. Lewis's words in *The Abolition of Man* (1996, 76). Although he did not attribute the quote to Lewis, Newbigin shortly thereafter referred to Lewis's dystopia in *That Hideous Strength*, saying that it represented "the carrying of one of the fundamental assumptions of our culture to its logical conclusion" (Newbigin 1986b, 84). Newbigin, like Lewis, thought that rationalistic scientism tended to produce a dominant elite governed only by irrational, amoral desires.

Newbigin decried epistemology that began with the autonomous human mind and reduced all things outside the mind to propositions without personhood or purpose. He charged that such an epistemology separated what belonged together and produced damaging dichotomies: reason vs. faith, facts vs. values, public vs. private (1986b, 16-19; 1989a, 17) mind vs. matter, objective vs. subjective, theory vs. practice (1993, 344-345; 1995b, 36-39).

Dominated by such dichotomies, modern Western culture claimed to be pluralistic, but was really dogmatic on matters purported to be public facts accessible to objective reason. The philosophy for public life was atheistic, dominated by the principles and procedures of mechanistic, depersonalized scientism (1986b, 13-18, 65-66).[10] Schools taught that science provided assured knowledge to be accepted by all (1994a, 149), while insinuating that religion and values were not "true accounts of how things are" but were merely cultural and personal options for people in a "supermarket society" to pick from and to enjoy in private (1985a, 244). According to Newbigin's diagnosis of the West, pluralism ruled in the private world of what some religious people believe, but pluralism was excluded from the public world of what all rational people know (1989a, 27; 1994a, 71).

In Newbigin's judgment, the assumptions and dichotomies of modern Western culture pervaded the church. He viewed fundamentalism

---

[10]In a public exchange, David Stowe criticized Newbigin for oversimplifying "the Western mind" and for overdoing his charges of widespread capitulation to scientism. Stowe also contended that if science was viewed as public scrutinizing and testing in pursuit of truth, then proximate justice and morality could be discovered through ongoing interaction and discussion, without directly asserting any particular faith (1988, 148-149). Newbigin replied that in the realm of morality, conversation without revelation could only produce popular opinion and assertions of will. Any remaining agreement about morality in Western societies rested on the lingering influence of Europe's long Christian history (1988b, 152). On this point, Charles West (1988) sided with Newbigin: secular values were leftovers of the Christian vision and could not be preserved unless idolatries were confronted. Newbigin countered Stowe's challenge about being too negative toward science by declaring that he actually wanted Christian thinking to be more scientific in the proper sense. Truly scientific method would reflect the nature of what was to be known. Modern experimental methods could be appropriate for investigating inanimate things; however, insisted Newbigin, "As we rise through the scale of living creatures and human beings to the supreme venture of knowing, the knowing of God, the proper method of seeking must change according to the changing nature of the reality we are seeking to know." God could not be known unless he revealed himself. Therefore, a properly scientific method would be attuned to that fact and would start with God's self-revelation, "not from a speculative philosophy, however optimistic, based on the generality of human experience" (1988b, 151-152).

and liberalism as "twin children of the Enlightenment," both pursuing "the false ideal of a kind of knowledge that is immune to doubt." Objectivist fundamentalists wanted "to affirm indubitable propositions about everything in earth and heaven," while subjectivist liberals immunized religious statements from doubt by treating them as symbolic expressions of "a purely inward, psychic experience" (1988a, 192). This split between objective and subjective poles of knowing, asserted Newbigin, appeared in each group's handling of Scripture. Fundamentalists treated Scripture as a collection of facts in a textbook and insisted that every proposition was historically and scientifically accurate, while liberals (accepting higher criticism's rationalistic denial of biblical testimony to God's words and actions in history) treated scriptural narratives as accounts of religious experience (1991, 30; 1994a, 165; 1994d, 72). Newbigin expressed sympathy with fundamentalist rejection of scholarship that denied biblical authority, but he thought fundamentalist defense of Scripture rested on "a surrender to the very forces threatening to destroy biblical authority" (1995b, 86).

Protestants in modern Western culture, complained Newbigin, were failing to challenge the public-private dichotomy. Religious conservatives emphasized personal transformation and the eternal destiny of individual souls, neglecting the Bible's call to transform culture and its public eschatology of a redeemed creation under God's reign (1983, 32-33; 1989a, 178-179; 1995a, 81). Meanwhile, charged Newbigin, liberals lobbied for political causes without biblical grounding and sought to blend Christianity with other religions rather than calling for individuals to trust Christ and his atonement (1985a, 231; 1991, 66; 1994a, 46; 1994b, 3). Both conservatives and liberals viewed churches as voluntary associations and formed various denominations, thus conforming to the privatized, consumerist structure that a secularized society assigned to religion. It followed logically, argued Newbigin, that denominations could not bring a missionary challenge to the culture, since they lacked authority to announce public truth and claimed only to be groupings of individuals who happened to have similar opinions (1986b, 145; 1994a, 64, 74). In these and other ways, the syncretistic church was immersed in modern Western assumptions and was unable to challenge them effectively.

In pressing the question, "Can the West be converted?" Newbigin explained that he was asking:

Can the Church offer, in the context of our culture, a new "fiduciary framework," a new way of grasping the totality of things that can replace, not the private religious worlds of individuals in our culture, but the public world into which all of us educated in a European language have, from childhood, been inducted and in which we have lived? For two and a half centuries theologians have labored to understand the Bible from within the 'fiduciary framework' of Western culture as it has developed since the end of the seventeenth century. Is it possible, in an intellectually coherent way, to undertake the reverse operation? (1994a, 108)

Newbigin's attempt to answer such questions is discussed in the next chapter.

CHAPTER 9

Newbigin's Prescription for Epistemology and Apologetics

In Newbigin's diagnosis, dichotomies that infected modern Western culture and its churches sprang from an epistemology that separated personal belief from impersonal knowledge. He responded by offering an epistemology of personal knowledge, which would apply to theology as well as science. At the same time, he insisted that apologetics had to take for its starting point and ultimate criterion God's self-revelation in Christ, as rendered in Scripture and in the church community's ongoing conversation and public witness. In this chapter, I sketch Newbigin's prescription for epistemology and apologetics.

Relational Epistemology for Science and Theology

Newbigin thought that in mission to the West, a primary intellectual task was "to recover a concept of knowledge that will heal the split in our culture between science and faith, between the public world and the private" (1994a, 112). He wanted to show that healthy science and healthy faith were more similar than was commonly supposed.

In modern Western culture, said Newbigin, the ideal for knowledge was the sort of data that could be gained through the senses and entered into a computer; other kinds of knowing were evaluated by how close they came to that standard. But this was not the only ideal available. The central tradition of Hinduism, said Newbigin, held that the senses were unreliable, even illusory, and that true knowledge was found by withdrawing from the senses into pure inwardness. Still another view, suggested Newbigin, was that of the Bible, where knowledge was rooted in relationships, mutual self-revelation, and trust. Knowledge rooted in personal relationship included knowledge of the supremely personal God; it also included every other kind of knowledge (1966, 79-80). Indeed, belief in a personal God with purposes had provided the original basis for confidence that the world was rational and contingent, giving impetus to the sciences' search for meaningful patterns (1986b, 65-94).

Newbigin's relational epistemology drew upon various sources, but his main debt was to scientist Michael Polanyi's *Personal Knowledge* (1958). Polanyi, as understood by Newbigin, denied "the objective-subjective dichotomy" and insisted that all knowing—including scientific knowing—"involves the personal commitment of the knower as a whole person" (1995b, 39). Drawing on Polanyi, various writings of Newbigin repeatedly stressed the following themes: Knowing is a skill developed through a personal process of learning. Knowledge occurs within a community of shared knowledge and is shaped by its plausibility structures. All knowledge begins within some accepted framework and must start with an act of faith, accepting some presuppositions as givens. Trust and doubt are both necessary in knowing, but trust must be primary as openness to reality, and doubt is secondary as a way to reduce error. Knowledge is gained through apprenticeship under the authority of a tradition and its acknowledged masters. Indwelling a tradition and its accepted framework instills a wealth of tacit knowledge. Tacit knowledge is seldom the focus of one's direct attention and cannot be fully expressed in propositions, but it provides the necessary background for gaining knowledge about any particular focus of inquiry. Discovery results not from obvious induction based on clear data but from heuristic passion to grasp reality more fully and from imaginative leaps that sometimes lead to paradigm shifts. Knowing is not robotic acceptance of proven certitudes but risky commitment to what is not immediately verifiable. Personal knowledge always has subjective dimensions but makes claims about objective reality, claims held with universal intent as true for all and not just for oneself. The claim is published, made known to others, as an invitation to consider and test it. A key measure of a claim's validity is whether it leads to new discovery and further knowledge of reality (1966, 80-88.; 1983, 20-32; 1986b, 79-83 1989a, 29-65; 1991, 45-59; 1994d, 61; 1995b, 39-44).

In commending this epistemology, Newbigin sometimes used the term *faith* not just to denote trust in God and his revelatory actions but to indicate beliefs accepted without prior proof. In this sense, an epistemological act of faith would not be inferior to knowledge but would be a precondition for all knowing. "We have to begin by believing the evidence of our senses, the veracity of our teachers and the validity of the tradition into which we are seeking apprenticeship." Even if such things might need to be questioned at some point, the questioning itself would inevitably be based on knowledge gained as a result of the initial "faith" and the apprenticeship in a tradition of knowing (1994d, 61).[1] Foust rightly observes, "This is not so much 'faith' as it is 'accepted understandings,'" which is not the same as biblical faith in Christ (2002b, 155). Newbigin sometimes blurred the distinction.

Accepting Polanyi's account of how science at its best really operates, Newbigin saw a resemblance to the relational epistemology of the Bible. He did note some differences. Newbigin said that science confines itself "to a limited set of questions about the rational structure of the cosmos," while the Christian tradition addresses "larger questions" of "ultimate meaning and purpose" and depends on "models, concepts, and paradigms" appropriate to "a more comprehensive rationality based on the faith that the author and sustainer of the cosmos has personally revealed his purpose." The scientific community's tradition "is one of human learning, writing, and speaking," whereas the Christian community's tradition is witness to God's revelatory actions centered in Christ (1989a, 49-50). Still, said Newbigin, both science and Christianity involve community, tradition, authority, personal commitment, publication, testing, and other similarities noted above.

---

[1] What Newbigin here called "faith" would be somewhat similar to "basic belief" as used by Plantinga (2000) and other "Reformed epistemologists." A properly basic belief is one that is not inferred from other beliefs but is a belief directly produced by properly functioning cognitive faculties operating in appropriate circumstances. Basic beliefs involve a sort of "faith" in one's cognitive faculties (perhaps including a faculty capable of sensing God's reality), but "faith" in one's knowledge-producing faculties is not identical to faith as an embrace of specifically Christian truths and a personal trust in the God who speaks in Scripture and comes to us in Christ. As Plantinga explains, Christian beliefs "do not come to the Christian just by way of memory, perception, reason, testimony, the *sensus divinitatis*, or any other of the cognitive faculties with which we human beings were originally created; they come instead by way of the work of the Holy Spirit, who gets us to accept... these great truths of the gospel. These beliefs don't come just by way of the normal operation of our natural faculties; they are a supernatural gift" (Plantinga 2000, 245).

In view of Newbigin's firm emphasis on revelation and his fierce critique of "the modern scientific worldview," it seems strange that he would use a scientist's account of the scientific community's knowing as a model for the Christian community's knowing.[2] Newbigin went so far as to depict Polanyi's epistemology as vital for a missionary encounter with the West and even for healing church divisions. The "Polanyi model," besides closing the gap between science and faith, could help end "the sad quarrel between our objectivist fundamentalists and our subjectivist liberals" (1991, 46).

Yet Polanyi himself expressed religious views that were a syncretistic mixture of liberalism and evolutionism. He depicted religion not in terms of biblical revelation but primarily as "the passionate search for God" (Polanyi 1958, 281). He praised "progressive Protestant theology," especially that of Paul Tillich, and agreed with Tillich's claim that knowledge of revelation "does not imply factual assertion" (Polanyi 1958, 283). Polanyi claimed that scientific study of evolution could be interpreted as a clue to God (1958, 285). He echoed Teilhard de Chardin and Henri Bergson in giving evolution quasi-religious status (1958, 388, 400). He spoke of "a prime cause emergent in time" and declared that "the appearance of the human mind has been so far the ultimate stage in the awakening of the world" (1958, 405). Polanyi's epistemology did not have its starting point and cornerstone in the crucified and risen Christ as God's ultimate revelation. His epistemology evidently left Polanyi vulnerable to many of the errors Newbigin elsewhere deplored. Therefore, whatever the strengths of Polanyi's epistemology, it is hard to see how it could mesh with Newbigin's view of revelation or perform the missionary wonders Newbigin expected of it.[3]

---

[2]Lamin Sanneh expresses unease "about the parallel lines drawn for science and religion" and suggests that Newbigin, still rooted in the Enlightenment, risked making Christianity "a look-alike or surrogate rationality" (Sanneh 1993, 166-167). In contrast, Michael Goheen denies "incipient rationalism" in Newbigin and states, "The analogy and parallel between the scientific community and the church reveal the significance of a hermeneutical community in maintaining and communicating a tradition of understanding." If Newbigin made any mistake in drawing on philosophy of science, suggests Goheen, it was in limiting himself to Polanyi, for more recent philosophers of science have stressed even more "the importance of the hermeneutical community" (Goheen 2000, 387-388, 417).

[3]Here I am not denigrating Polanyi's legitimate epistemological insights or Newbigin's agreement with many of them. I am doubting whether Polanyi's views fit with Newbigin's Barthian concept of revelation, and I am questioning whether Polanyi's epistemology would prevent disastrous theological missteps and renew mission to the

Richard Gelwick asserts that Newbigin neglected key distinctions in Polanyi. Empirical science focused on specific facts at a level of experience "suitable to verification." Religious worship involved a world picture of integrative meaning that made contact with reality and was "suitable to validation" but involved sacred experience "beyond the verifiable facts of science." Newbigin ignored this distinction between verification and validation, says Gelwick, thus making epistemology of science a norm for epistemology of religion, and becoming vulnerable to the scientific reductionism Polanyi sought to overcome (2000, 43).

In a rejoinder to Gelwick, George Hunsberger denies that Newbigin equated scientific fact with "the fact of Christ" and denies that Newbigin sought for Christian claims the kind of verification appropriate for scientific investigation. Rather, contends Hunsberger, Newbigin used Polanyi to show that "science is not so objective as the cultural attitude takes it to be, and religious believing is not so absolutely different from it. Science is more historically conditioned, and Christian faith more epistemologically valid, than the common take on things." Newbigin showed companionship—not identity—of scientific and religious knowing, says Hunsberger, so that Christians would not regard faith as merely subjective but would believe confidently and witness publicly and humbly (Hunsberger 2000, 24-25). In my estimation, Hunsberger accurately expresses the intent of Newbigin's epistemology.

Yet Newbigin's epistemology, in trying to heal the split between science and faith, sent a double message. One message was that he wanted Christianity to have science's factual authority; the other was that Christians ought simply to testify to the Bible's story from within the church's plausibility structure so that others would accept by faith the gospel's factuality and join the community. As Gelwick observes in reply to Hunsberger, "In this discrepancy between 'be like the authority of science in the public square' and 'be a part of the community of Christian faith,' Newbigin fails to distinguish well between the nature of knowing in science and theology" (Gelwick 2001, 18-20).[4]

West. Still, Christians can learn from Polanyi. For instance, Reformed evangelical philosopher Esther Lightcap Meek (2003) offers a stimulating philosophy of knowledge that builds on Polanyi's epistemology. Meek also draws upon Newbigin and Lewis, among others.

[4]In addition, Gelwick complains that Newbigin spoke of *the* gospel despite various Christian understandings, and was not open to what other religions discovered as their heuristic passion brought them into contact with reality and moved them to witness with universal intent. Kettle responds to this concern of Gelwick by emphasizing

Historically Embodied Rationality

In applying relational epistemology to both scientific claims and Christian claims, Newbigin professed "agreement with the postmodernists" that "all truth claims are culturally and historically embodied." However, he repudiated irrational skepticism, denied "surrender to subjectivity," and insisted that truth claims can be "really true" (1995b, 97-98).

The Enlightenment shifted "the location of reliable truth from the story told in the Bible to the eternal truths of reason." For those in the Enlightenment tradition, historical narrative was inferior to timeless truth. However, this notion was turned on its head by "Nietzsche and his disciples—the so-called postmodernists." They showed that "the eternal truths of reason are in fact products of particular histories." The Enlightenment's self-evident truths only seemed self-evident in a specific historical context "shaped by a particular story." Newbigin, accepting this aspect of postmodern analysis, took it to be "obviously true that all our eternal truths and all our metanarratives are products of particular human histories." Yet he insisted that it would be unwarranted to conclude that all truth claims and metanarratives therefore equally lacked an objective referent. "The (true) assertion that all truth claims are culturally and historically embodied does not entail the (false) assertion that none of them makes contact with a reality beyond the human mind" (1995b, 73-74).

Newbigin summarily rejected total skepticism, such as that advocated among some European intellectuals in earlier times and again in some postmodern circles: "Quite simply, it is an intellectual pose and not a genuine belief. So long as we continue to live we continually act on the assumption that certain things are true and others are not"

Newbigin's rejection of the dichotomy between ultimate commitment and truth-seeking, and Newbigin's insistence that all truth-seeking had a starting point and supreme criterion. A Christian with an ultimate commitment could still expect to learn truths from people with other ultimate commitments, but would grasp and integrate these truths in terms of ultimate commitment to Christ. One could be open to truth from various sources, but one could not hold multiple ultimate commitments; otherwise pluralism would become the ultimate commitment, replacing other ultimate commitments it claimed to embrace (Kettle 2002b, 20-22). I think Kettle's interpretation of Newbigin is sound on this matter, and I agree with Newbigin's rejection of pluralism and his call to learn from others while remaining faithful to our ultimate commitment. At the same time, I think Gelwick is right that Newbigin's rejection of pluralism marked a significant departure from the tone of Polanyi's comments about religion.

(1995b, 24). People had to explore and cope with a real world. They could be "right or wrong about it." Indeed, survival depended on being right, not just about physical things such as food or dangerous animals, but also about God and his reign. A "collapse into relativism and subjectivism" would bring doom (1995b, 35). Without the gospel truth of the personal God, the culture would deteriorate "into the irrational fanaticism that is the child of total skepticism." Newbigin thought that it might be "the greatest task of the church in the twenty-first century to be the bastion of rationality in a world of unreason" (1986b, 93-94).

Newbigin depicted reason not as a separate source of information or authority but as a faculty for grasping and arranging various parts of our experience in meaningful patterns. Rational striving to make sense of things could occur only within a specific, continuous tradition of language and culture. Rationality had to deploy words and concepts that embodied the way a particular society made sense of things. Any appeal to reason as a source of information or authority alongside Scripture or tradition would in reality be only an appeal to the plausibility structure of a specific tradition. Newbigin denied any culture-independent, neutral form of reason by which all particular traditions of rationality could be measured, but he also shunned surrender to utter relativism. All forms of rationality had to be tested by their adequacy for making sense of experience and coping with reality. Some rationalities were more adequate than others. A new way of seeing things, a paradigm shift, could not be justified by appeals to an overarching logical system. The new paradigm's superior rationality would shine forth in its adequacy to make sense of diverse phenomena and to stimulate and incorporate new discoveries, and in the courage and vigor with which its advocates used their rational faculty (1989a, 11, 53-57; 1994a, 90-92; 1994d, 79-81).

For Newbigin, rationality was not to be equated with (or judged by) universal, self-evident Reason abstracted from historical particulars. However, rationality did have to seek and show internal coherence and correspondence with reality.[5] Newbigin thus differed from relativistic,

[5]Kenneson, though applauding Newbigin's cultural analysis, finds him unsatisfactory because Newbigin still spoke of public truth and held a correspondence model of truth. Kenneson thinks evangelicals should instead opt for a version of Richard Rorty's (anti)epistemology, where beliefs are habits of behavior, and truth is internal to a community's web of beliefs, with no external referent. "We *always* know for certain what is true, because we are always in the grip of some belief" (Kenneson 1995, 155-170, 226-227). While crediting Newbigin with anticipating how "postmodernity

anti-realist versions of postmodernism, as Kettle (2002b, 21) and Weston (2004, 233-234) point out. According to Newbigin, all knowing "has an essential subjective pole. But equally it has an objective pole. It 'latches on' to some reality outside the knower. Otherwise it is not knowing at all. Its grasp may be limited and faulty, but nevertheless it is a grasping at something that is *there*, objectively" (1994a, 104-105). If objectivity meant excluding all subjectivity in knowing, it was "absurd to suppose that total objectivity is possible." However, Newbigin declared, "If objectivity means that we must aim for the greatest possible truthfulness in our thinking and speaking about realities beyond our own minds, then of course it is a proper goal" (1995b, 45).[6] In short, Newbigin held to a form of critical realism, though sometimes the realism was nearly obscured by the critical dimension, particularly when he placed extreme emphasis on the social construction of knowledge.[7]

---

would level the epistemological playing field," Kenneson laments that Newbigin remained "regrettably fixated on epistemological concerns." We should assume truth to be intersubjective, "not so much 'out there' or 'in here' as 'between' persons." Kenneson thinks this resonates with an anthropology based in Trinitarian perichoresis (2002, 76-82). In my judgment, Kenneson's view represents an incoherent, disastrous surrender to postmodern irrationalism.

[6]Winfried Corduan accuses Newbigin of misrepresenting and abandoning the correspondence theory of truth in favor of "a radical conventionalism" which severs ties to an objective referent and exempts itself from propositional analysis. Reacting especially against Newbigin's hyperbolical assertion that "the congregation is the only hermeneutic of the gospel," Corduan says that if Christians can only appeal to communal and pragmatic grounds, we have already lost. After all, pluralism's central claim is that "different world views function satisfactorily for different people" (Corduan 1997, 32-38). Corduan is mistaken in charging that Newbigin abandoned correspondence theory. Newbigin is best understood as a critical realist: from within a socially embodied tradition, he aimed for truthfulness "about realities beyond our own minds" (Newbigin 1995b, 45). Still, given Newbigin's penchant for overstatement and dialectic, Corduan's epistemological critique remains valuable in identifying elements in Newbigin's thought that went too far in the direction of conventionalism and weakened Christianity's ability to make its case.

[7]Douglas Groothuis says Newbigin's concept of truth is "unsteady" and "inconsistent" and involves statements that may be taken to distort and deny the correspondence view of truth. While accepting Newbigin's insistence that humans cannot attain a standpoint that rises beyond any human perspective, Groothuis insists that this does not affect correspondence as the measure of truth: "for a belief to be true, it must linguistically represent some *part* of reality *accurately*, from a perspective, not without any perspective" (2000, 152-154).

Authority and Fallibility in Community and Scripture

Newbigin contended for Jesus Christ as "absolute truth," the standard by which "*all* so-called knowledge must be tested" (1994a, 72). God's truth in Christ was to be appropriated and propagated not in timeless systems of thought but in the story conveyed by the church. Newbigin never tired of saying that Jesus did not write a book but formed a community (e.g. 1953, 20; 1982b, 228; 1989a, 133; 1994d, 70; 1995a, 52; 1995b, 89). This community constituted a plausibility structure, a tradition of rationality, based on faith that the clue to history's meaning was revealed in the biblical story culminating in Jesus. In Newbigin's opinion, the gospel's credibility did not depend on an infallible church, an inerrant Bible, or airtight arguments, but on the Spirit-guided communal life and authoritative public witness of believing congregations, who were the "only real hermeneutic of the gospel" (1989a, 227, 232; 1994a, 42, 146, 153, 176).

Newbigin insisted on the reality of God's revelation in Christ, to which the Bible and the church witnessed. Jesus' actions, teachings, death, and resurrection, though understood and explained with less than perfect accuracy, had to be confidently and clearly affirmed as our ultimate criteria, revealed by God and not accessible to mere "observation and induction from the human situation as we see it" (1994a, 50). These actual happenings, involving this concrete person, were "events in real history," not just "stories told to illustrate truths." Otherwise "the whole of Christian teaching would fall to the ground" (1989a, 66; see also 1994d, 76). Jesus' body was really raised; his tomb was really empty. Unlike myths, which "express eternal truths in story form," the church's story was historical and competed with accounts from secular historians. In telling the story of real historical events, the church through the ages affirmed that this story provided "the true interpretation of all human and cosmic history." While making this enormous claim, the church—past and present—was all too often flawed by confusion, wickedness, and apostasy. Even so, wrote Newbigin, the fallible church was chosen by God and entrusted with the only story that had power to correct the church itself and to convert the world; no other body existed to tell that story (1995b, 77).

As part of his epistemology and apologetic, Newbigin sought to relativize and weaken liberal approaches that subordinated the witness of the Bible and the church to the authority of critical scholarship. The historical-critical method of biblical scholarship desacralized the sacred book, said Newbigin, by locating it "in the world of objective facts that the scientist studies and classifies." Likewise, the techniques of anthropologists and sociologists desacralized the sacred society, the church. The use of Enlightenment methods to study Scripture and church brought to light valuable insights that could not be dismissed (1986b, 42-43). However, exalting such methodology and findings to a position of supreme intellectual authority was erroneous. The Bible's unique claims and promises, believed and embodied by the church, could not be subjected to any scientific test (1995b, 55).

Studying Scripture from a critical stance—illuminating as that might be in some respects—was not more objective than the church's traditional confession of biblical authority, observed Newbigin. The critical approach just exchanged one confessional stance for another, giving primacy to the modern scientific worldview. Postmodern critics took yet another step and examined Scripture to ask not about truth but about whose agenda was being advanced. Newbigin remarked that such a method could be turned on itself. By its own principles, such scholarship had to be viewed "not as the unveiling of any truth, but as a concealed effort (rather successful so far) to assert the authority of academics over ecclesiastics." Critical scholarship, despite legitimate insights, was self-contradictory in at least two ways. First, it relativized biblical truth claims by placing them in a particular culture but ignored that the critical method was "itself the product of a particular culture." Second, critics claimed to represent a scholarly majority but naïvely ignored that the vast majority of people in most ages and cultures who studied the Bible did so from a confessional acceptance of its authority. "If we take a global view and a long view, must we not say that the opinion of a very small minority in a culture that appears to be collapsing is asserting an authority that fits oddly with their real situation?" (1995b, 79-85, 101-102).

As the church did not have to be error-free in order to be the community chosen by God for mission to the world, so the Bible did not have to be error-free to bear reliable witness to Jesus. Although Newbigin saw merit in conservative critiques of liberal views of Scripture, he thought conservatives too often adopted "a style of certainty more in the tradition of Descartes than in the truly evangelical spirit." They were too fearful of new discoveries, too reluctant to reconsider long-held beliefs, and too prone to present Christianity as "a matter of demonstrable fact rather than a matter of grace received in faith" (1995b, 70). It was a mistake for fundamentalists to treat the Bible as "a collection of individual facts" akin to what science textbooks claimed to offer.[8] In contrast, Newbigin portrayed "the character of the Bible as a summons to the adventure of faith, calling for interpretation in different circumstances, requiring the exercise of fallible human judgment at every stage through the original writing and the many translations to the contemporary reader" (1994a, 165). Newbigin disparaged "a kind of fundamentalism which seeks to affirm the factual, objective truth of every statement in the Bible and which thinks that if any single factual error were to be admitted, biblical authority would collapse" (1995b, 85).

According to Newbigin, Jesus' disciples had "fallible memories." Accounts of his teachings and actions came "in varied versions filtered through the various rememberings and interpretings of different groups" (1995a, 52).[9] The Bible contained so much variety, even inconsistency, that critical reflection was necessary.[10] Scripture also contradicted "things we certainly know" through science (1989a, 97). The Spirit did not grant infallible accuracy to biblical writers. Even though the church recognized the Bible as "having a position of decisive authority within the entire ongoing tradition," wrote Newbigin, "that

[8]Newbigin warned that those affirming the full factual accuracy of the Bible would be "on a collision course with the findings of science in spite of the efforts of the creationists" (1994d, 73; see also 1994a, 104). Perhaps he was overly eager for Scripture to mesh with science, despite his repeated insistence that "revelation is contradiction."

[9]In accepting the fact of Jesus as absolute revelation but treating as fallible the biblical testimony to the implications of the Christ-fact, Newbigin fell into the very fact/value dichotomy he so abhorred. As Charles Smith points out, Newbigin left the gospel's meaning on "the subjective, values side of the equation." Without any "fixed and knowable" doctrine, we would be left only with different New Testament witnesses and subsequently with what different cultures and traditions take the Christ event to mean. According to Smith, "Newbigin wants the church to proclaim as 'public truth' a gospel the ultimate meaning of which is not clearly known by the church and over which the church should engage in never ending debate." Smith rightly insists that Scripture infallibly reveals not only the historical events centered in Christ but the doctrinal meanings of those events (1999, 115-119). Smith correctly sees Newbigin's denial of inerrancy as an indication that Newbigin "never really leaves the modernist paradigm for truth" (1999, 139).

[10]As examples of conflicting views within Scripture, Newbigin mentioned Joshua's ferocity in contrast to the Sermon on the Mount; exclusiveness in Ezra and Nehemiah as opposed to universalism in Ruth and Jonah; and Paul's view of Roman power as God's servant versus Revelation's depiction of that power as Satanic (1995b, 88-89).

does not mean that the conditions governing all human knowing of God do not apply within the biblical canon." Jesus did not make the Father known by writing a book of "infallible, unrevisable, irreformable statements." Rather, Jesus formed a community whose "witness comes to us in varied forms," so that we know few of Jesus' words and deeds exactly or "with the kind of certainty Descartes identified with reliable knowledge." Since this manner of community and scripture is God's appointed witness to revelation, declared Newbigin, "The doctrine of verbal inerrancy is a direct denial of the way in which God has chosen to make himself known to us as the Father of our Lord Jesus Christ" (1995b, 89-90).

Although biblical writers could be wrong at various points, said Newbigin, "the Bible, taken as a whole, fitly renders God." Like those authors, later Christians could sometimes be wrong in their efforts to address public events in their time and culture, but in such *praxis* (which knowing always involved) they would nevertheless trust the same God they met in the Bible. In the company of past and present believers, they could find fresh biblical insight (1986b, 59-61; 1994a, 50). What people believed about the Bible mattered less than what they did with it, declared Newbigin. They needed to take it in continually and digest it so that it would become "the all-surrounding ambience of daily life," shaping their thoughts, feelings, and actions (1995b, 87). Using Polanyi's terms, Newbigin said Christians had to "indwell" the biblical story so that it would function "as the *tacit* component in our endeavour to understand and deal with the world" (1994d, 76). Such saturation in Scripture occurred through deep involvement in a church community which provided the social context and plausibility structure for indwelling the gospel story (1986b, 58; 1989a, 228-232).

Misguided Apologetics

Newbigin's rejection of ecclesiastical infallibility and biblical inerrancy was matched by his vehement attacks on natural theology and apologetics which sought to make the gospel credible by marshalling evidence or using universal criteria for truth. Newbigin attacked at two levels: he alleged blindness to the cultural particularity of all human knowing, and he depicted traditional apologetics as tantamount to unbelief and idolatry.

On the first level, Newbigin insisted that since all reasoning occurred in a social context, no culture-independent rationality existed as a neutral standard by which to judge all others. Various traditions of rationality made universal claims that rivaled one another, but none could demonstrate their superiority by extricating themselves from their own particularity and making their case in terms of a context-independent rationality. Attempts to do so would naïvely mimic the Enlightenment in treating as universal and neutral what was in fact culture-specific. Therefore, apologists who tried to demonstrate Christianity on the basis of some supposed rationality besides that embodied in the Christian tradition of rationality were making an intellectual mistake (1989a, 64; 1994a, 142).

On the second level, Newbigin lodged much more serious accusations. In his judgment, the approach taken in traditional apologetics and natural theology was not just an intellectual misstep, but sinful departure from God and the gospel. Its evils were legion.

Proofs that appealed to autonomous reason, alleged Newbigin, treated God as a thing, not as a person. A personal being could not be known through impersonal methods of investigation and demonstration, but only through paying direct attention to the person's presence and communication through speech and action (1986b, 87-88; 1994d, 60). Knowing God was akin to knowing other people through sustained personal interaction, so it was disastrous to seek evidence and arguments for God as though the living Lord was merely lifeless matter to "be investigated by the autonomous human subject" (1994a, 93).

Newbigin conceded that because the personal God created all things, made humanity in his image, and "never left himself without witness in the mind and conscience of any people," natural theology was able to gather data supporting "the hypothesis that God exists." Yet there was "radical discontinuity" between this kind of knowledge and personal knowledge evoking receptivity and trust. "Natural theology," contended Newbigin, "is in no way a step on the way toward the theology which takes God's self-revelation as its starting point. It is more likely, in fact, to lead in the opposite direction" (1989a, 62).

Seeking a starting point outside the gospel to prove the gospel's reasonableness involved granting ultimate authority to the contemporary culture's plausibility structure, contradicting the gospel, and looking for a *logos* other than Jesus (1995b, 93-94). Newbigin charged that a claim to neutral rationality would inevitably involve grasping for certainty apart from grace, ignoring sin's impact, and denying the need not just for information but for God's revelation of forgiveness. The product of such reasoning, said Newbigin, would not be the living God but an idol. Natural theology and evangelical rationalism subverted faith and fell into a deadly trap (1994d, 67-68).

If God used particular events and words to reveal his purpose and to summon us to love and obey him, we might respond not by personal commitment but by a distant, calm evaluation of God's revelation and invitation. "But by doing so we would be asserting our right to make the final decision, and we have no means of proving that we have that right. It might be that we do not" (1986b, 41). Subjecting God and his revelation in Christ to our own criteria for rationality and our own right to determine the gospel's credibility was, in Newbigin's estimation, making oneself the judge, and God the one being judged.

Misguided apologetics was at odds with God's grace, insisted Newbigin. The gospel was not just information, but invitation, atonement, reconciliation, and salvation. Gospel assurance differed from the Age of Reason's certainty in at least two ways. First, faith placed confidence "not in the competence of our own knowing, but in the faithfulness and reliability of the one who is known." Second, faith did not claim to grasp final truth "but to be on the way that leads to the fullness of truth." It was absurd to claim full knowledge and absolute certainty about a fellow human's purposes, so it would be even more absurd to make such claims about God. Moreover, rationalistic slogans about being open to evidence and following truth wherever it led assumed that people were seeking truth and would recognize it when they encountered it. However, declared Newbigin, "We are not honest inquirers seeking the truth. We are alienated from truth and are enemies of it. We are by nature idolaters, constructing images of truth shaped by our own desires." The ultimate proof of this came when Truth became incarnate in Jesus, and the representatives of the best in human culture sought to destroy him. Thus, our own notions of pursuing truth had to be renounced. Confessing gospel truth involved "continual indebtedness to grace." Newbigin also stated that a Christian's understanding had to be "constantly open to revision and correction, but—and this is the crucial point—*only* and *always* within the irreversible commitment to Jesus Christ. If that commitment is questioned, then I am once again a clueless wanderer in the darkness, bamboozled by the products of my own imagination" (1995b, 65-70).[11]

---

[11]Newbigin has been criticized for being too exclusivist and dogmatic. Konrad Raiser charges Newbigin's apologetic with neglecting religious plurality (Raiser 1994, 50). Werner Ustorf opposes Newbigin's "new form of Christian apologetic." Ustorf

If God revealed himself to us through "an immeasurably costly act of self-giving for our redemption," it would be insulting to say, "Thank you, but I have other collateral sources of information." Newbigin contended that coming to know God is not a matter of "reasoning from our unredeemed experience." Rather, "Christ gives us the eyes through which we can begin to truly understand our experience in the world." Evangelical apologists who sought "context-independent criteria" to bolster Christian claims fell into the trap of Descartes, rather than recognizing "the certainty of faith as the only kind of certainty available." In addition, the pursuit of allegedly indubitable certainties often produced arrogance and "a kind of hard rationalism that is remote from grace" (1995b, 97-100).

Only God was context-independent, insisted Newbigin. Only when the Judge brought history to its finale would all evidence be available for absolute proof. Only then would Jesus' supremacy as the meaning of history be empirically and universally evident beyond doubt (1983, 50; 1986b, 60; 1989a, 65; 1994a, 79). Only then would the salvation or damnation of any individual be known for sure. Meanwhile, belief in Christ or lack thereof was no sure indicator of eternal destiny (1969, 60-61; 1982a, 151; 1989a, 180; 1994a, 129; 1995a, 78-81, 173-174).[12] God gave Jesus as the clue to history's goal, and the Spirit revealed Je-

---

applauds Europe's "disestablishment of Jesus Christ" and says that Christian beliefs are no longer taken as "sentences about 'what is the case.'" Ustorf reduces Jesus' divinity and atonement to just "one particular cultural (the Hellenistic) option." With a new "plurireligious awareness," writes Ustorf, Christian mission is "not about Christianizing the world," but about partnering "in the mission of other religions and also of (agnostic) humanism." Missionary spirituality should not "lead us to 'God'" but instead should "lead us to our fellow human beings" (Ustorf 2002, 128-144). Lynn Price similarly rejects Newbigin's emphasis on revealed truth to be made public. Price says Newbigin's approach feels like "a tightly controlled, white, Western-conceptual, male-dominated, authoritarian church compound with little traffic between it and the continuing life of the world." If truth is really personal, perspectival, and practical, contends Price, we should drop claims about the church as "community of the true." Price calls for "a radical attitude shift" in the direction of "faithful uncertainty" which accepts inconsistency and plurality, questions orthodoxy, and engages the wide variation within Christianity and outside it, assuming the Spirit is in everyone (Price 2002, 107-110). The pluralism of Price, Raiser and Ustorf is traitorous to Christian faith and mission. Newbigin was right in his irreversible commitment to Christ.

[12]Newbigin's evasiveness about salvation and damnation clouds the gospel's personal urgency. Various observers rightly object to Newbigin's equivocation and agnosticism about how individuals receive eternal life (Carson 1996, 287; Corduan 1997, 38-40; Hunsberger 1998, 225-234; Scrotenboer 1982, 153; Smith 1999, 160-164).

sus through the fallible biblical witness as further developed, proclaimed, and lived in the fallible church's witness in different cultures and eras. Until the end, Christians would have to walk by faith in God's revelation within history and become witnesses themselves, without seeking the kind of certainty that would come from a book of inerrant propositions or a system of irrefutable arguments. With the clue already given but certainty awaiting the end, eschatology was crucial for Newbigin's epistemology, as Schuster shows (2006, 335). Newbigin's "eschatological epistemology" (Foust 2002b, 162; Hunsberger 2000, 19) opposed any apologetic that claimed to provide demonstrable certainty.

Newbigin's attacks on what he saw as misguided apologetics stemmed largely from his epistemology. Foust helpfully portrays Newbigin in terms of "an internal dialectic or a dual discourse," involving an epistemology "from below" and another "from above." Epistemology "from below" limited all people to seeing the world through the accepted understandings of a particular tradition they inherited or chose. While this epistemology would bring freedom from scientism's claim to a monopoly on absolute certainty, it would also entail cultural relativism in religious or human studies, says Foust, making "all absolutes empty and all beginnings arbitrary." However, Newbigin's overriding missionary concern was for the factual and historical revelation in Christ, objectively originating "from above," which could already be known with confidence by insiders. While epistemology from below said that "there is no privileged position for knowing that is above all others," epistemology from above said that Christians know "the ultimate meaning of the universe." When thinking from below raised problems of relativism, Newbigin did not address the problems but simply moved to an emphasis on thinking from above, asserts Foust. Indeed, Newbigin frequently switched back and forth between positions without telling the reader (or perhaps without recognizing the switch himself). Thus Newbigin claimed that verification could only be eschatological, even as he contended for objective truth insiders can know. This dual discourse may be why theologians of quite different positions are drawn to Newbigin, suggests Foust (2002b, 160-162).

This dual discourse may also be why Newbigin has provoked complaints that seem mutually contradictory. For instance, Harold Netland (1994, 106-111) finds Newbigin's approach too presuppositional, while Charles Smith (1999, 119) criticizes Newbigin for being too evidential. I think Newbigin is more presuppositional than evidential, but his dialectical style and inconsistencies leave his writings open to very different understandings and assessments. According to Foust's dual-discourse analysis, Newbigin's epistemology was presuppositional in that it had foundations that could not be proven, but he did "not follow it through like a typical presuppositionalist approach." Instead, Newbigin granted fundamental epistemological importance to the very process of ongoing theological debate, while his eschatological epistemology denied certainty to any position (Foust 2002b, 162).

Newbigin's dual discourse fueled his intense opposition to apologetics other than his own. A striking case in point occurred in an exchange between Newbigin and Harold Netland. While Netland praised Newbigin's critique of modernity and his call to evangelize others and honor Jesus' lordship over all of life, Netland suggested that Newbigin conceded too much to presuppositionalism in basing all knowing on faith postulates and in denying the possibility of "context-independent criteria for evaluating worldviews." Netland argued that faith postulates could not really be an epistemological starting point since they rested on epistemologically prior basic beliefs such as non-contradiction, extra-mental reality, general reliability of senses and memory, and more. Furthermore, contended Netland, if one disallowed the possibility of non-arbitrary criteria and allowed only presuppositions bound to cultural context or personal choice, relativism was unavoidable. Rather than capitulate in this way to the relativism and skepticism of contemporary plausibility structures, Netland advocated positive apologetics. At a theoretical, transcultural level, positive apologetics would seek to identify and use context-independent criteria to objectively justify Christian claims. At an applied level, positive apologetics would present the gospel in a manner sensitive to particularities of cultural context and individual personality (1994, 96-111).

Newbigin's response to Netland was fierce but largely misguided. Although Netland plainly stated that transcultural criteria could be objectively valid even if denied by a flawed worldview, Newbigin alleged that Indian philosophy's denial of the principle of non-contradiction disproved the possibility of context-independent criteria. Newbigin wrongly equated Netland's concept of basic beliefs with the Enlightenment's "self-evident beliefs," using the failure of one to discredit the other. Newbigin charged that "context-independent" knowledge assumed a mechanistic cosmos, sought to stand outside history, denied God, contradicted Scripture, and fell away from faith into "the Cartesian trap" (1994d, 86).

However, when Netland used the phrase "context-independent," he was not endorsing a mechanistic cosmos or claiming to step outside history or denying the significance of cultural context and individual subjectivity. He was making an ontological claim that there are principles and criteria which transcend particular contexts, and he wanted apologists to identify and deploy these as far as possible. Just how far that might be was an epistemological question, distinct from the ontological claim that such criteria existed. Also, Netland was claiming that despite considerable differences throughout history and across cultures, some aspects of knowing were common to all (or nearly all) contexts. He was denying that cultures are so different as to make communication and evaluation impossible. Thus Netland was not playing God; he was asserting that human rationality and morality have more in common across the range of cultures than Newbigin supposed.

Netland suggested that the disagreement with Newbigin was less than it first appeared and that part of the difference may have been that they were "each reacting against quite different emphases within modernity." He saw Newbigin reacting against "an excessive confidence in the powers of reason," while Netland was responding to "the opposite extreme, an excessive irrationalism and loss of confidence in reason to settle cognitive disputes" (Netland 1994, 114-115 note 26). While there is truth in that assessment, I think Newbigin's denunciation of Netland was also at least partly due to the "dual discourse" running through Newbigin's epistemology. When an apologist such as Netland differed from Newbigin's culture-bound epistemology-from-below, Newbigin reacted hotly as though Netland was challenging epistemology-from-above and denying the need for revelation and regeneration.

Proper Apologetics

In rejecting some apologetic approaches, Newbigin did not totally repudiate apologetics but proposed a different approach. The church would be going down the wrong path if it tried to authenticate gospel truth "by reference to some allegedly more reliable truth claim." In that sense, the church could agree with postmodernists in replacing timeless truth with a story. Still, noted Newbigin, the church differed profoundly from postmodernism. "For the postmodernists, there are many stories but no overarching truth by which they can be assessed. They are simply stories. The church's affirmation is that the story it tells, embodies, and enacts is the true story and that others are to be evaluated by

211

reference to it" (1995b, 76).[13] God's revelation was "not a matter of co-ercive demonstration but of grace, of a love that forgives and invites." Grace guided confidence in speaking of God and the manner of com-mending gospel truth to others (1995b, 78). Those chosen by God and gripped by the gospel story were to be apologists in community through public testimony, personal commitment, and intellectual effort to show how, from the starting point of the gospel, new perspectives opened up which made more sense of a wide range of things.

Newbigin asserted that "the proper form of apologetics is the preaching of the gospel itself and the demonstration—which is not merely or primarily a matter of words—that it does provide the best foundation for a way of grasping and dealing with the mystery of our existence in this universe." Such demonstration could only be "partial and tentative" until God's final judgment. Jesus' incarnation, crucifix-ion, and resurrection could not fit into any plausibility structure based on other assumptions. "The reasonableness of Christianity will be demonstrated (insofar as it can be) not by adjusting its claims to the re-quirements of a preexisting structure of thought but by showing how it can provide an alternative foundation for a different structure." This approach did not involve abandonment of reason or "a blind leap in the dark," insisted Newbigin. Rather, it was "a personal response to a personal calling." Jesus did not offer provable certainties; he sum-

---

[13]George Hunsberger applauds Newbigin for helping Christians navigate the transition from modern to postmodern—in an era that was already post-Christian. Hunsberger says Newbigin's "postmodern apologetic" showed how we could hold things as true even if our grasp was only partial. Hunsberger finds in Newbigin's "log-ic of election" a sound link between divine revelation from above and historical, communal particularity from below, thus showing how something historically situated could have universal significance (Hunsberger 1998, 11-12, 82-112). Paul Weston hails Newbigin as a "postmodern missiologist" who accepted the force of objections to metanarratives and abuse of power, without sinking into relativism (2004, 232). Newbigin engaged postmodernity in a sustainable way, says Weston, by shunning linkage of Christianity to Enlightenment notions of Reason as a neutral stance for evaluating different viewpoints, by emphasizing gospel truth as story and not system, and by making demonstration of truth communal and practical. At the same time, says Weston, Newbigin avoided relativism by not making the Christian story a mere language game limited to its own sectarian boundary. "If modernity's outlook was about rational 'certainties,' and postmodernity's about a radical perspectivism, New-bigin models for us a third possibility: 'witness' to the truth from within a tradition" (Weston 2004, 244-245). Craig Van Gelder (1996, 65-68) and David Kettle (2002a, 207-209) likewise value Newbigin as a guide for how to affirm gospel authority in a postmodern context.

moned people to follow him. If ultimate reality was the personal, triune God, then responding with personal faith to a personal calling was the only way to know God's reality. Any claim that rational proof was cognitively superior to personal response would implicitly—and wrongly—be taking ultimate reality to be impersonal (1995b, 93-95).

Newbigin, following Barth, insisted that revelation meant contradiction, not continuity with previous understandings (1982b, 81, 93 102, 170). Bible passages about God's wisdom confounding the world's wisdom had to be taken with utmost seriousness. Yet discontinuity was not total, said Newbigin. Christian conversion had something in common with a paradigm shift in science: the new paradigm was not contained in the old and could not be reached by logical inference from the old, yet the old could "be rationally understood from the point of view of the new." Therefore, recognizing radical discontinuity did not mean giving in to irrationality. "Seen from one side there is only a chasm; seen from the other there is a bridge." A converted person's new understanding could "find a place for the truth that was embodied in the former vision and yet at the same time offer a wider and more inclusive rationality than the older one could." The new, wider rationality provided a standpoint from which the old could be embraced and not contradicted (1986b, 52-53).

The insights of modern culture could never provide a basis for proving the gospel's rationality, yet the gospel, if accepted by faith, could integrate scientific learning and other modern discoveries. "From one side the other looks quite irrational, but from the other side there is a rationality that embraces both." Conflicts between resurrection faith and modern, miracle-denying scientism could not be settled by logic. "The view will prevail that is seen to offer—both in theory and practice—the widest rationality, the greatest capacity to give meaning to the whole of experience. This is as much a matter of faithful endeavor and costly obedience as of clarity and coherence of argument." Conversion of the mind had to involve a paradigm shift leading to "a new vision of how things are" (1986b, 63-64).

Wary of "the reductionist trap" that prevented acknowledgement of purpose and personality, Newbigin testified, "I believe that all created beings have a sacramental character in that they exist by the creative goodness and for the redeeming purpose of God, that nothing is rightly understood otherwise." Taking the Incarnation and Trinity as the starting point for understanding the whole of reality, one could recognize human personhood as real and seek relationships with other persons. This could not be done from the standpoint of "the real but limited rationality of the reductionist views that try to explain the whole of reality in terms of the natural sciences from physics to biology." Christian thought did not allow such views to be autonomous or ultimate, yet it did recognize and include "these other kinds of explanations as proper and necessary at their respective levels." Rather than start at the bottom and reason upward from impersonal particles, Newbigin suggested that apologetics begin with ultimate personhood and purpose and work downward, showing how purpose was evident in humans and higher animals and "may be recognized throughout the whole range of nature . . . right down to the lowest levels" (1986b, 87-92).

According to Newbigin, "The territory which natural theology explores may be quite properly explored in the reverse direction," starting with God's revelation in Jesus and exploring "all its implications in the realm of philosophy" (1994d, 70). With the gospel as its starting point, the church could pursue "a proper kind of natural theology that deals with the same area natural theology addresses," covering the same field of inquiry but starting "from the other end." Rather than arguing from data or experience to the gospel, Christians were to show "how the Christian story enables us to understand and deal with the whole range of experience in both public and private life." This, declared Newbigin, "is a true and necessary form of apologetics" (1995b, 96).

The church community was to assert authority publicly not by proofs but by witnessing in Jesus' name, invoking the Trinity, and "offering a model for grasping human life" (1995a, 28). The church in each new era had to show the gospel paradigm's "adequacy to human experience" and "its power to 'make sense' of new situations." When the gospel was published as truth for all peoples and all aspects of life, wrote Newbigin, it would "prove itself so by opening the way to fresh discoveries and fresh coherences and fresh clarities" (1994a, 93, 108). A Christian witnessing to an unbeliever could not "justify the new pattern in terms of the old," but the Christian could say, "Stand here with me and see if you don't see the same pattern I do" (1989a, 11).

Newbigin usually insisted that it was impossible to judge between different plausibility structures and traditions of rationality by appealing to any standard of rationality beyond the competing systems. Yet occasionally he could sound as though the absurdity of materialistic scientism ought to be obvious, and the rational superiority of Christianity equally obvious. "What could be more absurd than the idea that the whole universe has come into existence by a series of accidents, and that it functions like a machine—constructed by nobody for no purpose?" Christianity "gives an infinitely more rational account of the universe and of our experience in it than does the contemporary creed" (1994a, 173).

Despite his fierce rhetoric against basing Christian belief upon arguments rather than an act of faith, Newbigin stated that philosophical analysis and argument could be "a very necessary part of the task of Christian witness."

> Any mind shaped by modernity will be fully furnished with beliefs and assumptions which seem to make Christian faith untenable or at least very questionable. Part of Christian testimony is to uncover the hidden assumptions behind these beliefs and to show how God's action in Christ, in redeeming and revealing, opened the way for a truer understanding of that which had been seen as calling it into question. This activity can have a very important role in helping others on the journey of faith. In that sense they may form part of the pathway to faith. But one must distinguish between the ways by which people are drawn to faith (which are as various as are the varieties of human nature and experience) and the foundation on which faith rests. This foundation cannot be anything provided by the philosopher. It can only be the action of God himself. The only ultimate authority in the new creation is its Author. (1994d, 70)

This distinction between faith's ultimate foundation and the various pathways to faith should have restrained Newbigin from premature attacks on evangelical apologists. So far as I know, most of these apologists regarded argument and evidence as means God could use to help certain types of people toward faith, not as substitutes for the Spirit's regenerating work or as competitors with God's authority in the incarnate Word and the written Word.

Public Truth

Newbigin denied that his epistemology of personal knowledge made the gospel merely subjective. He insisted on the gospel as public truth. Through world mission, the gospel was to summon all individuals and peoples to faith (1991, 33). Moreover, the gospel was to be public truth in that it was to permeate congregational life and to address every public institution and issue. Newbigin thought it insufficient to present the gospel as a theory, a worldview, or a religion. The gospel had to be "embodied in a society (the church) which is both 'abiding in' Christ and engaged in the life of the world" (1995b, 39). Christ crucified as ultimate revelation and authority would be credible only if congregations were vibrant and were engaging the full range of institutions and issues (1989a, 227; 1994a, 42).[14]

> The local congregation is the only effective hermeneutic of the gospel. Europe was originally evangelized from the top down. Kings were converted and their peoples followed. If it is to be reevangelized, it will be from the bottom up. The thousands of local congregations throughout Europe need to be reaffirmed, encouraged, and enabled to be the centers from which a new way of seeing the world can dawn on a society that has lost the belief that truth can be known. (1994a, 176)

Thus, for Newbigin, mission to the West meant not just witnessing to individuals but also challenging societal structures (1983, 33; 1986b, 95; 1987, 7; 1994a, 172).[15] The church had to proclaim Jesus' supremacy over principalities and powers. In discussing the powers, Newbigin said little about demonic tempters trying to influence or bring damnation on individual humans; instead, he spoke largely in terms of unmasking dominant ideologies (1982b, 210-211; 1989a, 198-210; 1991, 74). God's Word authorized the church to speak in God's name "to the state and to every other human institution." Religious freedom was not merely the church's freedom to do its own thing. Rather, the church's proper freedom was "inseparable from its obligation to declare the sovereignty of Christ over every sphere of human life without exception" (1991, 70-72).

---

[14]According to Wilbert Shenk, the Gospel and Our Culture program, which Newbigin helped launch, expressed his "consuming passion" to renew the Western church so that it could bring Christian witness "to bear on the whole of life . . . without reverting to 'Constantinian' forms and assumptions" (2000, 63).

[15]Forrester says that Newbigin offered "helpful, heady rhetoric" about public truth but said little about application. For the most part, Newbigin's sweeping language about the missionary necessity of engaging public policy floated "free of concrete earthing" and drew little attention outside the church (Forrester 2002, 8-10). Drew notes that Newbigin's call for public engagement was "light on explaining in detail" how to persuade others with different convictions (2005, 29). In a rare flash of specificity, Newbigin sought a Barmen-style declaration targeting Margaret Thatcher's policies. That attempt failed. Evidently few British Christians were convinced that Thatcher's policies constituted an evil comparable to Nazi ideology. In my opinion, this quixotic episode illustrates a hazard of Newbigin's overstatement that a gospel which does not engage public life is no gospel at all.

Newbigin urged that, without resorting to coercion or limiting freedom of religion, Christians should unashamedly seek "a privileged position for the Christian faith in the public life of the nation." He wanted not a new Christendom ruled by ecclesiastical officials but a society which contained large numbers of Christians who had thought through how to apply the Christian faith to various sectors of public life (Newbigin, Sanneh, and Taylor 1998, 157, 163-164). Congregations had to provide a setting for Christians to do this. The main activity of the church in the world would be "the action of its members in their daily work" (1994a, 154-156). [16] Newbigin suggested that in all sectors of public life—"industry, politics, medicine, education, local government, welfare, administration, the media, literature, drama, and the arts"—Christian lay people in each sector should join together and "examine the accepted axioms and assumptions that underlie the contemporary practice" (1994a, 73). A renewed influence of Christian truth in public life, permeating "the conversation of economists, psychiatrists, educators, scientists, and politicians," would not destroy legitimate gains of the Enlightenment, said Newbigin, but would preserve their fruits on the only basis that could resist the new barbarians (1991, 39, 64). Newbigin's call for a missionary sense of public engagement, though motivated by noble intentions and prompting some missiologists to pursue it further, has also raised various unresolved problems. [17]

[16]Goheen likes Newbigin's view that "the task of believers in their various callings in culture is the primary place where a missionary encounter takes place" (Goheen 2002b, 40). Goheen agrees with Newbigin that salvation touches not just human souls but the whole creation (2002b, 43). Yet Newbigin leaves us with an unresolved dilemma, observes Goheen: "If a Christian exercises political authority, where does s/he allow room for freedom and dissent and where is there a required submission to the law that has been fashioned in light of the gospel?" (2002b, 48-49).

[17]Douglas Ottati wonders how a state can endorse Christianity while defending religious freedom. If "the gospel" is to shape public life, which of the various viewpoints among differing Christian groups qualifies as *the* gospel? Which elements of pagan and secular culture will be eliminated if Christianity is the foundation for public life and if Christians hold privileged positions? (Ottati 1993). Hunsberger, though usually aligned with Newbigin, challenges Newbigin's eagerness for the gospel to provide the basis of the social order. Hunsberger opposes any suggestion that "a society might embrace the Christian vision as its basis apart from adherence to and allegiance toward Jesus the Christ." That was the problem with the old Christendom: "the society had the shell of the Christian faith's perspective and ethos while no longer holding its essential faith." The church must not "return in spirit or form" to a relationship with wider society "rooted in the memory or remnants of Christendom," lest it "forfeit the next stage of its calling" (Hunsberger 2002, 105).

CHAPTER 10

Comparison and Evaluation

This chapter highlights and evaluates key similarities and differences between Lewis and Newbigin in their diagnoses of intellectual hindrances to Christianity, their epistemological views, and their recommendations for missional apologetics. I identify points of comparison (drawing on chapters 5 through 9), assess strengths and weaknesses in each author's approach, and discuss the degree to which differences in their views might have been due to differences in the contexts experienced by each (as described in chapters 3 and 4).

Their Diagnoses of Intellectual Hindrances

Lewis and Newbigin both perceived Britain and the broader West to be engaged in an ongoing, accelerating movement away from Christendom. Both were ambivalent toward past Christendom, valuing some aspects but lamenting others, such as the use of force to impose a creed. Both wondered how broad or deep the earlier, coercive Christianization of Europe had been, and both saw a need to re-convert Europe, this time through mission rather than coercion. Both thought that post-Christian cultures were more resistant to the gospel than pre-Christian cultures. Both sought to identify and deal with intellectual hindrances to the gospel in their context. Lewis focused more on intellectual hindrances to the persuasion and conversion of individuals, while Newbigin paid more attention to intellectual factors that curbed the gospel's impact on various public spheres.

218

Both generalized about "the West" at times, but Lewis was more wary of such generalizations than Newbigin. Lewis stressed that intellectual and religious variety had long characterized "the West," and he stated that his diagnosis was based mainly on interaction with university students and with intelligent proletarians whom he met in the Royal Air Force. Newbigin, by contrast, painted with a broader brush and seldom specified which real people his observations were based upon when he spoke about "the West."

Both wrote of intellectual developments among educated elites, but Lewis suggested that the influence of such elites was in decline, while Newbigin's diagnosis gave more weight to intellectual history and to the potential trickle-down effect that a new missionary-driven epistemology could have. Ironically, the career missionary stressed the impact of highbrow intellectual trends more than the career scholar did. This difference may have been partly due to the very fact that Lewis spent so much time in a scholarly context. That context could foster awareness of complexity, sensitivity to nuance, and wariness of sweeping generalizations or overstatement. At the same time, it could provide exposure to a host of philosophical, literary, and artistic movements that were out of touch with ordinary people and seemed unlikely ever to have much impact on them.

There may have been a weightier factor, though, that moved Newbigin to emphasize the impact of intellectual elites more than Lewis did: a significant difference in the two men's actual level of interaction with people in Britain and the West. Lewis based his cultural assessment on decades of daily contact with students who were not yet elite scholars, on much give and take with intelligent proletarians, and on personal correspondence with thousands of people from various walks of life. Newbigin, on the other hand, lived outside the West for most of his adult life. Upon his return to Britain, his assessment of the West owed more to his reading of scholarly books than to interaction with a wide spectrum of less educated Britons and Americans in the late twentieth century context.[1] Moreover, Newbigin's core diagnosis of the West was not a discovery he made in later years through interaction with various kinds of people; rather, it was a reaffirmation of views he had learned from intellectual mentors already as a student back in the

---

[1] Newbigin claimed to find his "Archimedean point"—a perspective from which to look critically at his own culture—during his retirement years while reading books by Western thinkers focusing on the impact of the Enlightenment (1993c, 250-251).

early 1930s.[2] In his experience as a seventy-something pastor in the Birmingham context, Newbigin interacted mainly with immigrants and with white Christians who were elderly like him, not with young and middle-aged white people who were more typical of the majority of Britain's population.

Lewis and Newbigin both shared Pascal's antipathy to "the geometric spirit." Both saw problems in a methodology that sought to reduce all things to the mathematical and the mechanical. Both warned against a dichotomy between fact and value which explained away value and denied overarching purpose. Both saw in scientism an imperialistic lust for power, and both warned that abandonment of religious and moral truth about personhood tended to reduce all discourse to mere assertion of power. While Newbigin drew directly upon Lewis's critique of scientism, Newbigin placed somewhat more emphasis on the imperialistic dimension of modern Western rationality, perhaps reflecting the impact of his time in India during its break from British rule, his familiarity with complaints from non-Western participants in ecumenical discussions, and his reading of postmodern scholars who viewed metanarratives as assertions of power. Newbigin also stressed more than Lewis that a dichotomy between fact and value carried with it a split between public and private. This emphasis may have stemmed partly from differences in sociopolitical context: public institutions became less religious and more secular later in the century, when Newbigin wrote, than they had been in Lewis's time. Also, Newbigin moved in theological circles that underscored God's kingdom reign and emphasized social action and political engagement.

---

[2]Readers of Newbigin may get the impression that, after decades of living in India, his experience of the British context in the later 1900s jolted him into seeing the West as a post-Christendom mission field. Walls, for instance, says of Newbigin, "Perhaps like many another returning missionary, he never fully recovered from the culture shock of reentry. He analyzes his own culture as only someone can who has been used to analyzing somebody else's" (Walls 2002, 145). But already in 1933, Newbigin saw the West as a mission field and was convinced of "the radical departure of Europe from the Christian faith when it followed Descartes and the pioneers of the Enlightenment" (1985a, 25-26). When he settled back into his old homeland in the later 1900s, he may also have settled back into his old assessment of its root problems. His contacts with non-Western Christians, his mission experience, and his interactions with Britons in the late 1900s goaded him with new urgency to articulate a missionary critique of Western culture. But in the actual critique, he expanded on positions he had held for decades, and he augmented those earlier views mainly with material he found in books published by Western intellectuals.

Lewis and Newbigin both believed that scientism had roots in a major intellectual shift during the 1600s, in which Descartes was a major player. Lewis was more careful than Newbigin in his appraisal of this shift. Where Newbigin made Descartes a villain responsible for troubles of all sorts, Lewis thought that the shift associated with Descartes and the Enlightenment, considered by itself, was of limited importance for the wider culture. It was one among many intellectual and cultural strands, and was not especially dominant. Lewis placed greater emphasis on the subsequent effects of the Industrial Revolution and on the impact of scientism at a popular level, rather than focusing mostly on intellectual history as Newbigin did. Indeed, Lewis sometimes adapted apologetic arguments from Descartes.

Newbigin depicted the Enlightenment as a reversion to Greek rationalism, making God's revelation subordinate to reason. Lewis viewed Greek thought more positively. He saw Christianity less as the antithesis of Greek rationality than as the successful union of Hebrew and Greek thought in the Christian revelation. If Lewis erred, it was in the direction of downplaying the antithesis between Christianity and other intellectual traditions. If Newbigin erred, it was in the direction of exaggerating that antithesis.

In challenging reductionistic scientism, Lewis and Newbigin both resisted a cosmology that made evolution ultimate, but neither had much of a quarrel with biological theories of evolution as such. In my judgment, they may have conceded too much to the evolutionary narrative and may have slipped into a fact-value split of their own. They were willing to regard the Genesis creation account as a theologically profound folk tale and to grant the "facts" detailed in Darwinian science, so long as value-destroying assumptions of amorality and impersonality were not part of the package. Perhaps, as non-scientists, Lewis and Newbigin thought it best not to venture beyond their realm of competence, and therefore refrained from challenging evolutionary accounts of physical data. Still, given their insights into the provisional, constructed nature of scientific theory, they could have expressed more vigorous doubts about prevalent biological accounts. In doing so, they might also have been able to accept and defend a more straightforward reading of the early chapters of Genesis.

Lewis and Newbigin both raised concerns about syncretism in the thought patterns of churches and theologians. Lewis charged that theological liberals gave more credence to naturalistic assumptions and to faddish notions of progress than to historic Christian claims. Lewis spoke of liberalism as semi-Christian or non-Christian; meanwhile, he seldom criticized conservative evangelicals publicly. Newbigin, on the other hand, wrote at times as though liberalism and conservative evangelicalism ("fundamentalism") were equal and opposite errors, both rooted in syncretistic, idolatrous reliance on Enlightenment-based reason. Newbigin could sound as though evangelical affirmations of biblical inerrancy and apologetic argument were as seriously mistaken as liberal denials of Jesus' incarnation and resurrection. In such utterances, Newbigin lacked a sense of proportion. I think Lewis and Newbigin were both wrong to deny inerrancy, but at least Lewis did not compound his mistake by calling inerrancy a syncretistic product of modernity. Indeed, Lewis stated that most Christians for most of history had a view of biblical inspiration that verged on direct divine dictation (2007, 961). For Lewis, even if affirmation of inerrancy was mistaken, it was not an Enlightenment-based mistake, and it did little harm. For Newbigin, inerrantists and apologists were to be tarred with the same brush as liberals who denied Christian basics.

Newbigin's context may have contributed to such judgments. He spent much of his life in a context of ecumenical activism, pursuing organizational church unity. This probably made him reticent to regard theological liberals as outside the circle of Christian unity, and it may have magnified his distress at evangelicals, many of whom used their conception of truth to denounce the World Council of Churches. In addition, Newbigin's 1980s political context and his reaction to it may have colored his theological judgments. Viewing the policies of Thatcher and Reagan as comparable to Nazi ideology, Newbigin was horrified that so many American evangelicals supported Reagan. Newbigin was upset enough to condemn America's religious right as worse than Khomeini's Islamic revolution, and this wrath against politically conservative evangelicals may have fueled his blasts against theologically conservative evangelicals' views on inerrancy and apologetics.

Lewis and Newbigin both believed that a thought pattern common among many twentieth century Westerners was to make themselves judges over God and to be oblivious to their need for divine grace. Yet Newbigin's analysis differed from Lewis's. Lewis declared that a sense of sin had been lost, and he attributed this to incessant flattery of the self-satisfied masses, the loss of belief in objective moral standards, and psychologists' efforts to erase all guilt feelings. Newbigin stressed that people had enthroned their own reason, setting themselves up as the judges of truth, and had become complacent in an intellectual paradigm that was not based on Christ. Lewis sought to confront people with a moral standard outside themselves and to awaken a sense of sin, in order to prepare people to hear the gospel as good news. Newbigin disparaged attempts to make people aware of their guilt; such awareness, he said, would come only as Jesus and his cross were proclaimed. Any starting point but Christ would be a mistake; it would be a concession to the sort of proud intellectual autonomy that Newbigin saw as the West's chief problem. Lewis, in contrast, thought the cross would seem irrelevant unless people first saw their need for atonement.

In my estimation, Lewis's angle on this matter had more biblical warrant and greater likelihood of missionary effectiveness. Like Lewis, I think the gospel is unlikely to take root where a sense of sin is absent. Like Lewis, I believe that moral law—whether in codified form or in conscience—is the Spirit's chief instrument for bringing awareness of sin and preparing people to cry out for God's mercy in Christ. Still, I would not try to apply a single formula to every situation or deny that Newbigin's emphases could be applicable in certain cases. For some people, a sense of unworthiness comes only after hearing how Jesus loved us and laid down his life for us; for some, awareness of God's judgment may come almost simultaneously with trust in God's acceptance. Moreover, for some people, the sinful tendency to judge God may take the particular intellectual form of demanding that God provide evidence to meet our standards before we condescend to acknowledge God's claims. Thus Newbigin's insights could provide valuable guidance in some situations.

Lewis and Newbigin both saw that extreme rationalism led to reductionism, which in turn produced skepticism and relativism. Newbigin stressed that a Cartesian method of radical doubt could only produce more doubt, and he viewed nihilism as the outcome of a misguided quest for certainty. Lewis recognized that such things played a role, but he also saw other factors contributing to a growing irrationalism. He suggested that many English people were pragmatic, uninterested in finding truth for its own sake; they just wanted to improve their level of comfort and pleasure. Lewis also thought that sloppy popularizations of Freud's and Einstein's ideas had added credence to the notion that everything is relative. Further, Lewis thought that the spread of a vague pantheism was blurring truth and morality. Newbigin similarly posited a link between a pantheistic religious pluralism and distaste for doctrinal truth, but he portrayed pluralism mainly as a result of fact-value and public-private dichotomies emerging from the Enlightenment, whereas Lewis saw not only those factors but various others at work. Both Lewis and Newbigin thought that distaste for doctrine and embrace of irrationalism not only presented serious obstacles to Christian belief, but could also give the church an opportunity to stand out more clearly as a bastion of rationality in contrast to a nihilism that could not satisfy persons or sustain a culture.

When diagnosing intellectual challenges in their respective contexts, both authors expressed concerns about irrationalism as well as rationalism. Lewis had less of a tendency than Newbigin to depict intellectual history as a linear process in which rationalism preceded and produced irrationalism. Lewis saw ebb and flow in various intellectual fashions that might elude explanation by intellectual historians, and he thought Christians needed to recognize such fluctuations and to change their apologetic emphases accordingly. In the 1800s, for instance, "hard thinking seemed to be on the side of materialism," so the most pressing need for Christian thinkers "was to remind people that there is something which escapes discursive thought." But in Lewis's day, "spurious mysticism" was growing among leading opponents of Christianity, so Christians needed to remind people of objective truth and morality (2004b, 188-189). In some settings, anti-intellectual spirituality and scientific rationalism could both be influential simultaneously. Christians would then be in a two-front war. It seems that Lewis perceived this two-front challenge to be the case in his context and accordingly fought on both fronts: contending for objective truth and moral absolutes, and at the same time stressing that reality surpasses discursive thought and its constructs.

My sense of Newbigin is that, although he opposed both rationalism and irrationalism, he regarded rationalism as the main threat and irrationalism as a lesser corollary. When opposing pluralistic irrationalism, he placed most of the blame for it on its rationalistic predecessor: modernity was the progenitor of postmodernity. If modernity's methodology and quest for certainty could be identified and demolished, then postmodernity, too, might give way to a better, gospel-based paradigm. Newbigin saw scientistic rationalism dominating public fact, and pluralistic irrationalism dominating private value. He seemed to think that if he could break the grip of rationalism by relativizing its claims and reducing it to just one socially constructed outlook among many, a more chastened view of public truth would emerge, and pluralistic irrationalism would also lose strength as various communities made claims with universal intent. Newbigin's overriding concern with rationalism may have led him to underestimate the risk that his own approach would tilt toward irrationalism.

Their Epistemological Views

Lewis and Newbigin both were critical realists. Both affirmed realities independent of a person's mind, and both insisted that human thought is truthful to the degree that it is in touch with such realities. Both flatly rejected anti-realist skepticism; they regarded it as an intellectual pose, not a genuine belief. At the same time, Lewis and Newbigin both recognized that thought is framed in language and is often limited by the capacities of a particular linguistic system. Both perceived that historical, social, psychological, and physiological factors always condition, and sometimes distort, how people think. Both held that human thought involves constructs which are not exact mental replicas of reality. Both observed that a shift from one cosmological or theological model to another model could result from factors besides fresh evidence. Both sometimes expressed the critical dimensions of their epistemology so strongly that their realism could seem shaky. Still, while stressing the need to be aware of limits and fallibility in one's thinking and to be open to correction and further discovery, Lewis and Newbigin both opposed giving up on truth altogether. Instead, they called for diligence in pursuing truth and in sharing truth with others. In these respects, they were on the right track: critical realism seems a sound perspective for epistemology.

In addition to their critical realism, Lewis and Newbigin had other similarities in their epistemological views. Both dismissed the notion of autonomously learning everything from scratch. Both observed that most of what we know is learned from others and accepted on their authority. Both stressed the need for mentorship in a tradition of knowing and for fellowship in a community of shared belief. Both regarded the Bible as authoritative though not inerrant. If read regularly and taken as a whole, the Bible was a reliable witness to God and his ways and would bring sound knowledge of the real Jesus. However, Scripture contained some harmless errors of minor fact, and perhaps even conveyed some things that were evil and damaging unless corrected in light of the whole.

Without expanding on my own belief in biblical inerrancy, I think it is worth asking what the net impact of Lewis's and Newbigin's epistemology of the Bible has been in the West. In distancing themselves

225

from the camp of unbelieving higher critics of Scripture, while not going all the way into the camp of those who affirm inerrancy, Lewis and Newbigin occupied a place somewhere between. In commending that position, did they enable many non-believers who could not swallow inerrancy to at least take the Bible as authoritative? Did they provide space for many Christians with somewhat varying views of biblical authority to stop bickering and agree simply to honor its authority without bothering about inerrancy? Or have their views of the Bible pulled more people away from affirmation of inerrancy? In the absence of quantitative research to answer these questions, one can only guess. Still, Lewis and Newbigin have been more popular among evangelicals than among liberals, so my concern would be that the number of evangelicals drawn away from inerrancy could exceed the number of critics and unbelievers won over to trust in biblical authority.

Lewis and Newbigin both stressed that knowing is closely related to virtue, that sin impedes and distorts believing, that plausibility and practice are intertwined, that growth in holiness is yoked to growth in knowledge. They differed, however, on the degree to which humanity's fall into sin damaged our capacity to know. Newbigin, from his Reformed and Barthian theological context, considered sin's devastation of mind and conscience to be pervasive; God's revelation in Christ of the true and the good stood in contradiction to humanity's fallen mind and conscience. Lewis, on the other hand, understood the Bible—particularly Romans 7—to teach that sin damaged our knowledge of God's Law less than our ability to obey it (though he also held that the deeper one sank into sin, the less the mind and conscience could discern the true and the good). Granting that our moral perceptions were impaired, Lewis still insisted that "there is a difference between imperfect sight and blindness." If our idea of goodness were completely different from what God meant by goodness, then the claim that God is good would have no content, and authentic religion would be indistinguishable from devil worship (1967, 108).

Although Lewis's and Newbigin's views on the noetic effects of sin were in tension, it would be unwise simply to dismiss one perspective in favor of the other. Some of the tension may spring from different points made in Scripture itself—not contradictions, but variations of emphasis. Even when we choose to sin, we often know better. We are not merely ignorant of God's reality; we know truth but suppress it. About this Lewis was right. By the same token, the unregenerate mind is blind to God's glory in the face of Christ. The cross is foolishness to

226

the perishing. The gospel contradicts worldly wisdom. Newbigin was right to take seriously the mind's depravity. If Newbigin erred, it was in extrapolating from such truths a full-blown epistemology about non-Christian people that seemed mostly a negation. If Lewis erred, it was in underestimating sin's damage to human reasoning and the radical discontinuity between unregenerate thought and gospel truth.

Lewis and Newbigin both held that some things must be taken as givens, that all reasoning must start with at least some presuppositions. However, they sounded very different notes on what could be presupposed. Lewis posited self-evident absolutes and first principles of logic and morality; Newbigin attacked such notions. Both authors correlated the presuppositions of their epistemology with an ontology that made God the ultimate reality, but they did so in contrasting ways. Both affirmed the holy Trinity as ultimate reality. Both spoke of the sacramental character of all created things. Both looked to the Word (Logos), the second person of the Trinity, as the objective source and standard of truth and goodness. They differed, however, on the epistemological implications of this ontological conviction.

Lewis insisted that absolute, objective logic must be taken as a first principle, and he viewed human logic as an offshoot of the Logos. Likewise, Lewis declared that absolute, objective morality must be presupposed, and he regarded the moral *Tao* as the Word himself expressing God's righteous nature in temporal terms. For Lewis, logic and morality had absolute ontological grounding in the Logos, and people's minds and consciences could have some sense of timeless, Logos-based reality even if they did not know the historical incarnation of the Logos in Jesus and did not know Scripture.

Newbigin, on the other hand, disparaged claims to timeless truth and focused more exclusively on the historical manifestation of the Logos in Jesus, especially his death and resurrection. Seeking any other starting point for knowledge, charged Newbigin, was to look for a logos other than Jesus. That charge was not strictly accurate, as the case of Lewis showed. Lewis's view of logic and morality, though not revolving specifically around Jesus' death and resurrection, looked to the Logos. Lewis did not look for a logos besides the Logos who came to us in Jesus; he just took seriously the fact that the Logos pre-dated the incarnation and made himself known in various lesser ways besides manifesting himself most fully in Jesus. Jesus is not only the man from Nazareth who atoned for sin and conquered death; he is also the Word through whom all things were made, the one who fills the whole universe and in whom all things hold together (John 1:1-9; Eph 4:10; Col 1:15-17; Heb 1:2).

Lewis was fond of Plato, and it is understandable that some critics think Lewis's ideas about a transcendent, absolute Reason and *Tao* were framed too much along Platonic lines and should have been tempered by more specifically biblical conceptualization. However, in my view, Lewis's insistence on epistemological first principles of reason and morality do not contradict biblical revelation and are consistent with his Logos-based ontology. The Word's act of creation preceded his incarnation, crucifixion and resurrection. Newbigin's call to make Jesus' resurrection the starting point for knowing neglected the Word's prior role in creating an intelligible universe and endowing humans with intelligence.

For Lewis, first principles of thought and morality expressed universal, timeless truths that were not bound to any locale or era. Accordingly, Lewis stressed commonalities across cultures and continuities across time in logical and moral reasoning. For Newbigin, first principles were to be found only in a specific time and place, in the specific acts of a specific person (Jesus), who lived in a specific context and formed a community of chosen witnesses (the church) to bear specific testimony. Consequently, Newbigin stressed differences between historically conditioned cultures and incommensurability between their socially shaped plausibility structures.

Lewis characteristically treated similarities among various cultures as more significant than differences in logics, moralities, and myths. He often stressed a common "core." This was somewhat out of keeping with another position taken by Lewis. In his literary criticism, Lewis attacked "the method of The Unchanging Human Heart. According to this method the things which separate one age from another are superficial." Lewis sardonically granted "that if you remove from people the things that make them different, what is left must be the same, and that the Human Heart will certainly appear Unchanging if you ignore its changes" (1942, 61-62). Lewis himself might have been vulnerable to this very charge in his own emphasis on cross-cultural common ground in logical reasoning, morality, and myth. Commonalities were bound to loom large if differences were downplayed.

Newbigin, on the other hand, stressed cultural differences and historical conditioning to such a degree that his epistemology seemed to leave little room for discussion based on any shared principles of inference or morality. He implied that if cultures evidenced some variations from each other in their views of right and wrong, it meant that no common core of morality could be identified. Newbigin also seemed to think that if some in India denied the validity of inferential logic and regarded the physical world and other persons to be illusory, this showed that appeals to logic or basic beliefs were merely assertions of distinctively Western constructs. Newbigin suggested that such constructs seemed self-evident only because they had been socially reinforced for centuries in the West. I think Newbigin went overboard in minimizing commonalities across cultures and in stressing the social construction of knowledge. It is questionable whether most people, even in India, avoid inferential thinking or act as though the external world is unreal.[3] Those who do hold such notions might better be regarded as aberrations from what seems obvious to most people in most cultures, rather than as proof that various cultures' logics and moralities have little in common and are separated from each other by unbridgeable chasms.[4]

Lewis and Newbigin were both critical realists who recognized that language and thought could refer truthfully to reality but could not provide exact linguistic or mental replicas of reality. Yet the critical dimension of each author's critical realism took quite different form and expressed different emphases. Newbigin placed greater emphasis than Lewis on communal plausibility structures in the formation and reinforcement of beliefs, whereas Lewis paid more attention than Newbig-

[3]As Groothuis points out, "Newbigin fails to distinguish the common canons of logic and evidence from non-Christian plausibility structures." Groothuis agrees with Newbigin that apologists must not alter the gospel to make it conform to fallen thought patterns or sinful cultural trends, "but one may appeal to the light of conscience and reason available to all people made in the image and likeness of God who live within the revelation of creation (Gen 1:26; Ps 19; Acts 14:17; Rom 1-2)." Groothuis grants that in all our reasoning, we are embodied creatures in particular cultures. Even so, some principles "are universally true and applicable within and between worldviews" (Groothuis 2000, 157).

[4]Griffiths (1987) and Netland (2001, 293-296) find that many Eastern thinkers adhere to logical principles such as non-contradiction. Even if some in the East deny the law of non-contradiction, "there is literally no other way that thinking can proceed," insists Andrew Kirk. Moreover, human dignity involves coherent thought and consistency between thought and action. "In practice all people, whatever their theory may say to the contrary, act on the basis of fundamental beliefs. These are beliefs universally held by humankind and reflected in the common structure of all languages. Their negation is not merely false but absurd; they are necessary for engaging in the practical affairs of life." Modernity fell into idolatrous rationalism, but that did not discredit universal principles: "Reason itself is not at fault" (Kirk 1999, 167-170).

in to the epistemological importance of metaphor and myth. At times Lewis could sound perilously close to anti-realism in his discussions of how all discourse involved metaphors, images, and constructs. By the same token, Newbigin could go so far in emphasizing the impact of socially conditioned plausibility structures that some of his critics could accuse him of regarding truth as a social convention rather than as an accurate reference to reality. Still, both Lewis and Newbigin remained realists, and both offered insights that were valuable if kept within proper bounds.[5]

The different emphases—Lewis stressing the metaphorical, Newbigin the historical and social—reflected their interests and intellectual contexts. As a writer and literary critic, Lewis dealt constantly with metaphor. His inner circle of friends included authorities on myth and the history of language and metaphor, most notably Tolkien and Barfield. Moreover, Lewis sought to take account of, and defuse, claims in the academy and the church that metaphorical and anthropomorphic language in the Bible had to be demythologized. Part of his strategy was to show that other kinds of discourse that were alleged to be literal and scientific often turned out to be as metaphor-based as Scripture.

As for Newbigin, his greater stress on the historical, cultural, and social conditioning of knowledge bore something of the imprint of his context. Already as a theological student at Cambridge during the 1930s, Newbigin was taught to regard all thought as rooted in a tradition's particularity and to dismiss claims to universal, objective knowledge.[6] Newbigin spent decades in India meeting patterns of

[5]James Sire is a critical realist and seems to regard Newbigin as a critical realist too (Sire 1995, 117). Sire understands Newbigin as saying that "we can come to grasp some of the truth," though sometimes we are mistaken and must change our mind (1995, 117). Sire sees value in a postmodern critique insofar as it helps to humble the pretensions of autonomous reason. However, he says, many postmoderns still seem to accept philosophical certitude as the proper but unreachable goal. "Since it is unreachable, postmodernism falls back into despair of knowing anything approaching the truth. It's all or nothing at all. It can't be all. It will then be nothing" (1995, 120). If overconfident naïve realism is not tenable, the better alternative, Sire rightly contends, is not epistemological despair but critical realism. Sire thus affirms parts of Newbigin's epistemology but, unlike Newbigin, thinks it possible and advisable to compare worldviews using tools and criteria that apply across worldviews.

[6]From 1933 to 1936, Newbigin studied at Westminster College, Cambridge, where theologian John Oman was Principal (Newbigin 1985a, 28). Oman insisted that all knowledge must build on the foundation of a community's inherited tradition (Oman 1931, 346). He stressed that we can see things only from our own standpoint

thought much different from those of the society he grew up in. His late-1900s intellectual context gave him analytic tools and labels such as Polanyi's "personal knowledge," Thomas Kuhn's "paradigm shifts" and "community structures," as well as Peter Berger's "social construction of knowledge" and "plausibility structures." By Newbigin's last years, it had also become common among many intellectuals to speak of "postmodernism." Newbigin tried to articulate an epistemology that could incorporate legitimate elements of these intellectual currents while holding to historic Christian orthodoxy.

Newbigin expressed considerable agreement with postmodern emphases on cultural differences. His missionary experience and his distaste for colonialism made him wary of imposing one culture upon another. He tended to regard talk of shared rationality and of cross-cultural commonalities as Western imposition of Enlightenment notions on peoples who were culturally other. However, excessive emphasis on cultural difference and disjunction can produce problems of its own. Lewis saw this more clearly than Newbigin did. Lewis's kind of perspective may be gaining new traction. Though academic fashions have for some time tended to deny similarities across cultures, it is becoming evident that repudiation of cross-cultural commonalities is as likely to lead to harmful misuse of power as did the other extreme of regarding all peoples as being basically the same.[7]

---

as persons and that any claim to an objective "absolute standpoint" is "merest illusion" (Oman 1931, 358-359). Newbigin sounded similar themes in his writings of the 1980s and 1990s about mission to the West. Evidently Newbigin's view of all knowledge as historically situated and socially embodied came not only from his own missionary experience of other cultures or from studying late-1900s Western culture, but from studying under Oman. Thomas (1996, 16-21) identifies various elements in Oman's thought that left an imprint on Newbigin.

[7]"Lewis's argument about cross-cultural similarities has increasing credibility in contemporary postcolonial theory. Until recently, a main point of postcolonial theory has been that the Western assumption of a common human nature allowed colonial powers to impose on non-Western people changes dictated by specifically Western ideas that were mistakenly assumed to be universal. . . . Postcolonial theory, therefore, has understandably emphasized the differences between cultures. But theorists are beginning to recognize a violence that is a counterpart to the construction of the Same, namely, the construction of the Wholly Other. When we judge people of other cultures as people with whom we have nothing in common, we are free from having to take a genuine interest in them, from caring about their wellbeing, or from questioning our treatment of them. Distancing and excluding people under the construction of the 'Other' is potentially as violent as their inclusion under the construction of the 'Same'" (Kort 2001, 90).

Lewis, in giving considerable attention to the role of metaphor within epistemology, offered many stimulating and provocative epistemological insights. However, he was not always sufficiently careful. His overstatements asserting all language to be metaphorical were not meant to conflict with his insistence on objective logic and morality, but that impression could sometimes be hard to avoid. Also, in dealing with biblical revelation, Lewis's notion of metaphor and his distaste for overly systematized doctrine could sometimes lead in the wrong direction. A striking instance is his treatment of atonement. Lewis was right that various biblical pictures of atonement had metaphorical dimensions and revealed a richer reality than a single, univocal, systematic theory could convey. However, he erred in shortchanging the biblical centrality of substitutionary propitiation of God's wrath, and he paid too little heed to quite systematic uses of inference and argument by New Testament authors, especially Paul. When Paul discussed atonement, election, justification by faith, and other key doctrines, he was not merely offering various metaphors that could freely be accepted if they helped and discarded if they did not. Paul was frequently distinguishing truth from error in a rigorous manner. Lewis's epistemological emphasis on metaphor (together with his predisposition to seek common ground) sometimes resulted in smudging distinctions and obscuring what was at stake in difficult or divisive doctrinal questions, even on matters where firm definition and clear inference were deployed by biblical authors. Another result was that Lewis underestimated what was at stake in doctrinal disputes between the Reformers and Rome.

As noted earlier, Lewis affirmed the epistemological import of myth as a means of conveying universal reality through a particular story, and he regarded pagan myths as preparations for myth-become-fact in the Incarnation. He expressed these views in a context where various Christian thinkers were portraying Christianity more as the fulfillment of other religions than as their antithesis. Lewis's views on myth were part of his motivation to write stories with an underlying apologetic purpose, and those stories remain a valuable part of Christian witness still today. Also, much of value can be learned by grappling with Lewis's discussions of how myth and propositional truth convey reality in different ways, and by reflecting on his observations about the relationship between pre-Christian myths and God's revelation in Christ. Nevertheless, this area of his epistemology should be handled cautiously. The Bible gives little warrant for seeing pagan sacrifices or ritual resurrections in pagan fertility cults as gleams of divine light or as preparation for the gospel. Such things were viewed as evils to be swept away, not as partial revelations to be built upon. Some church fathers regarded pagan myths to be demonic deceptions. Lewis concurred that much in myth resulted from satanic counterfeiting, but the myth's core may still have originated in earlier revelatory stories that came from God but were corrupted over time, or in human reflection on observable patterns within the created world. Lewis, though eager to build upon good things held in common by non-Christian religions, was not blind to their idolatries and evils. In a 1961 letter, he wrote that in relation to "all the higher Paganisms," Christians had to pursue "a double task of reconciling and converting. The activities are almost opposites, yet must go hand in hand. We have to hurl down false gods and also elicit the peculiar truth preserved in the worship of each" (2007, 1300). At times Lewis the lover of myth may have been too quick to identify and endorse what he construed as the revelatory elements common to various mythic traditions, and not quick enough to "hurl down false gods."

Newbigin said less about myth than Lewis did; myth did not play a major role in Newbigin's epistemology. All the same, his view of missionary contextualization (like Lewis's) recognized the need to connect with the vocabularies and stories of the receptor culture, as well as the need to call the culture and its stories into question (Newbigin 1986b, 4-9). Both authors recognized the importance of both aspects of contextualization, but Lewis leaned toward more stress on commonality, whereas Newbigin tended to emphasize contradiction. Lewis was quicker to depict pagan myths as preparatory for Christianity. Newbigin was more inclined to present the cross as the contradiction and undoing of all that; the way forward did not lie through recapitulating Greek rationalism or pagan mythology.

Their Recommendations for Mission and Apologetics

Lewis and Newbigin both saw the West as a mission field. Both viewed proclamation of the historic Jesus and his acts of redemptions as the core of mission. Both perceived that this mission faced an intellectual atmosphere in the West that resisted making past history decisive for the present and that tended to deny the universal importance of particular events. Lewis sought to skewer chronological snobbery and thus to help people beyond it. Newbigin argued that all thinking was rooted in historical particularity and thus that gospel-based thinking, rooted in the history of Israel and Jesus, had as strong a claim to rationality and believability as any other claims to truth.

Both authors valued direct gospel preaching and deemed it central to mission. They differed on how apologetics related to preaching. Lewis viewed apologetics as a junior partner to preaching; apologetic arguments could help prepare some people to receive gospel preaching, and apologetics could help believers to fend off attacks against preached truths. Newbigin tended to denigrate most forms of apologetics and to stress preaching and testimony almost to the exclusion of apologetics: forthright preaching was itself the proper and primary form of apologetics.[8] At times Newbigin could speak of a need for Christians to expose modernity's hidden assumptions that caused people to find Christian preaching implausible, and he could support efforts to show that God's action in Christ helped make sense of things. In these respects, he could sound similar to Lewis. But a louder note in Newbigin was his denunciation of traditional apologetics as a concession to unbelief and his adamant insistence on proclamation. I find Lewis's position more helpful. Newbigin too often depicted preaching and apologetics in opposition rather than in alliance.

Lewis and Newbigin both saw Christian living as a very powerful form of witness and apologetics, often more effective than even the strongest arguments. Lewis, in stressing the winsomeness of holiness, did not deny the real, though modest, value of arguments and evidence. Newbigin too often suggested an opposition, in which the value of embodied faithfulness somehow indicated the worthlessness of verbal argumentation.

Both men saw Christian community, as experienced in local congregations and through a spirit of unity with the church around the world and across the centuries, to be vital for making Christianity plausible and for sustaining belief. Both thought that individuals would find it hard to maintain orthodox belief and vital trust apart from regular involvement in a congregation. Both regarded church divisions and ani-

---

[8]Groothuis correctly observes that preaching, as recommended by Newbigin, may help those who are already Christians and win some non-believers, but other people need "apologetical preparation" before they will give the gospel a hearing. One cannot reject all reasoning or evidence in support of Christian truths and still think that publication with universal intent provides escape from relativism, for "to publicly display one's belief does not make it objective or rational. All world religions and major worldviews do that in various ways." Newbigin leaves "no way to test a tradition against reality" (Groothuis 2000, 158).

mosities to be detrimental to gospel plausibility. However, Newbigin set up yet another false opposition: he used the importance of church to imply the uselessness—even the ungodliness—of most apologetic argumentation. His insistence on the local congregation's life as "the *only* hermeneutic of the gospel" might have been less misleading if it had been a one-time rhetorical flourish. But Newbigin used that phrase again and again in a variety of settings.[9] Lewis's example showed that it was possible to honor the apologetic importance of vibrant congregations and ecumenical harmony without denying the propriety of marshalling apologetic arguments.

Lewis and Newbigin both put forth efforts to raise doubts about bogus certitudes, especially those associated with reductionistic scientism. Both knew that mistaken presuppositions could block people from even taking Christian truth seriously. Both strove to show that many widespread, unquestioned assumptions in the West were better seen not as universal, timeless truths but as temporary, local opinions. Both depicted scientism as the product of a specific period with its own psychological preferences, power agenda, and canons of believability. Lewis, unlike Newbigin, did not inveigh against timeless truths as such. Lewis held that universal, timeless truths did exist and could be known—but were more likely to be found in moral commonalities or in rules of logic than in scientific theorems or in a contemporary cosmology. In contrast, Newbigin's strategy for relativizing the supposed certainties of scientism was to relativize *all* claims of universal, timeless truth, even claims about logic and morality. All notions about timeless, universal truth had to be relativized; the only absolute was God's historical, local revelation in Jesus, the cornerstone of all truth.

Lewis and Newbigin both had a sense of urgency about influencing societal plausibility structures. Both believed that winning individuals one at a time would be inadequate to produce widespread success in mission to the West. Both wanted more Christians to be stellar thinkers whose intellectual excellence and grasp of truth in various spheres of life would bring those spheres more into line with Christianity.

[9]It is ironic that while Newbigin called the congregation the only hermeneutic, he also diagnosed the Western church as syncretistic. It seems obvious that in order to make such a charge, Newbigin had to draw on some standard outside the church itself and needed some hermeneutic besides what was happening in those allegedly syncretistic congregations.

Lewis and Newbigin differed, however, on why such wide-ranging influence was a necessary part of mission. A major reason Lewis wanted Christians to address all areas of life was in order to cultivate a setting for a greater harvest of eternal souls. Lewis placed enormous emphasis on winning individual persons to Christ, so that even when he looked beyond direct persuasion of individuals and called for extending Christian thought to various cultural spheres, his main hope was that the overall cultural atmosphere would be conducive for more individuals to become Christians and follow the road to salvation. In contrast, Newbigin's notion of public truth stressed cultural transformation as much or more than the winning of individual souls. Newbigin certainly wanted conversions, but he was reluctant to label anyone as saved or lost, and he thought the church growth movement overemphasized the counting of converts. Newbigin's desire for mission to pervade all spheres of thought and all societal structures was motivated mainly by his insistence on the comprehensive application of God's reign to all spheres of life.

Lewis and Newbigin also differed on the tactics they favored for bringing Christian influence to bear in various spheres. Lewis wanted to infiltrate various realms of culture with latently Christian assumptions, thus producing a cultural context in which people's intellect and imagination would be more receptive to Christianity. He saw positive potential for indirect apologetics in books, periodicals, and radio; in highbrow scholarship, popular non-fiction, and in various genres of entertaining stories. Newbigin, when discussing plausibility structures, stressed more than Lewis the need for Christians to "seek access to the levers of power" in media, schools, and government—though somehow in non-coercive ways. Lewis rightly stressed that Christians can advance their mindset on many fronts in subtle but effective ways. Newbigin's approach was more likely than Lewis's to raise red flags about theocracy or clergy invading realms where they were incompetent. On the other hand, Lewis may have steered too far clear of power issues. Mission in the West can ill afford not to address the huge impact of institutions and the power interests that operate through them. Structural impediments to Christian plausibility and practice are real.

Newbigin, more than Lewis, showed how Enlightenment epistemology could affect public structures. Both men spoke of the fact-value dichotomy in Western thought, but Newbigin did more than Lewis to show how this dichotomy was used to justify the banishment of Christian conviction from the public sphere. Even if Newbigin overemphasized epistemology and intellectual history, he was right to draw attention to the reality that non-Christian ideas have consequences in the shaping of social structures—which in turn enshrine those ideas and impede acceptance of biblical ideas and structures.

Lewis and Newbigin both believed that Christian witness needed to be theologically orthodox and culturally relevant. Missionaries had to speak the culture's language and at the same time speak the gospel truth. Failure to translate the gospel into understandable language would make it incomprehensible and irrelevant. Failure to maintain sound, Bible-based theology would result in syncretism.

While Lewis and Newbigin both accepted these principles for mission, they differed in their diagnosis of the West and consequently weighted their mission priorities differently. Lewis often spoke of the clergy's failure to translate the Christian message into contemporary vernacular language. He also expressed concern that churchy talk and practices made gospel realities seem musty, dull, or sissified. In contrast, Newbigin said little about the clergy's failure to connect with the population; rather, he worried mostly about syncretism and charged that the churches were in danger of drowning their message by being too immersed in the culture. While Lewis called for translation of the gospel into terms that theologically uneducated people in Western culture could understand, Newbigin warned that the gospel was being swallowed up in the culture's assumptions and language. Lewis told clergy to study the language of ordinary people within and outside their congregations, and to speak that language without using the jargon current among theologians. Newbigin's writings about the West largely ignored such concerns; indeed, he often used such jargon.

Newbigin seldom addressed his books and lectures to Western people outside the church, or even to uneducated church people. Although he called for Christians to move beyond a Christendom ecclesiology that only addressed others within a context presumed to be Christian, his own books were mostly adaptations of lectures given to preachers and theologians. Perhaps Newbigin would have emphasized vernacular translation more, and adapted his own vocabulary accordingly, if his books had targeted an uneducated, unchurched readership. But Newbigin aimed his publications at helping Christian leaders to analyze Western culture from a mission perspective, rather than appealing directly to those who did not understand Christian basics. He was trying to embolden pastors, not persuade people outside the church. In his words, "I have felt that my main ministry was just to encourage ministers to be more confident in preaching the gospel" (1989a, 116). That was worth doing, but the fact that his writings were not even attempting to explain the gospel to the unchurched, or to persuade them of its truth, may partly explain his tendency to ignore the danger that British preachers were not presenting the gospel understandably nor arguing for it compellingly. Also, his antipathy to the use of apologetic evidence was easier to maintain when discussing mission in the abstract than it would have been in conversations with non-Christians who saw no grounds for taking Christian truth claims seriously.

Lewis and Newbigin both thought that too many people in the West had a mindset that blinded them to the activities of unseen powers. Both believed that people who found it implausible to believe in such powers were all the more vulnerable to the activity of evil powers. Therefore, a vital part of mission in the West was to raise awareness of the powers. Lewis wrote often of personal angels as servants of God, and he wrote of demons trying to lead individuals astray, as well as prompting false philosophies and causing havoc in wider realms. Newbigin's discussions of the powers focused more on entities acting in institutional norms, roles, and structures than in individual temptation. He depicted the powers more as impersonal forces (1989a, 198-210) than as fallen angels, individual centers of will. Newbigin warned against dismissing New Testament talk of the powers as outworn mythology, but his own treatment was stamped by modernity's preference to frame understanding in terms of depersonalized, demythologized abstractions and forces, rather than speaking of personal beings in the spirit realm.[10] Lewis seemed closer than Newbigin to a view of personal spirits such as that held in the Bible and in various cultures.

Lewis and Newbigin both saw apologetic value in comparing worldviews. Both contended that Christianity could account for more areas of thought and a wider range of experience than materialism or pantheism could do. Both argued that Christianity fostered further discoveries in the intellectual realm and better conduct in the practical realm. In short, both depicted Christianity as a more capacious and fruitful worldview than its competitors.

---

[10]Newbigin recalled that it came as a shock to his own Western rationalism when an evangelist in India spoke matter-of-factly about doing half a dozen exorcisms in recent months (1994a, 99). Newbigin could cite such memories as examples of how his own intellectual assumptions were challenged in a different cultural setting, yet in his own reflections he still said little about angels or demons as personal spirits.

The two missionaries differed, however, on the proper tactics for a Christian to use in conversation with someone holding a non-Christian worldview. Newbigin, taking a mainly presuppositional stance, thought the right approach was to stake out the ground held by Christians, to unmask and challenge assumptions held by non-Christians, and to invite them (at least as a thought experiment) to step over to the Christian standpoint. This would give non-Christians an opportunity to see things in a new light and to discern a pattern that could never be seen from the standpoint of old, non-Christian assumptions. In addition, such an approach was necessary in order to uphold God's revelation in Christ as the starting point of thought and the ultimate commitment. According to Newbigin, any attempt to argue for Christianity from beliefs that were part of the non-Christian's worldview, or to build a case on the basis of things allegedly held in common by different worldviews, could only lead to a syncretism which trimmed and twisted Christianity to fit some other ultimate commitment.

Like Newbigin, Lewis challenged mistaken assumptions in other worldviews. Also, Lewis often used his literary skills to help readers enter imaginatively into a Christian vision of things. Yet, unlike Newbigin, Lewis was willing to step into other people's non-Christian worldview, to help them take seriously the best of what they already knew, and to show how such knowledge was more consistent with the central claims of Christianity than with the central claims of the worldview they were espousing. Newbigin's approach was to tell a non-Christian, "Stand here with me and see if you don't see the same pattern I do" (1989a, 11). Lewis approved and used that approach at times, but he could also say, in effect, "I'll stand there with you and show that you know more clues to the Christian God than you might realize."

For Newbigin, a worldview that saw ultimate reality as personal was totally different from a worldview that viewed ultimate reality as impersonal; therefore, no more fundamental principle than either of these views could be found to serve as a basis for judging between them (1995b, 13-14). For Lewis, by contrast, one worldview could be shown better than another, not necessarily on the basis of a principle more fundamental than either worldview, but on the basis of what people from the two worldviews had in common. In contending against materialism and pantheism, Lewis thought that many people who paid homage to such worldviews nevertheless had an inescapable sense of their own personhood: they took mind, conscience, desire, and love seriously. These things, held in common and never totally effaced despite worldview differences, could serve as clues to lead people toward belief in a superpersonal ultimate reality and away from mistakenly making impersonality ultimate. Lewis did not claim that various traits of human personality had more ultimate *ontological* status than the reality of the Trinity, but he did think that many people could have more direct *epistemological* access to some dimensions of their own personhood than to knowledge of God. Hence, it was proper to help them take seriously what they already knew to be true by virtue of their own personhood and thereby to give them grounds to accept a worldview that could account for personhood.

In my estimation, Lewis was right about this, and Newbigin was mistaken to assert that every theistic argument was tantamount to exalting Enlightenment notions of universal rationality above the reality of God.[11] Likewise, he was wrong to claim that all visions of ultimate truth involve circular argument (1989a, 48, 63). Newbigin confused epistemology (knowing) and ontology (being). Arguing from premises accepted by both parties in a discussion does not mean the premises are claimed to rank higher ontologically than the conclusion. God's being is ontologically prior and superior to all else, but knowledge of God does not always precede all knowledge of other things. Sometimes what is known of those things may lead toward knowledge of God, and a skilled apologist may be of some help in bringing this about, without using circular argument and without demoting God to a lower status than a set of premises held in common across different worldviews.

Newbigin was too quick to embrace some elements in his intellectual context and to make of them a divine prohibition against traditional apologetics. He embraced Barth's theological insistence on revelation without apologetics; he adopted Polanyi's and Kuhn's emphasis on science making imaginative leaps rather than building incrementally on accumulating evidence; he cobbled together these theological and scientific accounts of discovery; and he concluded that a paradigm shift—not an accumulation of evidence—was the only proper model for conversion to Christian belief. He accepted a theological trend that construed the doctrine of election strictly in terms of a community chosen

---

[11]As Groothuis says, the Enlightenment was not wrong to search for objective truth; its error lay in arrogant, utopian assumptions about the power of autonomous reason and the attempt to reduce rational knowing to one perfect method. These Enlightenment flaws do not preclude Christian apologists from making a cumulative case that Christianity is rational and objectively true (Groothuis 2000, 144, 185).

to convey and embody God's message (explicitly repudiating election as God choosing specific individuals for eternal life); he espoused sociological accounts of plausibility structures; he patched together these theological and sociological explanations of knowing as rooted in particular community; and he concluded that the church community's distinctive tradition and fellowship—not argument based on broadly shared commonalities—constituted the only proper mode for interpreting the gospel to non-Christians. On rare occasions, Newbigin could offer remarks that seemed to vary from these positions, but he mostly emphasized paradigm shifts and communal knowing at the expense of building a case for belief.

Lewis and Newbigin both emphasized the reality of a personal God and the necessity of a personal relationship with him. Both did so against the backdrop of a cultural and intellectual context that they perceived to be highly depersonalized. Lewis took the challenge of depersonalized reductionism as an occasion to bring renewed attention to various aspects of human personhood and to argue for God as the source of personhood. Newbigin, in contrast, thought that it would be an improper concession to an impersonal worldview if Christians tried to make a case for God based on any form of inferential reasoning from propositions about something besides God's revelation in Christ—even if those propositions were about aspects of human personhood.

Lewis and Newbigin alike knew that it was not enough to hold propositional statements about God without responding to the personal, living Lord. Also, both observed that constructing an apologetic case *that* a God exists involved a truncated conception of God and omitted much that could be included in testimony about *who* God is, as revealed in the Bible and known through personal encounter. Lewis still thought that making an initial case for theism—despite all that had to be left out—could help some people. Newbigin, on the other hand, opposed apologetic arguments for theism, even though he granted that there was ample evidence in creation and conscience for making such a case.

Newbigin lodged a number of objections against arguments for theism, including the following: He thought such arguments would fail to convince someone whose worldview centered on other ultimate commitments. He thought it wrong to marshal evidence for God as though God were an inert thing instead of the present and personal Lord. Theistic argument would lead people away from the living God, not closer to him. Theism was not Christianity: the God of philosophical argument was not the living God revealed in the history of Israel and Jesus. Newbigin insisted that faith was a personal response of trust, not merely an assent to propositions. Therefore, healthy witness would omit theistic argument, testify to God's personal revelation of himself, and call for trust and obedience.

Lewis and Newbigin never directly debated each other, but Lewis's 1952 article "Is theism important?" (1970, 172-176) responded to complaints that were similar to those Newbigin would later bring against theistic arguments. Lewis disagreed with objectors who claimed that theism of the sort defended by philosophers was at best useless and at worst harmful. In Lewis's own journey, acceptance of theism had been a major step on his path to fully Christian belief. Also, his missionary experience indicated the worth of theism and of arguments for it: "Nearly everyone I know who has embraced Christianity in adult life has been influenced by what seemed to him to be at least probable arguments for Theism." The arguments might point only to "an aridly philosophical God," yet such a conception at least involved rejection of naturalism and affirmation of some sort of God, and such theism did not prevent further movement toward personal faith in a personal God (1970, 173-174).

Lewis distinguished between faith as "a settled intellectual assent" and faith as "a trust or confidence in the God who is thus assented to." Mere assent had little importance apart from trust, but assent was a pre-condition for trust and therefore mattered greatly. Philosophical arguments could aid assent but could not produce trust; trust was a divine gift. Those who reached the point of assent could go on to pray for the gift of trust. Most who did so, conceded Lewis, had "already had something like religious experience." Such quasi-religious experience of the numinous was not explicitly religious or creedal, but faith as assent could retrospectively transform "into religious experience what was hitherto only potentially or implicitly religious." Evidence and argument could perform the valuable service of helping people take such experiences as intellectually significant and remove an inhibition "which was preventing their development into religion proper" (1970, 173-174). Some people who had experienced signals of God's reality might not recognize them as such until their minds were persuaded of God's existence, sometimes with the help of argument.

Lewis asserted—no less vigorously than objectors to theistic argument—that the content of faith had to include the historical events of

242

God's dealings with Israel and his actions in Jesus. However, Lewis saw the revelation in history as cohering with, not contradicting, theism. "The object of faith is at once the *ens entium* [Being of beings] of the philosophers, the Awful Mystery of Paganism, the Holy Law given of the moralists, and Jesus of Nazareth who was crucified under Pontius Pilate and rose again on the third day." Christian faith was emphatically a response to historical events—but these events required "as their presupposition the existence of a Being who is more, but not less, than the God whom many reputable philosophers think they can establish" (1970, 172-175).

I resonate more with Lewis's view of apologetic argument as preparation for the gospel than with Newbigin's stark opposition to such argument.[12] Newbigin was right that the God pictured in theistic proofs lacked much that was conveyed in Christian testimony to the historical revelation. He was also right that discussing God as an object of investigation and argument was a far cry from knowing God through personal encounter. But Newbigin was wrong to posit utter opposition between the philosophical and the historical, between marshaling persuasive evidence and calling for personal response.[13] Lewis was no less

---

[12]Consider Newbigin's repeated insistence that Jesus' resurrection cannot fit any worldview except one of which it is the starting point. If Newbigin simply meant that we must let the resurrection account "speak for itself without revising it along secular lines, his point stands," says Groothuis. "But his comment seems to also imply that we cannot use any intellectual means outside of the proclamation of the resurrection itself to vindicate its truth to unbelievers." This Groothuis rejects as unhelpful for witness to people who wonder, "Why should anyone believe in Christ's resurrection in the first place?" Groothuis advocates building "a good philosophical case for theism," thus showing the possibility of miracles, and then offering historical evidence for the resurrection (Groothuis 2000, 155). Newbigin's writings mostly opposed argument from evidence, but his actual practice of witnessing may have been surprisingly similar to apologists whose methods he claimed to oppose. At a 1993 conference in Uppsala, Newbigin was asked what he would say to someone who dismissed Jesus' resurrection as just a legend. Newbigin replied that he would go over the historical evidence for Jesus' resurrection (Netland, personal communication).

[13]Ramachandra appreciates Newbigin but criticizes his "tendency to speak in either/or categories which simply do not ring true to the way in which most people come to believe from a position of total skepticism." Evidence, of itself, might not "prove" gospel truth, but evidence (such as that for the resurrection) may move a person toward true assumptions and beliefs. Ramachandra presses for a clearer distinction "between *grounds* for belief and psychological *certainty*. The former are matters for logical argument and persuasion." Since ultimate reality is personal and can be known only in a personal way, certainty comes from the Spirit, not from logic. Still, "the Holy Spirit is not a substitute for evidence" (Ramachandra 1996, 169-171).

aware of the relevant differences, yet he had a better sense than New-bigin that different approaches could be complementary, not just con-tradictory. Lewis recognized that if a person had no relationship to the Lord and no settled assent to God's reality, God would seem only a speculative question to that person. In such a case, an apologist could build a case to address questions and call for assent. If assent to God's reality was given, the inquirer no longer faced just an argument but a Person, and would have to move from "the logic of speculative thought" to "the logic of personal relations." Thus, "the logic of specu-lative thought" did not necessarily contradict or block personal faith but could play a (limited) part in moving a person another step along the path toward trust (Lewis 1960d, 26-30).

Lewis and Newbigin both believed that faith was a venture that went beyond evidence. Both said that indubitable, public proof would arrive only with Jesus' second coming. Both suggested that the interim absence of such proof provided opportunity to exercise personal trust in God's character without demanding absolute empirical verification. Both encouraged a tenacity of belief that did not merely fluctuate with the latest information. However, Newbigin stressed more than Lewis the eschatological tension of the already and the not yet: already Jesus' death and resurrection provided a decisive clue to history's goal, but there was not yet conclusive proof to demonstrate that Jesus was exalt-ed, nor was there clear knowledge of what the final consummation would be like.

Lewis gave a significant role to evidence and arguments before con-version, yet he stressed that after conversion, it was vital to maintain confidence in God's character even in the teeth of seemingly contrary evidence. Newbigin seemed to allow little room for presenting apolo-getic evidence and argument before a person's conversion, but after conversion he seemed to allow for considerable intellectual effort—and even critical second-guessing of much biblical doctrine—in response to new evidence and different contexts. In Newbigin's view, biblical wit-nesses ascribed various and sometimes conflicting meanings to the his-torical events centered in Christ. Our critical faculties and our ongoing dialogues would be vital for an ongoing process of interpreting Christ afresh for new situations. This may explain why Newbigin could be la-beled too presuppositional by some evangelical criticism, yet too evi-dential by other evangelical appraisal. Both charges could be correct. In my estimation, Newbigin was too presuppositional in that he did not allow apologetic evidence to function in areas where it could provide legitimate help, yet he was overly evidential at points where he should have accepted biblical revelation as infallible.

Newbigin helped some Christian leaders in the West to see society and church through missionary eyes. Newbigin was at his best in helping people to question many assumptions and in showing that what passed for public truth was often thinly disguised ideology. Some of his insights deserve to remain in the arsenal of missional apologetics, particularly his emphasis on the personal and communal dimensions of knowing and on ultimate reality as personal. But these insights can be included in the arsenal without casting away legitimate weapons of rational argument across cultural boundaries and without blunting the ultimate weapon of truth: the written Word of God. Newbigin was most helpful when he challenged comfortable assumptions, offered provocative insights, and stimulated further thinking. He was less helpful as a mentor for mapping a coherent, constructive approach to epistemology and apologetics.

Lewis, despite some shortcomings, provided a better, more practicable model. His diverse array of tactics can be used, adapted, and augmented in contemporary mission.

CHAPTER 11

Missional Apologetics Today

Having compared and evaluated Lewis's and Newbigin's views of the post-Christendom West, epistemology, and apologetics, I conclude this book by briefly reflecting on some considerations relevant for contemporary mission in Western societies. First, drawing on what we have seen thus far, I underscore some enduring lessons from Lewis and Newbigin. Then I explore a number of recent developments and discussions that relate to the applicability of Lewis and Newbigin for current missional apologetics.

Lessons from Lewis and Newbigin

Christian witness can benefit from careful attention to strengths and shortcomings of Lewis and Newbigin. Here I briefly highlight several points that I consider to be especially important for mission today. My highlights are far from exhaustive. Readers of previous chapters in this study may be struck by any number of things, some of which may impress them as more important or more urgent than items that receive special mention in this chapter. Such variations of judgment may well be appropriate for context-sensitive apologists. Different readers in different Western mission settings may rightly differ in their estimates of which findings in this book are most important for their specific situations. Here are some of the lessons that stand out for me.

1. The personal is crucial.

Christian witness in the West should stress the personal. Lewis's and Newbigin's diagnosis of reductionistic, depersonalizing thought patterns in the West is far from obsolete: too much academic and popular thought continues to regard dead matter or vaguely impersonal spirit as the most fundamental fact. Contemporary Christian witness would do well to carry on the precedent of Lewis and Newbigin in emphasizing the personhood of the tri-personal God, the personality of Jesus as the incarnate Word, the need for human persons to have personal faith and devotion to the Lord, and the flourishing of human personality and community centered in such relationship.

Unlike Newbigin, I do not think God's personhood precludes all use of theistic arguments and marshalling of evidence for Christian truth. All the same, it remains the case that arguments (and the assent they may help to produce) are far from sufficient; the goal is always personal trust, penitence, love, adoration, and obedience. Moreover, even in the very construction of a cumulative case for Christianity, some of the most compelling arguments are those that identify elements of human personality as clues to God. Lewis remains a helpful example for showing Christianity to be more plausible than competing views because it best accounts for vital elements of human personhood.

2. Epistemology matters.

Epistemology is of considerable importance for Christian belief and witness. Newbigin may have unduly exaggerated epistemology as *the* chief concern in mission to the West, but epistemology still remains *a* major element to be reckoned with. Newbigin oversimplified intellectual history, overstated the impact of presuppositions, and expected more missionary benefit from Polanyi's epistemology than it could deliver, but missiologists must not take such excesses as grounds for denying that epistemology matters greatly. Lewis and Newbigin remain instructive examples of missionary efforts to discern epistemological missteps in the West, to develop a sounder epistemology, and to pursue forms of witness in accord with such epistemology.

Healthy epistemology involves a critical realism that posits objective realities outside the individual subject; acknowledges the truth-discerning capacities and frequent failings of human logical and moral faculties; recognizes the impact of social relationships, institutions, and plausibility structures on individual thought; affirms the infallible truth of biblical revelation; and recognizes the Holy Spirit's impact on the mind. Lewis and Newbigin insisted on many of these points, and we can build upon their work. Unlike them, however, we should hold to biblical inerrancy, though not with a wooden or simplistic hermeneutic.

Missional epistemology in the West should follow Lewis and Newbigin in recognizing that science does not qualify for special epistemological privilege and is not somehow exempt from the influence of social arrangements and metaphorical constructs. We should also stress that Christianity offers not just sentiments but factual claims about reality.

Not every missionary, evangelist, or lay Christian needs a rigorously articulated epistemology in order to witness with integrity and effectiveness. Still, those who have keen awareness of epistemological matters can make a valuable contribution to the total witness of the Christian community and may prove to be especially helpful in reaching certain types of people. Moreover, awareness of factors that condition perceptions of plausibility or implausibility can affect missionary strategy. Of particular importance, in my judgment, is awareness of reigning assumptions and social plausibility structures. As Lewis and Newbigin stressed, Christians in the West should not confine their evangelistic strategy to individual persuasion but should also strive to influence the wider cultural atmosphere.

Missional epistemology must include, but not be limited to, philosophical and theological perspectives. Valuable insights can also be gained from the angle of the social sciences and their methodology. Lewis realized that human beliefs were affected by many factors, including social relationships and institutions. His observations on such matters were richer and ranged more widely than the efforts of some who focus too narrowly on intellectual history or the deployment of logic and evidence. In that regard, Lewis did well to consider some of the areas that the social sciences focus upon. Yet he tended to deride the methods employed in the social sciences and to ignore their findings. He rightly opposed the reductionistic scientism and anti-religious bias of some figures in psychology, sociology, and anthropology, but he gave too little heed to sounder practitioners of social science.[1] Mission-

---

[1] In a private letter, Lewis wrote of enjoying a work of anthropology, especially its insights into language (2004b, 75-76). However, in public he portrayed anthropologists as opponents of revealed religion and objective morality (1960b, 109-110; 1967,

aries in the West would be wise to go beyond Lewis and to recognize that judicious use of the methods and literature of the social sciences can be a valuable aid to understanding Western societies and how their thought patterns and epistemologies are shaped.

Newbigin interacted with some literature in the human sciences, especially sociology of religion. Some of this interaction was quite insightful and can serve to stimulate missional apologists working at the intersection of epistemology and social science. However, we must also learn from Newbigin's mistakes. He could seize upon a catchphrase such as "plausibility structure" but use it to mean something quite different from what sociologists meant by it. He could swing from one extreme wing of sociological debate to the other, as when he first declared secularization to be near-universal but later verged on denying secularization altogether. Contemporary missionaries dealing with epistemology would do well to join Newbigin in drawing some insights from the human sciences, but in a more balanced and careful manner than Newbigin did. In a similar vein, we can join Newbigin in being alert to institutional power factors that affect knowing, but we must find better ways to critique and influence institutions than Newbigin was able to suggest.

3. *Vital belief comes from the Holy Spirit.*

Epistemology must reckon with, and apologetics must depend upon, the Holy Spirit's empowerment of witnesses and his illumination of hearers. Lewis could have been more explicit and specific about the Holy Spirit's work. Still, Lewis insisted that living knowledge of divine truth and personal knowledge of God could come only as a divine gift, not as a human achievement. Lewis knew that apologetic and epistemological efforts would make a positive impact only if the Spirit blessed them and used them as preparatory measures for gospel proclamation fired by the Holy Spirit. Missional apologetics does not neces-

---

73-74; 1989, 36-37). He depicted sociology as pseudo-scientific, reductionistic, and manipulative. One of his noble fictional characters, expressing Lewis's own view, said that there was no such science as sociology and declared, "I happen to believe that you can't study men, you can only get to know them, which is quite a different thing" (1946a, 70-71). Lewis interacted somewhat more with psychology. He strove to defuse Freudian attacks on faith but also drew some insights from psychologists. Still, Lewis's general distrust of anthropology and his dismissal of sociology, together with his individualistic distaste for social structures, kept Lewis from using some analytic tools that could have proved valuable.

sarily clash with the Holy Spirit's work; it can be used by the Holy Spirit. Still, the West's ultimate need is not just more study and better arguments, but a mighty move of the Spirit.

Newbigin's emphasis on the centrality of epistemology, taken out of context, might seem to indicate that he thought a change in epistemology could save the West. However, we must keep in mind the nature of Newbigin's dual discourse of epistemology from below and epistemology from above, and we must recognize that the latter mattered most to him—and should matter most to us. Newbigin's paramount concern was that God's revelation in Jesus would be believed, proclaimed, and lived in the power of the Holy Spirit. Newbigin saw common epistemological assumptions as obstacles impeding openness to the Spirit's work in Scripture, community, and individual hearts and minds. His epistemology strongly stressed the historically conditioned and communally shaped character of all knowing, not because he wanted to exalt relativism, but because he believed that the historical events of Scripture and the plausibility structure of the church community were the Spirit's chosen means for revealing God's truth to human minds.

Contemporary missional apologists may need to disagree with Newbigin's thinking in various ways, but his ringing affirmations of the Holy Spirit's ministry deserve to be echoed. We seek, as Newbigin phrased it, for people to say, "'I know the Lord Jesus Christ as my personal Lord and Savior.' . . . We commend [the gospel] to all people in the hope that, by the witness of the Holy Spirit in the hearts of others, it will come to be seen by them for themselves as the truth" (1989a, 50). "Evangelism is the telling of good news, but what changes people's minds and converts their wills is always a work of the sovereign Holy Spirit" (1994a 42). "The character and the purpose of God are rendered apparent for us in the Scriptures, and are understood as we read them in the power of the Holy Spirit and in the fellowship of the whole Christian Church in all ages" (1994a, 50).

Careful attention to epistemology need not conflict with depending on the Holy Spirit. Indeed, a robust epistemology should forthrightly affirm the divine design of various human capacities for knowing, and the Holy Spirit's work in attuning those faculties to recognize and believe God's revelation of his existence, character, and saving purposes. Lewis and Newbigin, each in his own way, conveyed such things. Contemporary thinkers such as Alvin Plantinga (2000, 241-323) and William Craig (2000, 28-38; 2008, 43-60) explicitly commend an epistemological model that recognizes the inner testimony of the Holy Spirit as the primary cause of Christian belief and commitment, insisting that Spirit-prompted belief in God as Father and Jesus as Savior is imminently rational.

4. Imaginative storytelling complements rigorous argument.

Missional apologetics involves much more than precise, logical presentation of true propositions. Metaphor and myth, not just propositional absolutes and logical inference, can prepare people to receive the gospel. Stories can arouse interest and evoke a sense of wonder and longing in a way that step-by-step prose argument cannot. Lewis knew this, and his fiction may be his most powerful and enduring apologetic work.

Lewis's view of non-Christian myths as anticipatory of Christianity may have been questionable, but there is no question that he wrote his own stories with full awareness of the Christian revelation and with a desire for others to taste something of its reality. Even if we were to suppose the myths of other religions to be more demonic than divine, Lewis's fiction was a deliberate attempt to convey gospel grandeur, with considerable success.

Some contemporary Christians, upon discovering the richness and power of story, mistakenly depict narrative communication as at odds with, and superior to, rigorous reasoning. Lewis knew better. He produced stirring stories *and* insisted upon careful reasoning. Missionaries in Western cultures would be wise to look to Lewis as an example of how to stir imagination and desire through stories that convey a taste of biblical reality, without jettisoning confidence in absolute truth, sound logic, and universal moral standards. People have an inbuilt need for truth and uprightness, as well as for beauty and mystery.

In an earlier era, Pascal suggested a strategy of stirring the heart before persuading the head, of making people wish Christianity to be true and then providing compelling grounds to recognize Christianity as true. Lewis spoke of baptizing the imagination before the mind. There is much missionary wisdom in such strategies.

These are not universal prescriptions for Christian witness. Sometimes the logical force of Christianity persuades the mind before its glory captures the heart. In other cases, imagination runs ahead of belief. The order may vary, and the most pressing need may differ from person to person, from setting to setting, from age to age. As Lewis pointed out, sometimes hard thought is urgently needed, but at other times it is more urgent to make people aware of things that surpass discursive thought. Often it is valuable to do both. Few of us have a blend of analytic and imaginative gifts to the degree that Lewis did, but missional apologetics does not require any individual to be omnicompetent. So long as Christians recognize that evocative storytelling and rigorous argument can be complementary, Christian storytellers and Christian arguers can pursue their respective approaches within the full spectrum of apologetic tactics used by the total Christian community.

Having stressed these lessons, I turn to recent developments and discussions that relate to the applicability of Lewis and Newbigin for contemporary missional apologetics.

Analyzing Culture, Avoiding Caricature

Christians must, with Lewis and Newbigin, continue to view the West as a mission field and give careful attention to analyzing Western culture. Or, to put it more accurately, we must see the West as a cluster of related mission fields. The West has various nations, cultures, and subcultures, with some overlap but many differences as well. Newbigin made a major contribution by helping to put cultural analysis of the West high on the agenda of missiology. But those who carry on with missionary analysis of culture today should heed Lewis's keen sense of different traditions, social classes, and strands of thought within "the West." We need to improve upon the sort of oversimplified characterizations that marred some of Newbigin's cultural analysis. Unfortunately, Newbigin's generalizations about "Christendom" and "modernity" continue to be echoed—sometimes in even more simplistic form—in contemporary mission discussions.

In North America, The Gospel and Our Culture Network (GOCN) has spearheaded the "missional church" movement, looking to Newbigin as its chief inspiration and as the source of its main categories for missiological analysis (e.g., Guder 1998; 2000; Hall 1996; Hunsberger and Van Gelder 1996; Van Gelder 2005; 2007). GOCN missiologists commonly complain that despite Christendom's demise in North America, a Christendom ecclesiology remains prevalent: "We cling to a vision of culture and church as one, but they have separated" (Hunsberger and Van Gelder 1996, xiv). In my estimation, such authors give insufficient weight to at least two facts: First, American Christianity never had an equivalent to European Christendom. "The United States is the first major Western world power in which there has been no established church" (Escobar 2003, 51). Second, Christian belief, church involvement, outreach, and cultural impact remain higher in North America than in Europe. Missional church thinkers tend to overestimate the degree to which American ecclesiology has been Christendom-based, and they tend to underestimate the degree to which Christians and churches remain a major factor in American public life.

The eclectic "emerging church" movement draws on elements of missional church thinking and on Newbigin himself. According to some emerging church advocates, "The church is a modern institution in a postmodern world. The church must embody the culture of postmodernity for the Western church to survive the twenty-first century." This breathless pronouncement is based on a cultural assessment that two huge shifts have occurred in the West since the 1950s: Christendom has given way to post-Christendom, and modernity has given way to postmodernity. It is claimed that prior to these shifts, the West was a more static culture, so it was not as urgent for the church back then to keep updating its cultural analysis (Gibbs and Bolger 2005, 17-18). This caricature of the West's past and future makes Newbigin seem nuanced by comparison. "Christendom" and "modernity"—two foci of Newbigin's writings—may be useful rubrics in missional discussion, but these terms obscure more than they reveal if used as catch-all labels or—worse yet—as bludgeons against evangelicalism amid claims to offer a new, more authentic form of church.[2] The emerging church may have some merit as an array of attempts to contextualize the gospel for some specific settings and types of people in the West, but we must be wary of overly simplistic descriptions of the West and overly sweeping prescriptions for the church.

If Lewis could hear some "emerging church" leaders trumpet themselves as post-Christendom, postmodern, post-evangelical, and post-everything, I suspect he might yawn and remark that this sounds like yet another case of chronological snobbery, evolutionary infatuation with emergence and novelty, and other symptoms of the ongoing drive to be ever so *modern*. If Lewis could hear the simplistic generalizations about Christendom and modernity that are bandied about in some contemporary discussions on mission, he might repeat something he said more than fifty years ago: "all the 'spirits', 'meanings', or 'qualities' attributed to historical periods . . . are always most visible in the periods

---

[2]Gibbs and Bolger (2005) offer research on the emerging church from a positive perspective. Carson (2005) offers a more critical perspective.

we have studied least." He might remind us that "'periods' are a mischievous conception" even if they are sometimes "a methodological necessity." Those who analyze historical periods and cultural shifts "must beware of schematizing" and "must not impose either on the old things that were dying out (not all old things were) nor on the new things that were coming in (not all of them to stay) a spurious unity" (1954, 63-64).

If Newbigin could hear some contemporary calls for a post-Christendom ecclesiology that abandons existing forms of church and engages with the secular world, he might comment that it sounds very much like what he heard (and sometimes said) in the 1960s about the need to secularize theology and ecclesiology. He might urge us not to repeat the mistakes he made during his anti-Christendom, pro-secularization phase.

Cultural analysis of mission contexts in the West can be valuable, so long as we recognize the limits of our analysis and do not use cartoonish analysis of culture to justify sweeping prescriptions for church and mission. The cultural analyses practiced by Lewis and Newbigin provide examples that remain instructive for contemporary mission thinkers. We can learn from the wisdom, as well as from the shortcomings, of those who have preceded us.

The key trends Lewis and Newbigin remarked upon in their discussions of twentieth century Britain continue to require attention in any twenty-first century cultural analysis: declining church involvement and belief, post-Christian sexuality, and increasing diversity. Likewise, the institutions discussed by Lewis and Newbigin—school, home, media, government, and church—remain important areas for contemporary mission research and missionary engagement.

A gap in the mission vision of both Lewis and Newbigin seems to remain a gap in much contemporary thinking about mission in the West: how to make the home effective for intergenerational transmission of Christian faith and for attracting non-Christians to faith in Christ. It seems that more thought is given to what sort of church style can reach the latest generation than to why each succeeding generation seems to think itself so far removed from the preceding generation. A closer look at home life, the fading of family devotions, the age-segregated structure of schools, and the specific demographic targeting of entertainment and advertising might provide important clues.

Despite shortcomings in analyzing the West from a mission perspective, and despite some oversimplifications in contrasting Christendom and post-Christendom, it remains undeniable that significant religious changes have occurred in Britain and in other Western societies. "Post-Christendom" can serve as a useful umbrella term to cover many of those changes, so long as the limits of the term are kept in mind. The term is more applicable to Britain than to the United States, for reasons noted above.

Growing Gap Between Churchgoers and Others

In contemporary Britain, the gap continues to widen between the typical churchgoer (who is more committed and militant than the average churchgoer of earlier times) and unchurched compatriots (who have less Christian knowledge and involvement than ever before). This increasing distance can be seen as impeding Christianity's capacity to connect with the wider population (Brown 2001, 165-166, 190-198; 2006, 301). However, it can also be seen as "the liberation of religion" from a social order that not only reinforced but also domesticated religion (Hastings 1991, 583).

Hastings sees in English history various waves of zeal to "convert and truly Christianize a rather nominally Christian England," alternating with eras where "society thrusts religious things away from its functioning" after a dated form of religion weighs too heavily on social structures. Forced to adjust to the expulsion and stand on its own, religion can then "effectively resume its missionary task." In the past, religion has proved adept at finding new and compelling forms, insists Hastings. Moreover, present trends toward a post-industrial situation may heighten the importance of home and neighborhood and thus "favour the practice of religion" (Hastings 1991, 670-671).

Brown sees an ongoing trend in which British churches are marked by "increasing commitment from decreasing numbers of people" (2001, 198). Greater levels of commitment among Catholics and evangelicals may have "helped reduce the apathetic middle to a secular condition," suggests David Martin. "With the ending of Constantinian establishment, and as a further contribution to its dismantlement, Christians have raised the bar about what it means to be a Christian, and so inhibited the take-up." As Christians become more distinct from others, it becomes harder to achieve "any general re-Christianization of society." But this may be desirable. "In its self-understanding Christianity returns to what it originally aspired to be: the leaven in the lump, the salt that has not lost its savour" (Martin 2005a, 119).

Lewis regarded Britain's religious decline as the fading of nominal British folk religion, not as a collapse of real Christianity. Consequently, he thought that the claims of Christianity and the nature of Christian commitment would stand out more clearly. Newbigin viewed shrinking churches as evidence of divine pruning—and pruning often precedes fresh growth and fruitfulness. Both missionaries took a somber view of their religious context, yet they saw not grounds for despair but opportunities for mission. Such an outlook remains appropriate for the contemporary context.

As British society develops an identity less tied to churches, churches may also be developing an identity that is less conformed to society—a missionary identity. Increasing commitment may coincide with decreasing numbers for a time, but in the long term may lead to renewed growth. A time of pruning and recommitment often leads to reinvigorated evangelism and numerical growth. This ultimately rests in God's hands and depends upon the movement of his Spirit. Highly motivated churches may become more active and effective in evangelistic outreach than when they were larger and lukewarm. As churches grow in zeal and eventually in numbers, British Christians may influence various spheres of public life and move even the uncommitted to think in more Christian terms. As McLeod says, "a decisive role in religious history" is usually "played by smaller groups of the strongly committed" (2000, 288).

The passing of "Christendom" may be less a tragedy than an opportunity. Jacques Ellul once remarked, "Christendom astutely abolished Christianity by making us all Christians." Citing these words, Ramachandra says Christendom's passing "should lead not to nostalgia among European Christians, but to a celebration of the new hermeneutical as well as evangelistic possibilities the situation offers." European Christians can learn from believers elsewhere who must "live on terms set by other people" and adopt a missionary stance of humble, vulnerable engagement with others (Ramachandra 2005, 491). British believers may draw encouragement and insight from Christians in other countries on how churches can flourish without "Christian" hegemony over society. Remarking on similarity between the contemporary context and that faced by the early church before Constantine, Berger finds "this similarity inspiring rather than depressing . . . this means taking on the role of the missionary, even when one is, so to speak, 'at home'" (Berger 2003, 40-41).

Christian missionaries to Europe from other countries "are having results" (Stark 2001, 117), as are European Christians who are eager to evangelize. This does not mean that Britain can easily be won to Christianity by "entrepreneurial wizardry on the part of the churches" (Kirk 2005, 133). It does, however, signal that when Britain is approached as a mission field, rather than as a place where nominal Christianity is taken for granted, conversion may become more frequent and churches may again grow.

As Christians pursue mission with renewed urgency, and as British people find naturalism or vaguely eclectic spirituality unsatisfying, Britain may—by God's grace—experience a fresh advance of biblical, Christ-centered faith. The growing gap between churchgoers and others may be healthy in some respects. It may indicate movement away from the sort of syncretism that so concerned Newbigin.

However, as Lewis pointed out, Christians must beware of widening the gap needlessly by failing to speak in terms that unbelieving people can understand, by failing to convey grounds for taking Christianity seriously, by perpetuating religious forms that are vestiges of a bygone culture rather than expressions of living faith, or by avoiding close relationships with non-Christian people. Christians must not presume that the church's increasing distance from the surrounding society always signifies growth in holiness and sound doctrine; it may also indicate an ingrown subculture that uses its own jargon, huddles within its ecclesiastical plausibility structure, and hides its light under a bushel. Pious talk about faithfulness to the gospel and about refusal to pander to the world can sometimes cloak a stubborn, slothful rejection of missionary adaptability, a refusal to become all things to all people in order to save some (1 Cor 9:22).

The church must be distinctive in its beliefs, conduct, and vision, while at the same time constantly and publicly bringing its beliefs, conduct, and vision to bear on people and institutions outside the church. These emphases, prominent in both Lewis and Newbigin, must be maintained in contemporary mission.

Post-Christian Weightier Than Postmodern

In a book portraying two deceased missionaries in their specific historical and cultural contexts, the continuing relevance of the missionaries' insights for a particular contemporary context depends to some extent on how widely our setting differs from theirs. Context-sensitive apologetics accepts that tactics which were appropriate and effective in one setting might not be suitable for a different setting. But where substantial similarities remain, methods that were formerly effective may continue to bear fruit.

Some seem to claim that postmodernity presents an unprecedented challenge, and that any apologetic from an era before the turn to postmodernity is obsolete. I disagree. Postmodernity's importance can be overblown. Many people's lack of Christian heritage and of any church background whatsoever has changed the landscape for Western apologists more than postmodernity has done. Christian witness to people who are generations removed from any significant family involvement in church or Sunday school might need to differ in some ways from witness to people who directly experienced some sort of church ties during their younger years but later abandoned Christian belief and practice.

Relevance for Postmodern Ethos

Even if postmodernity were as dominant an ethos as some claim, Lewis and Newbigin would be far from irrelevant. Newbigin was still publishing not that long ago, so his work is too recent to be summarily dismissed as outdated. He spoke explicitly of postmodern thought. Indeed, missional thinkers who engage postmodernity often regard Newbigin as an important contributor. In my estimation, Newbigin sometimes went too far in stating that we live in a postmodern age, but at any rate he was certainly attentive to postmodern tendencies and was himself critical of modernity.

Lewis died nearly a half-century ago, so it might be tempting to regard him as less relevant for contemporary mission. Some observers, familiar with a few of Lewis's more evidential or syllogistic passages, might allege that Lewis's approach is so steeped in a "modern" approach that it cannot connect with a new, postmodern context. In this view, intellectual and cultural changes in the decades since Lewis's death render Lewis's approach to missional apologetics obsolete.

This view involves at least two errors. One error assumes that because intellectuals have "moved on" to other views, the masses have also moved on. However, an argument that sophisticated scholars see as demolition of a straw man, may in fact be an effective address to real errors held by many real people. Moreover, clear thought and plain talk often connect with the masses even when an educated elite has other preferences. Continuing interest in Lewis's books makes it hard to deny his contemporary relevance for at least some people.

A second error in thinking that the "new" postmodern milieu outdates Lewis is a failure to see that very little of what is called postmodern would be new to Lewis. He knew Hume, Freud, Marx, and Nietzsche before the appearance of latter-day champions of skepticism and the hermeneutics of suspicion. Lewis knew as well as any postmodernist that the stated rationale for something may spring from unstated desires for power and pleasure. Lewis saw problems with imperialism and colonialism. He saw that much science sprang from pursuit of control, not just love of knowledge. Before Thomas Kuhn wrote of paradigm shifts in science, Lewis wrote of "the change of Models." Before Stanley Fish's literary criticism, Lewis stated that all use of language entailed an element of control.[3] Before Peter Berger analyzed "plausibility structures," Lewis wrote of "a taste in universes" and of what would be "believed by the great mass of unthinking people." Lewis knew, better than most, the limits of language and logic, the power of "storying," and the impact of community in shaping individual thought and behavior. Lewis anticipated much of what is now labeled postmodern—perhaps because the "postmodern" is an extension of the modern, not a sharp break from it.[4] Lewis utilized some sound insights that now tend to be associated with a postmodern perspective, and at the same time he foresaw and opposed the irrationality and amorality into which (post)modernity was plunging.[5]

---

[3]Lewis wrote, "I do not think that Rhetoric and Poetry are distinguished by manipulation of audience in the one and, in the other, a pure self-expression, regarded as its own end, and indifferent to any audience. Both these acts, in my opinion, definitely aim at doing something to an audience and both do it by using language to control what already exists in our minds" (1942, 53).

[4]"Lewis never treated postmodernity directly (he died four years before Derrida published *Of Grammatology*), but he foresaw its coming" (Vanhoozer 2005b, 76).

[5]Wesley Kort observes that Lewis and postmodern literary studies "share a penchant for autobiography and personal reference, an intense but critical interest in culture, including popular culture, a skepticism toward the prevailing centers of academic and social power, and a strongly polemical style. But Lewis reveals that these interests and styles are not necessarily wedded to skeptical or self-serving motives and results but can also serve positive, public moral and spiritual ends" (Kort 2001, 17). In Kort's opinion, "the cultural criticism that Lewis aimed at modernity continues largely to be relevant to our own situation. While it is far from uniform, modernity has retained most of the characteristics that Lewis deplored and attacked. . . . Lewis's cultural critique and his alternative way of giving an account of the world continue to apply" (Kort 2001, 162).

The alleged gap between modern and postmodern is often exaggerated and does not consign Lewis's work to obsolescence. [6] Of course, gospel communicators should always keep updating their use of words and keep expanding their arsenal of methods. Lewis himself would not want contemporary mission to limit itself to parroting his every word and aping his every move: he insisted that Christian truth be translated into the vernacular language of each nation or locale and each new generation. He also recognized that even in his own time, his tactics were suitable only for a certain kind of apologist seeking to reach a particular kind of audience. We must update gospel language and apply it in fresh ways to differing contexts. Even so, Lewis continues to remain relevant for many people in the West, even for those who could in some sense be called postmodern. [7]

Increasingly Post-Christian Context

If a major shift in context has occurred that might limit somewhat the applicability and effectiveness of Lewis's or Newbigin's approaches, it is less the shift from modern to postmodern, and more the shift from Christian to post-Christian. Since Lewis and Newbigin were both converts from atheism to Christianity, it might seem that they would, from their own experience, have a strong sense of how non-believers think and feel. They would indeed be intimately acquainted with a particular kind of unbelief; but there are different varieties, and different backgrounds, of unbelief. Lewis and Newbigin were not merely non-

[6]William Craig sees postmodernism as a "faddish movement" and says, "We do not, in fact, live in postmodern times." Because "postmodernism is unlivable . . . there can be no postmodern society. Rather, we live in post-Christian times, and what has replaced Christianity is not postmodernism but rather what has been aptly called 'the new absolutism.'" Openness and tolerance are not only valued but demanded. "Nor do most people, including academics, think that there is no objective truth. No one uses a postmodernist hermeneutic when reading the label of a medicine bottle. Theologians tend to think that postmodern pluralism and relativism are all the rage, when in fact such thinking is largely confined to the literature, social sciences, and religious studies departments at universities" (2000, 181).

[7]Gene Veith (1997) writes of Lewis as "Evangelist to the postmodernists." Meanwhile, Reed Jolly (1997) calls Lewis "Apostle to Generation X," and George Musacchio (1997) depicts "Lewis as evangelist to the modernists." Admiration for Lewis can be so excessive that he becomes the solution to every problem, the mission template for every context and era. Such an extreme must be avoided, yet Lewis's versatility and continuing relevance for various audiences is undeniable. "The great value of Lewis as apologist was his many-sidedness" (Farrer 1965, 25).

believers who became Christians; both grew up in churchgoing families and were familiar with much Christian vocabulary, thought, and practice even when they were not Christians. That was common for many of their generation in Britain. In contemporary Britain, however, it is far less common for people outside the church to have experience with church life or familiarity with church teaching. On the one hand, this means that fewer people need help to deal with memories of troubling, trivial, boring, or illogical aspects of church life. On the other hand, it also means that newer generations of unchurched people in Britain have less vestigial Christianity that might resonate with an apologist's presentation.

Lewis's direct apologetic arguments were most appropriate for a context of "orthodoxy in discredit; an age full of people talked out of a faith in which they were reared," according to Lewis's friend, theologian Austin Farrer. Such a context "provides an opening to the apologetic approach. 'You have been rattled and browbeaten,' says the apologist. 'You have been sold a false image of faith and an inflated estimate of her enemies. Give faith her rights, and you will again believe.'" This fit the situation of English people in the 1930s and 1940s, and it still fits the situation of many Americans. Already by the time of Lewis's death, he was vastly more popular in America than in Britain. As Farrer observed, "America is a far less de-Christianized country than England. Where the erosion of orthodoxy has gone beyond a certain point, other champions and different arms are called for" (Farrer 1965, 24-25). Lewis himself may have recognized the need for "different arms." This might be part of the reason that after the late 1940s, he worked more on stories and indirect apologetics, and less on the kind of direct arguments he had often used in earlier years.

Newbigin lived to see Britain move still further from Christianity than it had been in Lewis's time, yet Newbigin's style of apologetic would seem—even more than Lewis's—to match the contours drawn by Farrer: urging people not to be intimidated by attacks on Christian belief, and helping them to give Christian faith its due as understood and lived within the church's plausibility structure. That might be of some help to people with a church background, but it would seem less helpful to the growing number of people in Britain (and elsewhere in the West) for whom the church played little or no role in their own, their parents', or even their grandparents' lives. The foremost challenge for a missional apologist in relation to such people would be how to get them to pay attention and grant any credence to Christian claims in the first place.

The kind of mission and apologetic that can reach Westerners who have little or no church background may need to be different in certain respects from approaches favored by Lewis or Newbigin. Missional apologetics in the West would benefit from more research into the work of Christians and churches that have had some success evangelizing in Europe among people several generations distant from church. Of course, even if an increasingly post-Christian context limits to some degree the applicability of Lewis's and Newbigin's approaches, this does not render them completely irrelevant. Contemporary missional apologists seeking to reach Western non-believers with no church background can glean much insight from Lewis and Newbigin and adapt it for a new context and audience. Also, there are still sizeable numbers of unchurched, uncommitted people in the West (especially in America) who have some background in church, Sunday school, or a Christian family. Such people ought to remain a high priority for mission and apologetics, and they have much in common with the sort of people Lewis and Newbigin understood best.

Uniting Presuppositional and Evidential Apologetics

Dulles writes of "the tension between two Christian attitudes that recur in every generation—an apologetically inclined mentality, which seeks to find as broad a common ground as possible with the non-Christian, and a strictly dogmatic stance, which would safeguard the integrity of the faith even at the price of placing severe limits on the free exercise of reason" (Dulles 2005a, 109-110). The former mentality was more characteristic of Lewis, the latter of Newbigin. Yet Lewis, while emphasizing common ground with non-Christians, insisted on Christian orthodoxy. And Newbigin, while declaring a dogmatic starting point and denying that "reason" could referee between worldviews with opposing presuppositions, sought to show the gospel's rationality according to its own criteria.

Doctrinal fidelity and apologetic persuasiveness are not mutually exclusive, though some degree of tension may be unavoidable. In contemporary mission, we must not truncate or dilute the gospel to make it more palatable for non-Christians. By the same token, we must not shy away from making a persuasive case for the gospel. Orthodoxy and apologetics belong together. Dulles charges that all too often, abandoning apologetics goes together with less desire to bring the gospel to others and less clarity and confidence in Christians' own beliefs. "Recognizing that faith is enfeebled if its rational grounds are denied, committed Christians are returning to apologetics." In the United States, "Evangelical Protestants are taking the lead. . . . And their method succeeds. The churches that combine a concern for orthodoxy with vigorous apologetics are growing." Among Roman Catholics too, a renewal of apologetics is occurring, "albeit more slowly" (Dulles 2004, 20).

Dulles shows at considerable length the historical role of apologetics in Christian mission and theology, and he contends that "the apologetical task will have to be carried on" in the present generation and beyond:

> In view of all that has been learned from depth psychology about the unconscious, from sociology about ideologies and plausibility structures, from comparative religion about the faiths of other peoples, and from linguistic analysis about the hazards of metaphysical discourse, the contemporary believer can scarcely stave off the real difficulties by an easy appeal to "blind faith." (Dulles 2005a, xxiii)

Reasoned argument is not the only, nor the most basic, form of Christian witness—but it is still very important.

> It is commonly said that if rational argument is so seldom the cause of conviction, philosophical apologists must largely be wasting their shot. The premise is true, but the conclusion does not follow. For though argument does not create conviction, the lack of it destroys belief. What seems to be proved may not be embraced; but what no one shows the ability to defend is quickly abandoned. Rational argument does not create belief, but it maintains a climate in which belief may flourish. (Farrer 1965, 26)

Newbigin was right that Christians who came to faith in response to gospel proclamation within the plausibility structure of a Christian congregation did not need to justify their beliefs in terms of some other plausibility structure in order for those beliefs to qualify as rational. Lewis made much the same point, but he did not think this ruled out the value of making a cumulative case for Christianity through theistic arguments and various other lines of evidence. I think Lewis was right. With various presuppositional thinkers and Reformed epistemologists, I think that belief in God and in biblical revelation can come directly, without needing demonstration based on allegedly more foundational truths. At the same time, with proponents of various strands of evidential apologetics, I think that evidence and arguments can be used by the Spirit to help some non-believers to find Christianity more plausible and can strengthen inquisitive or wavering Christians in their faith.[8]

William Craig offers a helpful "distinction between *knowing* Christianity to be true and *showing* Christianity to be true" (2000, 28). For some people, knowing may arise as a basic belief produced by the proper function of one's faculties within the proper setting, or by the direct testimony of the Holy Spirit. But others, who do not yet believe Christian claims, may benefit from being shown Christianity's plausibility in terms of evidence and arguments that make sense to them. These people might not be helped much by Christians who merely assert their own location within a Christian plausibility structure and declare the rightness of presupposing Christian truth. Even if such Christians are right and rationally justified in their knowing, their non-Christian acquaintances may need some showing through evidence and argument. I largely agree with Craig that "the presuppositionalists were right about knowing and the evidentialists about showing" (2000, 317; see also Craig 2008, 43-60).

An approach that unifies presuppositional and evidential thinking will recognize the legitimacy of knowing acquired from Scripture in the context of Christian community, while also granting importance to God's general revelation through creation and conscience, and offering reasons for non-Christians to take Christian claims seriously. Such an approach will expose hidden assumptions held by non-Christians that need to be discarded before they can give the gospel a fair hearing, but it will also identify aspects of the non-Christian's thought that are true and that may serve as clues to the reality of God in Christ.

[8]In *Five views on apologetics*, evangelical apologists represent five distinct approaches, identified as classical, evidential, cumulative case, presuppositional, and Reformed epistemology. In a less specific categorization, the first three could be loosely labeled evidential, and the latter two presuppositional. It is noteworthy that among contributors to this volume, those with a more evidential emphasis nevertheless agree with their more presuppositional colleagues that Christian belief can be rational even if acquired in a direct manner without supporting arguments. Meanwhile, those articulating more presuppositional approaches grant that evidence and argument can also serve useful purposes. Editor Steven Cowan identifies the following areas of agreement among the different contributors: "*1. The need for both positive and negative apologetics... 2. The value of theistic arguments and Christian evidences... 3. The noetic effects of sin... 4. The importance of the Holy Spirit in apologetics... 5. The existence of common ground with unbelievers... 6. A rejection of postmodern relativism*" (Cowan 2000, 375-376).

By faith I can presuppose biblical truth and proclaim the gospel on the authority of God himself. I can also come alongside people who do not yet acknowledge the authority of the Bible or of God, and I can identify some shared truths that may point them in the right direction. Such an approach fits with a critical realism that affirms the human capacity to know important things about reality, while remaining critically aware of our situatedness, fallibility, and use of constructs. Such an approach is also compatible with biblical inerrancy, even though critical realists such as Lewis and Newbigin did not affirm inerrancy. As a critical realist, I recognize that the concepts I communicate are partial, provisional vessels for God's treasure, and that my hearers may receive the treasure from God's inerrant Word into somewhat different conceptual vessels than the vessels I have used. As a critical realist engaging in missional apologetics, I depend on God's Holy Spirit to convey the realities revealed in the Word and to accomplish the purposes of God the Missionary.

References

Adey, Lionel. 1978. *C. S. Lewis's 'Great War' with Owen Barfield*. Victoria: University of Victoria.

_____. 1998. *C. S. Lewis: Writer, dreamer, and mentor*. Grand Rapids: Eerdmans.

Aeschliman, Michael D. 1983. *The restitution of man: C. S. Lewis and the case against scientism*. Grand Rapids: Eerdmans.

Allen, E. L. 1945. The theology of C. S. Lewis. *Modern Churchman* 34 (January-March): 317-324.

Anscombe, G. E. M. 1981. *The collected philosophical papers of G. E. M. Anscombe*, vol. 2. Minneapolis: University of Minnesota Press.

Armstrong, John H. 2010. *Your church is too small: Why unity in Christ's mission is vital to the future of the church*. Grand Rapids: Zondervan.

Aupers, Stef, and Dick Houtman. 2006. Beyond the spiritual supermarket: The social and public significance of New Age spirituality. *Journal of Contemporary Religion* 21, no. 2: 201-222.

Badham, Paul. 1989. Some secular trends in the Church of England today. In *Religion, state, and society in modern Britain*, ed. Paul Badham, 23-33. Lewiston, N.Y.: The Edwin Mellen Press.

_____. 1994. Religious pluralism in modern Britain. In *A history of religion in Britain: Practice and belief from pre-Roman times to the present*, ed. Sheridan Gilley and W. J. Sheils, 488-502. Oxford: Blackwell.

Bailey, Edward. 1989. The folk religion of the English people. In *Religion, state, and society in modern Britain*, ed. Paul Badham, 145-158. Lewiston, N.Y.: The Edwin Mellen Press.

Balsbaugh, Jon. 1997. The pagan and the post-Christian: Lewis's understanding of diversity outside the faith. In *C. S. Lewis: lightbearer in the shadowlands*, ed. Angus J. L. Menuge, 191-210. Wheaton: Crossway Books.

_____. 1965. Introduction. In *Light on C. S. Lewis*, ed. Jocelyn Gibb, ix-xxi. New York: Harcourt Brace Jovanovich.

Barfield, Owen. 1973 [1928]. *Poetic diction*. Third edition. Middletown, Conn.: Wesleyan University Press.

_____. 1989. *Owen Barfield on C. S. Lewis*. Edited by G. B. Tennyson. Middletown, Conn.: Wesleyan University Press.

Bebbington, David. 1992a. *Evangelicalism in modern Britain: A history from the 1730s to the 1980s*. Grand Rapids: Baker Books

_____. 1992b. The secularization of British universities since the mid-nineteenth century. In *The secularization of the academy*, ed. George M. Marsden and Bradley J. Longfield, 259-277. New York: Oxford University Press.

_____. 1993. Evangelicalism in modern Britain and America: A comparison. In *Amazing grace: Evangelicalism in Australia, Britain, Canada, and the United States*, ed. George A. Rawlyk and Mark A. Noll, 183-212. Grand Rapids: Baker.

_____. 1994. Evangelicalism in its settings: The British and American movements since 1940. In *Evangelicalism: Comparative studies of popular Protestantism in North America, the British Isles, and beyond, 1700-1990*, ed. Mark A. Noll, David W. Bebbington, and George A. Rawlyk, 365-388. New York: Oxford University Press.

Berger, Peter. 1967. *The sacred canopy*. Garden City, N.Y.: Doubleday.

_____. 1979a. *The heretical imperative: Contemporary possibilities of religious affirmation*. New York: Doubleday.

_____. 1979b. Facing up to modernity. Harmondsworth: Penguin Books.

_____. 1999. The desecularization of the world: A global overview. In *The desecularization of the world*, ed. Peter L. Berger, 1-18. Grand Rapids: Eerdmans.

_____. 2001a. Postscript. In *Peter Berger and the study of religion*, ed. Linda Woodhead, Paul Heelas, and David Martin, 87-100. London: Routledge.

_____. 2001b. Reflections on the sociology of religion today. *Sociology of Religion* 62, no. 4: 443-454.

_____. 2002. The cultural dynamics of globalization. In *Many globalizations: Cultural diversity in the contemporary world*, ed. Peter L. Berger and Samuel P. Huntington, 1-16. New York: Oxford University Press.

_____. 2003. Orthodoxy and the pluralistic challenge. *Greek Orthodox Theological Review* 48: 33-41.

_____. 2005. Religion and the West. *The National Interest* (Summer): 112-119.

Bevans, Stephen B., and Roger P. Schroeder. 2004. *Constants in context: A theology of mission for today.* American Society of Missiology Series. Maryknoll, N.Y.: Orbis Books.

Beversluis, John. 1985. *C. S. Lewis and the search for rational religion.* Grand Rapids: Eerdmans.

Blamires, Harry. 1998. Teaching the universal truth: C. S. Lewis among the intellectuals. In *The pilgrim's guide: C. S. Lewis and the art of witness*, ed. David Mills, 15-26. Grand Rapids: Eerdmans.

Bosch, David J. 1991. *Transforming mission.* Maryknoll, N.Y.: Orbis Books.

Brewer, Derek. 1992. The tutor: A portrait. In *"C. S. Lewis at the breakfast table" and other reminiscences*, ed. James T. Como, 41-67. New York: Harcourt, Brace, Jovanovitch.

Brierley, Peter. 2000. *The tide is running out: What the English church attendance survey reveals.* London: Christian Research.

Brown, Callum G. 1995. The mechanism of religious growth in urban societies: British cities since the eighteenth century. In *European religion in the age of great cities 1830-1930*, ed. Hugh McLeod, 239-262. London: Routledge.

_____. 2001. *The death of Christian Britain: Understanding secularization, 1800-2000.* London: Routledge.

_____. 2003. The secularisation decade: What the 1960s have done to the study of religious history. In *The decline of Christendom in Western Europe, 1750-2000*, ed. Hugh McLeod and Werner Ustorf, 29-46. Cambridge: Cambridge University Press.

_____. 2006. *Religion and society in twentieth-century Britain.* Harlow, UK: Pearson Education.

Bruce, Steve. 1995. The truth about religion in Britain. *Journal for the Scientific Study of Religion.* 34, no. 4: 417-430.

_____. 1996. *Religion in the modern world: From cathedrals to cults.* New York: Oxford University Press.

_____. 1998. Cathedrals to cults: The evolving forms of the religious life. In *Religion, modernity, and postmodernity*, ed. Paul Heelas, David Martin, and Paul Morris, 19-35. Oxford: Blackwell Publishers.

_____. 2001a. Christianity in Britain, R. I. P. *Sociology of Religion* 62, no. 2: 191-203.

_____. 2001b. The curious case of the unnecessary recantation: Berger and secularization. In *Peter Berger and the study of religion*, ed. Linda Woodhead, Paul Heelas, and David Martin, 87-100. London: Routledge.

_____. 2002a. *God is dead: Secularization in the West*. Oxford: Blackwell Publishing.

_____. 2002b. Praying alone? Church-going in Britain and the Putnam thesis. *Journal of Contemporary Religion* 17, no. 3: 317-328.

Budziszewski, J. 2003. *What we can't not know: A guide*. Dallas: Spence.

Bultmann, Rudolph. 1962. *Kerygma and myth*. London: SPCK.

Burson, Scott. R., and Jerry L. Walls. 1998. *C. S. Lewis & Francis Schaeffer: Lessons for a new century from the most influential apologists of our time*. Downers Grove, Ill.: Intervarsity Press.

Caldecott, Stratford. 1998. Speaking the truths only the imagination may grasp: Myth and 'real life.' In *The pilgrim's guide: C. S. Lewis and the art of witness*, ed. David Mills, 86-97. Grand Rapids: Eerdmans.

Campbell, Jonathan G. 1994. The Jewish community in Britain. In *A history of religion in Britain: Practice and belief from pre-Roman times to the present*, ed. Sheridan Gilley and W. J. Sheils, 427-448. Oxford: Blackwell.

Carnell, Corbin Scott. 1974. *Bright shadow of reality: C. S. Lewis and the feeling intellect*. Grand Rapids: Eerdmans.

_____. 1997. Longing, reason, and the moral law in C. S. Lewis's search. In *C. S. Lewis: Lightbearer in the shadowlands*, ed. Angus J. L. Menuge, 103-114. Wheaton: Crossway Books.

_____. 1998. Imagination. In *The C. S. Lewis readers' encyclopedia*, ed. Jeffrey A. Schultz and John G. West, Jr., 214-215. Grand Rapids: Zondervan.

Carson, D. A. 1996. *The gagging of God*. Grand Rapids: Zondervan.

_____. 2005. *Becoming conversant with the emerging church: Understanding a movement and its implications*. Grand Rapids: Zondervan.

Casanova, José. 1994. *Public religions in the modern world*. Chicago: The University of Chicago Press.

Chadwick, Owen. 1975. *The secularization of the European mind in the 19th century*. Cambridge: Cambridge University Press.

Chaves, Mark. 1994. Secularization as declining religious authority. *Social forces* 72, no. 3: 749-774.

Chesterton, G. K. 1990 [1908]. *Orthodoxy*. New York: Doubleday.

_____. 1993. *The everlasting man*. San Francisco: Ignatius.

Christensen, Michael J. 1979. *C. S. Lewis on Scripture*. Preface by Owen Barfield. Introduction by Clyde S. Kilby. Waco: Word.

Clark, Kelly James. 2000. Reformed epistemology apologetics. In *Five views on apologetics*, ed. Steven B. Cowan, 265-284. Grand Rapids: Zondervan.

Colson, Charles W. 1976. *Born again*. Old Tappan, N.J.: Chosen Books.

Como, James T., ed. 1992. *"C. S. Lewis at the breakfast table" and other reminiscences*. New York: Harcourt, Brace, Jovanovitch.

Conn, Harvie M. 1960. Literature and criticism. *Westminster Theological Journal* 23, no. 1: 16-32

Corduan, Winfried. 1997. Ambivalent truth: A response to Lesslie Newbigin. *Philosophia Christi* 20, no.1: 29-40.

Cox, Jeffrey. 2003. Master narratives of long-term religious change. In *The decline of Christendom in Western Europe, 1750-2000*, ed. Hugh McLeod and Werner Ustorf, 201-217. Cambridge: Cambridge University Press.

Cox, John D. 1977. Epistemological release in *The silver chair*. In *The longing for a form: Essays on the fiction of C. S. Lewis*, 159-168. N. p.: The Kent State University Press.

Craig, William Lane. 2000. Classical apologetics. In *Five views on apologetics*, ed Steven B. Cowan, 25-55, 173-183, 314-328. Grand Rapids: Zondervan.

_____. 2008. *Reasonable faith: Christian truth and apologetics*. Third edition. Wheaton: Crossway.

Crim, Keith R. 1993. North America. In *Toward the 21st century in Christian mission*, ed. James M. Phillips and Robert T. Coote, 98-106. Grand Rapids: Eerdmans.

Darwin, Charles. 1887. *The life and letters of Charles Darwin including an autobiographical chapter, vol. 1*. Edited by Francis Darwin. London: D. Appleton and Company.

Davie, Grace. 1994. *Religion in Britain since 1945: Believing without belonging*. Oxford: Blackwell Publishing.

_____. 1999. Europe: The exception that proves the rule? In *The desecularization of the world*, ed. Peter L. Berger, 65-83. Grand Rapids: Eerdmans.

_____. 2000. *Religion in modern Europe: A memory mutates*. Oxford: Oxford University Press.

_____. 2001. The persistence of institutional religion in modern Europe. In *Peter Berger and the study of religion*, ed. Linda Woodhead, Paul Heelas, and David Martin, 101-111. London: Routledge.

_____. 2002a. *Europe: The exceptional case—parameters of faith in the modern world*. London: Darton, Longmann and Todd.

_____. 2002b. Praying alone? Church-going in Britain and social capital: A reply to Steve Bruce. *Journal of Contemporary Religion* 17, no. 3: 329-334.

Dobbelaere, Karel. 1999. Towards an integrated perspective of the processes related to the descriptive concept of secularization. *Sociology of Religion* 60, no. 3: 229-247.

Dorsett, Lyle. 1989. C. S. Lewis: Some keys to his effectiveness. In *The riddle of joy: G. K. Chesterton and C. S. Lewis*, ed. Michael H. Macdonald and Andrew A Tadie, 215-225. Grand Rapids: Eerdmans.

_____. 2004. *Seeking the spiritual place: The spiritual formation of C. S. Lewis*. Grand Rapids: Brazos Press.

Downing, David C. 1992. *Planets in peril: A critical study of C. S. Lewis's Ransom trilogy*. Amherst: The University of Massachusetts Press.

_____. 2002. *The most reluctant convert: C. S. Lewis's journey to faith*. Downers Grove, Ill.: Intervarsity Press.

_____. 2005a. *Into the region of awe: Mysticism in C. S. Lewis*. Downers Grove, Ill.: Intervarsity Press.

_____. 2005b. *Into the wardrobe: C. S. Lewis and the Narnia Chronicles*. San Francisco: Jossey-Bass.

Drew, Gavin. 2005. The gospel as public truth in a pluralist world. *Stimulus: The New Zealand Journal of Christian Thought and Practice* 13, no.3: 21-30.

Driscoll, Mark, and Gerry Breshears. 2008. *Vintage church: Timeless truths and timely methods*. Wheaton: Crossway.

Dulles, Avery Cardinal. 2004. The rebirth of apologetics. *First Things* 143: 18-23.

_____. 2005a. *A history of apologetics*. Second edition. San Francisco: Ignatius Press.

_____. 2005b. Mere apologetics. *First Things* 154: 15-20.

Duriez, Colin. 1998. The romantic writer: C. S. Lewis's theology of fantasy. In *The pilgrim's guide: C. S. Lewis and the art of witness*, ed. David Mills, 98-110. Grand Rapids: Eerdmans.

Duriez, Colin, ed. 2000. *The C. S. Lewis encyclopedia: A complete guide to his life, thought and writings*. Wheaton: Crossway Books.

Dyrness, William. 1983. *Christian apologetics in a world community*. Downers Grove, Ill.: Intervarsity Press.

Edwards, Bruce L. 1998a. Miracles: A preliminary study. In *The C. S. Lewis readers' encyclopedia*, ed. Jeffrey A. Schultz and John G. West, Jr., 82-83. Grand Rapids: Zondervan.

_____. 1998b. A thoroughly converted man: C. S. Lewis in the public square. In *The pilgrim's guide: C. S. Lewis and the art of witness*, ed. David Mills, 280-281. Grand Rapids: Eerdmans.

Escobar, Samuel. 2003. *The new global mission: The gospel from everywhere to everyone*. Downers Grove, Ill.: Intervarsity.

Fairfield, Leslie P. 1998. Fragmentation and hope: The healing of the modern schisms in *That hideous strength*. In *The pilgrim's guide: C. S. Lewis and the art of witness*, ed. David Mills, 145-160. Grand Rapids: Eerdmans.

Farrer, Austin. 1965. The Christian apologist. In *Light on C. S. Lewis*, ed. Jocelyn Gibb, 23-43. New York: Harcourt Brace Jovanovich.

Forrester, Duncan B. 2002. Lesslie Newbigin as public theologian. In *A scandalous prophet: The way of mission after Newbigin*, ed. Thomas F. Foust, George R. Hunsberger, J. Andrew Kirk, and Werner Ustorf, 3-12. Grand Rapids: Eerdmans.

Foust, Thomas F. 2002a. *Christology, restoration, unity: An exploration of the missiological approach to modern Western culture according to Lesslie Newbigin and Dean E. Walker*. Birmingham: University of Birmingham.

_____. 2002b. Lesslie Newbigin's epistemology: A dual discourse? In *A scandalous prophet: The way of mission after Newbigin*, ed. Thomas F. Foust, George R. Hunsberger, J. Andrew Kirk, and Werner Ustorf, 153-162. Grand Rapids: Eerdmans.

Foust, Thomas F., and George R. Hunsberger, ed. 2002. Bishop J. E. Lesslie Newbigin: A comprehensive bibliography. In *A scandalous prophet: The way of mission after Newbigin*, ed. Thomas F. Foust, George R. Hunsberger, J. Andrew Kirk, and Werner Ustorf, 249-325. Grand Rapids: Eerdmans.

Foust, Thomas F., George R. Hunsberger, J. Andrew Kirk, and Werner Ustorf, eds. 2002. *A scandalous prophet: The way of mission after Newbigin*. Grand Rapids: Eerdmans.

Freshwater, Mark Edwards. 1988. *C. S. Lewis and the truth of myth*. Lanham, Md.: University Press of America.

Gelwick, Richard. 2000. Christian faith in a pluralist society. *Tradition and Discovery (The Polanyi Society Journal)* 27, no. 2: 39-45.

_____. 2001. Heuristic passion and universal intent: A response to George R. Hunsberger. *Tradition and Discovery (The Polanyi Society Journal)* 28, no. 1: 16-22.

Gibb, Jocelyn, ed. 1965. *Light on C. S. Lewis*. New York: Harcourt Brace Jovanovich.

Gibbs, Eddie, and Ryan K. Bolger. 2005. *Emerging churches: Creating Christian community in postmodern cultures*. Baker Academic.

Gilbert, Alan D. 1994. Secularization and the future. In *A history of religion in Britain: Practice and belief from pre-Roman times to the present*, ed. Sheridan Gilley and W. J. Sheils, 503-521. Oxford: Blackwell.

Gill, Robin. 2002. A response to Steve Bruce's "Praying Alone." *Journal of Contemporary Religion* 17, no. 3: 335-338.

Gill, Robin, C. Kirk Hadaway, and Penny Long Marler. 1998. Is religious belief declining in Britain? *Journal for the Scientific Study of Religion* 37, no. 3: 507-516.

Goheen, Michael W. 1999. Toward a missiology of western culture. *European Journal of Theology* 8, no. 2: 155-168.

_____. 2000. "As the Father has sent me, I am sending you": J. E. Lesslie Newbigin's missionary ecclesiology. Ph.D. diss., University of Utrecht.

_____. 2002a. Liberating the gospel from its modern cage: An interpretation of Lesslie Newbigin's Gospel and Modern Culture project. *Missionalia* 30, no. 3: 360-375.

_____. 2002b. The missional calling of believers in the world: Lesslie Newbigin's contribution. In *A scandalous prophet: The way of mission after Newbigin*, ed. Thomas F. Foust, George R. Hunsberger, J. Andrew Kirk, and Werner Ustorf, 37-54. Grand Rapids: Eerdmans.

Green, Deirdre. 1989. Buddhism in Britain: "Skillful means" or selling out? In *Religion, state, and society in modern Britain*, ed. Paul Badham, 275-290. Lewiston, N.Y.: The Edwin Mellen Press.

Green, Roger Lancelyn, and Walter Hooper. 1974. *C. S. Lewis: A biography*. New York: Harcourt Brace Jovanovich.

Griffiths, Alan Bede. 1992. The adventure of faith. In *"C. S. Lewis at the breakfast table" and other reminiscences*, ed. James T. Como, 11-24. New York: Harcourt, Brace, Jovanovitch.

Griffiths, Paul J. 1987. Philosophizing across cultures: Or, how to argue with a Buddhist. *Criterion* 26 (Winter): 1-13.

Groothuis, Douglas. 2000. *Truth decay: Defending Christianity against the challenges of postmodernism*. Downers Grove, Ill.: Intervarsity Press.

Guder, Darrell L., ed. 1998. *Missional church: a vision for the sending of the church in North America*. Grand Rapids: Eerdmans.

Guder, Darrel L. 2000. *The continuing conversion of the church*. Grand Rapids: Eerdmans.

Haldane, J. B. S. 1928. *Possible worlds and other papers*. New York: Harper & Brothers.

_____. 1946. Auld Hornie, F.R.S. *Modern Quarterly* (Autumn): 32-40.

_____. 1948. God and Mr. Lewis. In *The rationalist annual: 1948*, ed. Frederick Watts, 78-85. London: Watts & Co.

Hall, Douglas John. 1996. *The end of Christendom and the future of Christianity*. Christian mission and modern culture, ed. Alan Neely, H. Wayne Pipkin, and Wilbert R. Shenk. Harrisburg, Pa.: Trinity Press International.

Harwood, A. C. 1992. About anthroposophy. In *"C. S. Lewis at the breakfast table" and other reminiscences*, ed. James T. Como, 25-32. New York: Harcourt, Brace, Jovanovitch.

Hastings, Adrian. 1991. *A history of English Christianity 1920-1990*. Third edition. London: SCM Press.

Heck, Joel D. 1997. *Preparatio evangelica*. In *C. S. Lewis: Lightbearer in the shadowlands*, ed. Angus J. L. Menuge, 235-258. Wheaton: Crossway Books.

_____. 2005. *Irrigating deserts: C. S. Lewis on education*. St. Louis: Concordia Academic Press.

Heelas, Paul. 2006. The infirmity debate: On the viability of New Age spiritualities of life. *Journal of Contemporary Religion* 21, no. 2: 223-240.

Heelas, Paul, and Linda Woodhead. 2005. *The spiritual revolution: Why religion is giving way to spirituality*. Oxford: Blackwell Publishing.

Helm, Paul. 2000. *Faith with reason*. Oxford: Oxford University Press.

Hervieu-Leger, Daniele. 2001. The twofold limit of the notion of secularization. In *Peter Berger and the study of religion*, ed. Linda Woodhead, Paul Heelas, and David Martin, 112-125. London: Routledge.

Hick, John. 1995. A pluralist view. In *Four views on salvation in a pluralistic world*, ed. Dennis L. Ockholm and Timothy R. Phillips, 29-59. Grand Rapids: Zondervan.

Hiebert, Paul G. 1985a. Epistemological foundations for science and theology. *TSF Bulletin* 8, no. 4: 5-10.

_____. 1985b. The missiological implications of an epistemological shift. *TSF Bulletin* 8, no. 5: 6-11.

_____. 1991. Beyond anticolonialism to globalism. *Missiology: An international review* 19, no. 3: 263-282.

_____. 1994. *Anthropological reflections on missiological issues*. Grand Rapids: Baker.

_____. 1996. The gospel in our culture: Methods of social and cultural analysis. In *The church between gospel and culture: The emerging mission in North America*, ed. George R. Hunsberger and Craig Van Gelder, 139-157. Grand Rapids: Eerdmans.

_____. 1999. *Missiological implications of epistemological shifts: Affirming truth in a modern/postmodern world*. Christian mission and modern culture, ed. Alan Neely, H. Wayne Pipkin, and Wilbert R. Shenk. Harrisburg, Pa.: Trinity Press International.

Hoedemaker, Bert. 1999a. The ends of the earth and the end of time. In *To stake a claim: Mission and the western crisis of knowledge*, ed. J. Andrew Kirk and Kevin J. Vanhoozer, 205-216. Maryknoll, N.Y.: Orbis Books.

_____. 1999b. Toward an epistemologically responsible missiology. In *To stake a claim: Mission and the western crisis of knowledge*, ed. J. Andrew Kirk and Kevin J. Vanhoozer, 217-233. Maryknoll, N.Y.: Orbis Books.

_____. 2002. Rival conceptions of global Christianity: Mission and modernity, then and now. In *A scandalous prophet: The way of mission after Newbigin*, ed. Thomas F. Foust, George R. Hunsberger, J. Andrew Kirk, and Werner Ustorf, 13-22. Grand Rapids: Eerdmans.

Holmer, Paul L. 1976. *C. S. Lewis: The shape of his faith and thought*. New York: Harper and Row.

Hooper, Walter. 1979. *Past watchful dragons: The Narnian Chronicles of C. S. Lewis*. New York: Collier Books.

_____. 1992. Oxford's bonny fighter. In *"C. S. Lewis at the breakfast table" and other reminiscences*, ed. James T. Como, 137-185. New York: Harcourt, Brace, Jovanovich,

_____. 1996. *C. S. Lewis: A complete guide to his life and works*. New York: Harper San Francisco.

Howard, Thomas. 1987. *C. S. Lewis: Man of letters*. San Francisco: Ignatius Press.

Hunsberger, George R. 1998. *Bearing the witness of the Spirit: Lesslie New-bigin's theology of cultural plurality*. Grand Rapids: Eerdmans.

_____. 2000. Faith and pluralism: A response to Richard Gel-wick. *Tradition and Discovery (The Polanyi Society Journal)* 27, no.3: 19-29.

_____. 2002. The church in the postmodern transition. In *A scandalous prophet: The way of mission after Newbigin*, ed. Thomas F. Foust, George R. Hunsberger, J. Andrew Kirk, and Werner Ustorf, 95-106. Grand Rapids: Eerdmans.

Hunsberger, George R., and Craig Van Gelder, eds. 1996. *The church between gospel and culture: The emerging mission in North America*. Grand Rapids: Eerdmans.

Hussain, Amjad. 2004. Islamic education: Why is there a need for it? *Journal of Beliefs & Values: Studies in Religion and Education* 25, no. 3: 317-323.

Hyatt, Douglas T. 1997. Joy, the call of God in man: A critical appraisal of Lewis's argument from desire. In *C. S. Lewis: Lightbearer in the shadowlands*, ed. Angus J. L. Menuge, 305-328. Wheaton: Crossway Books.

Jackson, Eleanor. 2001. *Walking in the light: A biographical study of Lesslie Newbigin*. Carlisle: Paternoster.

Jacobs, Alan. 2005. *The Narnian: The life and imagination of C. S. Lewis*. New York: Harper San Francisco.

Johansson, Lars. 1999. Mystical knowledge, New Age, and missiology. In *To stake a claim: Mission and the western crisis of knowledge*, ed. J. Andrew Kirk and Kevin J. Vanhoozer, 172-204. Maryknoll, N.Y.: Orbis Books.

Johnson, Mark. 1993. *Moral imagination: Implications of cognitive science for ethics*. Chicago: The University of Chicago Press.

Jolley, Reed. 1997. Apostle to generation X: C. S. Lewis and the future of evangelism. In *C. S. Lewis: Lightbearer in the shadowlands*, ed. Angus J. L. Menuge, 79-100. Wheaton: Crossway Books.

Jongeneel, Jan A. B. 1998. Is missiology an academic discipline? *Transformation: An International Journal of Holistic Mission Studies*, 15, no. 3: 27-32.

Keller, Tim. 2001. The missional church [article online]. Available from www.redeemer2.com/resources/papers/missional.pdf; internet.

Kenneson, Philip D. 1995. There's no such thing as objective truth, and it's a good thing, too. In *Christian apologetics in the postmodern world*, ed. Timothy R. Phillips and Dennis L. Okholm, 155-170, notes 215-220. Downers Grove, Ill.: Intervarsity Press.

_____. 2002. Trinitarian missiology: Mission as face-to-face encounter. In *A scandalous prophet: The way of mission after Newbigin*, ed. Thomas F. Foust, George R. Hunsberger, J. Andrew Kirk, and Werner Ustorf, 76-83. Grand Rapids: Eerdmans.

Kettle, David. 2002a. Gospel, authority, and globalization. In *A scandalous prophet: The way of mission after Newbigin*, ed. Thomas F. Foust, George R. Hunsberger, J. Andrew Kirk, and Werner Ustorf, 201-214. Grand Rapids: Eerdmans.

_____. 2002b. Newbigin, Polanyi, and impossible frameworks. *Tradition and Discovery (The Polanyi Society Journal)* 28, no. 2: 20-22.

Kilby, Clyde S. 1964. *The Christian world of C. S. Lewis*. Grand Rapids: Eerdmans.

_____. 1971. The creative logician speaking. In *C. S. Lewis: Speaker and teacher*, ed. Carolyn Keefe, 13-34. Grand Rapids: Zondervan.

_____. 1977. *Till we have faces*: An interpretation. In *The longing for a form: Essays on the fiction of C. S. Lewis*, 171-181. The Kent State University Press.

King, Alec, and Martin Ketley. 1939. *The control of language: A critical appraisal to reading and writing*. London: Longman, Green.

Kirk, J. Andrew. 1999. Christian mission and the epistemological crisis of the West. In *To stake a claim: Mission and the western crisis of knowledge*, ed. J. Andrew Kirk and Kevin J. Vanhoozer, 157-171. Maryknoll, N.Y.: Orbis Books.

_____. 2005. Secularization, the world church, and the future of mission. *Transformation* 22, no. 3: 130-138.

Kirk, J. Andrew, and Kevin J. Vanhoozer, eds. 1999. *To stake a claim: Mission and the western crisis of knowledge*. Maryknoll, N.Y.: Orbis Books.

Knot, Kim. 1989. Hindu communities in Britain. In *Religion, state, and society in modern Britain*, ed. Paul Badham, 242-256. Lewiston, N.Y.: The Edwin Mellen Press.

Kort, Wesley A. 2001. *C. S. Lewis then and now*. New York: Oxford University Press.

Kreeft, Peter. 1988. *C. S. Lewis: A critical essay*. Front Royal, Va.: Christendom College Press.

_____. 1989. C. S. Lewis's argument from desire. In *The riddle of joy: G. K. Chesterton and C. S. Lewis*, ed. Michael H. Macdonald and Andrew A Tadie, 249-272. Grand Rapids: Eerdmans.

_____. 1994. *C. S. Lewis for the third millennium: Six essays on* The abolition of man. San Francisco: Ignatius Press.

_____. 1998. *C. S. Lewis: A critical essay*. Front Royal Virginia: Christendom College Press.

Kuhn, Thomas S. 1970 [1962]. *The structure of scientific revolutions*. Second edition, enlarged. Chicago: The University of Chicago Press.

Kuzmic, Peter. 1993. Europe. In *Toward the 21ˢᵗ century in Christian mission*, ed. James M. Phillips and Robert T. Coote, 148-163. Grand Rapids: Eerdmans.

Lakoff, George, and Mark Johnson. 1999. *Philosophy in the flesh: The embodied mind and its challenge to Western thought*. New York: Basic Books.

_____. 2003 [1980]. *Metaphors we live by*. With a new afterword. Chicago: The University of Chicago Press.

Lambert, Yves. 1999. Religion in modernity as a new axial age: Secularization or new religious forms? *Sociology of Religion* 60, no. 3: 303-333.

_____. 2003. New Christianity, indifference and diffused spirituality. In *The decline of Christendom in Western Europe, 1750-2000*, ed. Hugh McLeod and Werner Ustorf, 63-78. Cambridge: Cambridge University Press.

_____. 2004. A turning point in religious evolution in Europe. *Journal of Contemporary Religion* 19, no. 1: 29-45.

Lewis, C. S. 1936. *The allegory of love: A study in medieval tradition*. Oxford: Clarendon Press.

_____. 1938. *Out of the silent planet*. New York: Macmillan.

_____. 1939. *Rehabilitations and other essays*. London: Oxford University Press.

_____. 1942. *A preface to* Paradise Lost. London: Oxford University Press.

_____. 1946a. *That hideous strength: A modern fairy-tale for grown-ups*. New York: Macmillan.

_____. 1946b. *The great divorce*. New York: Macmillan.

_____. 1947. *Miracles: A preliminary study*. New York: Macmillan.

_____. 1952. *Mere Christianity*. New York: Macmillan.

_____. 1954. *English literature in the sixteenth century, excluding drama*. The Oxford History of English Literature 3. Oxford: Clarendon Press.

_____. 1955a. [1940] *The problem of pain*. New York: Macmillan.

_____. 1955b. *Surprised by joy: The shape of my early life*. New York: Harcourt, Brace, Jovanovich.

_____. 1956. *Till we have faces*. New York: Harcourt.

_____. 1958. *Reflections on the Psalms*. New York: Harcourt, Brace, & World.

_____. 1960a. *The four loves*. New York: Harcourt Brace Jovanovich.

_____. 1960b. *Miracles: A preliminary study*. [1947] Revised. New York: Harper San Francisco.

_____. 1960c [1942]. *The Screwtape letters*. Revised edition. New York: Macmillan.

_____. 1960d. *The world's last night and other essays*. New York: Harcourt.

_____. 1961. *An experiment in criticism*. Cambridge: Cambridge University Press.

_____. 1962. *De descriptione temporum*. In *They asked for a paper*, 9-25. London: Geoffrey Bles.

_____. 1964. *The discarded image*. Cambridge: Cambridge University Press.

_____. 1967. *The seeing eye and other selected essays from* Christian reflections. New York: Ballantine.

_____. 1970. *God in the dock: Essays on theology and ethics*. Grand Rapids: Eerdmans.

_____. 1973 [1964]. *Letters to Malcolm: Chiefly on prayer*. New York: Harvest.

_____. 1980. *The weight of glory and other addresses*. Revised and expanded edition. New York: Macmillan.

_____. 1982. *On stories: And other essays on literature*. New York: Harcourt Brace Jovanovich.

_____. 1986. *Present concerns*. Edited by Walter Hooper. New York: Harcourt.

_____. 1989 [1933]. *The pilgrim's regress: An allegorical apology for Christianity, reason, and romanticism*. Grand Rapids: Eerdmans.

_____. 1994a [1954]. *The horse and his boy*. New York: HarperCollins.

_____. 1994b [1956]. *The last battle*. New York: HarperCollins.

_____. 1994c [1950]. *The lion, the witch, and the wardrobe*. New York: HarperCollins.

_____. 1994d [1955]. *The magician's nephew*. New York: Harper-Collins.

_____. 1994e [1951]. *Prince Caspian: The return to Narnia*. New York: HarperCollins.

_____. 1994f [1953]. *The silver chair*. New York: HarperCollins.

_____. 1994g [1952]. *The voyage of the* Dawn Treader. New York: HarperCollins.

_____. 1996 [1944]. *The abolition of man*. New York: Touchstone.

_____. 2003 [1944]. *Perelandra*. New York: Scribner.

_____. 2001 [1961]. *A grief observed*. San Francisco: Harper San Francisco.

_____. 2004a. *The collected letters of C. S. Lewis. Vol. I, Family letters 1905-1931*. Edited by Walter Hooper. New York: Harper San Francisco.

_____. 2004b. *The collected letters of C. S. Lewis. Vol. II, Books, broadcasts, and the war 1931-1949*. Edited by Walter Hooper. New York: Harper San Francisco.

_____. 2007. *The collected letters of C. S. Lewis. Vol. III, Narnia, Cambridge, and Joy 1950-1963*. Edited by Walter Hooper. New York: Harper San Francisco.

Lindskoog, Kathryn. 1998. Anthroposophy. In *The C. S. Lewis readers' encyclopedia*, ed. Jeffrey A. Schultz and John G. West, Jr., 82-83. Grand Rapids: Zondervan.

Lindsley, Art. 2005. *C. S. Lewis's case for Christ: Insights from reason, imagination and faith*. Downers Grove, Ill.: Intervarsity Press.

Lundin, Roger.1993. *The culture of interpretation: Christian faith and the postmodern world*. Grand Rapids: Eerdmans.

Marsden, George M., and Bradley J. Longfield, eds. 1992. *The secularization of the academy*. New York: Oxford University Press.

Martin, David. 1965. Towards eliminating the concept of secularization. In *Penguin survey of the social sciences*, ed. Julius Gould, 169-182. Harmondsworth: Penguin.

_____. 1978. *A general theory of secularization*. Oxford: Blackwell.

_____. 1991. The secularization issue: Prospect and retrospect. *The British Journal of Sociology* 42, no. 3: 465-474.

_____. 1999. The evangelical protestant upsurge and its political implications. In *The desecularization of the world*, ed. Peter L. Berger, 37-49. Grand Rapids: Eerdmans.

_____. 2005a. *On secularization: Towards a revised general theory*. Burlington, Vt.: Ashgate Publishing Company.

_____. 2005b. Secularisation and the future of Christianity. *Journal of Contemporary Religion* 20, no. 2: 145-160.

Martindale, Wayne. 1997. Shadowlands: Inadvertent evangelism. In *C. S. Lewis: Lightbearer in the shadowlands*, ed. Angus J. L. Menuge, 31-53. Wheaton: Crossway Books.

Maudlin, Michael. 1993. 1993 *Christianity Today* book awards. *Christianity Today* 37, no. 4: 28.

McLeod, Hugh. 2000. *Secularisation in Western Europe, 1848-1914*. New York: St. Martin's Press.

_____. 2003. Introduction. In *The decline of Christendom in Western Europe, 1750-2000*, ed. Hugh McLeod and Werner Ustorf, 1-26. Cambridge: Cambridge University Press.

McLeod, Hugh, and Werner Ustorf, eds. 2003. *The decline of Christendom in Western Europe, 1750-2000*. Cambridge: Cambridge University Press.

Medcalf, Stephen. 1991. Language and self-consciousness: The making and breaking of C. S. Lewis's personae. In *Word and story in C. S. Lewis*, ed. Peter J. Schakel and Charles A. Huttar, 109-146. Columbia, Mo.: University of Missouri Press.

Meek, Esther Lightcap. 2003. *Longing to know: The philosophy of knowledge for ordinary people*. Grand Rapids: Brazos Press.

Meilaender, Gilbert. 1978. *The taste for the other*. Grand Rapids: Eerdmans.

_____. 1991. Theology in stories: C. S. Lewis and the narrative quality of experience. In *Word and story in C. S. Lewis*, ed. Peter J. Schakel and Charles A. Huttar, 147-156. Columbia, Mo.: University of Missouri Press.

_____. 2000. *Things that count: Essays moral and theological*. Wilmington, Del.: ISI Books.

Menuge, Angus J. L., ed. 1997. *C. S. Lewis: Lightbearer in the shadowlands*. Wheaton: Crossway Books.

Menuge, Angus J. L. 1997. God's chosen instrument: The temper of an apostle. In *C. S. Lewis: Lightbearer in the shadowlands*, ed. Angus J. L. Menuge, 115-142. Wheaton: Crossway Books.

Mews, Stuart. 1994. Religious life between the wars, 1920-1940. In *A history of religion in Britain: Practice and belief from pre-Roman times to the present*, ed. Sheridan Gilley and W. J. Sheils, 449-466. Oxford: Blackwell.

Midgley, Mary. 1992. *Science as salvation: A modern myth and its meaning*. London: Routledge.

Mills, David. 1998. To see truly through a glass darkly: C. S. Lewis, George Orwell, and the corruption of language. In *The pilgrim's guide: C. S. Lewis and the art of witness*, ed. David Mills, 111-132. Grand Rapids: Eerdmans.

Mills, David, ed. 1998. *The pilgrim's guide: C. S. Lewis and the art of witness*. Grand Rapids: Eerdmans.

Milward, Peter. 1995. *A challenge to C. S. Lewis*. Cranbury, N.J.: Associated University Presses.

Mitchell, Basil. 1973. *The justification of religious belief*. New York: Seabury.

Mitchell, Christopher W. 1997. University battles: C. S. Lewis and the Oxford University Socratic Club. In *C. S. Lewis: Lightbearer in the shadowlands*, ed. Angus J. L. Menuge, 79-100. Wheaton: Crossway Books.

_____. 1998. Bearing the weight of glory: The cost of C. S. Lewis's witness. In *The pilgrim's guide: C. S. Lewis and the art of witness*, ed. David Mills, 3-14. Grand Rapids: Eerdmans.

Musacchio, George. 1997. Exorcising the *Zeitgeist*: Lewis as evangelist to the modernists. In *C. S. Lewis: Lightbearer in the shadowlands*, ed. Angus J. L. Menuge, 329-352. Wheaton: Crossway Books.

Myers, Doris C. 1994. *C. S. Lewis in context*. N.p.: Kent State University Press.

_____. 1998. Growing in grace: The Anglican spiritual style in the Narnia Chronicles. In *The pilgrim's guide: C. S. Lewis and the art of witness*, ed. David Mills, 185-202. Grand Rapids: Eerdmans.

_____. 2004. *Bareface: A guide to C. S. Lewis's last novel*. Columbia, Mo.: University of Missouri Press.

National Statistics. 2006. Focus on ethnicity and religion, [report online]. Accessed 18 January 2007. Available from http://www.statistics.gov.uk; internet. Crown copyright.

Neill, Stephen. 1986. *A history of Christian missions*. Second edition. Revised by Owen Chadwick. The Penguin History of the Church. London: Penguin Books.

Netland, Harold. 1988. Toward contextualized apologetics. *Missiology: An International Review* 16, no. 3: 289-303.

_____. 1994. Truth, authority and modernity: Shopping for truth in a supermarket of worldviews. In *Faith and modernity*, ed. Philip Sampson, Vinay Samuel, and Chris Sugden, 89-115. Oxford: Regnum Books.

_____. 2001. *Encountering religious pluralism: The challenge to Christian faith and mission*. Downers Grove, Ill.: Intervarsity.

_____. 2006. Introduction: Globalization and theology today. In *Globalizing theology: Belief and practice in an era of world Christianity*, ed. Craig Ott and Harold A. Netland, 14-36. Grand Rapids: Baker.

Neuhaus, Richard John. 2005. Secularization doesn't just happen. *First Things* 152: 58-61.

Newbigin, J. E. Lesslie. 1953. *The household of God: lectures on the nature of the church*. London: SCM Press.

_____. 1961. *A faith for this one world?* London: SCM Press.

_____.1963. *Trinitarian doctrine for today's mission*. Carlisle: Paternoster Press.

_____. 1966. *Honest religion for secular man*. Philadelphia: Westminster Press.

_____. 1969. *The finality of Christ*. London: SCM Press.

_____. 1982a. Cross-currents in ecumenical and evangelical understandings of mission. *International Bulletin of Missionary Research* 6, no. 4: 146-151.

_____. 1982b. *The light has come: An exposition of the fourth gospel*. Grand Rapids: Eerdmans.

_____. 1983. *The other side of 1984: Questions for the churches*. Geneva: World Council of Churches.

_____. 1985a. *Unfinished agenda*. Geneva: WCC Publications

_____. 1985b. The welfare state: A Christian perspective. *Theology* 88 (May): 173-182.

_____. 1986a. England as a foreign mission field. Address given to the Assembly of the Birmingham Council of Christian Churches. Accessed 20 May 2007. Available from http://www.newbigin.net; internet.

_____. 1986b. *Foolishness to the Greeks: The gospel and Western culture*. Grand Rapids: Eerdmans.

_____. 1987. "Can the West be converted?" *International Bulletin of Missionary Research* 11, no. 1: 2-7. See also: *Princeton Seminary Bulletin* 6, no. 1 (1985): 25-37.

_____. 1988a. Religion, science, and truth in the school curriculum. *Theology* 91: 186-193.

_____. 1988b. Response to David M. Stowe. *International Bulletin of Missionary Research* 12, no. 4: 151-153.

_____. 1989a. *The gospel in a pluralist society*. Grand Rapids: Eerdmans.

_____. 1989b. Gospel and culture—but which culture? *Missionalia* 17, no. 3: 213-215.

_____. 1989c. Mission in the 1990s: Two views. *International Bulletin of Missionary Research* 13, no. 3: 98-102.

_____. 1990a. Christianity and culture. Accessed 20 May 2007. Available from http://www.newbigin.net; internet.

_____. 1990b. Muslims, Christians, and public doctrine. *The gospel and our culture* 6 (Summer): 1-2.

_____. 1991. *Truth to tell: The gospel as public truth.* Grand Rapids: Eerdmans. Oosterhaven Lecture series at Western Theological Seminary, Holland, Michigan.

_____. 1993a. Certain faith: What kind of certainty? *Tyndale Bulletin* 44, no. 2: 339-350.

_____. 1993b. Pluralism in the church. *ReNews* (Presbyterians for Renewal) 4, no. 2: 6-7).

_____. 1993c. *Unfinished agenda: An updated autobiography.* London: Saint Andrew Press.

_____. 1994a. *A word in season: Perspectives on Christian world missions.* Grand Rapids: Eerdmans.

_____. 1994b. Ecumenical amnesia. *International Bulletin of Missionary Research* 18, no.1: 2-5.

_____. 1994c. Reply to Konrad Raiser. *International Bulletin of Missionary Research* 18, no. 2: 51-52.

_____. 1994d. Truth and authority in modernity. In *Faith and modernity*, ed. Philip Sampson, Vinay Samuel, and Chris Sugden, 60-88. Oxford: Regnum Books.

_____. 1995a [1978]. *The open secret: An introduction to the theology of mission.* Revised edition. Grand Rapids: Eerdmans.

_____. 1995b. *Proper confidence: Faith, doubt, and certainty in Christian discipleship.* Grand Rapids: Eerdmans.

_____. 1996a. On the gospel as public truth: Response to the colloquium. Accessed 20 May 2007. Available from http://www.newbigin.net; internet.

_____. 1996b. *Truth and authority in modernity.* Valley Forge, Pa.: Trinity Press International.

Newbigin, Lesslie, Lamin Sanneh, and Jenny Taylor. 1998. *Faith and power: Christianity and Islam in 'secular' Britain.* London: SPCK.

Nielsen, Jorgan S. 1989. Islamic communities in Britain. In *Religion, state, and society in modern Britain*, ed. Paul Badham, 225-241. Lewiston, N.Y.: The Edwin Mellen Press.

Oman, John. 1931. *The natural and the supernatural*. Cambridge: Cambridge University Press.

Orchard, Ronald K, ed. 1964. *Witness in six continents: Records of the meeting of the Commission on World Mission and Evangelism of the World Council of Churches held in Mexico City, December 8ᵗʰ to 19ᵗʰ, 1963*. New York: Friendship Press.

Ott, Craig. 2006. Conclusion: Globalizing theology. In *Globalizing theology: Belief and practice in an era of world Christianity*, eds. Craig Ott and Harold A. Netland, 309-336. Grand Rapids: Baker.

Ott, Craig, and Harold A. Netland. 2006. *Globalizing theology: Belief and practice in an era of world Christianity*. Grand Rapids: Baker.

Ottati, Douglas F. 1993. Whose gospel? Which culture. *Insights* 109: 41-57.

Oury, Scott. 1977. "The thing itself": C. S. Lewis and the value of something other. In *The longing for a form: Essays on the fiction of C. S. Lewis, 1-19*. N.p.: The Kent State University Press.

Packer, J. I. 1998. Still surprised by Lewis. *Christianity Today* (September 7): 54-60.

Pascal, Blaise. 1966. *Pensees*. Translated by A. J. Krailsheimer. London: Penguin Classics.

Payne, Leanne. 1995. *Real presence: The Christian worldview of C. S. Lewis as incarnational reality*. Grand Rapids: Baker.

Peach, Ceri. 2006. Muslims in the 2001 Census of England and Wales: Gender and economic disadvantage. *Ethnic and Racial Studies* 29, no. 4: 629-655.

Pearcy, Nancy R. 2008. *Total truth: Liberating Christianity from its cultural captivity*. Wheaton: Crossway.

Peters, Thomas C. 1998. The war of the worldviews: H. G. Wells and scientism versus C. S. Lewis and Christianity. In *The pilgrim's guide: C. S. Lewis and the art of witness*, ed. David Mills, 203-220. Grand Rapids: Eerdmans.

Phillips, Justin. 2002. *C. S. Lewis in a time of war: The World War II broadcasts that riveted a nation and became the classic* Mere Christianity. New York: Harper San Francisco.

Pinnock, Clark H. 1995. An inclusivist view. In *Four views on salvation in a pluralistic world*, ed. Verlyn D. Verbrugge, 93-123. Grand Rapids: Zondervan.

Pittenger, W. Norman. 1958a. Apologist versus apologist. *The Christian Century* 75 (October 1): 1104-1107.

_____. 1958b. Letter to the editor. *The Christian Century* (December 24): 1485-1486.

_____. 1981. C. S. Lewis: Combative in defense. *Studies in the Literary Imagination* 14, no. 2: 13-20.

Plantinga, Alvin. 1977. *God, freedom, and evil.* Grand Rapids: Eerdmans.

_____. 1993. *Warrant and proper function.* New York: Oxford University Press.

_____. 1996. Darwin, mind and meaning. *Books & Culture* (May-June): 8-11.

_____. 2000. *Warranted Christian belief.* New York: Oxford University Press.

Polanyi, Michael. 1958. *Personal knowledge: Towards a post-critical philosophy.* Chicago: University of Chicago Press, 1958.

Postman, Neil. 1985. *Amusing ourselves to death: Public discourse in the age of show business.* New York: Penguin Books.

Price, Lynn. 2002. Churches and postmodernity: Opportunity for an attitude shift. In *A scandalous prophet: The way of mission after Newbigin,* ed. Thomas F. Foust, George R. Hunsberger, J. Andrew Kirk, and Werner Ustorf, 107-114. Grand Rapids: Eerdmans.

Priest, Robert J. 2006. Experience-near theologizing in diverse human contexts. In *Globalizing theology: Belief and practice in an era of world Christianity,* ed. Craig Ott and Harold A. Netland, 180-198. Grand Rapids: Baker.

Pullman, Philip. 2001. The republic of heaven. *The Horn Book Magazine* (November/December): 655-667.

Purtill, Richard L. 1981. *C. S. Lewis's case for the Christian faith.* San Francisco: Harper & Row.

_____. 1998. Apologetics. In *The C. S. Lewis readers' encyclopedia,* ed. Jeffrey A. Schultz and John G. West, Jr., 83-85. Grand Rapids: Zondervan.

Raiser, Konrad. 1994. Is ecumenical apologetics sufficient? A response to Newbigin's "Ecumenical amnesia." *International Bulletin of Missionary Research* 18, no. 2: 50-51.

Ramachandra, Vinoth. 1996. *The recovery of mission.* Carlisle: Paternoster Press.

_____. 2005. Global religious transformations, political vision and Christian witness. *International Review of Mission* 94, no. 375: 477-492.

Redden, Guy. 2005. The New Age: Towards a market model. *Journal of Contemporary Religion* 20, no. 2: 231-246.

Reppert, Victor. 2003. *C. S. Lewis's dangerous idea: A philosophical defense of Lewis's argument from reason.* Downer's Grove: Intervarsity Press.

Robinson, John A. T. 1963. *Honest to God.* London: SCM Press.

Root, Jerry. 1997. C. S. Lewis and the problem of evil. In *C. S. Lewis: Lightbearer in the shadowlands*, ed. Angus J. L. Menuge, 353-366. Wheaton: Crossway Books.

_____. 1998. Tools inadequate and incomplete: C. S. Lewis and the great religions. In *The pilgrim's guide: C. S. Lewis and the art of witness*, ed. David Mills, 221-235. Grand Rapids: Eerdmans.

Rorty, Richard. 1995. Untruth and consequences. *The New Republic* (July 31): 32-36.

Ryken, Philip G. 1997. Winsome evangelist: The influence of C. S. Lewis. In *C. S. Lewis: Lightbearer in the shadowlands*, ed. Angus J. L. Menuge, 55-78. Wheaton: Crossway Books.

Sandhurst, B. G. 1948. *How heathen is Britain?* Revised and enlarged ed. Preface by C. S. Lewis. London: Collins.

Sanneh, Lamin. 1989. *Translating the message: The missionary impact on culture.* Maryknoll, N.Y.: Orbis Books.

_____. 1993. *Encountering the West: Christianity and the global cultural process.* Maryknoll, N.Y.: Orbis Books.

_____. 2003. *Whose religion is Christianity? The gospel beyond the West.* Grand Rapids: Eerdmans.

Sayer, George. 1988. *Jack: C. S. Lewis and his times.* San Francisco: Harper & Row.

Schakel, Peter J. 1984. *Reason and imagination in C. S. Lewis: A study of* Till we have faces. Grand Rapids: Eerdmans.

_____. 1998. Reason. In *The C. S. Lewis readers' encyclopedia*, ed. Jeffrey A. Schultz and John G. West, Jr., 348-350. Grand Rapids: Zondervan.

Schultz, Jeffrey A., and John G. West, Jr., ed. 1998. *The C. S. Lewis readers' encyclopedia.* Grand Rapids: Zondervan.

Schuster, Jurgen. 2006. The significance of the kingdom of God in its eschatological tension for the theology of mission of Lesslie Newbigin. Ph.D. diss., Trinity International University.

Scrotenboer, Paul G. 1982. Responses to the article by Lesslie Newbigin. *International Bulletin of Missionary Research* 6, no. 4: 152-153.

Shenk, Wilbert R. 1996. The culture of modernity as a missionary challenge. In *The church between gospel and culture: The emerging mission in North America*, ed. George R. Hunsberger and Craig Van Gelder, 69-78. Grand Rapids: Eerdmans.

_____. 2000. Lesslie Newbigin's contribution to mission theology. *International Bulletin of Missionary Research* 24, no. 2: 59-64.

Sire, James W. 1995. On being a fool for Christ and an idiot for nobody: Logocentricity and postmodernity. In *Christian apologetics in the postmodern world*, ed. Timothy R. Phillips and Dennis L. Okholm, 101-127. Downers Grove, Ill.: Intervarsity Press.

Smith, Christian. 2003. Introduction: Rethinking the secularization of American public life. In *The secular revolution: Power, interests, and conflict in the secularization of American public life*, ed. Christian Smith, 1-96. Berkeley: University of California Press.

Smith, Charles Frederick. 1999. An evangelical evaluation of key elements in Lesslie Newbigin's apologetics. Ph.D. diss., Southwestern Baptist Theological Seminary.

Smith, Stephen M. 1998. Awakening from the enchantment of worldliness: The Chronicles of Narnia as pre-apologetics. In *The pilgrim's guide: C. S. Lewis and the art of witness*, ed. David Mills, 168-184. Grand Rapids: Eerdmans.

Sommerville, C. John.. 2003. Review of *God is dead: Secularization in the West*. *Journal for the Scientific Study of Religion* 42, no. 2: 305.

Stark, Rodney. 1985. From church-sect to religious economies. In *The sacred in a secular age*, ed. Phillip E. Hammond, 139-149. Berkeley: University of California Press.

_____.1999. Secularization, R. I. P. *Sociology of Religion* 60, no. 3: 249-273.

_____. 2001. Efforts to Christianize Europe, 400-2000. *Journal of Contemporary Religion* 16, no. 1: 105-123.

Stark, Rodney, and Laurence R. Iannaccone. 1994. A supply-side reinterpretation of the secularization of Europe. *Journal for the Scientific Study of Religion* 33, no. 3: 230-252.

_____. 1995. Truth? A reply to Bruce. *Journal for the Scientific Study of Religion* 34, no. 4: 516-519.

Stark, Rodney, and Roger Finke. 2000. *Acts of faith: Explaining the human side of religion*. Berkeley: University of California Press.

Starr, Charlie. 2002. The triple enigma: Fact, truth, and myth as the key to C. S. Lewis's epistemological thinking. Ph.D. diss., Middle Tennessee State.

Stowe, David M. 1988. Modernization and resistance: Theological implications for mission. *International Bulletin of Missionary Research* 12, no. 4: 146-151.

Suggate, Alan M. 1994. The Christian churches in England since 1945: Ecumenism and social concern. In *A history of religion in Britain: Practice and belief from pre-Roman times to the present*, ed. Sheridan Gilley and W. J. Sheils, 467-487. Oxford: Blackwell.

Talbott, Thomas. 1998. A grief observed. In *The C. S. Lewis readers' encyclopedia*, ed. Jeffrey A. Schultz and John G. West, Jr., 193-194. Grand Rapids: Zondervan.

Taylor, Jenny. 2002. Lesslie Newbigin's understanding of Islam. In *A scandalous prophet: The way of mission after Newbigin*, ed. Thomas F. Foust, George R. Hunsberger, J. Andrew Kirk, and Werner Ustorf, 215-226. Grand Rapids: Eerdmans.

Thomas, V. Matthew. 1996. The centrality of Christ and inter-religious dialogue in the theology of Lesslie Newbigin. Ph.D. diss., St. Michael's College, University of Toronto.

Tiénou, Tite. 2006. Christian theology in an era of world Christianity. In *Globalizing theology: Belief and practice in an era of world Christianity*, ed. Craig Ott and Harold A. Netland, 37-51. Grand Rapids: Baker.

Ustorf, Werner. 2002. The emerging Christ of post-Christian Europe. In *A scandalous prophet: The way of mission after Newbigin*, ed. Thomas F. Foust, George R. Hunsberger, J. Andrew Kirk, and Werner Ustorf, 128-144. Grand Rapids: Eerdmans.

Van Gelder, Craig. 1996. A great new fact of our day: America as a mission field. In *The church between gospel and culture: The emerging mission in North America*, ed. George R. Hunsberger and Craig Van Gelder, 57-68. Grand Rapids: Eerdmans.

Van Gelder, Craig, ed. 2005. *Confident witness—changing world: Rediscovering the gospel in North America*. Grand Rapids: Eerdmans.

_____, ed. 2007. *The missional church in context: Helping congregations develop contextual ministry*. Missional Church Series. Grand Rapids: Eerdmans.

Van Heerden, L. 1958. Letter to the editor. *The Christian Century* (December 24): 1485.

Vanhoozer, Kevin J. 2005a. Pilgrim's digress: Christian thinking on and about the post/modern way. In *Christianity and the postmodern turn: Six views*, ed. Myron B. Penner, 71-103. Grand Rapids: Brazos Press.

_____. 2005b. Disputing about words? Of fallible foundations and modest metanarratives. In *Christianity and the postmodern turn: Six views*, ed. Myron B. Penner, 71-103. Grand Rapids: Brazos Press.

_____. 2005c. *The drama of doctrine: A canonical-linguistic approach to Christian theology.* Louisville: Westminster John Knox Press.

Van Leewen, Arend Theodoor. 1964. *Christianity in world history: The meeting of the faiths of East and West.* New York: Scribner.

Vaus, Will. 2004. *Mere theology: A guide to the thought of C. S. Lewis.* Downers Grove, Ill.: Intervarsity.

Veith, Gene Edward. 1997. A vision, within a dream, within the truth: C. S. Lewis as evangelist to the postmoderns. In *C. S. Lewis: Lightbearer in the shadowlands,* ed. Angus J. L. Menuge, 367-387. Wheaton: Crossway Books.

Verkuyl, Johannes. 1978. *Contemporary missiology: An introduction.* Translated and edited by Dale Cooper. Grand Rapids: Eerdmans.

Voas, David, and Steve Bruce. 2004. The 2001 Census and Christian identification in Britain. *Journal of Contemporary Religion* 19, no. 1: 23-28.

Voas, David, and Alasdair Crockett. 2005. Religion in Britain: Neither believing nor belonging. *Sociology* 39, no. 1: 11-28.

Voye, Liliane. 1999. Secularization in a context of advanced modernity. *Sociology of Religion* 60, no. 3: 275-288.

Wain, John. 1992. A great clerke. In *"C. S. Lewis at the breakfast table" and other reminiscences,* ed. James T. Como, 68-76. New York: Harcourt, Brace, Jovanovitch.

Wainwright, Geoffrey. 2000. *Lesslie Newbigin: A theological life.* New York: Oxford University Press.

Walls, Andrew F. 1996. *The missionary movement in Christian history: Studies in the transmission of faith.* Maryknoll, N.Y.: Orbis.

_____. 2002. Enlightenment, postmodernity, and mission. In *A scandalous prophet: The way of mission after Newbigin,* ed. Thomas F. Foust, George R. Hunsberger, J. Andrew Kirk, and Werner Ustorf, 145-152. Grand Rapids: Eerdmans.

Walsh, Chad. 1965. Impact on America. In *Light on C. S. Lewis,* ed. Jocelyn Gibb, 106-116. New York: Harcourt Brace Jovanovich.

_____. 1979. *The literary legacy of C. S. Lewis.* New York: Harcourt Brace Jovanovich.

Ware, Kallistos. 1998. God of the fathers: C. S. Lewis and Eastern Christianity. In *The pilgrim's guide: C. S. Lewis and the art of witness,* ed. David Mills, 53-69. Grand Rapids: Eerdmans.

Weber, Max. 1948. *From Max Weber: Essays in sociology.* Translated and edited by and with introduction by H. H. Gerth and C. Wright Mills. London: Routledge & Kegan Paul.

West. Charles C. 1988. Mission to the West: A dialogue with Stowe and Newbigin. *International Bulletin of Missionary Research* 12, no. 4: 153-156.

_____. 1996. Gospel for American culture: Variations on a theme by Newbigin. In *The church between gospel and culture: The emerging mission in North America*, ed. George R. Hunsberger and Craig Van Gelder, 214-227. Grand Rapids: Eerdmans.

Weston, Paul. 2004. Lesslie Newbigin: A postmodern missiologist? *Mission Studies* 21, no. 2: 229-248.

Williams, Sarah. 1995. Urban popular religion and the rites of passage. In *European religion in the age of great cities 1830-1930*, ed. Hugh McLeod, 216-236. London: Routledge.

Wilson, A. N. 1990. *C. S. Lewis: A biography*. New York: Norton.

Wilson, Bryan. 1966. *Religion in secular society: A sociological comment*. London: C. A. Watts.

Worrall, B. G. 1988. *The making of the modern church: Christianity in England since 1800*. London: SPCK.

Wright, N. T. 2007. Simply Lewis: Reflections on a master apologist after 60 years. *Touchstone* (March): 28-33.

Wuthnow, Robert. 1985. Science and the sacred. In *The sacred in a secular age*, ed. Phillip E. Hammond, 187-203. Berkeley: University of California Press.

ABOUT THE AUTHOR

David Feddes (Ph.D., Trinity International University) is Provost of Christian Leaders Institute. Formerly he hosted the international Back to God radio broadcast, directed the Center for Advanced Studies at Crossroad Bible Institute, and served as a pastor, evangelist, and church planter.